Adrian Mikhalchishin
Georg Mohr

The CENTER
A modern strategy guide

Chess
Evolution

Cover designer
Piotr Pielach

Typesetting
Piotr Pielach ‹www.i-press.pl›

First edition 2016 by Chess Evolution

ISBN 978-83-945362-9-9

All sales or enquiries should be directed to Chess Evolution
2040 Budaors, Nyar utca 16, Hungary

e-mail: info@chess-evolution.com
website: www.chess-evolution.com

Printed in Hungary

TABLE OF CONTENTS

KEY TO SYMBOLS

=	Equality or equal chances
⩲	White has a slight advantage
⩱	Black has a slight advantage
±	White is better
∓	Black is better
+-	White has a decisive advantage
-+	Black has a decisive advantage
∞	unclear
=∞	with compensation
⇆	with counterplay
↑	with initiative
→	with an attack
Δ	with the idea
□	only move
N	novelty
!	a good move
!!	an excellent move
?	a weak move
??	a blunder
!?	an interesing move
?!	a dubious move
+	check
#	mate

EDITORIAL PREFACE

There is a blank spot in the huge world of chess literature: systematically presented middle- game. Therefore authors, both long-term chess trainers, decided to fill this vacuum. With a series of books about the middle-game, we would like to present different topics of chess tactics and strategy in a slightly different way. Books, which will be published in the coming years as part of the series, are planned to cover all frequently discussed themes, as well as many others topics — those about which chess players and also trainers usually do not think as deeply as they should in order to achieve better results.

We are starting our series with a book about the centre. We will take two different approaches to this topic: the classical one, which will help us to discover all fundamental knowledge about the centre. This study is crucial for good understanding of chess. The second approach is more modern: we will think about the centre more dynamically, through the eyes of a grandmaster, a practical chess player. We will try to copy this two-part structure in the future books, in which planning, analysing, move decisions, pawn structures and various other topics will be discussed.

The authors are not imagining that our book will cover every aspect of presented topic. Knowledge about the centre is so important and wide chapter that it is virtually impossible to explain every detail in a single book. Moreover, there are countless of different perspectives on particular problems or procedures in the centre and we could not take into the account every one of them. However, we have wished to write a book, which would offer us 3600 view of the centre, enable an individual study to any aspiring student and help trainer in their work. Advices of the experienced coaches (we have boldly put ourselves into this category) are always welcomed for successful chess training.

To fulfil our objectives, we will publish an additional workbook accompanying each book. It will contain many exercises, puzzles and practical questions, which will further your understanding of the presented topic.

Yours,
Adrian Mikhalchishin and Georg Mohr

THE CENTER – BASICS

by Georg Mohr

One of the first concepts that a player comes across when learning how to play chess is the center, more accurately its role and its meaning. The name itself tells us that it has to do with something in the middle and in our case that represents the middle, or the center, of the board.

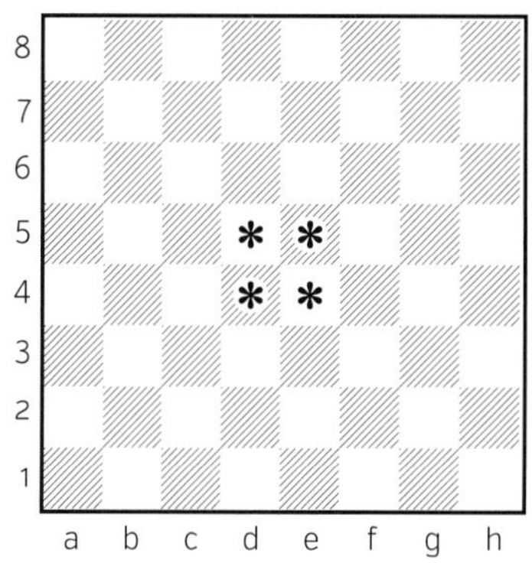

The small center

Sometimes we encounter the concept of the big center.

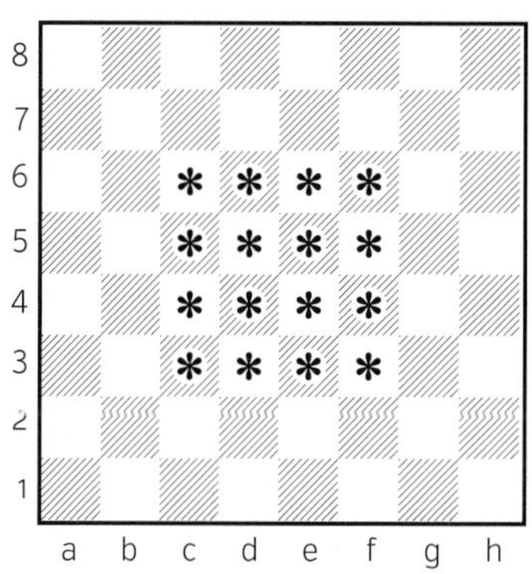

The big center

Most of the rules can be used for both centers, but we need to be careful! If a certain rule can be used in most of the cases, it certainly does not mean that we can definitely use it in all our own positions. Beginners usually do not know why the center so important. It is not like we can win the game there. The kings are not in the center and logically there are no mates. A material advantage can be achieved in every part of the board and it is also true that the center is not directly connected with the result at the end of the game. Its importance is tactical and strategic. Control over the center leaves a player with a positional advantage and this book will show you how to use that kind of advantage properly. The meaning of the center will be easier to understand if we get to know the power of the pieces in different parts of the board. For example, the queen in the center controls 27 different squares.

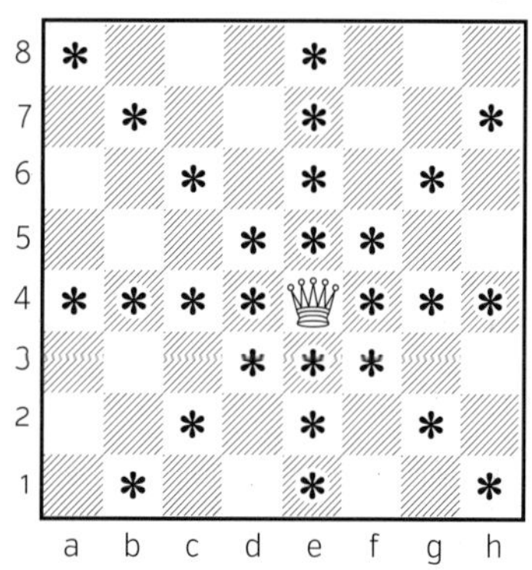

On the contrary, on the edge of the board or in the corner (the a3 square) the queen controls only 21 squares. An even more illustrative example is the knight, which controls eight squares in the center:

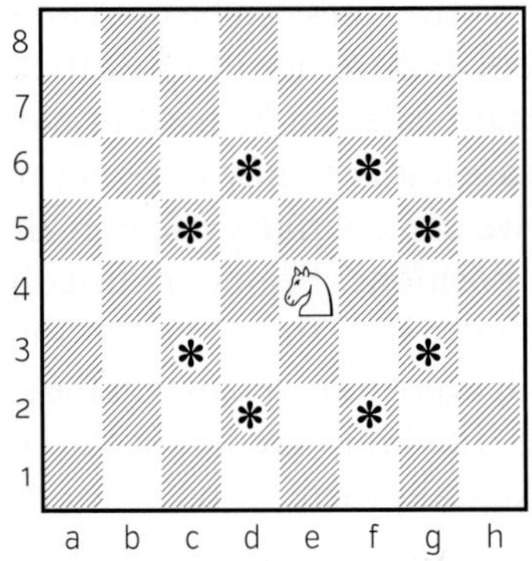

On the edge (a3) four squares and only two from the corner (h1).

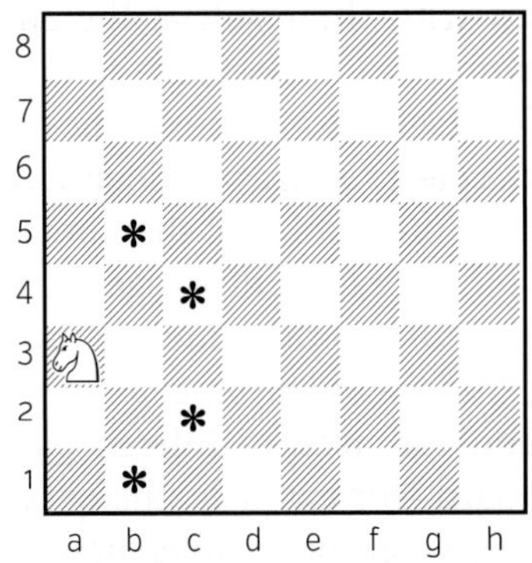

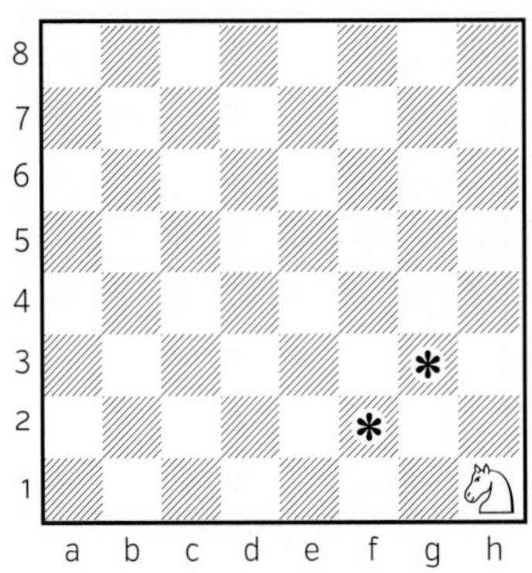

The center represents the part of the board from where the pieces can reach other, more distant parts. We can see that especially with the knight, and even more so with the king — which usually comes to a dominant position in the center in the endgame. That kind of dominant position can be decisive due to the space advantage (because the opposing kings cannot touch each other and the other king is automatically located outside of the center).

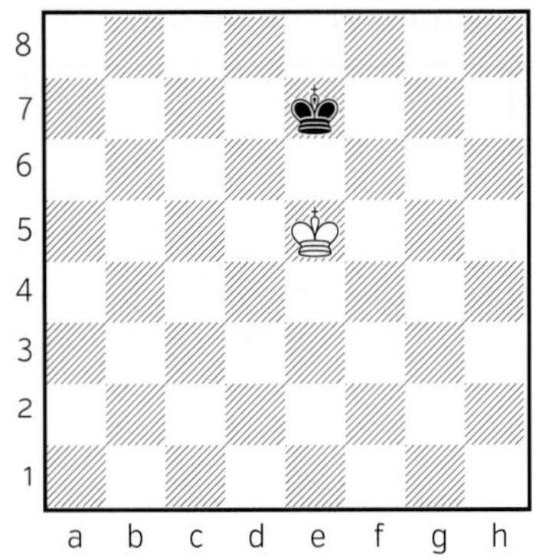

Control over the center leaves a player with the space advantage even earlier — in the middlegame. The pieces in the center are putting pressure on the opponent's pieces, which are forced to move backwards or defend themselves from positions which are usually distant from the center.

The fight for the center begins already in the opening. There are many ways of doing it: the usual way is that both players put their pawns in the center and then try to control it with them. Around 100 years ago that was the only known way and the only way that was accepted (1.e4 e5; 1.d4 d5).

The first World Champion Wilhelm Steinitz taught that having control over the center meant a big or even a decisive advantage and his lessons were popularized by German Dr. Siegbert Tarrasch the "teacher of the nation". Steinitz later on found another possibility, some kind of a 'pawn & pieces' center, where pawns and pieces help each other to reach the goal.

Only after the breakthrough of the small group of free-minded chess players (nowadays we call them hyper-modernists: Aron Nimzowitsch, Richard Reti and others) the wider knowledge about the center was produced. Hyper-modernists said — and also theoretically and practically proved — that there exist other possibilities of fighting for the center. The best-known is "control from a distance", where we control the central squares with the pieces (for example the e4 square in closed openings: after 1.d4 both moves 1...d5 and 1...♘f6 have the same effect, they both take control over the e4-square). An even more drastic possibility is to deliberately give up the center in order to later on restrain or attack it. The Grunfeld Defence and Alekhine's Defence are the most illustrative examples of these new principles. White can use similar tactics in, for example, the Reti opening.

There are many classifications of the center. The classic one concerns itself with center 'types': which vary with different pawn constructions. The mobile (moving) center, where one of the players has a pawn more in the center (usually one or two) and the opposing pawn cannot stop them from moving forward. The classical example is the e4 and d4 pawns against the d6-pawn.

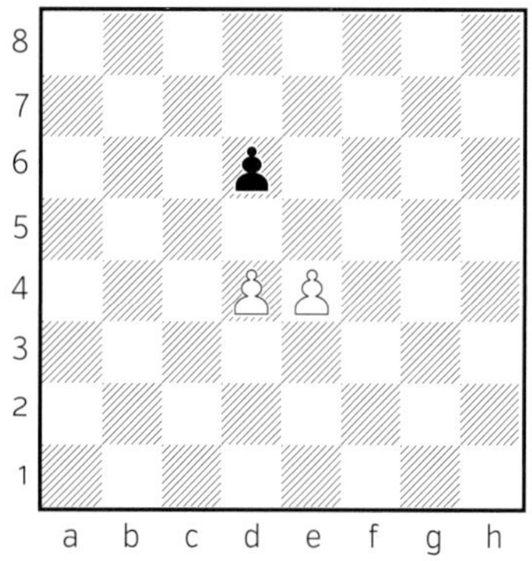

When and how to move forward? What does Black need to be careful of? The opposite represents the fixed (blocked) center, where the pawns cannot move forward and they can only disappear from the board (or capture away from the center). These kinds of positions are shown in the next two diagrams.

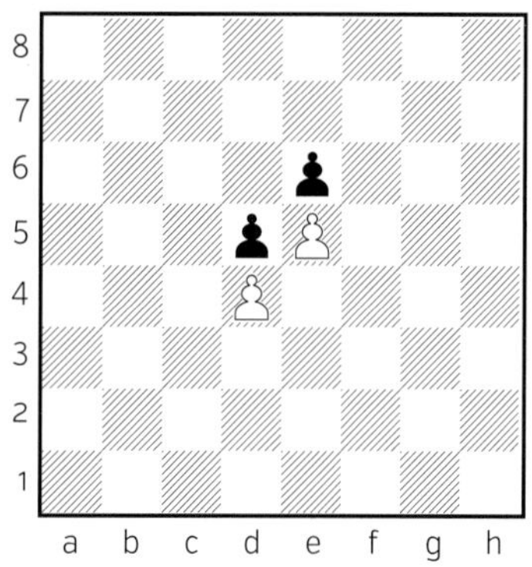

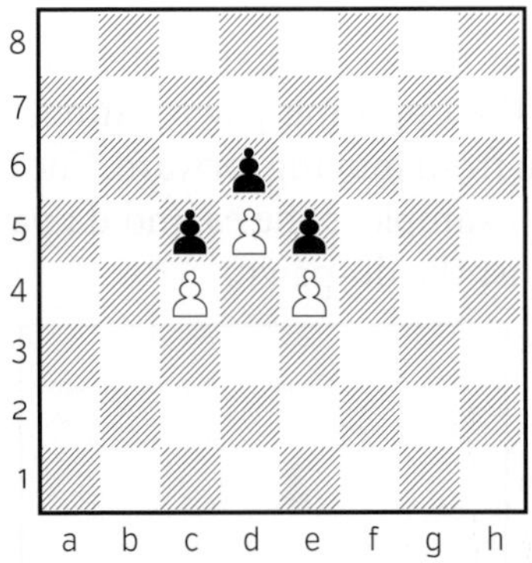

When we talk about the blocked center, the play is logically moved to the flanks and both players are trying to gain control over the center using a flank strategy.

We know many other types of centers: **the symmetrical center**, where two pawns are standing in front of each other:

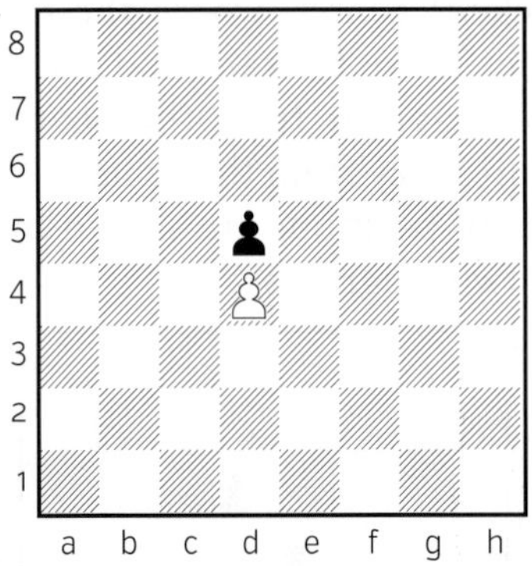

and the battle takes place on the other open central files. The **static center** means that the placement of the pawns has a specific shape and therefore every move with a pawn is extremely delicate and can even mean a material loss. **The dynamic center** (see next diagram) means that there is no direct contact between the pawns, but they are watching each other and they need to pay attention to any kind of movement among them. And there is also **the open center**, where there are no pawns in the center and the main role is played directly (by placement in the center) or indirectly (with control from a distance) by the pieces.

Every type of center mentioned is marked by pawns. Their general placement and most of all their placement in the center is called the **pawn structure**. There are many types of pawn structures and we would probably need many books to study them all.

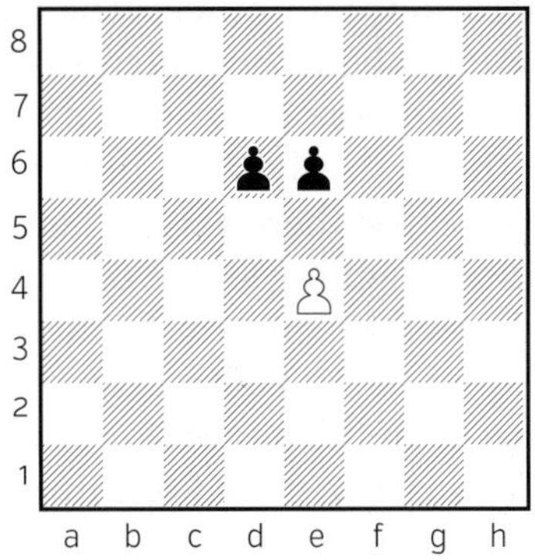

Dynamic center.

For each kind of structure there are typical and clear strategic plans, and pawn structures in the center are important mostly because they represent the result of the play in certain openings. The player, as a rule with his choice of the opening, also chooses a pawn structure and that is why knowledge of them and understanding of the subsequent play are so important.

Some of these rules have been known for decades (the position with an isolated pawn; the position with hanging pawns: the Carlsbad pawn structure), some of them were discovered in modern chess and that does not make them any less important (the Scheveningen structure; the Maroczy pawn structure; the structure with a backward d-pawn; structures with doubled pawns). In this book we will not look at them specifically, but the basic information about them will be found in the chapters on the different kinds of centers.

The positions will be studied based on whole games, because only in this way will you be able to understand the importance of the center, the pawn structures and their direct link with the openings, the middlegame and the endgame. The chosen games will be, in most cases, classical: the games of the old masters are as a rule clearer and easier to understand regarding the basic principles. In modern chess and in games that are being played today there are too many factors that are influencing them.

I hope that the basic knowledge about the center and about the most representative pawn structures will encourage you to study chess more deeply. The book is appropriate for chess beginners and much of the advice could also be used by more qualified chess players. I recommend to you to go through the book alone — it is easy to understand, and the best way to learn how to play chess is to study it by ourselves.

Overall I recommend the book to all trainers: the knowledge about the center is basic for the successful playing of chess. Many different examples and detailed descriptions of what is happening on this the most important part of the board will definitely come in handy with their work.

ABOUT STRATEGIC PLAY IN THE CENTER

IGNORING THE CENTER

It was said in the introduction that control over the center is one of the most important strategic elements in chess. Usually both players face this problem of the center responsibly and with varying tactics. They put their pawns in the center and use them to control the central squares, or one of the players gives up his control of the center and leaves it to the opponent — and then tries to weaken the opponent's pawn structure or even destroy it. Every square in the center is important, because even if you control only one square it could leave you with the advantage. The placement of a certain piece in the center, knowing that it cannot be driven away by any of the opponent's pawns, is beneficial for the development of the game. But it doesn't bring you an automatic advantage as we will see later on.

In any case, control over the center is of great importance. It is not important if we control it with the pawns or with the pieces, but what is important is to control it. The next example will demonstrate the dangers present if we give up the center.

1

▷ **Botvinnik**
▶ **Capablanca**
Amsterdam 1938 [E49]

1.d4 ♘f6 2.c4 e6 3.♘c3 ♗b4 4.e3 d5 5.a3 ♗c3 6.bc3 c5 7.cd5 ed5

Nowadays we are familiar with the fact that White has an advantage in this kind of position due to the good chances of advancing with his pawns in the center. In 1938 players did not know that — the Nimzo-Indian Defence as well as knowledge about the center had only started to develop.

8.♗d3 0–0 9.♘e2 b6 10.0–0 ♗a6

It looks like Black's position is great. He has a good pawn structure, no special weaknesses and his development is easy and simple. After the exchange of the light-squared bishops he will reach the most important strategic goal: the exchange of White's best placed piece.

11.♗a6 ♘a6 12.♗b2?

At first sight this is a very strange move, but it is fighting for the center! What is White's plan? Definitely the e3–e4 move in the center (after the f2–f3 move). The move will be difficult to perform without an appropriate defence of the d4 square, where

Black's pressure is focused. So both of the plans are clear and simple: first of all White needs to strengthen the d4 square and after that prepare the e3–e4 move. In the meantime Black will be putting pressure on the d4 square and will be placing his pieces on their optimal squares.

12...♕d7 13.a4 ♖fe8?!

Black can also put pressure on the d4 square indirectly, that is why the exchange of the pawns is necessary. After 13...cd4 14.cd4 ♖fc8 and 15...♖c4 the e3–e4 move would not be so easy to perform. The bishop on b2 would have a mainly defensive role.

14.♕d3 c4??

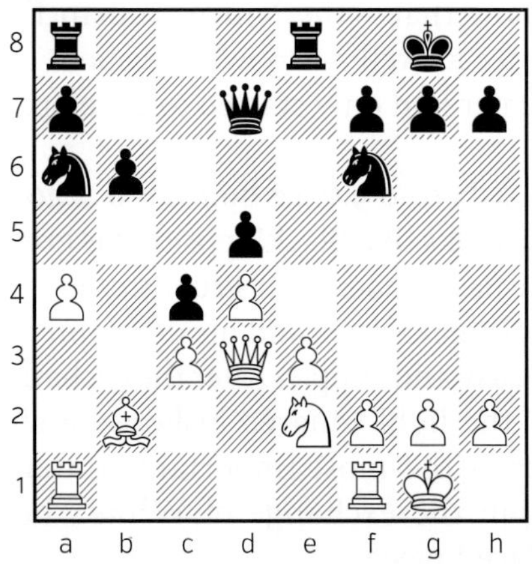

This is a very serious positional mistake and it represents a moment which needs to be examined more closely. It is known that White wants to play the e3–e4 move, and that Black is making his work harder with the pressure that he is putting on the d4 square. After the move played by Black — and White did not force him to play it — he has voluntarily released the pressure and subsequently left White with no obstacles. Black could choose from different plans, for example ...♘a6–b8–c6–a5–b3 or 14...♕b7.

The great Cuban was of course aware of the fact that he was giving up on the center with the move played, but he hoped that swift action on the queenside would bring him success.

15.♕c2 ♘b8 16.♖ae1

White follows his strategic plan — he moves his pieces to the squares which control the e4 square.

16...♘c6 17.♘g3 ♘a5

After 17...♘e4 there would follow 18.♘h1! (with the idea f3, and ♘f2, or back again ♘g3) and White would continue peacefully with his plan. For example: 18...f5 19.f3 ♘d6 20.♗a3 g6 21.♘g3 and there is no defence against the e3–e4 move. (Kasparov)

18.f3 ♘b3 19.e4 ♕a4 20.e5 ♘d7

Both players have realized their strategic plans. We can easily see that White has the positional advantage: he is threatening ♘g3–f5–d6 or an advancement of the f-pawn. Black will have to pass several tests before realizing the pawn-up advantage which he won on the queenside.

21.♕f2

We need to be careful when it comes to realization of the plans. Black threatens, with the tactical ♘b3–c5 move, to save his knight which is currently stranded on the queenside.

21...g6 22.f4 f5!

After this blockage White has no choice: he needs to take and open the e-file, where the exchange of the rooks will occur.

23.ef6 ♘f6 24.f5 ♖e1 25.♖e1 ♖e8 26.♖e6!

26.fg6 hg6 27.♖e8 ♘e8.

26...♖e6

After 26...♔g7 27.♖f6! ♔f6 28.fg6 White will lead out a strong attack; 26...♔f7 27.♖f6! ♔f6 28.fg6.

27.fe6 ♔g7 28.♕f4 ♕e8

29.♘f5 gf5 30.♕g5 was threatened.

29.♕e5 ♕e7

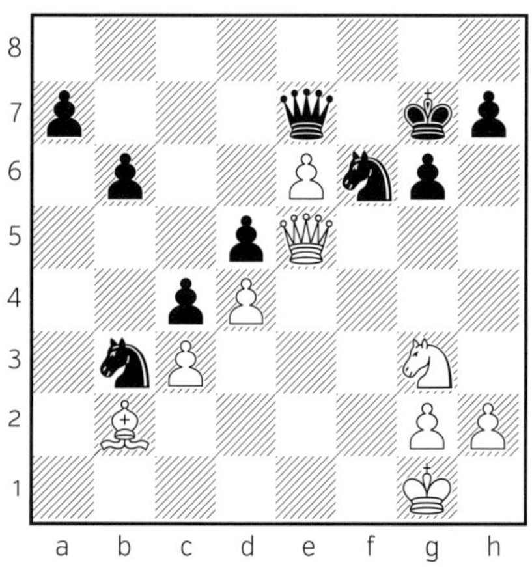

In front of us is one of the best-known positions in all of chess history, the highlight of White's entire strategy.

30.♗a3!!

A glorious sacrifice based on deflection.

30...♕a3 31.♘h5 gh5 32.♕g5 ♔f8 33.♕f6 ♔g8 34.e7

Care is required as White could still fall for the trick: 34.♕f7 ♔h8 35.e7? ♕c1 36.♔f2 ♕d2 37.♔g3 ♕g5 38.♔f3 ♘d4! 39.cd4 ♕g4 and it's only a draw because of the perpetual checks.

34...♕c1 35.♔f2 ♕c2 36.♔g3 ♕d3 37.♔h4 ♕e4 38.♔h5 ♕e2 39.♔h4 ♕e4 40.g4 ♕e1 41.♔h5 1:0

Weak squares in the center

Weakening the central squares can have fatal consequences. That is why we need to be careful when it comes to moving the pawns in the center: every movement leaves behind — and all around — weakened squares, which an experienced player can exploit quickly.

Let's take a look at two practical examples from the former World Champion Alexander Alekhine. In both games the players were incautious when it came to advancing the f-pawn — the movement of which left behind weak squares all along the e-file.

1

▷ **Winter**
▶ **Alekhine**
Nottingham 1936 [C01]

1.d4 e6 2.e4 d5 3.ed5 ed5

The Exchange Variation of the French Defence promises a symmetrical center with equal play. The development plan is simple for both players and they have no weaknesses.

4.♗d3 ♘c6 5.♘e2 ♗d6 6.c3 ♕h4 7.♘d2 ♗g4 8.♕c2 0–0–0 9.♘f1 g6 10.♗e3 ♘ge7 11.0–0–0 ♗f5 12.♘fg3 ♗d3 13.♕d3 h6

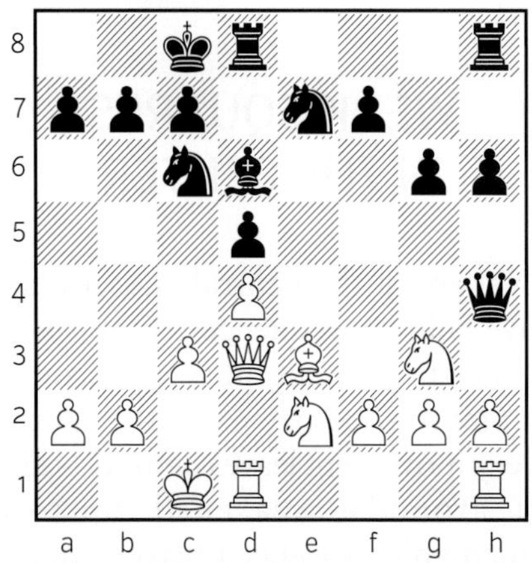

The position is more-or-less equal, although Black may have a slight initiative due to the more active placement of his pieces and a better bishop. When we try to decide which bishop is better and which one is worse, it helps to loojk at the pawn structures, especially with fixed pawns. In the center there are two fixed pawns, the d4-pawn and the d5-pawn. White‘s bishop is restricted by his pawn and Black‘s bishop is attacking the opponent‘s pawn. White wanted to destroy the co-ordination of Black‘s pieces and so he decided to play:

14.f4?

This move is bad, because it weakens many squares along the e-file (e.g. e3, e4). The soon to be again World Champion will exploit that with the maneuver of his knight to an eternal base (this represents a square from which the knight cannot be attacked by any of the opponent‘s pawns) and with the occupation of the e-file.

14…♕g4 15.h3 ♕d7 16.♖hf1 h5 17.♘g1 h4 18.♘3e2 ♘f5

The first part of the plan is fulfilled; the knight has moved to a wonderful square. Next follows a systematic conquest of the e-file.

19.♘f3 f6 20.♘h2 ♖de8! 21.♗d2 ♖e6! 22.♘g4 ♖he8! 23.♖de1 ♖8e7! 24.♔d1 ♕e8! 25.♕f3 ♘a5

The position is so good that Black is able to aid his strategy with a nice tactic.

26.b3

26.♕d5 ♖e2 27.♖e2 ♖e2 28.♕a5 ♘g3 29.♖f3 ♕e4! with a decisive attack.

26…♘c4! 27.♗c1

Bad would be 27.bc4, because of 27…♕a4 28.♔c1 ♗a3 29.♔b1 ♖b6 30.♔a1 ♕c2. Here you can see how easy it is to bring centralized pieces into play.

27...♘ce3 28.♗e3 ♘e3 29.♘e3 ♖e3 30.♕f2 ♕b5 31.♘c1 ♖c3 32.♖e7 ♗e7 33.♕e1 ♔d7 34.f5 ♖e3 35.♕f2 g5 36.♖e1 ♖e4 37.♖e4 de4 38.♔d2 ♗d6 39.♔c2 ♗f4 0:1

2

▹ **Alekhine**
▸ **Yates**
London 1922 (D64)

1.d4 ♘f6 2.c4 e6 3.♘f3 d5 4.♘c3 ♗e7 5.♗g5 0–0 6.e3 ♘bd7 7.♖c1 c6 8.♕c2 ♖e8 9.♗d3 dc4 10.♗c4 ♘d5 11.♘e4

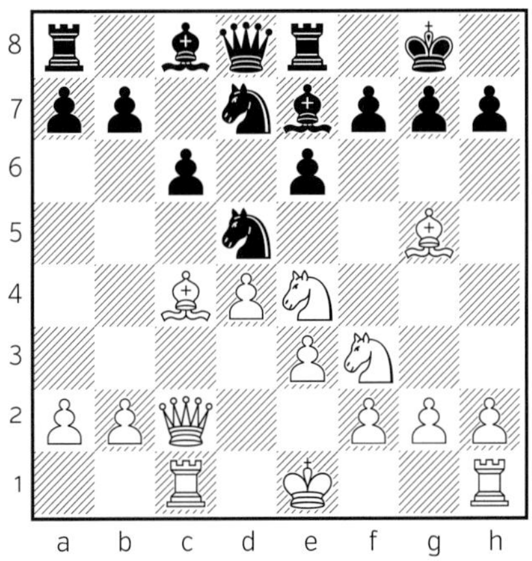

In this entirely normal position, with a still undefined center, Black wanted a little bit too much:

11...f5?

This move of the pawn weakens numerous squares along the e-file and the f-file.

12.♗e7 ♕e7 13.♘ed2 b5?

And now additional weaknesses appear. Black wanted to develop the bishop on c8 at any cost. It would have been wiser to play 13...♘5b6 14.♗d3 g6, with the gradual preparation of the liberating ...e6–e5 move.

14.♗d5 cd5 15.0–0 a5 16.♘b3 a4 17.♘c5 ♘c5 18.♕c5 ♕c5 19.♖c5 b4 20.♖fc1 ♗a6

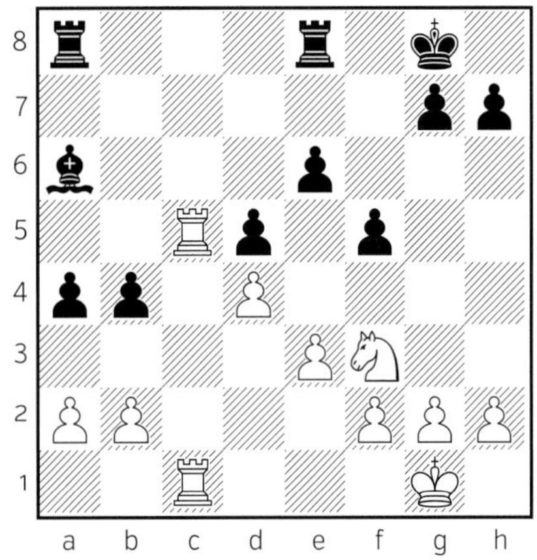

21.♘e5

The centralized knight on the eternal outpost puts pressure on Black's fortifications.

21...♖eb8

It is not possible to play 21...♖ec8 22.♖c8 ♖c8 23.♖c8 ♗c8 24.♘c6.

22.f3!

White's king will become involved in the play.

22...b3 23.a3 h6 24.♔f2 ♔h7 25.h4 ♖f8 26.♔g3 ♖fb8

White is the master of the open file, which means that he has the positional advantage. Next follows the penetration of the rooks to the seventh rank.

27.♖c7 ♗b5 28.♖1c5 ♗a6 29.♖5c6 ♖e8 30.♔f4 ♔g8 31.h5 ♗f1 32.g3 ♗a6 33.♖f7 ♔h7 34.♖cc7 ♖g8 35.♘d7 ♔h8 36.♘f6 ♖gf8 37.♖g7 ♖f6 38.♔e5 1:0.

THE WEAK SQUARE AS A TRUMP!

As with every rule, this one also has exceptions. One of them was demonstrated by Emanuel Lasker, who shocked — in one of the most famous games of all time — Jose Raul Capablanca with a seemingly irrational move. A premature move or a deep strategy?

1

▷ **Lasker**
▶ **Capablanca**
St. Petersburg 1914 [C68]

1.e4 e5 2.♘f3 ♘c6 3.♗b5 a6 4.♗c6
The Spanish Exchange Variation is a very special opening, and helped Lasker to some nice victories. Later on it was forgotten but some decades later it was brought back to life by Robert Fischer who used it to beat many unprepared opponents. Nowadays the variation is chosen by many players, even ones with high ratings. The exchange on c6 defines the pawn structure. After 4...dc6 and a later d4-ed4 White's superiority will be shown on the kingside, where he has four pawns against three pawns. On the other hand on the queenside Black has the same advantage, but he has troubles with the double pawns. Black, though, has other compensation.

4...dc6 5.d4 ed4 6.♕d4 ♕d4 7.♘d4 ♗d6 8.♘c3 ♘e7 9.0–0 0–0 10.f4 ♖e8 11.♘b3 f6

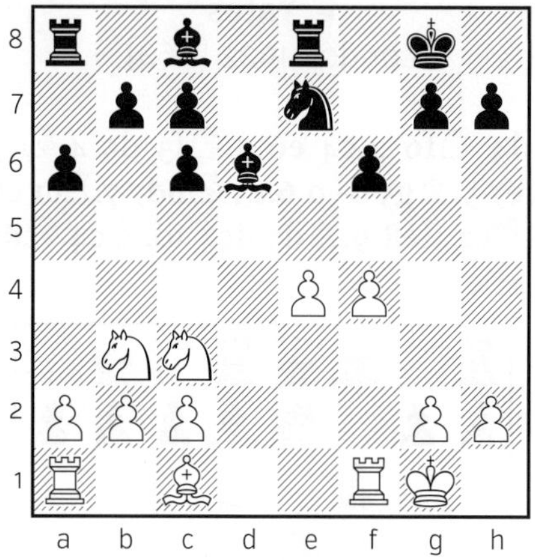

In the diagram we can see the famous position in which Dr. Lasker shocked his opponent with the following move:

12.f5!
Against all respected principles at the time! The movement of the f-pawn gives up its only advantage — the potential passed pawn on the kingside. "The careless advance" also leaves Black with the important central e5-square, but Lasker had foreseen a bit more. With his move he achieved three things: he opened the way for his dark-squared bishop, simultaneously he restricted Black's knight which wanted to settle down on g6

(and after a subsequent f4-f5 then ♘e5) and he started to build a fort on e6 for the knight — and with that he wanted to paralyze the entirety of Black's play.

12...b6

Maybe passive defence would be better — 12...♗d7 13.♗f4 ♖ad8. Black has chosen a plan which is connected with a counterattack on the e4-pawn, but it is very slow and weakens the critical e6-square.

13.♗f4 ♗b7?

With this unfortunate decision Black brings serious troubles upon himself. In principle he is trying to get rid of the doubled pawns, but this time, after the exchange of the pawns, the d6-pawn will be turned into an eternal weakness. Better would have been 13....♗f4! 14.♖f4 c5! with an approximately equal position as shown by Capablanca after the game...

14.♗d6 cd6 15.♘d4 ♖ad8 16.♘e6 ♖d7 17.♖ad1 ♘c8 18.♖f2 b5 19.♖fd2

White strengthens the pressure on the d6-pawn.

19...♖de7 20.b4

Preventing the c5 move and Black is strategically destroyed.

20...♔f7 21.a3 ♗a8?!

The last chance was hidden in the exchange sacrifice — 21...♖e6 22.fe6 ♖e6.

22.♔f2 ♖a7 23.g4

White controls the center and moves the play to the kingside.

23...h6 24.♖d3 a5 25.h4 ab4 26.ab4 ♖ae7 27.♔f3 ♖g8 28.♔f4 g6 29.♖g3 g5

The last of Black's move to be criticized by commentators (e.g. Kasparov) Now it is a little too late for wise advice: 29...gf5 30.ef5 d5 31.g5! hg5 32.hg5 fg5 33.♘g5 ♔f8 34.f6 ♖a7 35.♔e5! etc.

30.♔f3 ♘b6 31.hg5 hg5 32.♖h3!

Lasker was not tempted by the material goods on offer and rather prevents his opponent's counterplay. After 32.♖d6 ♖h8 and ♘c4.

32...♖d7 33.♔g3

The preparation of the end.

33...♔e8 34.♖dh1 ♗b7

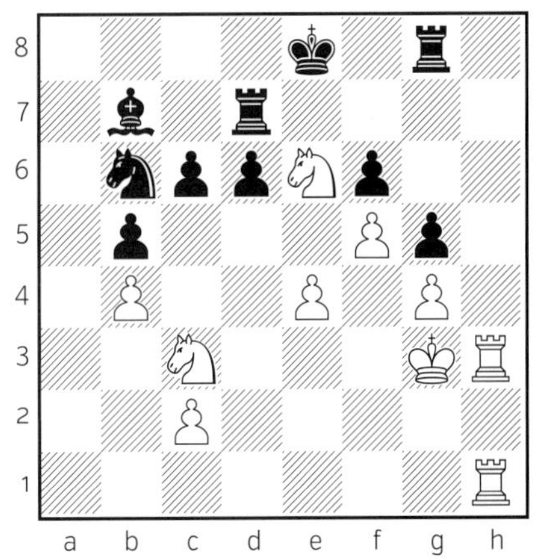

35.e5!

After 23 moves (from 12.f5) White's e-pawn manages to advance! With the e4-e5 move White clears the square for his knight.

35...de5 36.♘e4 ♘d5 37.♘6c5 ♗c8 38.♘d7 ♗d7 39.♖h7 ♖f8 40.♖a1 ♔d8 41.♖a8 ♗c8 42.♘c5 1:0.

COMPLETE CONTROL OVER THE CENTER

Let's have a look at yet another classical example on the theme of complete control of the center. In this game White voluntarily gave up the center, without even thinking of trying to attack it. Black firstly gains control over the center and later on over the both wings as well. White had no choice but to wait and to play without any plan due to his very passive position.

1

▷ **Lisitsin**
▶ **Botvinnik**
Leningrad 1932 [A30]

1.♘f3 c5 2.c4 ♘f6 3.g3 d5 4.cd5 ♘d5 5.♗g2 ♘c6 6.0–0 e5 7.d3 ♗e7 8.♘bd2 0–0 9.♘c4 f6 10.♗e3 ♗e6 11.a4

With this move White solidifies his knight's position, but he has also weakened himself on the queenside.

11...♕d7 12.♕d2 b6 13.♖fc1 ♖ac8 14.♕d1 ♔h8 15.♗d2 ♖fd8 16.♕b3 ♘c7 17.♗c3 ♖b8 18.♕c2 ♘d5 19.♘fd2 ♖bc8 20.♘f1 ♘d4!

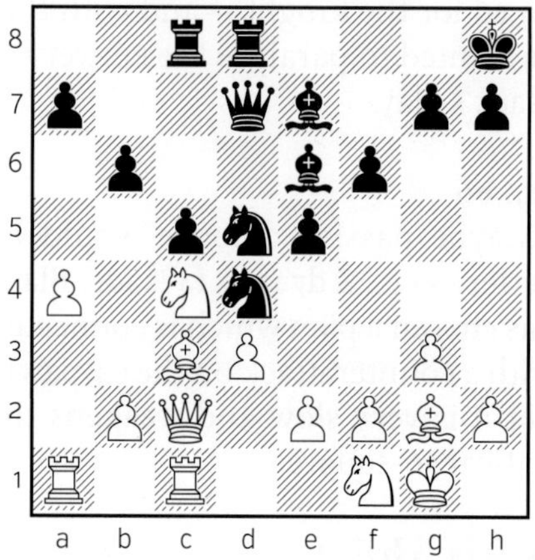

We have seen that White is moving the pieces without any real sense or purpose — his manoeuvres with the queen proving that he has no appropriate strategic plan. In the meantime Black's plan is clear and concrete. With the planned move of his knight to d4 he wants to force the opponent to capture his knight on d4 after which Black can start to put pressure on the e-file.

21.♕d1 ♗g4 22.♗d4

It is difficult for White to play the e2-e3 move because he would decisively weaken his d3-pawn. The concentration of Black's pieces in the center is so strong that it does not allow White to start any counterplay.

22...ed4 23.♕d2 ♗f8

Opening access to the e-file.

24.♖e1 ♖e8 25.h4 ♗h3 26.♗f3 ♖e7 27.♘h2 ♖ce8 28.♔h1 ♗e6! 29.b3 ♘b4! 30.♗g2 ♗d5! 31.♘f3 ♖f7

Black wants to bring his bishop on f8 into play.

32.♔h2 ♗d6 33.♗h3 ♕d8 34.♖ab1 ♖fe7 35.♘g1 ♗c7 36.♘a3 ♗b7!

With the threat 37...♕d5.

37.♗g2 ♗g2 38.♔g2 ♘d5 39.♘c2 ♕d6

A known manoeuvre: after gaining control in the center the play is moved to the wing. After 40...♘e3 there is no defence.

40.♘a3 ♘e3 41.♔h1 ♘g4 42.♕f4

If 42.♖f1, then 42...♕d5, if 42.♔g2 ♘f2!

42...♕f4 43.gf4 ♘f2 44.♔g2 ♘d3 0:1

EXCHANGES IN THE CENTER

A very important element, one which we will come across constantly, represents exchanges in the center. When to exchange, what to exchange and how to exchange? The exchanges in the center usually transforms the type of center or even changes the entire pawn structure.

Therefore it is very important to know different kinds of positions and to pick the most appropriate one for us from among them.

1

1.e4 e5 2.♘f3 ♘c6 3.♗c4 ♗c5 4.♘c3 ♘f6 5.d3 d6 6.♗e3

The exchange 6...♗e3 is not recommended. Black creates doubled pawns for White, but with that he has made White's position in the center stronger: White gains control over the d4 square and the e4 square is not in danger and so the help from the f-pawn does not make a difference. Besides that White also gained the open f-file that he will use later on.

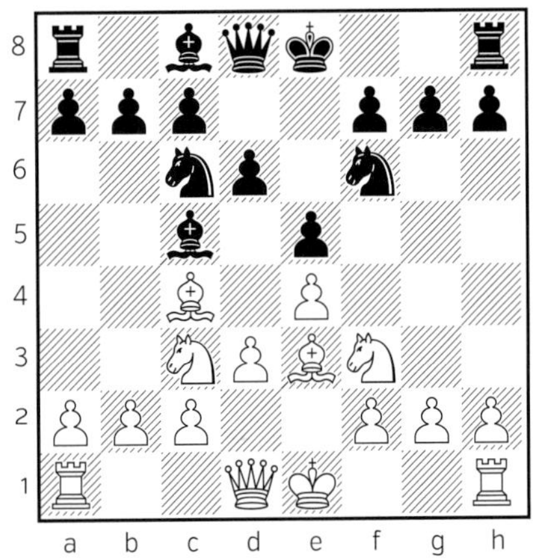

1.e4 c5 2.♘f3 ♘c6 3.d4 cd4 4.♘d4 ♘f6 5.♘c3 d6 6.♗e2 e5

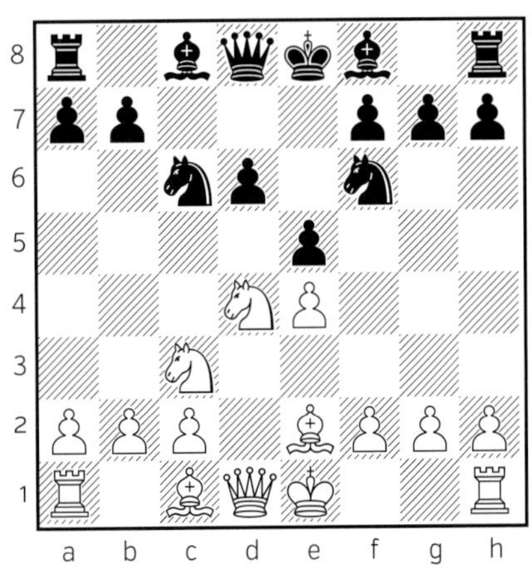

The exchange with 7.♘c6 is not recommended. The pawns are as a rule stronger the closer they are to the center and White only helps Black with this exchange. The b-pawn has moved a file closer to the center, and with it the d6-pawn gains a helper for when he advances.

The exchanges are good for the player when they free a square for certain pieces.

2

1.e4 e6 2.d4 d5 3.♘d2 c5 4.ed5 ed5 5.♘gf3 ♘c6 6.♗b5 ♗d6

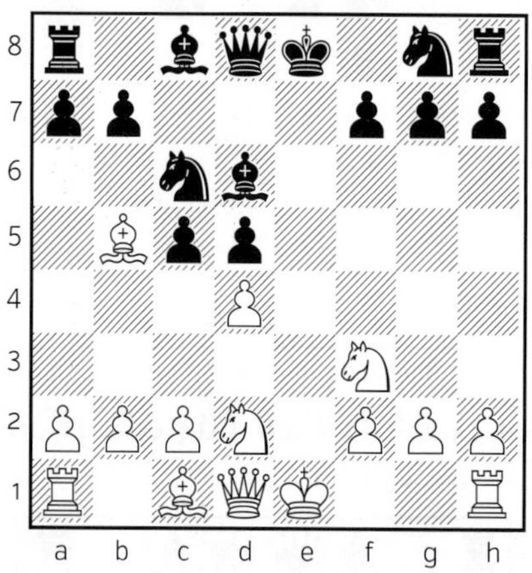

The exchange 7.dc5 is good for White, as it frees the d4-square for his knight (or his bishop).

Or an example from the game Alatortsev : Levenfish, Tbilisi 1937:

1.d4 ♘f6 2.c4 e6 3.g3 ♗b4 4.♗d2 ♗d2 5.♘d2 ♘c6 6.♘gf3 d6 7.♗g2 e5 8.d5 ♘e7 9.0–0 0–0 10.e4 ♘d7 11.♘e1 f5 12.♘d3 f4! 13.gf4?

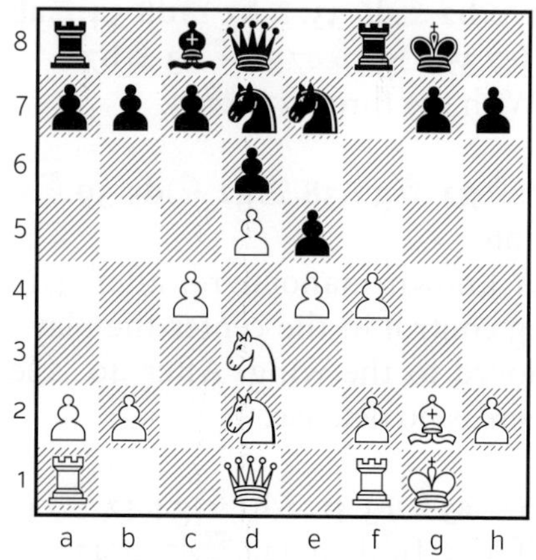

A serious mistake. Who knows what White was counting on? Black, of course, took with the pawn and thereby freed the e5-square, on which he will later put his knight or some other piece. For example 13...ef4 14.♘f3 ♘g6 15.♘d3 ♕e7 and then the knight comes to e5.

At the end of the 19th century the foundations for the positional school of chess were put in place by Wilhelm Steinitz. His conclusions were revolutionary and their value was even higher, because he was constantly proving them correct in his games. The earlier understanding about the center and the statements about the advantage of the player that has his pawn in the center were torturing Steinitz. Later on he understood that not all exchanges in the center are bad, on the contrary he thought that, even though we might lose some tension, the exchanges can be useful:

when we get rid of our pawn in the center we open the way for the rook that will subsequently attack the opponent's pawn on the now semi-open file. If this kind of attack is supported by other pieces, it already means a specific system to the play. Steinitz also tried out his plan in practice. In some variations of the Spanish Opening (Ruy Lopez) he started to (with the Black pieces) voluntarily take on d4, passing the space advantage to his opponent but planning to attack the e4-pawn.

Later on this sort of play was used by many great masters and the tactic is used in many openings even today.

3

▷ **Spassky**
▶ **Larsen**
Malmö 1968 [C46]

1.e4 e5 2.♘f3 ♘c6 3.♘c3 g6 4.d4 ed4 5.♘d4 ♗g7 6.♗e3 ♘f6 7.♗e2 0–0 8.0–0 ♖e8 9.♘c6 bc6 10.♗f3 ♗b7 11.♕d2 d6

You can see here an example of the previously described way of playing. Black took on d4 and made peace with White's knight in the center — and also with his apparently passive position in this part of the board. Black's d6-pawn is managing to stop White's e4-pawn and Black's pawns are so compactly connected that there is no visible way in which White could attack them before the endgame. That is why White would like to see the e4-e5 move happen, to clear the position in the center, but there is no simple way to force it. Meanwhile Black will be strengthening the pressure on the e4-pawn, along the e-file, on which he will place his heavy pieces — and also with the help of his light pieces.

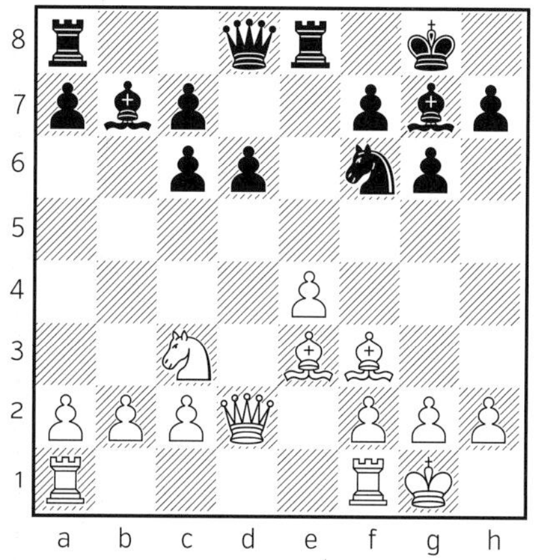

12.♗h6?

It would be better for White to play 12.♗g5 trying to disable Black's attack on his e4-pawn.

12...♗h6 13.♕h6 ♖e5 14.♖ae1 c5 15.♖e3 ♕e7 16.♖fe1 ♖e8

After a couple of moves, the position has drastically changed: all Black's pieces are actively attacking the e4-pawn and White's pieces are playing a solely defensive role. There is no way for Black to bring yet another piece into action and that is why he needs to get rid of one of the opponent's defensive pieces. The most vulnerable is the bishop on f3 and that can be disturbed by the ...g5-g4 move.

17.h4 ♕e6 18.♕f4 ♔g7 19.b3 h6 20.♕g3 ♕d7 21.♕f4 ♖8e7 22.♘d5?

White lost his nerve and the result will be shown in the endgame — his bishop on f3 restricted by his own pawns, against Black's powerful knight on e5 that controls everything.

22...♗d5 23.ed5 g5 24.hg5 hg5 25.♕g3 ♕f5 26.c4 ♖e3 27.fe3 ♖e5 28.♗d1 ♕d3 29.♗f3 ♕c3 30.♔h2 a5 31.♔h1 ♔f8 32.♖f1 ♕e3 33.♕h3 ♔g7 34.g3 ♕d4 35.g4 a4 36.♗d1 ♖e3 37.♕g2 ♖d3 38.♗e2 ♖d2 39.ba4 ♕e5 0:1

Black players quickly realized that the tactic is a sly one and started looking for numerous other variations where they could give up the center. In the next example Black took with his d5-pawn on e4, leaving White with his d4-pawn. Black later starts to restrict it with the c6 and e6 moves and then begins to pressure it.

4

▷ **Klovans**
▶ **Chistiakov**
USSR 1967 (C13)

1.e4 e6 2.d4 d5 3.♘c3 ♘f6 4.♗g5 de4 5.♘e4 ♗e7 6.♗f6 gf6 7.♘f3 b6 8.♗d3 ♗b7 9.♕e2 ♘d7 10.0–0–0 c6

Black has set up his blockade: he is not worried about White's slight advantage due to the almost complete blockage in the center, where White will not be able to create a real threat for some time.

11.♖he1 ♕c7 12.♔b1 0–0–0 13.g3 ♔b8

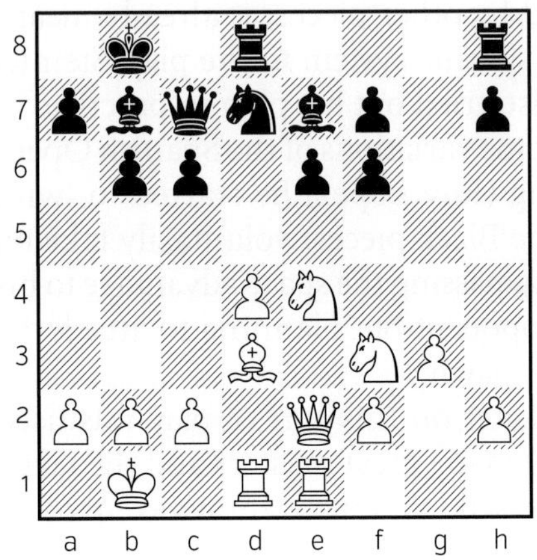

14.♗a6

When opponent has a Bishop pair, to change one is a logical decision.

14...♗a6 15.♕a6 ♖hg8 16.♕e2 f5 17.♘ed2 h5 18.♘c4 h4 19.♖d3 hg3 20.hg3 ♖h8 21.a3 ♗f6 22.♖ed1 b5 23.♘e3 ♘b6 24.♖c1

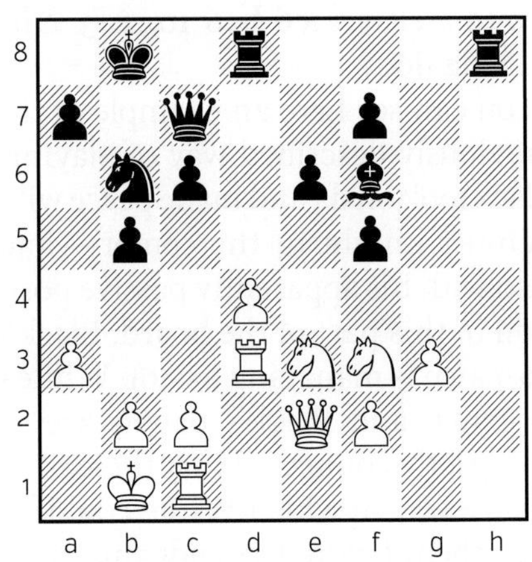

Black has reached an almost ideal position. He is putting pressure on the d4-pawn and White cannot start any action in the center. The d4-pawn is fixed on a black square and is creating around itself a complex of weak light-squares that will become the targets for development.

Of course Black will have to show something more if he wants to win. The active plans are connected with the advancement of the pawn on both wings.

24...f4 25.♘g4 ♗g7 26.♘ge5 fg3 27.♕e4 ♖d6 28.fg3 f6 29.♘g6 ♖e8 30.♖h1 ♘d5 31.g4 ♕f7 32.♖h7 ♖d7 33.♖d1 ♔a8 34.♖e1 ♖b7 35.♖hh1 b4 36.ab4 ♖b4 37.♔c1 ♕b7 38.b3 ♕a6 39.♔b2 ♕c4 40.♖e3 ♘e3

And Black is an exchange up with which he won the game.

In the years that followed after the Second World War, a similar idea — although an improved one — was launched in the world of the masters by the young Soviet grandmasters, starting with David Bronstein and Efim Geller.

We are of course talking about the King's Indian Defence and the variations that see Black taking on d4. Later many new variations evolved on this theme.

THE BLOCKADE OF THE CENTER WITH THE PIECES

A very efficient, but also very hard to realize, method of play is the blockade of the center with the pieces. What we have in mind are the positions where we move our pawns away from the center and replace them with pieces that are able to put more pressure on the opponent from the squares in the center. When we talk about that we cannot ignore Aron Nimzowitsch, the father of the teaching about the blockade and its consequences. Let us have a look into a blocked position with which Nimzowitsch enchanted millions of chess players from different nations:

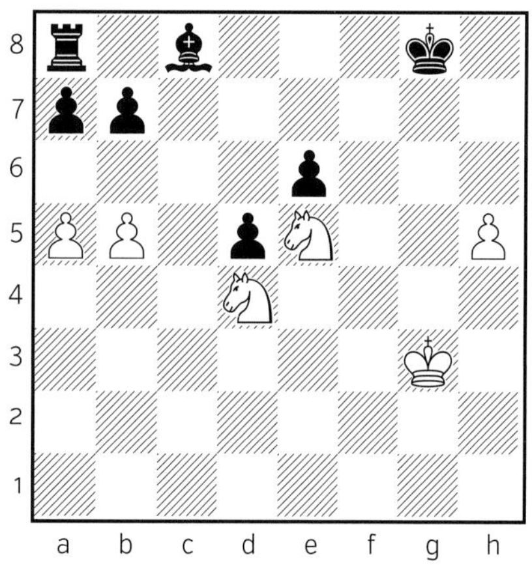

Even though White has less material, and that there are only a few pieces left on the board and White has no special threats, he is the one who is trying to win!

The position is, of course, not real and is a figment of Nimzovitsch's imagination. But his ideas were also shown in practice.

1

▷ **Nimzowitsch**
▶ **Salwe**
Karlsbad 1911 [C02]

1.e4 e6 2.d4 d5

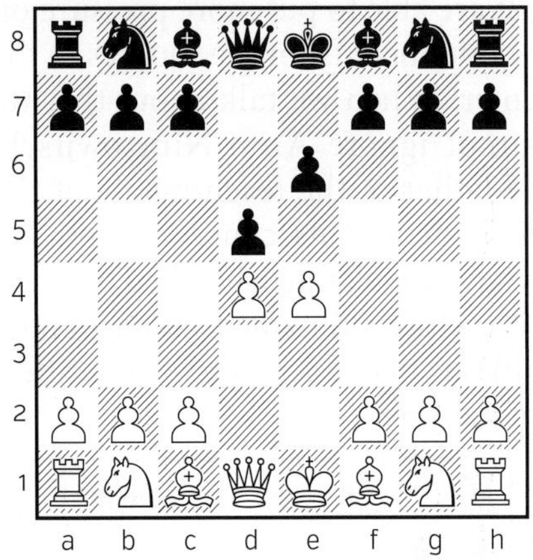

3.e5

The Advance Variation of the French Defence was one of Nimzowitsch's favourites. The continuation is quite simple: Black will try to destroy White's center. Nimzowitsch managed to prove that White is able to play against that with the pieces, and not just with the pawns- which was the belief at that time.

3...c5 4.c3 ♘c6 5.♘f3 ♕b6 6.♗d3

Nowadays they more often play 6.♗e2 or 6.a3, which prepares the next blockade — on the queenside: it is interesting that Black can also after 6.a3 decide on a blockage: 6...c4!? after which follows a complicated strategic battle.

6...♗d7

Black is preparing to take on d4, which was not possible immediately: 6...cd4 7.cd4 ♘d4? 8.♘d4 ♕d4 9.♗b5.

7.dc5!? ♗c5 8.0–0 f6

Black follows his strategy and is hoping that he will manage to somehow open the center. If he is able to play the ...e6-e5 move, his bishop will come into play and all the worries would be forgotten. White will face him in the center with his pieces.

9.b4!

A good strategy, which leaves White with the complete control over the dark-squares
(c5, d4, e5).

9...♗e7 10.♗f4

The additional defence of the decisive e5-square.

10...fe5 11.♘e5 ♘e5 12.♗e5

Nimzowitsch: "The new blockage piece (the bishop) does not do its job any worse than the knight."

12...♘f6

12...♗f6? with the plan of trying to exchange the unpleasant bishops, is not possible: 13.♕h5 g6 14.♗g6 hg6 15.♕g6 ♔e7 16.♗f6 ♘f6 17.♕g7+-.

13.♘d2

Nimzowitsch: “Trying to help the blockage piece!”

Play concentrated on winning the h7-pawn: 13.♕c2? 0–0! 14.♗f6 ♖f6 15.♗h7 ♔h8 16.♗g6 e5!–+ would be completely wrong, because it would liberate Black.

13...0–0 14.♘f3 ♗d6 15.♕e2 ♖ac8 16.♗d4 ♕c7 17.♘e5

Nimzowitsch:”Now White is controlling both central squares”

17...♗e8

Black opened both files for his rooks (c and f), but that does not do him any good. White has control over the center, but it is still not enough to win the game. Attention: when we have the advantage in the center we need to move the play to the wing and finish the task.

18.♖ae1 ♗e5 19.♗e5 ♕c6 20.♗d4 ♗d7 21.♕c2!

The queen is being activated in order to attack Black’s king.

21...♖f7 22.♖e3!

The last pieces are headed into battle.

22...b6 23.♖g3 ♔h8

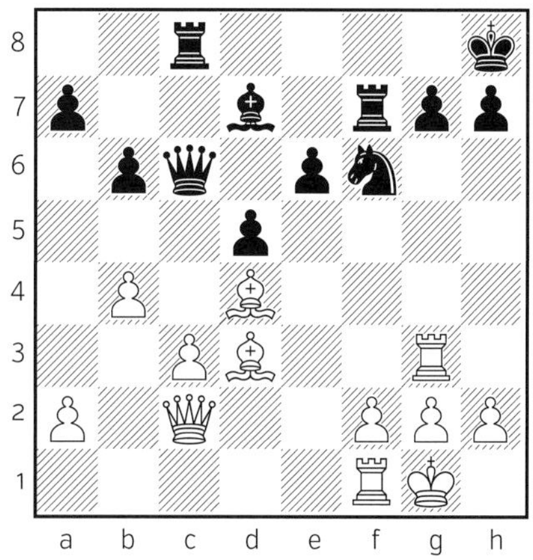

24.♗h7! e5

24...♘h7 25.♕g6!+-.

25.♗g6 ♖e7 26.♖e1 ♕d6 27.♗e3 d4 28.♗g5 ♖c3 29.♖c3 dc3 30.♕c3 ♔g8 31.a3 ♔f8 32.♗h4 ♗e8 33.♗f5 ♕d4 34.♕d4 ed4 35.♖e7 ♔e7 36.♗d3 ♔d6 37.♗f6 gf6 38.♔f1 ♗c6 39.h4 1:0.

THE TYPES OF CENTERS

In the following chapters we will get to know some basic types of centers and recommended methods of playing for both sides. All will be shown with the help of games from the great chess masters. The goal is for you to see that they too spend a lot of time thinking about this most important part of the board.

THE MOBILE CENTER

It is very easy to describe the mobile center: we can talk about the mobile center when one of the players has some pawns in the center (at least two) and the other player has one or even none. For example: e4, d4 : e6 or e4, d4 : d6 or d4, e5, f5 : c6, f7 or e3 : d5, e5, f5.

We talk about mobility, because one of the attacker's pawns is able to move freely due to not having any pawns in front of him. These kind of positions are usually very tense and the value of every move is very high. Every tempo can be decisive for the end result of the game. There is no room here for slow manoeuvres, for standing still, but only for a concrete action supported by accurate calculations.

It is clear that a player with the mobile center has the positional advantage. The pawns (the two pawns) are putting pressure on the opponent and are taking his space. The attacker will try to progress with his three pawns as far as he can and so push his opponent into an even more defensive role and also fix his pieces. After the advancing of the mobile pawns, there are two realistic effects:

The attacker will create a passed pawn: e5, d5 : c7, f7 — 1.e6 or 1.d6.

The attacker will increase his pressure on the opponent's pieces and will later move the play to the wing.

Seemingly, the defender's play is also quite simple. His first wish will be to attack the opponent's center in order to block or even destroy it. To achieve the blockade, he needs to undermine the center, but he needs to be careful. And yet another very important rule: when there is an active, mobile center, the defender needs to forget about any kind of wing activity!

IGNORING THE MOBILE CENTER

To begin with, let's see how dangerous the mobile center can be and how catastrophic the consequences can be if you play incautiously and ignore the center. In the Giuoco Pianissimo an incautious beginner could end up like this:

1.e4 e5 2.♘f3 ♘c6 3.♗c4 ♗c5 4.c3 ♘f6 5.0–0 a6?

Previously mentioned, this is an incautious move. Black needed to bravely take on e4.

6.d4 ed4 7.cd4 ♗a7 8.d5 ♘e7 9.e5!

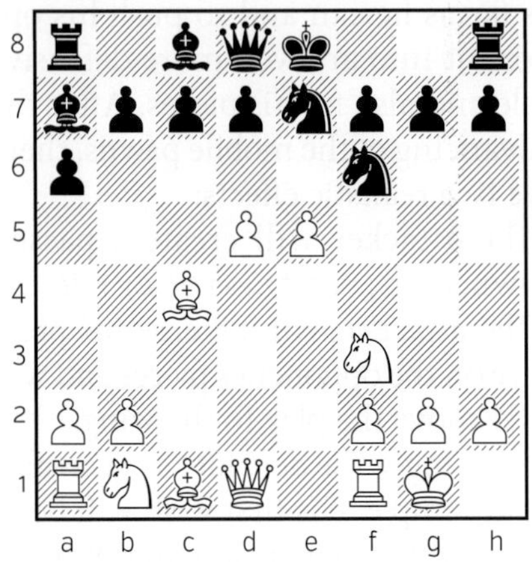

White's pawns are frightening and they will help to open the e-file causing grief to Black's king.

9...♘g4 10.h3 ♘h6 11.d6 ♘g6 12.♗g5 f6 13.ef6 gf6 14.♖e1 ♔f8 15.♗h6 mate!

An instructive game — I hope that it is clear now why a mobile center must not be ignored.

THE DOMINATION OF THE MOBILE CENTER

We got to know the classical mobile pawn center in the game between Botvinnik and Capablanca. White's pawns were advanced gradually, pushing Black's pieces away from the center and into a defensive role. When White had gained enough space, a mating attack followed. In that game the Cuban managed to defend thoughtfully, but generally the games end with more-or-less the same result.

1

▹ **Polgar**
▸ **Boensch**
Dortmund 1990 [D36]

1.d4 ♘f6 2.c4 e6 3.♘c3 d5 4.cd5 ed5 5.♗g5 c6 6.e3 ♗e7 7.♕c2 ♗g4 8.♘ge2 ♗e2 9.♗e2 ♘bd7 10.0–0 0–0 11.♗d3 ♖e8

The Exchange Variation of the Queen's Gambit offers White, as a rule, a potential mobile center. White's e-pawn is not facing any other pawns and that is why the preparation of the e3-e4 move is one of the basic plans in this position.

12.f3

As planned, though White will not be rushing with the e3-e4 move. Before that safety must be taken care of and, above all, the d4-pawn needs to be strengthened as it will be turned into a weakness after e4 — de4. Due to that, White will first move her bishop to f2 and then play the "mysterious" ♖ad1 move.

12...♘f8

Black decides to wait. The only possible solution to prevent White's plan is the ...c6-c5 move, but Black obviously did not like the position after the d4xc5 capture.

13.♗h4 a6 14.♖ad1 ♘g6 15.♗f2 ♗d6

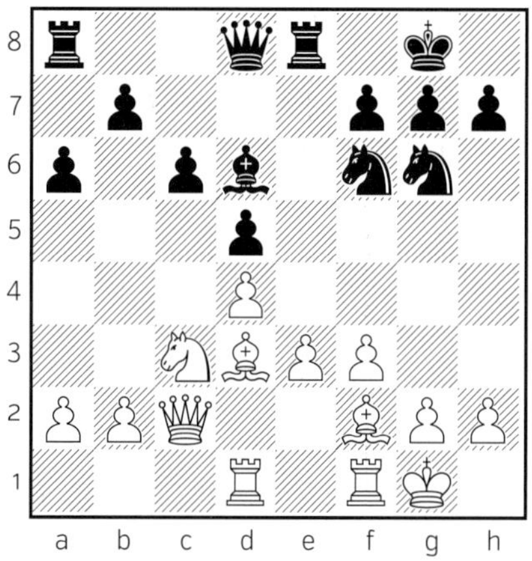

Now everything is prepared and there is no more reason to wait.

16.e4 de4

Black evidently has no choice but to take. Otherwise would follow 17.e4-e5 and Black's pieces would be pushed into passive defensive roles.

17.fe4

You can see here a classical position with a mobile center.

17...♘g4 18.e5

A very important moment. Every single step that is made by one of the mobile pawns in the center can be decisive and can impact the following course of the play. With the 18.e5 move, which was, of course, foreseen by White, Polgar decided to attack the king and for that she was willing to sacrifice her dark-squared bishop (which had no good spot to move to anyway).

The e4-e5 move is important also for another reason: the advancement of one of the two pawns creates a hole into which the opponent can place one of his pieces. After 18.e5 this hole is located on the d5-square (after the possible d5-move, the hole would be on e5). These holes are the reason why the movements of the pawns can be complicated and one must think about them very carefully.

18...♗c7

Worse is 18...♘f2? because of 19.♕f2.

19.♗c4 ♖e7 20.♔h1

Withdrawal of the king from the dangerous diagonal and also a preparation for withdrawal of the bishop — ♗g1. Therefore it is necessary for Black to take.

20...♘f2 21.♕f2 ♕d7 22.♘e4

The attack is now joined by the knight.

22...♖f8 23.♕f3

It is hard to lose a game with only one weakness. White is attacking the f7-square and Black is suitably defending it. But White's space advantage, because of the e5-pawn, makes it possible for White to create another weakness on the kingside. And it will be difficult for Black to defend two weaknesses in such a pressed position! Now, where should White attack? On the h7-square, of course!

23...♕e8 24.♕h5 ♔h8

This was really necessary — the threat was 25.♘f6 gf6 26.ef6 R... 27.♕h6.

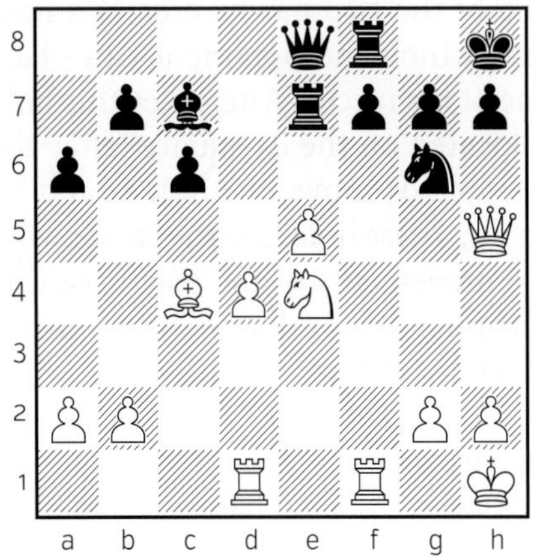

25.♖d3!

White's final piece joins the attack.

25...h6 26.♖df3 ♘e5

Black is completely helpless and is trying to somehow complicate matters but the former World Champion will be careful till the end.

27.de5 ♖e5 28.♖f7! ♖f7 29.♕f7 1:0.

Black is pinned all over: 29.♕f7 ♕f7 30.♖f7 ♖e4 31.♖f8 ♔h7 32.♗d3.

A FEELING FOR TIME

For appropriate play in positions with the mobile center a good feeling for the tempo aspect is needed, as is the preservation of the initiative. One of the best masters of this kind of play was Alexander Alekhine. Let us see how he, with the appropriate usage of tempos and consistent pressure, took down the American, Frank Marshall.

1

▷ **Alekhine**
▶ **Marshall**
Baden-Baden 1925 [Q06]

1.d4 d5 2.c4 ♘f6?

This move is bad because White can built a strong pawn center with no obstacles.

3.cd5 ♘d5 4.e4 ♘f6 5.♗d3 e5!?

The right choice of strategy — Black starts to undermine White's center. The sacrifice of the pawn is only temporary because White cannot keep it.

6.de5 ♘g4 7.♘f3

Worse would be 7.f4 ♗c5 8.♘h3 ♕h4, then 0–0 and Black would have great compensation with his play against White's king.

7...♘c6 8.♗g5!

White is not interested in the defence of the won pawn (8.♗f4 ♘b4!?) and instead he follows his plan to gain a mobile center.

8...♗e7 9.♗e7 ♕e7 10.♘c3 ♘ce5 11.♘e5 ♕e5 12.h3 ♘f6

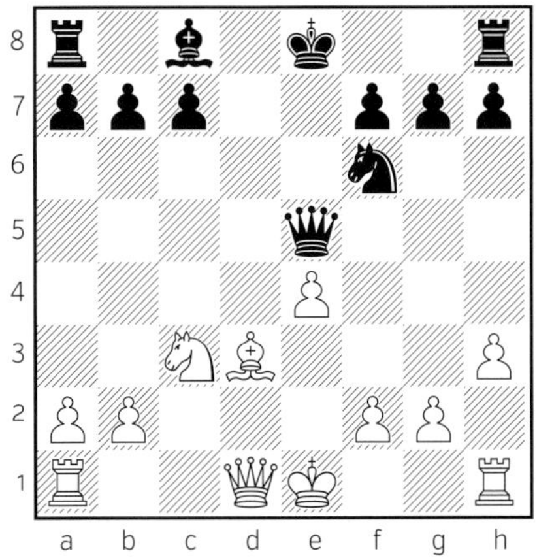

13.♕d2!

Alekhine demonstrates his feeling for dynamism with this move. After the incautious 13.0–0 Black would strike with 13...g5! Now 13...g5 is worse, because White would be castling on the queenside instead.

13...♗d7 14.♕e3!

Again showing great style — this move prevents long castling.

14...♗c6 15.0–0–0 0–0

With this opposite-sides castling Black is clearly in danger — but he needs to castle sooner or later.

16.f4!

The mobile center starts to invade Black's territory.

16...♕e6

Or 16...♕a5 17.e5 ♘d5 18.♘d5 ♗d5 19.♗h7 and 20.♕d3.

17.e5! ♖fe8 18.♖he1 ♖ad8

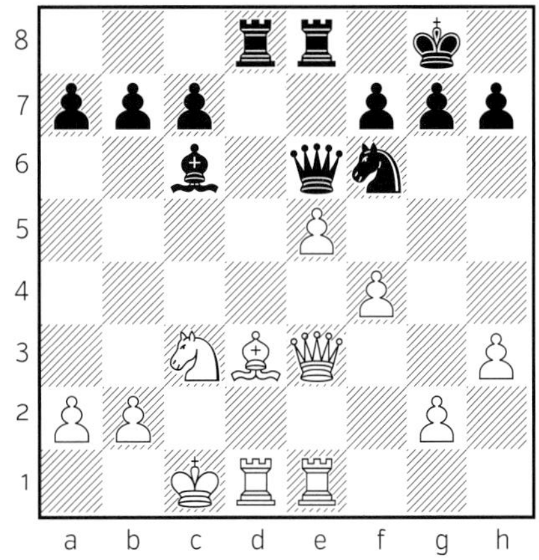

19.f5! ♕e7

First the opponent needs to be pushed back and then follows the attack! The rest of the game is all about the technique of calculating different variations.

20.♕g5 ♘d5 21.f6! ♕f8 22.♗c4 ♘c3 23.♖d8 ♖d8 24.fg7 ♘a2

If 24...♕e8, then 25.♗f7 ♔f7 26.♖f1 ♔e6 27.♖f6 ♔d5 28.♖f8 +-

25.♔b1 ♕e8 26.e6 ♗e4 27.♔a1 f5

27...fe6 28.♗e6 ♕e6 29.♕d8 ♔g7 30.♕d4 and 31.♖e4.

28.e7 ♖d5 29.♕f6 ♕f7 30.e8♕ 1:0

Black did not manage to orient himself. First he gave up the center without a battle, after which he was correct in breaking with the 5...e5 move, but then he started to philosophize and started to calculate the ...g7-g5 move. White in the meantime calmly waited for him and when the time was right he send his mobile pawns into battle and ended the game with a lightning-like attack.

PASSED PAWNS IN THE CENTER

The defender faces even more problems when there are no obstacles in front of the mobile pawns in the center. Let's take a look at a classical example of ignoring the mobile pawns in the center, and an example of the complete helplessness when the center is taken over by the opponent's pawns. It is very important to have the possibility of undermining them and the possibility of pressuring them. When a player has no potential for doing that, his position will soon turn into a disaster.

1

▹ **Gligoric**
▸ **Szabo**
Helsinki 1952 [E42]

1.d4 ♘f6 2.c4 e6 3.♘c3 ♗b4 4.e3 c5 5.♘ge2 d5 6.a3 cd4 7.ed4 ♗e7 8.c5

This move reveals White's plans; he wants to play actively on the queenside. The old rule states: ⊕Against action on the wing you must strike in the center!"

8...0–0 9.b4 b6 10.g3 bc5 11.dc5

Everything is clear: White thinks that he will gain a decisive initiative with the rapid advancement of his pawns on the queenside, while Black is not afraid of this advance and in the meantime wants to conquer the center.

11...a5 12.♖b1 ab4 13.ab4 ♘c6 14.♗g2 ♖b8 15.♗a3

White chose a plan, but then started to complicate matters. It is true that the advance does not bring him any riches: 15.b5 ♗c5! 16.bc6 ♖b1 17.♘b1 ♕b6 (or 17...♘g4, with great compensation for the lost piece).

15...♗d7 16.0–0 ♘a7

Black's play is simple: firstly he will block any kind of advance of White's pawns, and the rest will take care of itself.

17.♖e1 ♘e8 18.♗c1 ♗f6

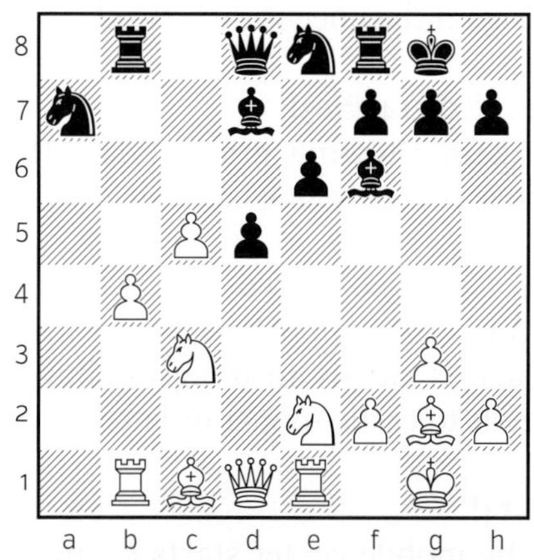

A very interesting position! It is obvious that White voluntarily gave up the central pawns and now wants Black to advance them as far as possible. White's plan would then be to undermine them or place a piece among them. In order to do that he chose a very provocative plan, which is literally inviting Black to progress.

The fearless Hungarian took up the challenge.

19.♗f4!? e5 20.♗d2 d4 21.♘d5 ♗c6 22.♘f6 ♕f6 23.♗c6 ♕c6

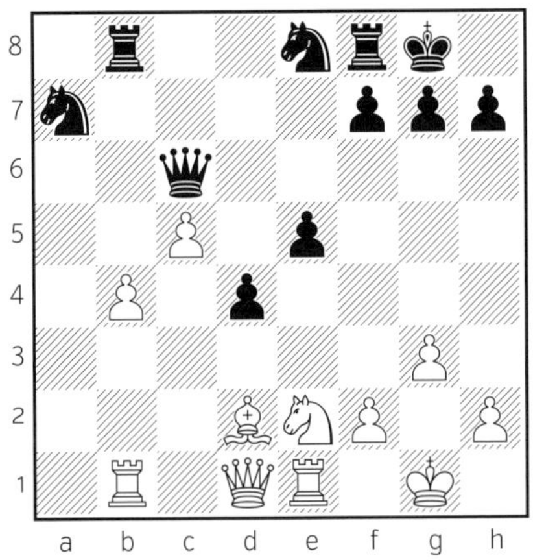

Next follows the undermining, for which Black is well-prepared.

24.f4 f6!

After the swap on e5 Black's pawns truly do not have support from the sides, but that kind of support is now not needed as White's play is paralyzed.

25.♕b3 ♔h8 26.♖f1 ♘c7 27.♕c4 ♘ab5!

An excellent move, which blocks all White's pawns and also defends the d4- pawn. The ...e5-e4 move is in the air.

28.♖be1 h6 29.g4

What else? White has no power on the queenside and he is beaten in the center. All he is left with is to try to attack on the kingside. It is wonderful to watch how Szabo systematically improved his position, without rushing things.

29...♖be8 30.f5 ♕d5

Black offers a transposition to the endgame, where White's chances would be the highest. Despite that, White wanted more than just a difficult endgame and so avoids the exchange.

31.♕c1 ♔h7 32.♘g3

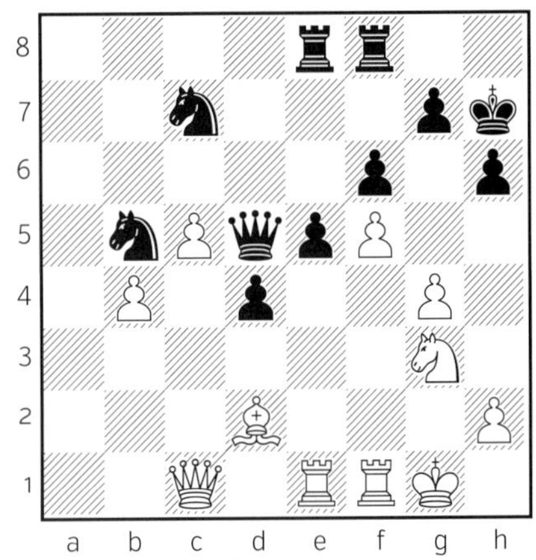

A splendid position! The time has come to start the pawn advances as Black naturally does not want the move ♘e4 to appear. Black's manoeuvres are very instructive: careful movement of the pawns and prevention of any blockade by White being able to place a piece among them.

White is left with just a desperate attack. We know that attacks on the wing can be successful only if you have the control over the center, so...

32...e4! 33.♗f4 e3 34.♕d1 ♕c4 35.h4 ♘d5 36.g5 d3!

Moving forward a rank!

37.♕g4 ♖g8!

A last prevention — White threatened to take on h6 followed by ♕g6.

38.♘h5 ♖e4 39.g6 ♔h8 40.♕g3

White gave up before Black could even respond **0:1.**

We have seen how strong the connected pawns can be in the center when there is no obstacle in front of them, but we don't encounter this kind of position too often in tournament practice. More common are the positions where one of the pawns is facing an obstacle and in this case the attacker (the player with the mobile center) usually tries to remove whatever obstacle is in his way. Let's see an example!

2

▹ **Bachtiar**
▸ **Bilek**
Skopje 1972 [A40]

1.d4 g6 2.g3 ♗g7 3.♗g2 c5 4.c3 ♕b6 5.dc5

But wait a second: we already figured it out that the pawns have a higher value the closest they are to the center, so why is it necessary to exchange a central pawn for the one on the file next to it?

5...♕c5 6.♘f3 ♘f6 7.0–0 0–0 8.♘bd2 d6 9.♕a4 ♘bd7 10.♕h4 ♕c7 11.♘g5

This aggressive action of White's seems a little forced and has no foundations in control over the center. It is also not good in a development sense, nor is it an appropriate placement of the pieces.

11...a5 12.♘de4

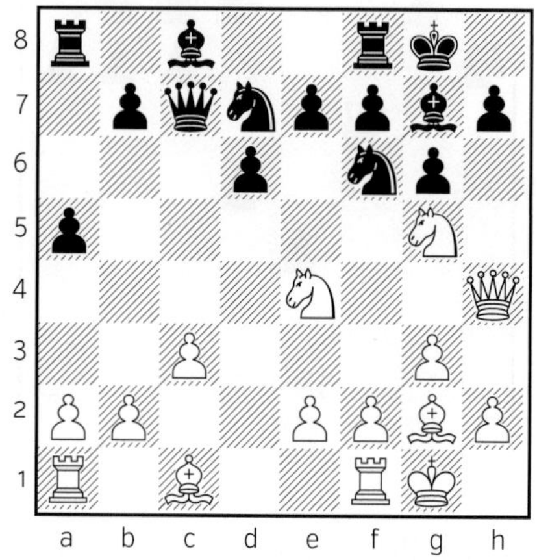

12...a4!

Black wants to force the a2-a3 move, because he is following the basic positional principle: when the opponents only have a bishop left on the board, the one that places his pawns on the squares that have the opposite colour to that of the bishops, has the advantage. Since there are dark-squared bishops on the board, the pawns need to be placed on the light squares!

13.♗d2 h6 14.♘f6 ♘f6 15.♘e4 ♘e4 16.♗e4 ♔h7 17.♗d3

If White had understood where the traps in the position are, than he would definitely move his bishop to the g2-square, from where it would be easier to fight against Black's pawns in the center. White did move his bishop to a seemingly active square, but from there Black's king cannot realistically be attacked.

17...e5 18.♖ac1 f5

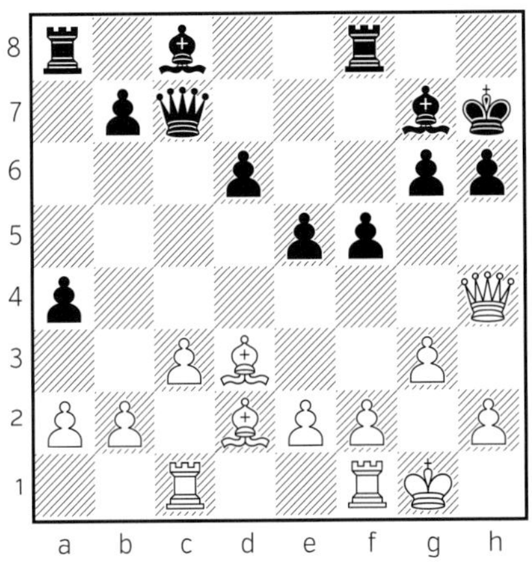

19.e4

Black's pawns need to be stopped, but White can only succeed in this temporarily: Black will prepare the d6-d5 move.

19...♕f7 20.ef5

The threat was 20...f4 followed by ...g6-g5.

20...gf5 21.♕b4 d5

Black has gained the control over the center and is stealing White's space. The attempt at a blockade will not work, however, and even less so with the upcoming unprincipled swap of the light-squared bishops.

22.f4 e4 23.♗b5?! ♗d7 24.♗e3 ♖fc8 25.♗d7 ♕d7 26.♖fd1

It looks like White has succeeded. Black's pawns in the center are blocked and ♗d4 is threatened, with the appropriate blockade. He also threatens to undermine the center with the c3-c4 move. However, Black evaluated the position more deeply:

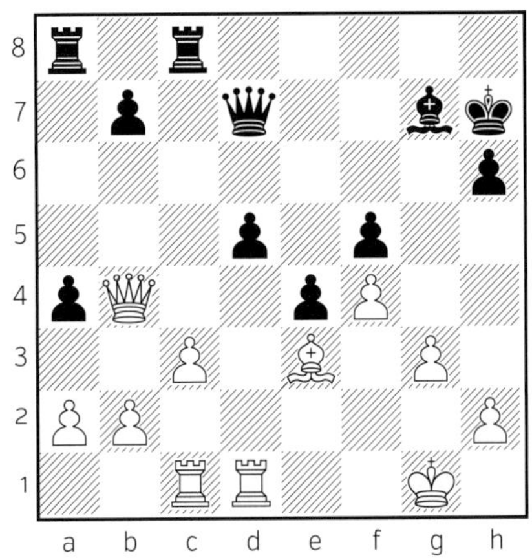

26...b5!

Preventing the undermining and he also indirectly preventing the blockade due to the threat 27...♖c4 forcing 28.♕a3.

27.b3 ab3 28.ab3 ♖a2

The next positional element on the list is — the seventh rank!

29.c4

With this move White frees the way for Black's d-pawn but again it is too late for sage advice. Let's take a look at a few variations: 29.♖d2 ♖d2 30.♗d2 ♗f8 31.♕a6 ♗c5; 29.♖e1 ♗f8 30.♕d4 ♗c5 31.♕c5 (31.♕e5 ♗e3) 31...♖c5 32.♗c5 b4.

29...d4 30.c5 d3 31.♖d2 ♖d2 32.♕d2 ♗d4 33.♕f2

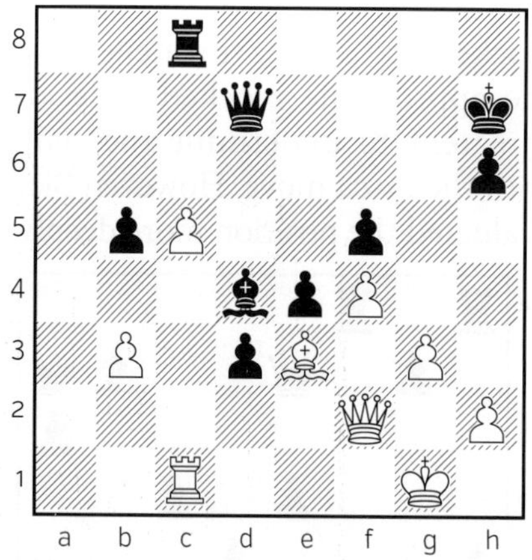

33...♖c5! 34.♖c5 ♗c5 0:1

Black's central pawns are unstoppable.

THE DEFENSIVE PLAY

Of course, the defender in not immediately lost when he is playing against the mobile center. But it is very important for him to know a lot of possibilities for he can defend against this kind of center. We will get to know the basic ones — pressuring the mobile center with the pieces:

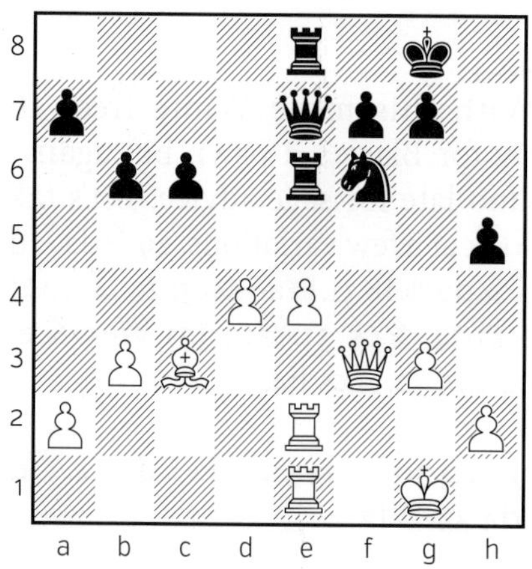

Black attacks the e4-pawn, which now has no choice but to advance. Now an empty space is left on d5 for Black's knight and after that it will become — a blocked mobile center:

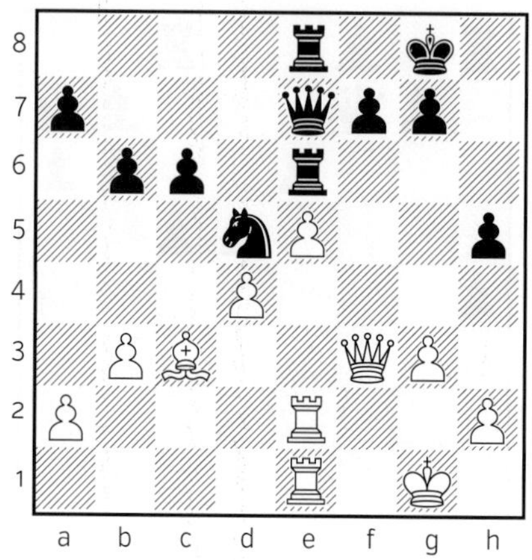

White is completely helpless in the position. The "wrong" bishop is left on the board and White's pawns are standing on the squares of the "wrong" colour. Black's main strategy is to open the position at the right moment and seek a favourable outcome — destroying the center:

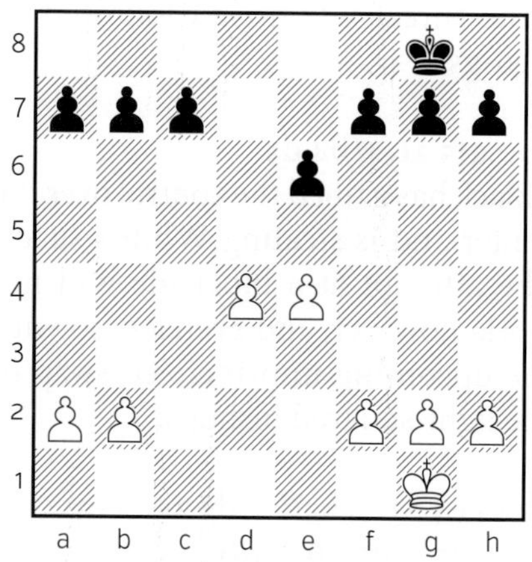

A typical placement of the pawns, where Black undermines White's center with the move 1...c7-c5! (There are still other pieces on the board that can make the c7-c5 move happen).

White is facing a problem: if he waits for the capture on d4, or if he takes on c5, then the mobile center can easily turn into an (almost) symmetrical center. The best possibility for him is to advance and to try to create a passed pawn (1...c5 2.d5 ed5 3.ed5) and after that the positions need to be, once again, evaluated very accurately.

The second possibility of trying to undermine the center with 1...f7-f5 is less recommended, because White can either take, or advance e4-e5, and most of all he can defend the center with the f2-f3 move.

The destruction of the mobile center — represents the most efficient way of fighting against the mobile center.

And now let us see how previously described possibilities were used in actual games. Pay attention to how cold-blooded the defenders must be and how self-confident the attackers can be.

THE PRESSURE AND THE BLOCKADE

1

▷ **Konstantinopolsky**
▶ **Kotov**
Baku 1946 [A14]

This time we will not be paying any attention to the introductory moves:

1.♘f3 ♘f6 2.c4 e6 3.b3 d5 4.♗b2 ♗e7 5.g3 0–0 6.♗g2 b6 7.0–0 ♘bd7 8.cd5 ed5 9.♘d4 ♗b7 10.♘f5 ♖e8 11.♘e7 ♕e7 12.♘c3 c6 13.d4 ♘e4 14.e3 ♘df6

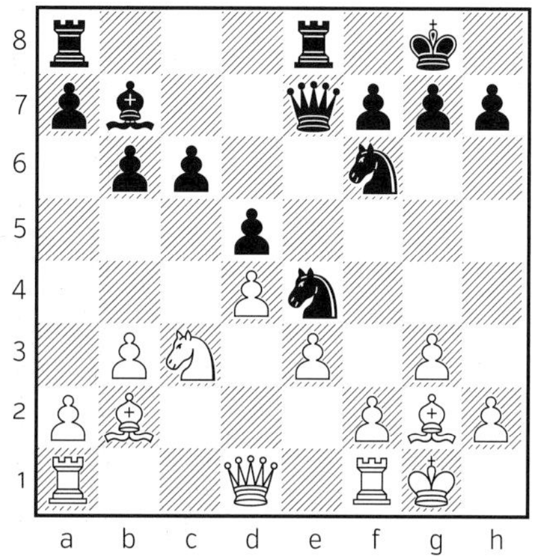

The decisive battle revolves around the e4-square. White wants to prepare the e3-e4 move, but there are still a few moves missing in the center before that. From the opposite side, we see that Black is preventing the afore-mentioned move and is over-protecting the (already protected by the pawn d5) square with his pieces.

15.♖e1 ♗c8 16.f3 ♘c3 17.♗c3 ♗f5!

We can understand — since we know the plans of both players — the moves that were played. Black really has taken care of the e4-square and he is controlling it in five different ways! Now how can White get what he wants?

White will not just give up: he will double his rooks and wait for his opportunity, so Black cannot just stand still forever. The rule says: "**When**

you gain control over the center, move the play to the wing!"

18.♕d2 h5! 19.♖e2 ♕d7 20.♖ae1 ♗h3!?

Maybe it would be better for Black to first double the rooks on the e-file, but that kind of mission is complicated. If he chooses ...♖e6 and ...♖ae8 he covers up his h3-c8 diagonal and after that he will not be able to play ...♗h3. The rook on e7 is being controlled by the dark-squared bishop (Bb4). Due to that, Black decided to play the ...♗h3 move first (and with that he loses some control over the e4-square) and only later will he double his rooks.

21.♗h1 ♖e6

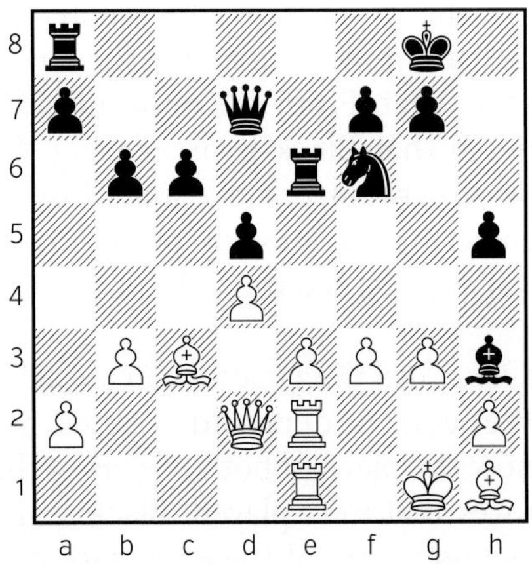

22.e4!?

White is in a hurry — this is his only chance to play the e3-e4 move. Both players probably accurately studied the forced outcome of this push.

22...de4 23.fe4 ♖ae8

Black's strategy is the right one because he will start to put pressure on the mobile center with his pieces. His wish is for White to advance one of his pawns and if possible Black wants him to do that with the e4-e5 move because after that both the d5- and f5-squares would be weak.

24.♗f3

This move is logical because it threatens 24...♗g4 25.♖e3 ♕e7 26.♕c2 ♘d5.

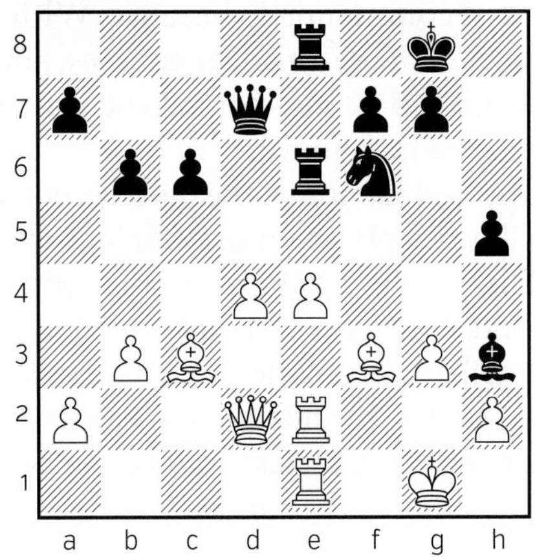

24...♗g4!

A move that "plays itself". Black gets rid of the defender of the critical square, because with the exchange he will force the e4-e5 move and with that the transition to the superior endgame with the knight against the dark-squared bishop.

25.♕f4 ♗f3 26.♕f3 ♕e7 27.e5

This position is already familiar to us. Black has reached his goal and now follows the technical part of the game.

27...♘d5 28.♗d2 ♕a3

White's center is blocked and Black moves the play to the wing. However the commentators suggested the 28...h4 move first and that needs to be followed by the penetration with the queen.

29.♖f2 f6 30.♕h5 ♕a2 31.♖ef1 ♕b3 32.♕g6 ♖8e7

Because of his impatient play, Black made it possible for White to complicate the position. Bad was 32...fe5, because of 33.♖f8 ♖f8 34.♕e6 ♔h7 35.♖f8 ♕d1 36.♖f1 and that is why Black needs to be careful.

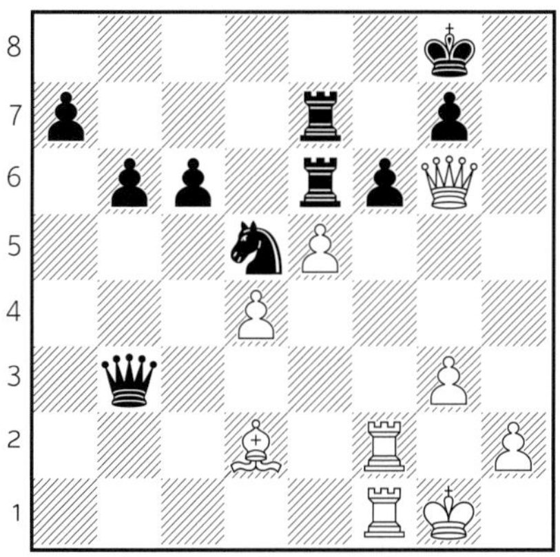

33.♗g5 ♖f7 34.ef6 ♕c4 35.♗h6 ♖ef6 36.♖f6 ♘f6 37.♗g7 ♕d4 38.♖f2 ♖g7 39.♕f6 ♕f6 40.♖f6

Black has managed to stop White's action, has made some exchanges and transposes to an unusual rook endgame a pawn up.

40...♖c7 41.♖d6 a5 42.♖d8 ♔f7 43.♖a8 ♔e6 44.♔f2 c5 45.♔e3 ♔d5 46.♖b8 ♖c6 47.h4 c4 48.♔d2 ♔c5 49.h5 ♔b4 50.♖g8 b5 51.♖g6 ♖c5 52.g4 ♔b3 53.♖e6 c3 54.♔c1 ♖c4 55.♖e3 b4 56.♖e1 ♖g4 57.♖h1 ♖g2 58.♔b1 ♖b2 0:1

THE TACTICAL FIGHT AGAINST THE CENTER

It is even better if the defender manages to destroy the mobile center. In order to do this he uses moves from the side or even sacrifices. Like in the next delightful miniature:

1

▹ **Shevcov**
▸ **Golovko**
USSR 1968 [C32]

1.e4 e5 2.f4

The King's Gambit is an opening in which the battle for the center takes place from the very beginning of the game. White is already trying to destroy Black's center with the second move, the gambit move. Black is facing a decision as to whether to accept the gambit (and use one of the known defensive techniques in order to play against the mobile center) or to instead make his own sacrifice and to try to create some tension in the center.

2...d5 3.ed5 e4 4.d4 ♘f6 5.c4
White is trying to keep his powerful, mobile mass of pawns in the center, but he is forgetting about development and the safety of his king.

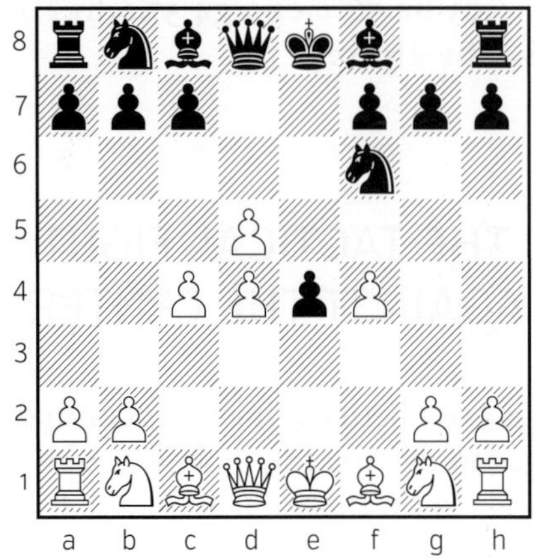

5...b5!
Black is back in action — the systematic breaking of White's center has begun. The e4-pawn represents a huge obstacle for White's development, and now it is clear that White should have started to break Black's center earlier with 4.d3.

6.b3 ♗b4 7.♗d2 a5!
He continues to put pressure on White's center, which is hard to believe. However, after the incautious 8.a3 would follow 8...♗d2 9.♘d2 a4! and White's chain is breaking.

8.a4 bc4 9.bc4 0–0 10.♘a3
White has no good moves to play, while on the contrary Black continues with his plan.

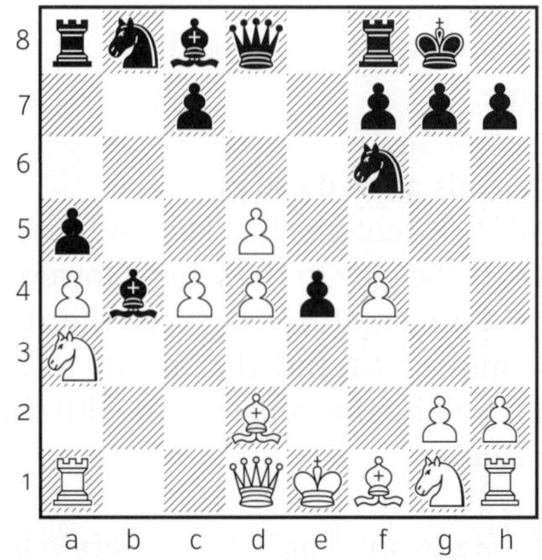

10...c6!
A new undermining.

11.♘c2 e3!
Black's advantage is already so huge that he is able to force events. After 12.♘e3 ♖e8 White has no choice left.

12.♗b4 ab4 13.♗e2
The pawns are untouchable because White can be attacked on the a5-e1 diagonal or on the e-file. There follows an efficient kill.

13...♖e8 14.♔f1 b3 15.♘e1 ♘e4 16.♘d3 ♘d2 17.♔e1 ♕a5 18.g4 ♗a6 19.♖c1 cd5 0:1.

THE UNDERMINING OF THE MOBILE CENTER

In chess we will most likely come across White's mobile center with the d4-e4 pawns. The pawns are just screaming out for the reaction of moves from the sides like...c7-c5 or...f7-f5. The placement of the pieces is crucial and besides that also the placement of the pawns, especially the ones that help to defend the center. If White's pawn is already standing on the c4-square then the most likely move is the ...c7-c5 move, which will without fail bring with it play on the dark squares. White can take on c5, wait for Black to take on d4 or he can advance the pawn d4-d5, but in all cases he leaves behind holes (d4, e3, c5, ...) that are the objects for Black's future counterplay.

On the other side of the board it is the same: if White has his pawns on d4, e4 and f4, he needs to be afraid of the f7-f5 move. Just like in the following classical game...

1

▷ **Rubinstein**
► **Grünfeld**
Ostrava 1923 [Q78]

Ernst Grünfeld was one of the brightest personalities of hyper-modernism and a very popular opening was even named after him — The Grünfeld Defence. This is one of the first games in that opening, which hides inside a deep, but risky idea: Black will leave the pawn center to White — and later on he will try to undermine it.

1.d4 ♘f6 2.c4 g6 3.g3 c6 4.♘f3 ♗g7 5.♗g2 d5 6.0–0 0–0 7.♕b3 dc4 8.♕c4 ♕b6 9.♘c3 ♗e6 10.♕d3 ♘a6 11.e4 ♖ad8 12.h3 ♘b4

White is building a powerful pawn center, but Black is not disturbed by it at all. With experienced manoeuvres he will ensure that he has no weaknesses. The swap of the queens is good for him due to the space advantage White holds, which would support continued threats for an organized attack against his king.

13.♕e2 ♕a6! 14.♕a6 ♘a6 15.♗e3 h6 16.♖ac1 ♖c8 17.♖fd1 ♖fd8 18.♘e5 ♘d7 19.♘d3

White avoids exchanging the Knights, as it would solve Black's space problems.

19...♘b6 20.♘f4 ♗d7

Black is pulling back peacefully, because White's pieces do not have any good squares to move to.

21.♗f1 ♘c7 22.b3 ♘e6 23.♘fe2

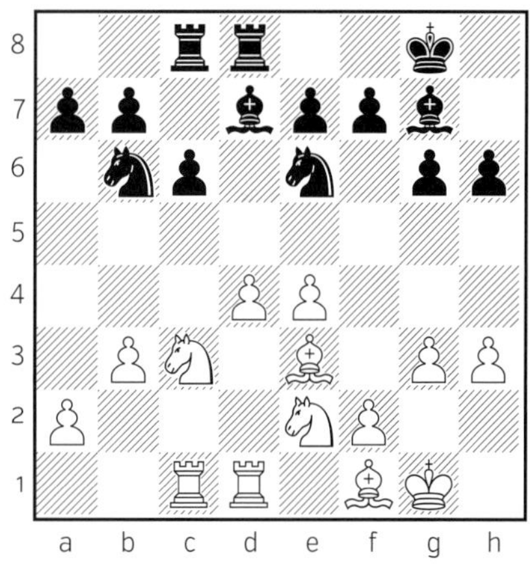

23...♘g5!

A provocative move! Rubinstein was a chess player with a strict classical style of play and so was surely confused by Black's tactic. A free build of the center and also with tempo...

24.f4 ♘e6 25.g4

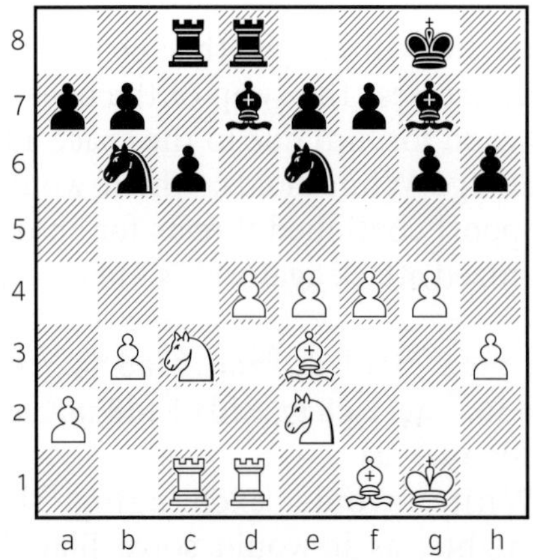

A famous position that forced the defenders of the classical principles to stop and think for a moment. White is dominating in the center where he has placed a lot of pawns. But Black has waited for his opportunity and after the next move White's center will begin to collapse.

25...f5! 26.♗g2

After 26.gf5 gf5 27.ef5 ♘c7 Black would gradually regain the pawn and transpose into the endgame.

26...♘c7!

Aimed at the d5-square, which will become the most important one when the e4-pawn leaves the scene.

27.♗f3 fe4 28.♗e4 ♘bd5

With this kind of dominance over the d5-square, Black has nothing to be afraid of. After a few moves the opponents agreed to a draw, but if they were to play on Black would be the one trying to win!

29.♔f2 ♗e8 30.♘d5 ♘d5 31.♘g1 ♖d6 32.♘f3 ♖cd8 33.♖d2 ♗f7 34.♗d5 ♗d5 35.♘e5 ♗e4 draw.

THE C6–E6 PAWNS AGAINST THE D4-E4 PAWNS

A typical defensive tactic for Black, which can often be found in modern chess, is the placement of the pawns on e6 and c6 (after the exchange of the d-pawn for White's e-pawn or c-pawn). This kind of position can be formed out of different openings, but it is very complicated and it is hard to say that White has an advantage due to his center.

Let us have a look at a position in which White has a pair of pawns on d4 and e4 and where Black has two defenders on c6 and e6. White does not have much to choose from: one plan is connected with the d4-d5 move, which will clear the center (look back — the open center) and the player that will have the advantage will be the one with the more active pieces.

The second plan is connected with the e4-e5 move. This is a strategically risky move, because White is voluntarily giving up control over the d5-square. So what is the e4-e5 move good for? Well, especially if White starts an attack against Black's king with that move: the freed e4-square will serve as a jumping-off point for White's pieces that will be transferring to the kingside. At the same time if White gets his pawn to e5, he also removes an important defender from the f6 square (usually the knight). But if Black played (besides the move ...e7-e6) also the ...g7-g6 move then there would be a hole left on f6, which would probably be filled by one of White's pieces.

But Black does not need to wait passively. In his reserves are two plans to undermine White's center — with the ...c6-c5 move and with the ...e6-e5 move. In both cases he needs to be aware of the consequences of the advance d4-d5, with which White gains a passed pawn. If White chooses not to advances there usually occur some exchanges in the center, and then there can appear some symmetrical positions, or positions with the majorities on either side.

To begin with, let us see an example on the theme of advancing with e4-e5. You will see how efficiently White exploited the e4-square for the transportation of his pieces and how he, with the help of his experience, managed to finish the attack after he had transferred his pieces in front of Black's king.

1

▷ **Forgacs**
▶ **Cohn**
St. Petersburg 1909 [Q53]

1.d4 d5 2.♘f3 e6 3.c4 ♘f6 4.♘c3 dc4 5.♗g5 ♗e7 6.e4 h6 7.♗f6 ♗f6 8.♗c4 ♘d7 9.0–0 0–0 10.e5

White advances the e5-pawn, even though Black has not yet played the ...c7-c6 move. This fact is not very important, because White is threatening with the advancement also the d4-d5 move and he is not afraid of the ...c7-c5 move (with which Black would seemingly save a move).

10...♗e7 11.♕e2 ♖e8 12.♖ad1 c6

Black has no choice — 13.d4-d5! was threatened.

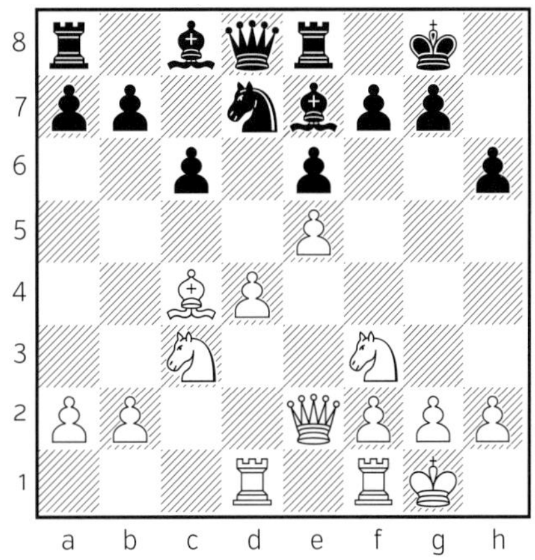

13.♕e4

The first White piece exploits "the jumping-off spot" for its transportation to the kingside.

13...♕c7 14.♖fe1 ♘f8 15.♕g4 b6 16.♕h5 ♗b7 17.♖e4

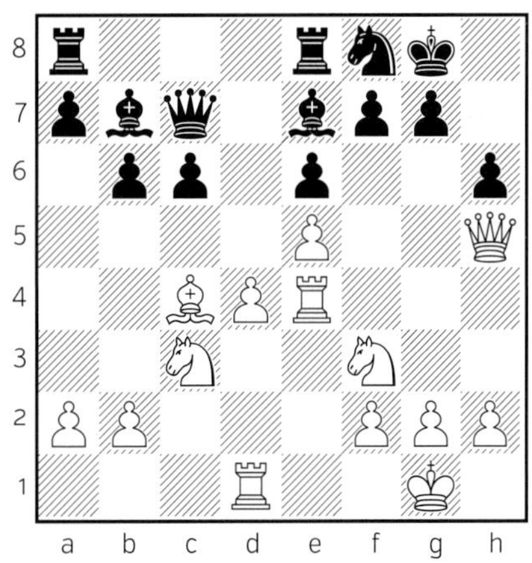

The e4-square is being exploited by yet another of White's heavy piece. It is important that Black is not able to play the 17...c5 move, because of 18.d5.

17...♗b4

With a desire to destroy the knight on c3, the next piece that wishes to exploit the e4 square.

18.♖g4 ♗c3 19.bc3

After 19.♕h6 would follow 19...♘g6, but White is not in a hurry.

19...♔h8 20.♘g5 ♖e7

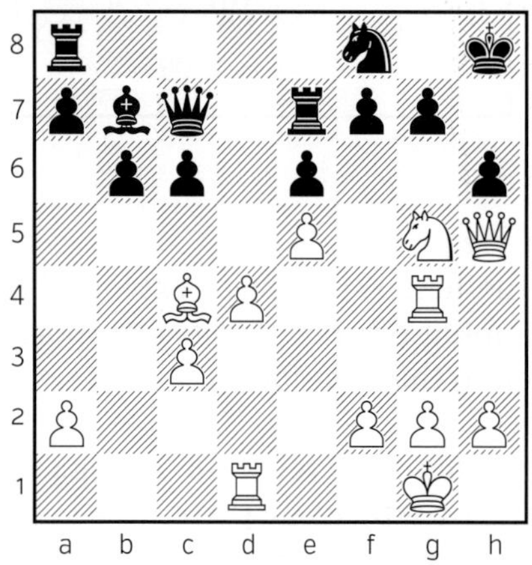

21.♘e4

A third pieces on the e4-square!

21...♖d8 22.♖d3 c5 23.♘f6

With the threat of 24.♕h6 gh6 25.♖g8 mate!

23...♘g6 24.♖h3 1:0

The position at the end is horrifying. All White's pieces joined the attack and there is no defence to be found against 25.♕g5 and 26.♖h6.

2

▹ **Gheorghiu**
▸ **Smyslov**
Buenos Aires 1978 [Q15]

1.♘f3 d5 2.c4 c6 3.d4 ♘f6 4.♕b3 ♕b6 5.♘c3 dc4 6.♕c4 ♗f5

The Slav Defence is a typical opening which brings us to "our" pawn setting. The difference between the previous game and the present game lies in the fact that this time Black has already developed his light-squared bishop before he setting up a defensive wall made of pawns.

7.g3 e6 8.♗g2 ♕b4 9.♘e5 ♘bd7 10.♕b4 ♗b4 11.♘d7 ♘d7 12.0–0 0–0 13.♗f4 ♖ad8 14.♖ac1 ♘b6 15.♖fd1 ♖d7 16.e4

The e2-e4 move takes space in the center, but it is strategically risky. We can see that Black will attack the d4-pawn and that is why White decided to follow a plan that includes many exchanges.

16...♗g6 17.a3 ♗e7

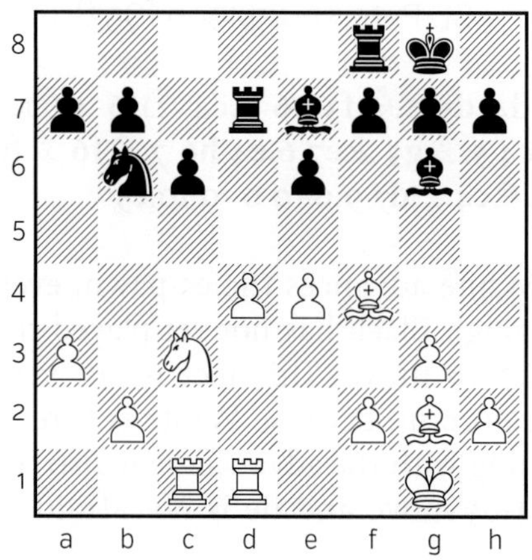

18.d5

There was no wiser choice for White because he is not supposed to allow ...♖fd8, a move that would prevent any strikes in the center from happening. What will follow next? If Black exchanges twice, White will place his piece on the d5-square and start to put pressure on Black with it. For example 18...cd5 19.ed5 ed5 20.♘d5 ♘d5 21.♖d5 ♖d5 (21...♖fd8 22.♖d7) 22.♗d5 b6 23.♖c7 and White pieces dominate the board. This is why Black needs to be careful.

18...cd5 19.ed5 ♖fd8!

A move that allows the e6-square become a weakness, but this will become meaningless after the many exchanges, because there will be no pieces left for White to attack the weakness with.

20.de6 fe6 21.♖d7 ♖d7 22.♖d1 ♖d1 23.♘d1 ♘d5 draw.

An example of an excellent defence was demonstrated by Alexander Alekhine in the famous match for the World Champion title against Jose Raul Capablanca, in Buenos Aires in 1927.

3

▷ **Capablanca**
▶ **Alekhine**
Buenos Aires 1927 [Q52]

1.d4 d5 2.c4 e6 3.♘c3 ♘f6 4.♗g5 ♘bd7 5.e3 c6 6.♘f3 ♕a5

The Queens Gambit, especially the Cambridge Springs Variation, marked the famous match, where all the games started with this very same opening accept from one! The Queens Gambit is the opening that most often leads to our structure.

7.♘d2 ♗b4 8.♕c2 dc4 9.♗f6 ♘f6 10.♘c4 ♕c7 11.a3 ♗e7 12.♗e2 0–0

A first chance for 12...c5.

13.0–0 ♗d7

And a second opportunity for Black to clarify the position with the 13...c5! move.

14.b4 b6

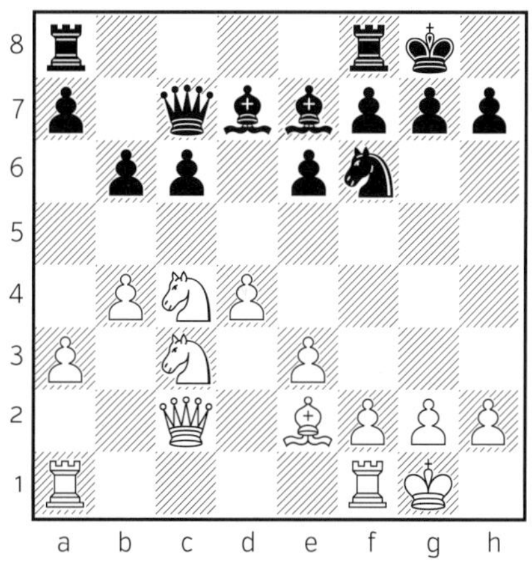

15.♗f3! ♖ac8!

Black is being careful and is strengthening the defence of the c6-pawn and the c-file generally.

16.♖fd1 ♖fd8 17.♖ac1 ♗e8

The opening has finished and both players placed their pieces where they wanted. White has more space and Black has the two bishops and not many weaknesses. If he manages to strike in the center — and thereby open the position for his bishops — his future will be bright.

18.g3 ♘d5 19.♘b2 ♕b8 20.♘d3 ♗g5 21.♖b1 ♕b7

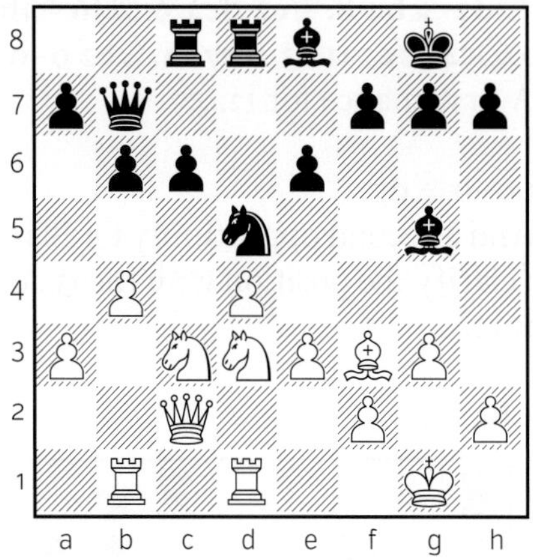

Risky is 21...♘e3 22.fe3 ♗e3 23.♔h1 ♗d4 and White is better (Müller), and after 21...♗e3 22.♗d5!+-

22.e4

It was a success — Capablanca wants more than a draw! It was not easy for Black to realise a freeing ...c5 or ...e5 move and he has had to wait for a long time. White helped him with the e3-e4 move and now Black's plan is simple — an attack on the d4-pawn!

22...♘c3 23.♕c3 ♕e7?!

It seems like Black did not understand the position yet, the 23...♕e7 move is simply bad. It would be more logical to play 23...♖c7.

24.h4!

White's only chance is hidden on the kingside.

24...♗h6 25.♘e5 g6 26.♘g4?!

This square is not optimal for the knight, therefore it would be better placed following 26.♘c4! ♗g7 27.e5! and 28.♘d6.

26...♗g7 27.e5

White has no wise alternatives left; 27...c5 was threatened.

27...h5 28.♘e3

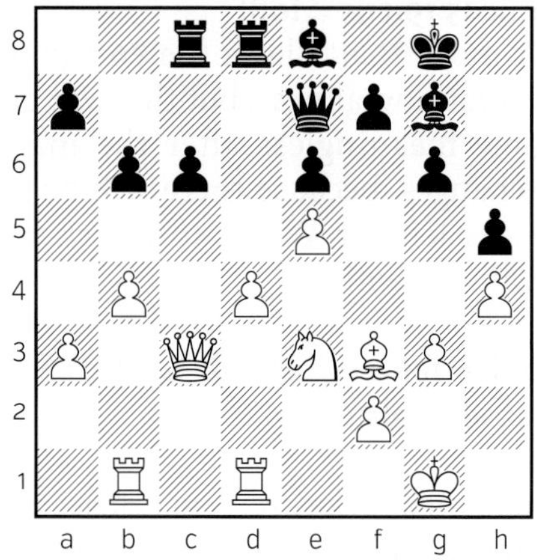

28...c5!

After all! With this strike from the side Black manages to break White's center. From now on the object of desire will become the e5 square, which cannot be defended by White.

29.bc5 bc5 30.d5?!

After this move Black is already better. Most likely the game would end in a draw after 30.♖b7 ♖d7 31.♖d7

♗d7 32.d5 ed5 33.♘d5 ♕e6 34.♘f4 ♗e5=.

30...ed5 31.♘d5 ♕e6

Of course not 31...♕e5? 32.♕e5 ♗e5 33.♘e7.

32.♘f6?

Better would be 32.♖b7 ♗e5 33.♕a5 with good chances of finding the solution.

32...♗f6 33.ef6 ♖d1 34.♖d1 ♗c6! 35.♖e1 ♕f5 36.♖e3 c4! 0:1

And Black has reached his ideal position, which was later on turned into a whole point...

THE d4-e4 PAWN AGAINST THE e6 PAWN

For our knowledge about the center and pawn structures, even more important is the position with a pawn pair d4-e4 against the e6 pawn. This position represents a huge problem for many chess masters!

White is a pawn up in the center and Black is a pawn up on the queenside — which is good for the endgame. White's plans are similar to the ones in the previous example (where Black had a pawn on c6). Everything revolves around the d4-d5 move, or around the e4-e5 move. In the first case White will place his bets on the passed d-pawn that will disturb the co-ordination between Black's pieces. After the exchange on d5 White in some cases takes with the piece when he thinks that the active pieces would bring him more benefits than a passed pawn. In the second case White is placing his bets on the attack on the king. A version of the second possibility is also very important where White sacrifices d4-d5 and after the taking he does not recapture, but rather advances with e4-e5 and a sharp attack (the d-pawn is being sacrificed to block the dark-squared bishop's way and thus destroys the co-ordination between the defence pieces).

Let's get to know some classic games on the previously described themes, which will help you to understand how difficult this pawn structure is.

1

▷ **Keres**
▶ **Geller**
Moscow 1962 [D41]

1.d4 ♘f6 2.c4 e6 3.♘f3 d5 4.♘c3 c5 5.cd5 ♘d5

This time the pawn structure comes from an improved Tarrasch Defence variation, where Black takes on d5 with the knight instead of with the pawn like in the original Tarrasch.

6.e3 ♘c6 7.♗c4 ♘c3

This exchange is maybe premature. Black could have chosen 7...cd4 8.ed4 ♗e7, leading to positions with a passed pawn and other types of play that will be shown in the following chapters.

8.bc3 ♗e7 9.0–0 0–0 10.e4 b6 11.♗b2 ♗b7 12.♕e2 ♘a5 13.♗d3 ♖c8 14.♖ad1 cd4 15.cd4

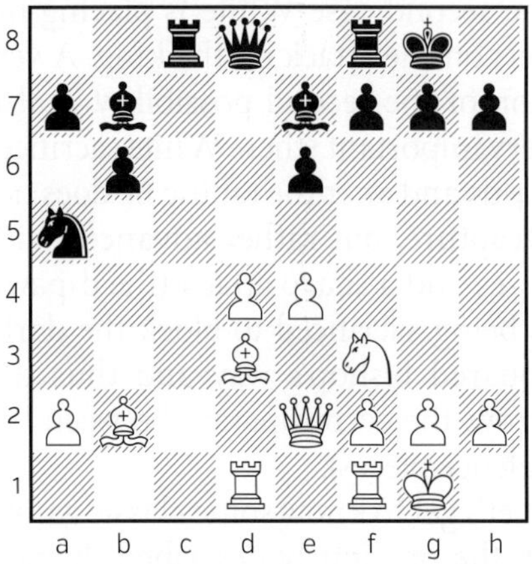

A classic position on our theme. White's bishops are placed behind the pawns, but there is great attacking potential in them. It is clear that in these type of positions the center needs to be opened. The advance with e4-e5 makes less sense here, because it would close the dark-squared bishop. That is why White is left with the advance of the d4-d5 move.

15...♗b4?

Due to the what was just described it would be better to play 15...♗f6.

16.d5! ed5 17.ed5 ♕e7

It is hard to give Black any wise advice. Bad is 17...♗d5? 18.♕e5 f6 19.♕h5 g6 20.♗g6 hg6 21.♕g6 ♔h8 22.♕h5 ♔g7 23.♖d5 or 17...♗c3 18.♗f5! ♖c4 19.♘e5. Best would be 17...♖e8 18.♘e5 (with the threat 19.♗h7) 18...♕h4 19.♗b5 ♖ed8 20.♗d7 and White always has an advantage.

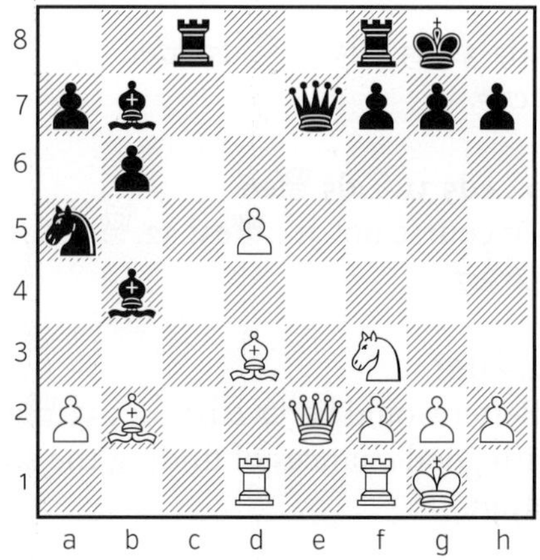

18.♘e5

"After this move, there is no defence." (Kasparov)

18...f6

Also hopeless would be 18...♗d6 19.♕h5 g6 20.♘g4!! (Keres) or 18...♖fd8 19.♕e4 g6 20.♕d4! ♖d5 21.♘g6! fg6 22.♕h8 ♔f7 23.♕h7 ♔e8 24.♗b5! ♖b5 25.♕g8 ♕f8 26.♕g6 ♕f7 27.♖fe1! ♗e1 28.♖e1 ♔f8 29.♕h6! (Rybka, Kasparov).

19.♕h5! g6

19...fe5? 20.♗h7 ♔h8 21.♗g6.

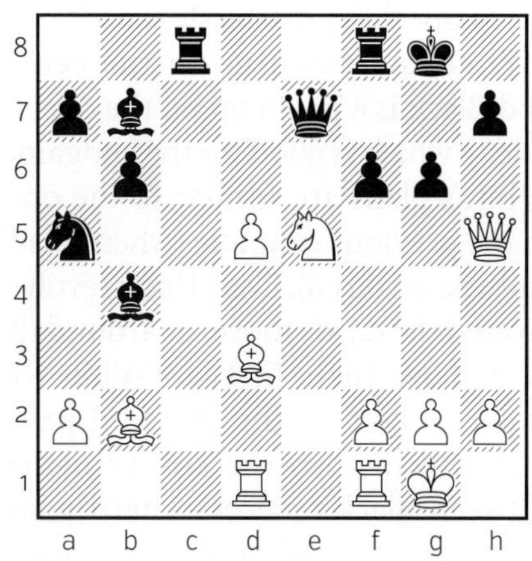

20.♘g6! hg6 21.♗g6 ♕g7

This move leads to a quick loss, but Black is already lost. For example 21...♗a6 22.d6! or 21...♖c7 22.♗f5!

22.♖d3 ♗d6

22...♗a6 23.♖g3 ♗f1 24.♗h7 ♔h8 25.♗f5+-.

23.f4 ♕h8 24.♕g4 ♗c5 25.♔h1 ♖c7 26.♗h7! ♔f7 27.♕e6 ♔g7 28.♖g3 1:0

The theme of the next game is the d4-d5 advance, along with e4-e5 and also another kind of attack.

2

▷ **Keres**

► **Fine**

Ostende 1937 (D41)

1.♘f3 d5 2.d4 ♘f6 3.c4 e6 4.♘c3 c5 5.cd5 ♘d5 6.e4 ♘c3 7.bc3 cd4 8.cd4 ♗b4

Among the theoreticians this exchange variation was for a long time considered to be one of the basic variations that ends in a draw and it was indeed used by all the "great draw players" in chess history. The move itself points to a difference between this and the previous variation — after the exchange of the dark-squared bishops White's attacking potential will minimize.

9.♗d2 ♗d2

For some time the players with the Black pieces tried to play 9...♕a5, until the great Akiba Rubinstein discovered the 10.♖b1 move!

10.♕d2 0–0 11.♗c4 ♘d7

The second possibility is 11...♘c6, and we will look at this in the next game.

12.0–0 b6 13.♖ad1 ♗b7 14.♖fe1 ♖c8 15.♗b3 ♘f6 16.♕f4 ♕c7 17.♕h4 ♖fd8

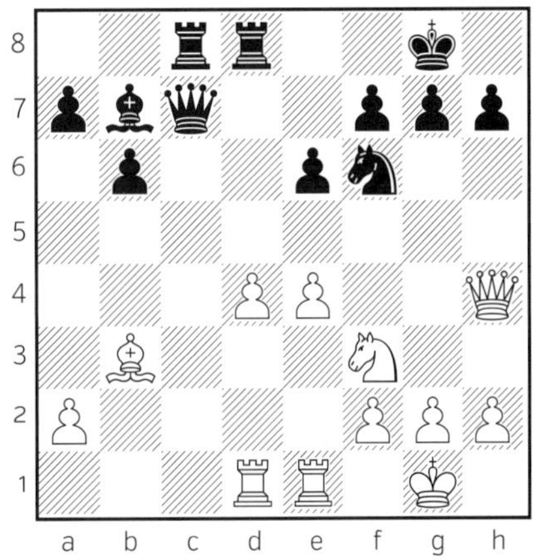

A very important moment! White is standing at a crossroads: if he wants to achieve anything, he will need to move one of the central pawns. The d4-d5 penetration and the big exchanges do not do him any good and that is why he started to fancy the 18.e5 move. The move is logical, because White opens a potential diagonal for his bishop and at the same time gets rid of the knight on f6, from where it is able to defend the king. He is also creating a known trampoline on the e4-square for his pieces, above all for his knight that will — with the help of the ♘g5-e4 manoeuvre — join the attack. For example: 18.e5 ♘d7 19.♘g5 ♘f8 20.♘e4 or 18.e5 ♘d5 19.♘g5 h6 20.♘e4 ♘c3 21.♘f6! But Keres decided on another kind of penetration, a motif which was unknown until then.

18.♖e3 b5! 19.♖de1 a5!

Black has managed to achieve nice counterplay — White's bishop is in danger.

20.a4 20...b4?

This move frees White's hands and above all it gives White some extra time or a tempo for an opening of the action. Correct is 20...ba4 21. ♗a4 h6 and White's attack is stopped.

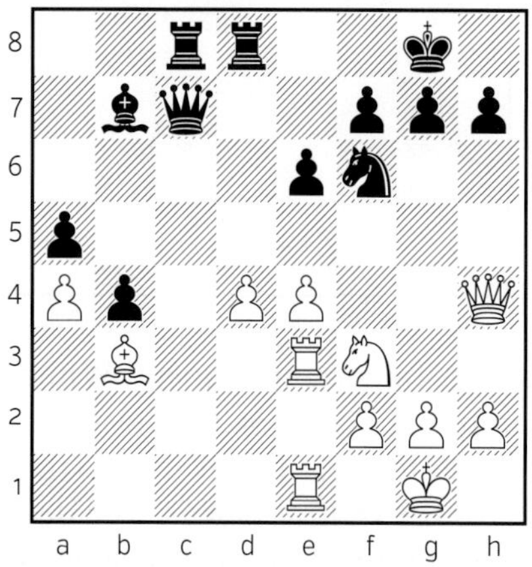

21.d5! ed5 22.e5!

Fine was surely not expecting that.

22...♘d7 23.♘g5 ♘f8

More resistant would be 23...h6, when White's attack would continue like this: 24.e6! hg5 25.ef7 ♔f7 26.♖e7.

24.♘h7! ♘h7 25.♖h3 ♕c1 26.♕h7 ♔f8 27.♖he3 d4 28.♕h8 ♔e7 29.♕g7 ♖f8 30.♕f6 ♔e8 31.e6 1:0

When the attacker, after the penetration, takes with the piece then there are some different kinds of dangers present, which the defender must face.

3

▹ **Spassky**
▸ **Petrosian**
Moscow 1969 [D41]

1.c4 ♘f6 2.♘c3 e6 3.♘f3 d5 4.d4 c5 5.cd5 ♘d5 6.e4 ♘c3 7.bc3 cd4 8.cd4 ♗b4 9.♗d2 ♗d2 10.♕d2 0–0 11.♗c4 ♘c6 12.0–0 b6 13.♖ad1

This move and the placement of the rooks on d1 and e1 were prepared by Spassky especially for this match. Alekhine preferred to play 13.♖fd1, but what Spassky had in mind was the penetration in the center, a theme which we have just encountered.

13...♗b7 14.♖fe1 ♖c8

Later on players, with more success, tried 14...♘a5 15.♗d3 ♕d6.

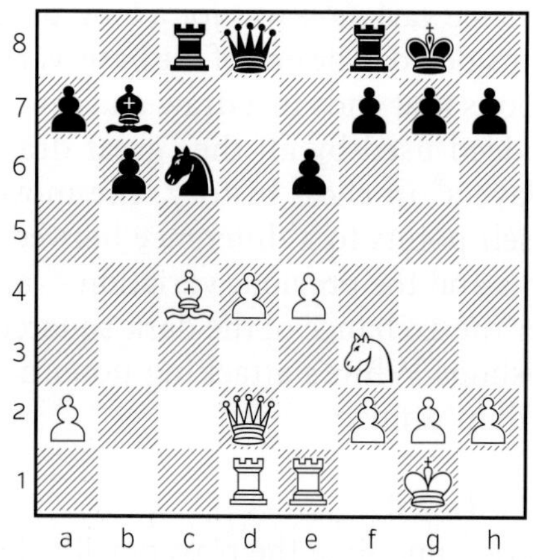

15.d5 ed5 16.♗d5

Playing on the domination of the pieces in the center. With the bishop on c4 it is hard for White to count on the attack and due to that it would be worse to play: 16.ed5 ♘a5 17.♗f1 ♕d6 18.♘g5 ♕h6!

16...♘a5 17.♕f4 ♕c7

The swap of the queens is usually in favour of the player who is defending.

18.♕f5 ♗d5 19.ed5

Without the white-squared bishops the passed pawn is a decisive factor on the board. It is supported by both White's rooks and by the queen and Black will not be able to set up the basic defensive plan in the battle against the passed pawn — the blockade.

19...♕c2

Too slow is 19...♘c4 20.♘g5 g6 21.♕h3 h5 22.♘e4± or 19...♕d6 20.♘g5 ♕g6 21.♕g6 hg6 22.d6! ♘b7 23.d7 ♖cd8 24.♖e7 ♘c5 25.♖d5! +-.

20.♕f4! ♕a2 21.d6!

White is proving how powerful a passed pawn can be with great play.

21...♖cd8 22.d7 ♕c4 23.♕f5 h6 24.♖c1 ♕a6 25.♖c7 b5 26.♘d4 ♕b6 27.♖c8! +- ♘b7

27...b4 28.♖e8 ♕d4 29.♖f8 ♖f8 30.♖f8 ♔f8 31.♕c5!!+-; 27...g6 28.♖d8 ♕d8 29.♕b5+-; 27...♕d4 28.♖d8 ♖d8 29.♖e8+-.

28.♘c6 ♘d6 29.♘d8!! ♘f5 30.♘c6 1:0

THE TACTICAL GAME – THE e4-e5 (...e5-e4) MOVE

There are a lot of cases when the opponent's mobile center is seemingly blocked by the defender. The critical square that would make the breakthrough possible -and that is the object of the strategic battle — is well defended, and now the defender is looking for an attack. And at that time in spite of everything the critical square breaks: the sacrifice of the pawn turns everything upside down. The action erupts there or on the other wing and the battle begins, for which the defender is usually not well prepared.

An example on this theme, where the opponent should not have taken the pawn on the critical square, was demonstrated by legendary Akiba Rubinstein.

1

▹ **Verlinsky**
▸ **Rubinstein**
Moscow 1925 (A09)

1.♘f3 d5 2.c4 d4 3.b4 c5 4.♗b2 g6 5.e3 ♗g7 6.d3 ♘h6 7.♘bd2 0-0 8.ed4 cd4 9.g3 e5 10.♗g2 a5 11.b5 a4 12.♗a3 ♖e8 13.0-0 f5 14.♘e1 ♘d7 15.♖c1 ♘f7 16.♘c2 ♗f8 17.♗f8 ♔f8 18.♘b4 ♘c5 19.♖e1 ♕d6 20.♖b1 ♗d7 21.♗d5 ♖ad8 22.a3 ♗c8 23.♖b2 ♖e7 24.♘f3 ♘h6 25.♖be2 ♖de8 26.♕d2 ♔g7 27.♕b2 ♘g4 28.♕b1

♘f6 29.♔g2 h6 30.♕d1 g5 31.h3 ♘h7 32.♔h2 h5 33.h4 g4 34.♘d2 ♘f6 35.♕b1

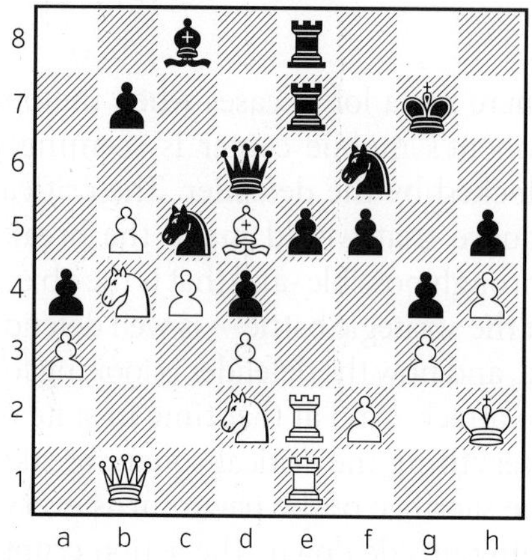

35...e4!

Black attacks on the most defended square on the board. Everything is possible due to the fact that White cannot take the pawn: after 36.de4 fe4 37.♘e4 ♘fe4 38.♗e4 White would be at least an exchange down — 38...♗f5! and now Black has the initiative:

36.♕a1 e3 37.♘f1 ♘b3 38.♕b2 f4 39.gf4 ♕f4

And from here he outplayed his opponent, even though there is no visible way of an immediate win. Most likely that also made the great Rubinstein mad, who started to complicate things more and more until the sensational defeat!

40.♔g2 ♔g6 41.fe3 de3 42.d4 ♘d4 43.♘d3 ♘d5 44.♘f4 ♘f4 45.♔h1 ♘de2 46.♖e2 ♘e2 47.♕e2 ♗f5 48.♘g3 ♖d8 49.♕f1 ♗e4 50.♔g1 ♖f7 51.♕c1 ♖fd7 52.♕e3 ♖d1 53.♘f1 ♗f3 54.♔f2 ♖8d3 55.♕e6 ♔g7 56.♘e3 ♖1d2 57.♔g3 ♔f8 58.♔f4 ♖d4 59.♔g5 ♖d6 60.♕e5 ♔f7 61.♘f5 ♖g6 62.♔f4 ♖e2 63.♕c7 ♔f8 64.♘d6 ♖ee6 65.♕f7 1:0

But the defender can rarely wait calmly after the e4-e5 (...e5-e4) move. In most cases he is forced to take and after that follow some interesting outcomes. One of them is connected with the exchange in the center — these kinds of positions are usually formed in the attack of the four pawns against the King's Indian Defence and others are formed from a passing by (...de5 — f5!), where the attacker is playing on the weakened position of the opponent's king.

2

▷ **Mikenas**
▶ **Vladimirov**
Moscow 1963 [A69]

1.d4 ♘f6 2.c4 c5 3.d5 g6 4.♘c3 d6 5.e4 ♗g7 6.f4 o-o 7.♗e2 e6 8.♘f3 ed5 9.cd5 ♖e8

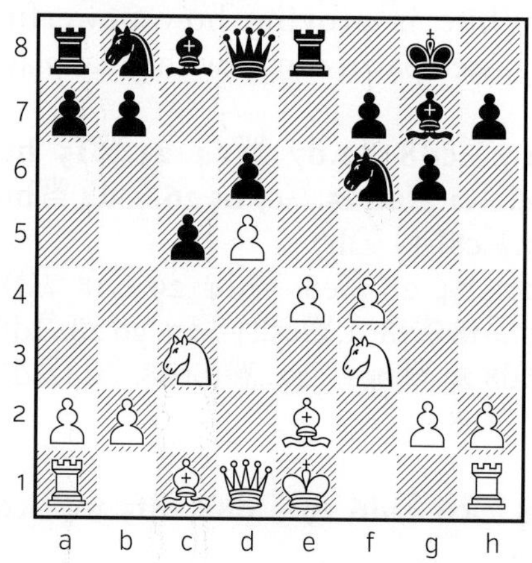

White is prepared to play the e4-e5 move, which is connected with a pawn sacrifice. Will a quick development, an open file and a diagonal be enough to replace the material loss? White will receive yet another trump — the passed d5-pawn, which has an open path ahead of it.

10.e5!? de5 11.fe5 ♘g4 12.♗g5 ♕b6 13.0–0 ♘e5 14.♘e5 ♗e5

A theoretical position which illustrates our theme. White has undoubted compensation and from now on the time factor (every lost/won tempo) will become very important.

15.♗c4 ♗f5

Black has more than one defensive plan. It is possible to take yet another pawn on b2 and the in-between 15...♕b4 is also possible. All this can be found in the opening manuals.

16.♗b5!

A tricky move — White is challenging Black's bishop to return back. Black's rook is in trouble because it cannot move to the f8-square (16...♖f8 17.♗e7 and d6), and also not possible is 16...♘d7? in view of 17.♖f5 and 17.♗d7. All that is left is the withdrawal to c8 or the return of the bishop, where after 16...♗d7 17.♕f3! White gains some new attacking tempos.

16...c4 17.♔h1 ♖c8 18.♕f3

White is constantly making his opponent angry by not allowing him to finish his development. The threats on the f-file are very serious and due to that Black decided to 'cover-up' the file.

18...f6 19.♖ae1 ♕d4 20.♗f4!

A transposition to the endgame, where White will gain back the pawn and where he will be left with a passed pawn and a clear advantage.

20...♕f4 21.♕f4 ♗f4 22.♖f4 ♘a6 23.g4! ♗d3 24.♗a6 ba6 25.♖f6 ♖ab8 26.♖e7 ♖e8

The only move. White is already winning, but he still needs to solve some technical problems.

27.♖e8 ♖e8 28.♖a6 ♖b8 29.d6 ♖b7 30.♖c6 ♖d7 31.♔g1 ♔f7 32.♘a4! ♔e6 33.♘c5!

A very accurate calculation of the transposition to a winning pawn endgame.

33...♔d5 34.♘d7 ♔c6 35.♘e5 ♔d6 36.♘d3 cd3 37.♔f2 ♔d5 38.♔e3 ♔c4 39.g5 a6 40.h3 a5 41.a4 d2

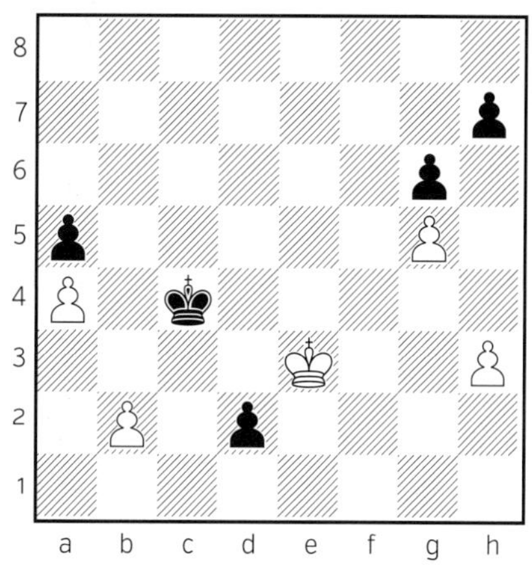

42.♔d2 1:0

A very nice end position where White is winning: 42...♔b3 43.♔d3 ♔b2 (43...♔a4 44.♔c4) 44.♔c4.

THE CONCLUSION

To achieve a mobile, full center is considered to be advantageous. The player that manages to achieve it has a space advantage, because the opponent's pieces are held back and they need to wait. We can evaluate the position only after some time has passed, because every move and every won tempo is important. Undoubtedly there is no room here for sleepy play and slow manoeuvres!

The attacker will try to advance his pawns and squeeze the opponent even more. With the manoeuvre in the center he will gain a passed pawn or he will move the play to the wing, from where he will start to attack the opponent's weaknesses.

The defender has no choice. He will try to block the opponent's center first and then try to break it with the strikes from the sides and, hopefully, finally destroy it. It is important to know that as a rule there is no room for the defender's actions on the wing in this kind of position (we attack on the wing when there is a fixed center).

THE SYMMETRICAL CENTER

We can talk about a symmetrical (we can also come across with the word static) center when the pawns on the central squares are having trouble moving. Or there is a pawn in front of them and in that case it is possible that they cannot move at all or that any kind of movement would bring material (or positional) losses. That is the reason why the pawns in this kind of center are usually 'resting' and the play takes place either besides them or on the wings.

There is a difference between a symmetrical center and a blocked center: in a blocked center, the word tells us that the center is completely occupied by pawns and as a result the play with the pieces (and with other pawns) is moved to the wings. On the contrary there are only few pawns in the center (often there are only two) when we talk about a symmetrical center. A classic example of a symmetrical center is with pawns on d4 and d5, without c and e pawns. It is similar when the pawns are standing on e4 and e5, but in that case it does not often happen that the f-pawns are not placed on the board, which can make the undermining possible (f2-f4 or ...f7-f5).

We will get to know the positions in the diagram in detail. First we need to ask ourselves what the players want in this kind of position. The initiative is very important — if one of the players manages to conquer a central square and later put his piece there (we call that kind of square a base or outpost, because Black has no pawns with which to get rid of the piece), it will always make the defender angry or uncomfortable. It is similar with the open-lines that are placed besides the central pawns: the advantage will be with the player who can gain control over the line first and later, with the help of it, prepare manoeuvres in the center and so make room for the action on the wing.

The symmetrical center can be formed out of many modern and nowadays very popular openings: out of the Nimzo-Indian Defence, the Russian Defence, the Queen's Gambit — and also out of some variations of the French Defence.

THE INITIATIVE ON THE QUEENSIDE AND THE TRANSPOSITION TO THE ENDGAME

To begin with let's have a look at two games of the fourth World Champion, Alexander Alekhine. In the first game the then World Champion was defeated by a young, Russian Mikhail Botvinnik, who over a decade later took Alekhine's place as World Champion.

"I thought that I made the position equal, but the fact is that I was already lost at that time! A very dangerous position, a very unpleasant structure," moaned Alekhine after the game.

1

▷ **Botvinnik**
▶ **Alekhine**
Amsterdam 1938 [D41]

1.♘f3 d5 2.d4 ♘f6 3.c4 e6 4.♘c3 c5 5.cd5 ♘d5 6.e3 ♘c6 7.♗c4 cd4 8.ed4 ♗e7 9.0–0 0–0 10.♖e1

Botvinnik loved positions with the passed pawn, which you will get two know in the second part of this book. He was one of the first researchers of this very sensitive area and he also knew the transpositions to other kinds of positions. One of them will be demonstrated in the game.

10...b6?!

Today we know that this decision was not a very good one. Black would first need to take on c3 (10...♘c3 11.bc3) and only then develop his bishop on the long diagonal: 11...b6 12.♗d3 ♗b7. Of course White will not just stand still, but he will immediately take the initiative on the kingside, where Black has too few defensive pieces: 13.h4! ♗h4 (14.♘g5 was threatened) 14.♘h4 ♕h4 15.♖e3, with a very strong initiative in exchange for the sacrificed pawn. (Kasparov)

11.♘d5! ed5

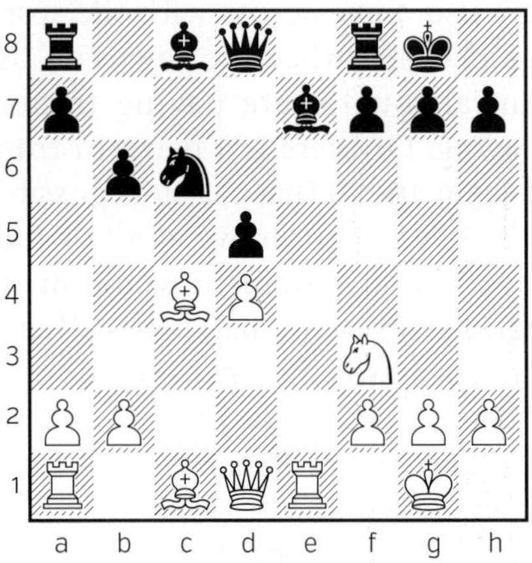

White has transformed the center into a symmetrical center, which brings him a pretty large advantage due to his better development and the initiative (he has the move). It is instructive to watch just how accurately Botvinnik was able to preserve the initiative and how finely he exchanged the pieces leaving only those on the board which would bring him the final success.

12.♗b5

Black is sentenced to a passive defence. Now the weaknesses on the c-line and on the e-line become obvious. Because of this every further exchange could be fatal. Alekhine did not evaluate the position well enough and he started to prepare the exchange of the light-squared bishops (following the principle: to exchange a bad bishop for better one).

12...♗d7?

The problem that Black faces after the exchange are the holes in his territory, especially the hole on c6. Better would be 12...♗b7 13.♕a4 ♖c8 14.♗f4 a6! and Black could hope to gradually equalize.

13.♕a4 ♘b8

A passive move, but here it is hard to give any wise advice to Black. For example 13...♖c8 14.♗f4 and Black has no good move; White is threatening ♖a1–c1, with a decisive advantage.

14.♗f4 ♗b5 15.♕b5 a6 16.♕a4 ♗d6

A classical defensive technique in a pressed position: after every exchange the defender has more space and more possible solutions to his problems.

17.♗d6 ♕d6 18.♖ac1

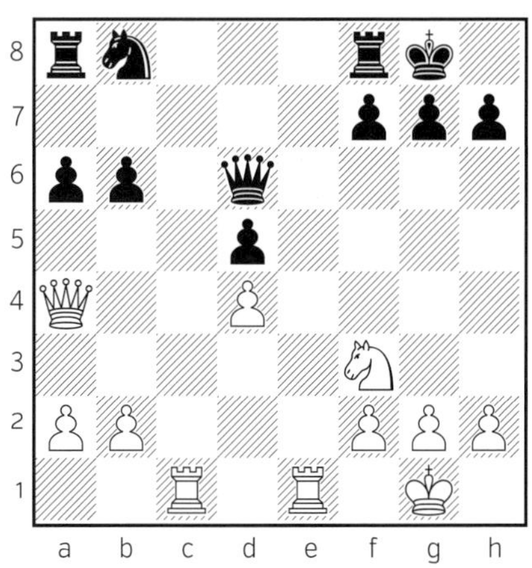

A very interesting position! The pawns are placed almost symmetrically and it is hard to say that one of them is weak. On the top of this there are only a few left and there are not many pieces either (there are already three pairs missing from the board).

There are two open files in the center and they are both under White's control: even though there are no direct effects of the control to be seen, Black is having difficulties due to not having a good plan. He desperately wants to swap the last piece, but the knight on b8 is sentenced to a passive role and it also needs to control the penetration squares of White's rook.

18...♖a7 19.♕c2

White has no troubles just playing. He evaluates that it will be easier for him to penetrate through the c-file than through the e-file, the latter of which could be defended by Black's king...

19...♖e7

The moment that proves that the exchanges are good for White: 19...♘d7 20.♕c6 ♕c6 21.♖c6 with a won endgame. After 19...f6, with which he defends the critical e5-square (where White wants to place his knight) and after 20.♕f5 White starts to exploit the next critical light-square in Black's territory — e6.

20.♖e7 ♕e7 21.♕c7! ♕c7 22.♖c7

White cold-bloodedly agrees to yet further exchanges. He penetrates with a rook to the seventh rank, from where he is able to paralyze Black.

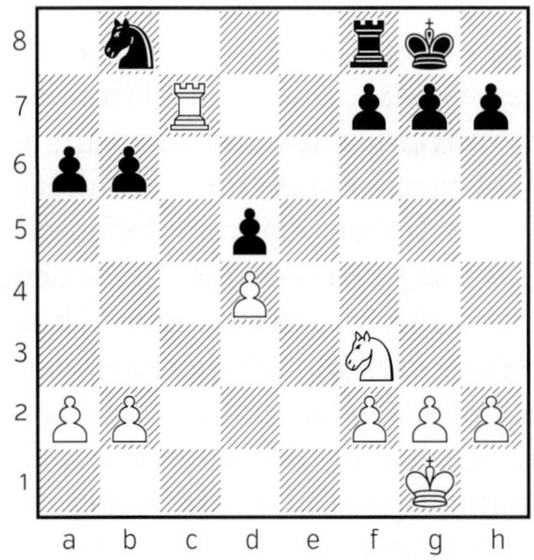

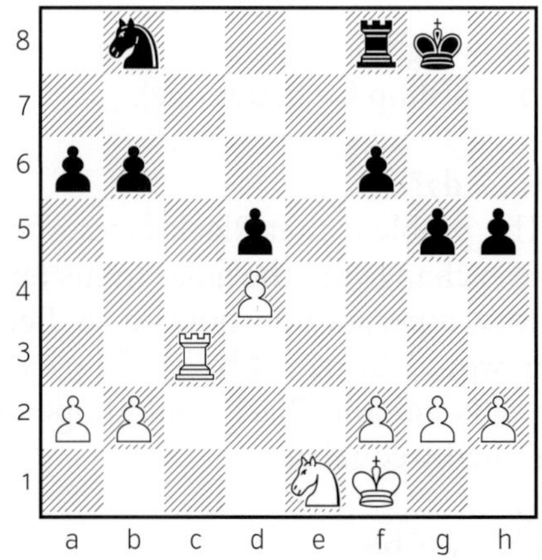

22...f6!

Black wants to swap rooks (with ...♖f7) and he did not get scared by the move 23.♖b7, because he would obtain nice counterplay after 23...♖c8! White saw that he would need to leave the seventh rank.

23.♔f1 ♖f7 24.♖c8 ♖f8 25.♖c3!

An outstandingly instructive game! With the help of the in-between check he has managed to return Black's rook to the eighth rank and now White also temporarily withdraws. And everything is supported by accurate calculations as we will soon get to see.

25...g5

Alekhine defends himself cleverly — with the advance of the pawns on the kingside the seventh rank lose some of its power and also the domination over Black's rook weakens.

26.♘e1 h5

Black continues with his defensive strategy.

27.h4!!

A surprise on the wing where Black surely did not expect it! White wants to weaken Black's pawns on the kingside.

27...♘d7

The capture 27...gh4 28.♘f3 would be much worse; 27...♔f7 is most likely the best choice, even though White would, after 28.hg5 fg5 29.♘f3 ♔f6 30.♘e5, keep a clear advantage. Look at the placement of the knights!

28.♖c7

Complete control!

28...♖f7 29.♘f3! g4 30.♘e1

The knight moves to the f4-square, which was taken over with skilful moves of the pawns and by provocations from the knight.

30...f5 31.♘d3 f4

Black was facing a sad choice: whether to leave the knight on f4 or to place there his pawn, which will be constantly under attack.

32.f3

Botvinnik was not thinking about winning a pawn after 32.♘b4, instead he rather fixes Black's additional weakness. He knew very well that the material would wait for him. Next follows a slow, almost sadistic realization of his advantage.

32...gf3 33.gf3 a5 34.a4 ♔f8 35.♖c6 ♔e7 36.♔f2 ♖f5 37.b3 ♔d8 38.♔e2 ♘b8

A desperate attempt at activation.

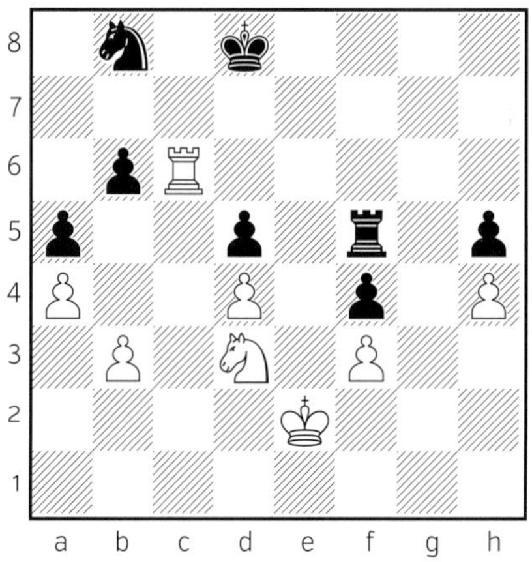

39.♖g6!

White is certainly not thinking about 39.♖b6? ♔c7, where Black would be left with a chance for a counterplay after 40...♘c6.

39...♔c7 40.♘e5 ♘a6 41.♖g7

After 41.♖g5 White would have won a little faster, but that does not change the result.

41...♔c8 42.♘c6 ♖f6 43.♘e7 ♔b8 44.♘d5 ♖d6 45.♖g5 ♘b4 46.♘b4 ab4 47.♖h5 ♖c6 48.♖b5 ♔c7 49.♖b4 ♖h6 50.♖b5 ♖h4 51.♔d3 1:0.

"I was completely helpless!" (Alekhine)

The World Champion memorized the lesson deeply. And only a year after he got the chance to demonstrate what his compatriot taught him...

2

▷ **Alekhine**
▶ **Eliskases**
Buenos Aires 1939 [D41]

1.e4 c6 2.d4 d5 3.ed5 cd5 4.c4 ♘f6 5.♘c3 e6 6.♘f3 ♗e7 7.cd5 ♘d5 8.♗b5! ♗d7 9.♗d7! ♘d7 10.♘d5 ed5

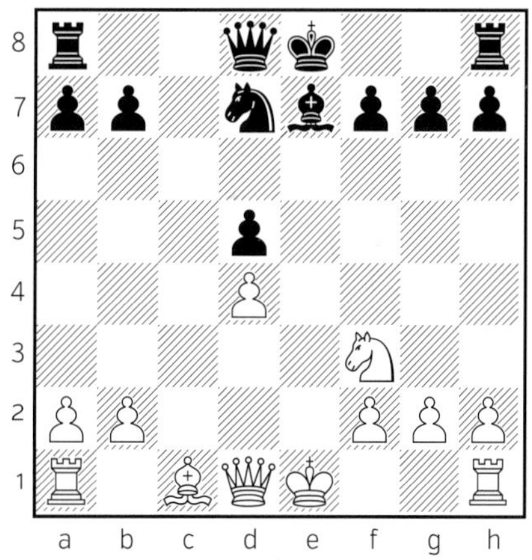

The position in the diagram is very similar to the diagram from the previous game...

11.♕b3 ♘b6 12.0–0 0–0 13.♗f4 ♗d6

Black is following the same logic as his opponent a year ago: every exchange makes it easier to defend.

14.♗d6 ♕d6 15.♖fe1 ♖ac8 16.♖ac1

The story repeats itself: Black has no direct weaknesses, but he is completely squeezed and without a real plan.

16...h6 17.♘e5 ♖c7 18.g3 ♖fc8 19.♖c7 ♖c7 20.♕b5

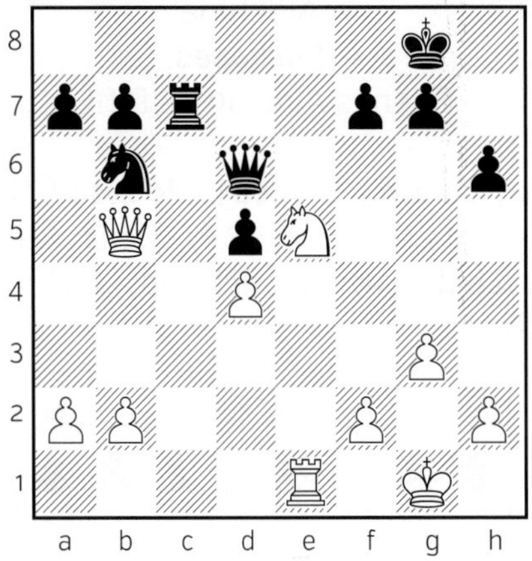

Black exchanged a pair of rooks and took control over the c-file. He managed to achieve a lot more that Alekhine did a year ago. How to evaluate the position? White undoubtedly has the initiative and that is why Black could only save himself by making the right exchanges. It would be the best to neutralize White's pressure on the e-file: 20...♖e7 21.♕a5 f6 22.♘g6 ♖e1 but with the respective positions of the knights White will keep all the luxuries of the position.

20...♘d7 21.♘d7 ♖d7 22.♖e8 ♔h7 23.h4! a6

Black cannot block with 23...h5, due to 24.♖a8! a6 25.♕e2 with a double threat (♕h5 or ♕e8).

24.♕e2 ♖d8 25.♖e7 ♖d7 26.♖e5 g6

Black is having a really hard time: h4-h5 is threatened, as well as a check on the diagonal and the penetration to the eighth rank.

27.h5 ♕f6 28.♕e3 ♖d6

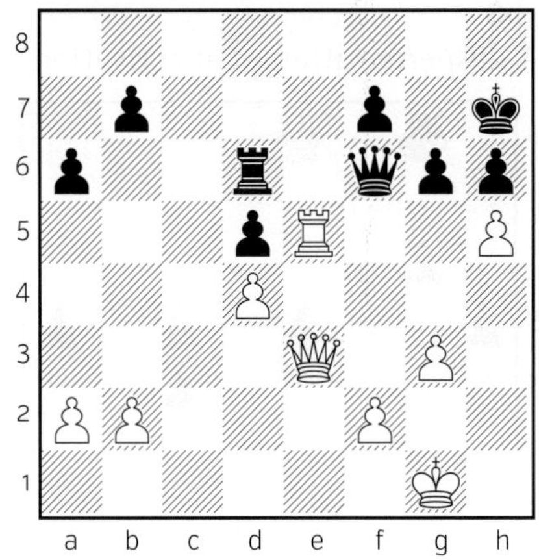

29.♕b3!

The d5-pawn is lost. In exchange Black will win a pawn on b2, but this will do him no good until the endgame, and that is still far away.

29...♖b6 30.hg6 ♕g6 31.♕d5 ♖b2 32.♖f5 ♖b5?

Better would be 32...♔g8.

33.♖f7 ♔g8 34.♖f6 ♖d5 35.♖g6 ♔h7 36.♖b6 ♖d4 37.♖b7 ♔g8 38.♖b6 ♖a4 39.♖h6 ♖a2 40.♔g2 a5 41.♖a6 a4 42.♖a7 a3 43.g4 ♔f8 44.g5 ♔g8 45.♔g3 ♖a1 46.♔g4 ♖g1 47.♔f5 ♖g2 48.f4 a2 49.♔f6 1:0

Let us see one more modern game, which will help us to believe that the basic rules about the center which were true in the past, are also true today!

3

▹ **Ivanchuk**
▸ **Karpov**
Linares 1991 [E54]

1.d4 ♘f6 2.c4 e6 3.♘c3 ♗b4 4.e3 0–0 5.♗d3 d5 6.♘f3 c5 7.0–0 cd4 8.ed4 dc4 9.♗c4 b6 10.♗g5 ♗b7 11.♖c1 ♘c6 12.a3 ♗e7 13.♕d3

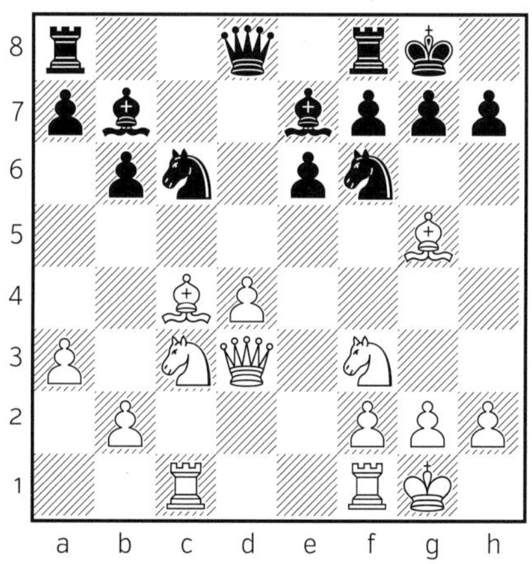

13...♘d5?!

Black is offering a transposition into the positions that are good for White and which we have already got to know. 13...♖c8 14.♗a2! ♖c7!? 15.♗b1 g6 16.♗h6 ♖e8 17.♖fe1 ♖d7 or 13...h6 (Anand) 14.♗h4 ♖c8.

14.♗d5! ed5

14...♗g5 15.♘g5 ♕g5 16.♗e4 f5 17.♗c6 ♗c6 18.f3 ♖fd8 19.♘e2.

15.♗e7 ♘e7 16.♖fe1 ♖c8 17.h4!

This motif was already used in the game Alekhine : Eliskases. White wants to occupy the space on the kingside and fix the pawns in front of Black's king. He also wants to take the g6-square away from the knight. Another possibility is 17.♖e3 ♕d6 18.♖ce1, with pressure on the e-line.

17...h6 18.h5 ♖c7 19.♘b5?!

An unnecessary exchange. We already know that exchanges are good for the defender and the move played made it possible for Black to get rid of his light-squared bishop, his worst piece. White would keep a stable advantage after 19.♖e3 ♕c8 20.♖ce1 ♕f5 21.♕d2.

19...♖c1 20.♖c1 ♗a6 21.a4 ♗b5 22.♕b5 ♘f5 23.g3 ♘e7 24.♘e5

Despite the mistake on the 19th move White has kept a clear advantage. His pieces are more active, he is controlling the open file and Black has a lot of weak squares. It is hard for Black to get rid of the knight on e5 without weakening his position even more.

24...♕d6 25.♕a6 ♘f5 26.♕d3 ♘e7 27.♕f3 a5 28.♔g2

Anand later showed a simple move: 28.b3!± with which White would keep his big advantage

28...f6?!

Black could find counterplay with the move 28...g5! because it is unwise for White to open the f-file. The threat would be ...f7-f6-f5 and White's king would be in danger.

29.♘d3

Worse would be 29.♘g6 (Anand) 29...♘g6 30.hg6 f5!

29...♖c8 30.♖e1

White does not want to exchange rooks. After 30.♖c8 ♘c8 31.♘f4 ♘e7 his advantage would be only symbolic.

30...♖c4 31.♘f4

Yet another inaccurate move. The commentators proved in their long analysis that better would be 31.♕g4!? and 31...f5!? 32.♕h4 ♘c6, followed by a nice variation: 33.♖e8 ♔f7 34.♖c8 ♘d4 35.♖d8 ♕e6 36.♖d7 ♔g8 37.♕d8 ♔h7 38.♖e7! ♖c8 39.♖e6 ♖d8 40.♖b6±.

31...♖d4 32.♘g6 ♘g6 33.hg6 ♔f8!

The queen ending is lost after 33... ♖e4?! 34.♖e4 de4 35.♕e4 ♔f8 36.♕a8 ♔e7 37.♕b7 (Anand).

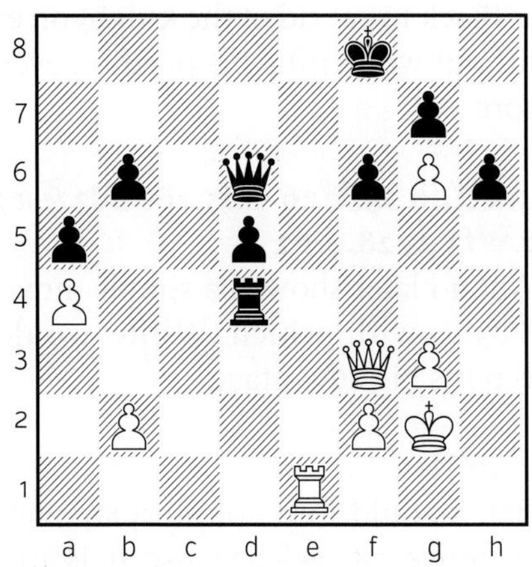

34.♕f5! ♖c4 35.g4 ♕f4 — Black ran out of time — 1:0.

White has good compensation, but the road to the victory would still be long and complicated. For example: 36.♕d5 ♕g4 (36...♕c7 37.♕g8!+-) 37.♔f1 ♕h3 38.♔e2 ♕g4 39.♔d3+- or 35...♕b4 36.♖e3 ♖g4 37.♔f3 or 35...d4 36.♖e6 ♕d8 37.♕b5± or the best 35... ♖c6 (Anand) 36.g5 d4!?

THE OUTPOST ON e5 (e4)

It is clear that when there is a symmetrical pawn structure, the two central squares that are being controlled by the opponent's pawn are very important. In the positions we are looking at White's outposts are the e5-square and c5-square and Black's outposts are the e4-square and the c4-square. Due to White's first move advantage it is logical that he will be the first to occupy an outpost. And it is not hard to choose which: In the opening it is easier for the knight to reach the e5-square than the c5-square.

Let us see an example on this theme which proved successful for Karpov, the victim from the previous game. Obviously he also learned from his defeats...

1

▷ **Karpov**
▶ **Morovic Fernandez**
Las Palmas 1994 (D32)

1.c4 ♘f6 2.♘f3 e6 3.d4 d5 4.e3 c5 5.♘c3 ♘c6 6.cd5 ed5 7.♗b5 ♗d6 8.0–0 0–0 9.h3 cd4 10.ed4 h6 11.♖e1 ♗d7

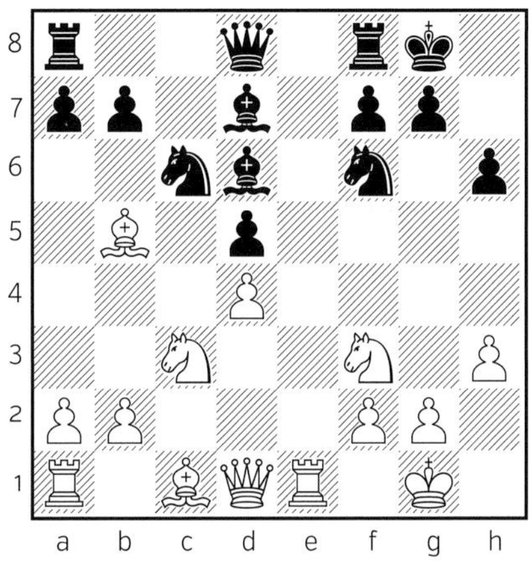

We see here the position that allows a jump on e5. We already know the structure, and the difference from the other games is undoubtedly the number of pieces on the board. When there is a full board it is hard for White to exploit his positional advantage and he needs to use a new strategic plan.

12.♘e5!
This move does not represent a decisive threat, but it is very unpleasant. What should Black do? He will not be able to tolerate the knight forever and he needs to devote some time to this problem. The possible capture would be (at least for now) very bad, because White would take with the pawn and so gain a majority on the kingside and he would also isolate and weaken Black's d5-pawn.

12...♖c8 13.a3 a6
Possible is 13...♖e8, where White quietly strengthens his outpost — 14.♗f4.

14.♗a4
The bishop wants to be placed on the b1-h7 diagonal, but there is still no concrete mission for him there. That is why in the meantime he will put pressure on the defenders of Black's center which forces Black to contemplate some unpleasant decisions.

14...b5
Almost forced, but we can see with the naked eye that the move leaves holes behind, which will not be easy to shore up.

15.♗b3 ♗e6 16.♗c2
The motive is simple: to move the queen to d3 and to get rid of the knight on f6.

16...♕b6 17.♗e3 ♖fd8
For the first time Black is threatening to take: if he had the move, he would play 18...♗e5 19.de5 d4!

18.♘g4!
Black has no choice but to take the knight with the bishop. He must not give up the knight on f6, because he desperately needs it for the defence.

18...♗g4 19.hg4 ♗b8 20.♗f5 ♖c7 21.a4!

The play over the whole board is a distinctive feature of the great masters. White is threatening to take on b5, with which he would weaken Black's b5-pawn.

21...b4 22.a5!

A nice pawn sacrifice, the beginning of the final attack.

22...♘a5 23.♘a4 ♕d6

Or 23...♕b5 24.♘c5, with the idea 25.♗d3 or 25.♕a4.

24.g3!

White is marvellously moving the play from wing to wing — just as in football, where similar transfers are practically undefendable. He is now threatening 25.♗f4.

24...♖a7 25.g5 hg5 26.♗g5 ♘c6

Quickly back into defence, but sadly it is too late for Black.

27.♖c1!

This time White is threatening 28.♗f4 indirectly. An interesting variation is 27...♘e7 28.♗f4 and the queen is trapped in the middle of the board!

27...♘a5 28.♖c5 ♘c4 29.b3 ♘a3

Once more: 29...♘b6? 30.♗f4+-

30.♔g2

The final operation: the rook goes to h1.

30...♖e7 31.♖h1 ♖de8 32.♖h8! ♔h8 33.♕h1 ♔g8 34.♗f6 ♕g3 35.fg3 ♖e2 36.♔h3 gf6 37.♔g4 1:0.

THE COUNTERPLAY

Counterplay is connected with a few elements. The first and the most important one is the withdrawal of the pieces away from the center or the neutralization of the possible pressure on the open lines.

It is clear that the defender can turn into an attacker, if he manages to switch roles (if he chases away the attacker's pieces from the center and he himself occupies the outpost or if he takes away the control over the open file from the opponent). But usually this kind of heroism does not work out for him and he needs to face the attacker's pressure.

In this case it is better to dig oneself in and to be careful that the position does not get any weaker and at the same time search for the possible weaknesses within the opponent's territory. It is very important to evaluate the position regularly — the positional elements can quickly change and it is very important that one exploits every possible moment for action. When we defend ourselves these kinds of moments are not common and we cannot afford to miss any of them!

1

▷ **Timman**
▶ **Yermolinsky**
Elista 1998 [B30]

1.e4 c5!

The exclamation mark is placed here because we will see that an absolutely symmetrical pawn structure can be formed also out of the sharpest opening in the world.

2.♘f3 ♘c6 3.♗b5 e6 4.0–0 ♘ge7 5.c3 a6 6.♗e2 d5 7.ed5 ed5 8.d4 cd4 9.♘d4 ♘d4 10.cd4?!

Even though we would lose a few tempos, White really needs to take with the queen.

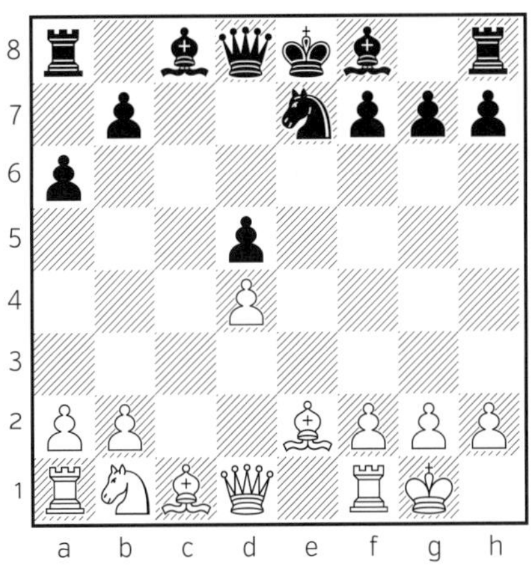

10...g6! 11.♘c3 ♗g7

Black is developing his pieces ideally, they are looking at the d4-pawn and are also controlling the potential outpost on the e5-square. White already has a few minor problems to worry about: first of all it is important how he intends to defend the d4-square?

12.♗g5 0–0 13.♖e1 h6 14.♗h4?

Correct would be 14.♗e7 ♕e7 15.♘d5 ♕h4 16.♘b6 ♖b8 17.♘c8 ♖fc8 18.♗g4 ♖d8 19.♖e4 ♕f6, with more-or-less equal play.

14...g5!

The start of forced play.

15.♗g3 ♘c6 16.♗f3 ♗e6 17.♗e5 ♘e5 18.de5 d4 19.♘a4 ♕a5!

It is interesting that White is already in serious trouble — even though he has not played any very bad moves yet.

20.♗b7 ♖ad8 21.♖c1 d3 22.♖e4 ♗d7 23.♗c6

Better would be 23.♘c5, although Black would keep his advantage: 23...♗f5 24.♖a4 ♕b6 25.b3 d2 26.♖cc4 ♖fe8!

23...♗c6 24.♖c6 ♕d5 25.♖cc4 ♗e5∓ 26.♘c3 ♕d6 27.h4 d2 28.hg5 hg5 29.♖e3 ♗f4 30.♘e4? ♕e6–+ 31.♖ec3 f5 32.g3 fe4 33.gf4 ♖f4 34.♖g3 ♕c4 0:1

2

▷ **Damljanovic**
▶ **Yusupov**
Belgrade 1989 [D58]

1.d4 ♘f6 2.♘f3 e6 3.c4 d5 4.♘c3 ♗e7 5.♗g5 0–0 6.e3 h6 7.♗h4 b6 8.♕b3 ♗b7 9.♗f6 ♗f6 10.♖d1 c6 11.e4 ♘d7 12.cd5 ed5 13.ed5 ♖e8 14.♗e2 cd5 15.0–0 ♘f8

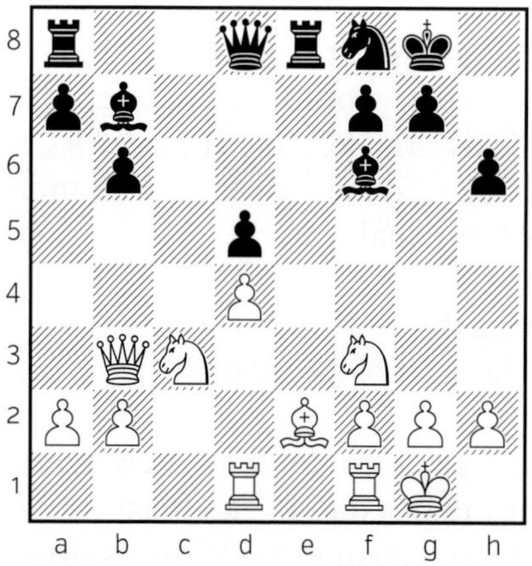

White has formed our structure and has forced Black to develop his bishop on a passive b7-square. But Black has his trumps: first of all the pair of bishops, which makes it easier to defend the outpost on the e5-square and at the same time offering preliminary conditions for the attack on the d4-pawn. White would be better if he could jump into the e5-square, but the jump is not possible at the moment.

16.♖fe1 ♘e6

The ideal square for the knight, from where he attacks the d4-pawn and defends the sensitive c7-square.

17.♗b5?!

This move is connected with a loss of time, so the withdrawal to the f1-square would be better.

17...♖e7 18.♖e3 ♕d6!

The queen will move to f4 and it strengthen the pressure on the d4-pawn.

19.g3 a6 20.♗f1 b5

Preparing the advance of the pawns to b4 and a5 with the conquest of space on the queenside. Black needs to open the position a bit more because his bishops demand it!

21.♗g2 ♖c8 22.♘e2 b4 23.♕d3 a5

The light-squared bishop will join play via the a6-square.

24.♕f5 ♖ce8 25.h4 ♗c8 26.♕c2 ♗a6 27.♘c1 ♖c8

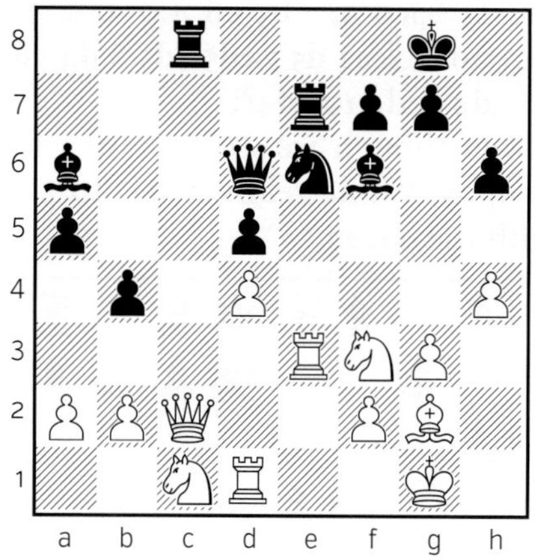

28.♕a4

This move leads directly to defeat! After 28.♕f5 White could still resist.

28...♘d4!

First we saw exemplary strategic play and for the end a lovely tactical stroke.

29.♘d4 ♗d4 30.♖d4 ♖e3 31.fe3 ♕g3! 32.♘b3 ♕e3 33.♔h2 ♖c2 34.♕d7 ♕e5 35.♔h1 ♖b2 36.♕d5 ♖b1 0:1

THE OPEN CENTER

We can talk about the open center when there are no pawns of either side placed within it. Manoeuvres with the pieces are characteristic for this kind of positions and both players place their pieces in the center. The manoeuvres are connected with the occupation of the open lines in the center and also of the important squares. Possible weaknesses in the opponent's camp, especially the ones near the center, have a double significance.

The placement of the pieces in the center is also important because it adds power to the pieces, especially to the light pieces in the center. When a bishop is placed in the center, it controls 13 squares (in the corner only seven), whereas a knight can, from the center, jump to eight different squares — a lot more than when it is placed in the corner or on the edge of the board. And there is something else important to know: if we place a bishop, for example on the e5-square, it will control the whole board on two long diagonals. A knight, which has difficulties with moving from one side of the board to another because its manoeuvres are slow, becomes alive in the center and can quickly reach even the most remote squares on the board.

When there is an open center it is hard to give advice. It is clear that the player who occupies the center with his pieces will try to create weaknesses in the opponent's camp. If he manages to do that, he will quickly move the play there. It is also clear that the defender will try to prevent that and he will try to defend his position with the pieces and with hardly any movements with the pawns (any movement with the pawns leaves behind empty holes!)

1

▷ **Reti**
▶ **Capablanca**
New York 1924 [A15]

1.♘f3 ♘f6 2.c4 g6 3.b4

Richard Reti was one of the pioneers of chess hyper-modernism. In practice the famous Czech successfully defended wing openings — the attempt at controlling the center from a distance. Jose Raoul Capablanca was his opposite — a marvellous classical player with a refined feeling for clear positions. We can imagine that the unusual opening placements which were chosen by hyper-modernists, were confusing to him.

3...♗g7 4.♗b2 0–0 5.g3 b6!?

Capablanca also decides on a hypermodernistic "double fianchetto".

6.♗g2 ♗b7 7.0–0 d6 8.d3 ♘bd7 9.♘bd2 e5

"Black played through the opening simple and 'nice' and the chances are balanced". (Alekhine)

10.♕c2 ♖e8 11.♖fd1 a5

Action in the center is premature: 11...e4 12.de4 ♘e4 13.♗g7 ♔g7 14.♘d4.

12.a3 h6?!

A move that is hard to understand, and the very beginning of later Black's troubles. Until this game the Cuban had not lost a game for several years and later on he apologized that he was sick when the game started. "I have never beaten a healthy opponent!" joked Dr. Emanuel Lasker.

13.♘f1 c5 14.b5 ♘f8

The activation in the center with 14...d5 would again not be good: 15.cd5 ♘d5

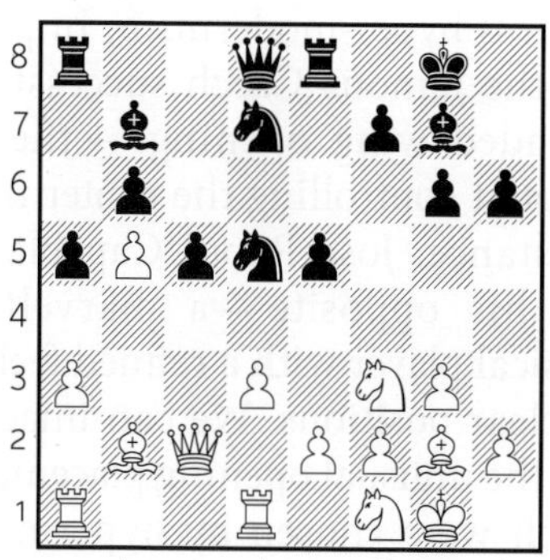

16.♘3d2! ♕e7 17.♘c4 ♖ad8 18.♘fd2! (the knight's marvellous manoeuvres) and White has the advantage.

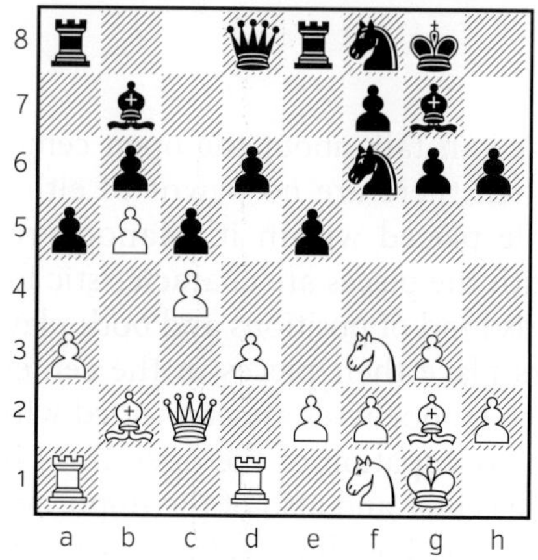

15.e3!?

A very important moment for White to decide about his plans in the center. One possibility was 15.e4 and ♘e3-d5, but the Czech rightly evaluated that the opening of the center would bring him more.

15...♕c7 16.d4 ♗e4 17.♕c3 ed4 18.ed4 ♘6d7?

Alekhine later wrote that better would have been: 19...♖ad8 20.dc5 dc5 21.♗g7 ♔g7 22.♕b2 ♔g8 23.♘e3, where White would be just a little better. It is clear that White will manage to open the center completely, but the question is who will be able to occupy it with the pieces first and more successfully? The following manoeuvres answer this question.

19.♕d2! cd4 20.♗d4 ♕c4 21.♗g7 ♔g7 22.♕b2 ♔g8 23.♖d6

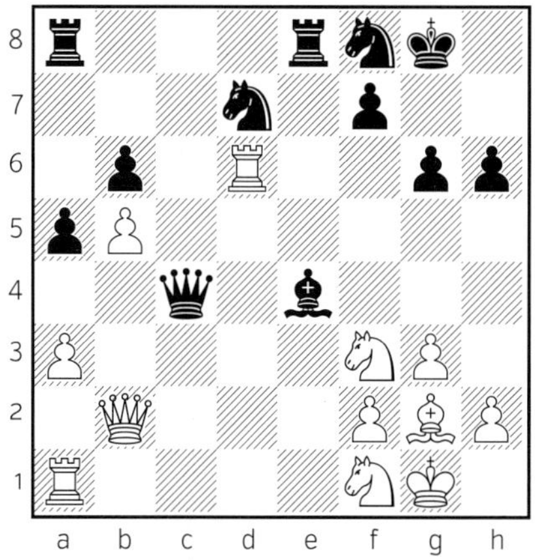

Along the way the opponents removed the c-pawns and now the center is completely open. It is threatening 24.♘3d2, which was not able immediately due to 23...♕c2.

23...♕c5 24.♖ad1

With the pieces in the center White controls the d-file and has the initiative because of the attack on the knight.

24...♖a7 25.♘e3 ♕h5

The unpleasant 26.♘g4 +- was threatened.

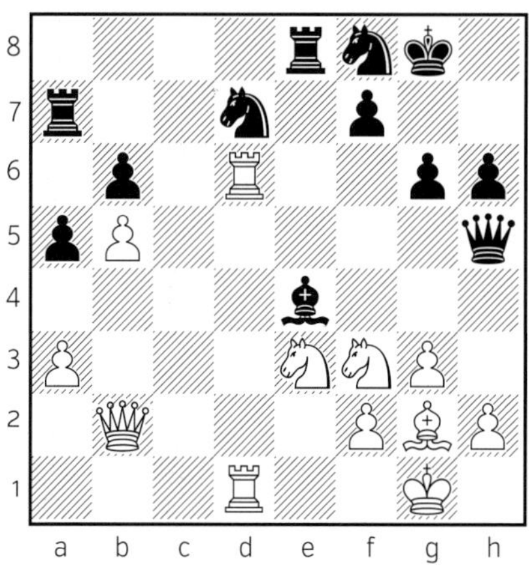

26.♘d4!

The best! Look at the domination by White's pieces in the center, from where they control the entire board. Black's pieces are fully pinned: the knight on d7 defends the b6-pawn and the rook on a7 and the knight on f8 defends the knight on d7. The queen is alone on the kingside and the rook on e8 controls nothing.

Reti held his greed for the queen in check and gave up the opportunity of the attractive 26.♖1d5 ♗d5 27.g4, where White would — after 27...♗f3 28.gh5 — win the queen for his rook, knight and pawn, but would have difficulties with the realization of the advantage, as in the game.

26...♗g2 27.♔g2 ♕e5?

Black tries to patch himself up, even though the move 27...♘e5 would definitely be better. Of course he could not play 27...♖e3? 28.fe3 ♕d1 29.♘e6.

28.♘c4 ♕c5

"The unfortunate queen cannot find any safe shelter". (Alekhine)

29.♘c6 ♖c7 30.♘e3

White's predominance in the center is horrifying. We already said that the knight can move very quickly from the center to the wing. White's knights successfully combine between attacks on the queenside, where they paralyzed Black, and quick jumps on the kingside where there are holes around Black's king. Now ♘g4 is threatened again, but the game was finished after Capablanca overlooked:

30...♘e5 31.♖1d5 1:0

PROVOKING THE WEAKNESS

Provoking a weakness, against which the attackers strategy will be based, represents the basic plan in this position. Let us have a look how Mikhail Botvinnik handled these types of positions.

1

▹ **Kotov**
▸ **Botvinnik**
USSR 1939 [E33]

1.d4 ♘f6 2.c4 e6 3.♘c3 ♗b4 4.♕c2 ♘c6 5.♘f3 d5 6.e3 0–0 7.a3 ♗c3 8.♕c3 ♗d7

Black , in exchanging off the pair of bishops, develops lightening-like. The player who has the advantage in development needs to open the position and usually that is connected with the opening of the center. That is why White needs to be careful.

9.b3 a5 10.♗d3 a4 11.♘d2?

This move is against all basic principles of play in the opening. The knight leaves the center and moves again without White firstly finishing his development.

11...♖e8 12.0–0

It clear that Black's plan is to open the center with the strike ...e6-e5. That's why 12.f2-f4 was interesting, but it takes squares away from the dark-squared bishop and also creates new holes on the light-squares. Black would continue with 12...♘a5! and after the big exchange on c4 the bishop would start to play.

12...e5 13.de5

Yet another inaccurate move: when we fall behind in development we do not open the game up. Better would be 13.♗b2, without fear of 13...e4.

13...♘e5 14.♗b2 ab3 15.♘b3 ♘e4!

The beginning of the occupation of the center with the pieces — preparation for complete opening of the center.

16.♕c2 ♘c4 17.♗c4 dc4 18.♕c4

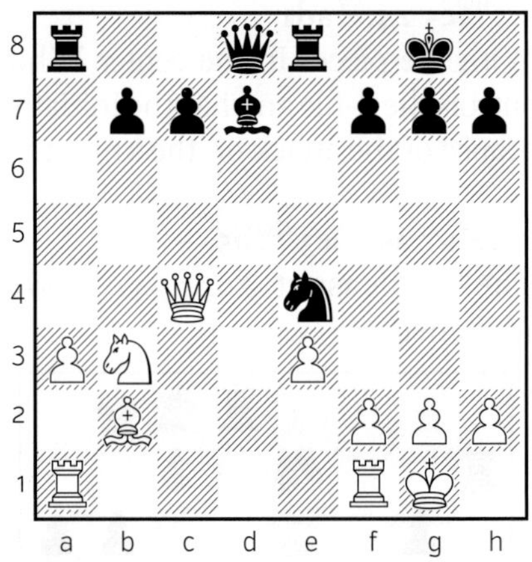

18...♕g5!

An excellent move, which forces White to weaken himself. There are two threats: 19...♗h3 and 19...♗b5 due to which White has few choices.

19.f4 ♕g6

Threatening ...♗e6-♗b3 and ...♘d2, winning the exchange. Grabbing the pawn with 20.♕c7 would be incredibly dangerous: 20...♗h3 21.♕c2 ♖ac8 22.♕e2 ♘d6! with many different threats.

20.♖fd1 ♘d6! 21.♕d3 ♗f5 22.♕c3 ♗e4 23.♖d2 ♗c6 24.♕d3 ♘f5

Black strengthen himself in the center with nice manoeuvres and combines his dominance with threats on the light-squares. Many things are threatened: directly 25...♖e3 or more indirectly 25...♗e4 26.♕c3 ♘h4.

25.♗e5 f6 26.♗c7 ♖e3

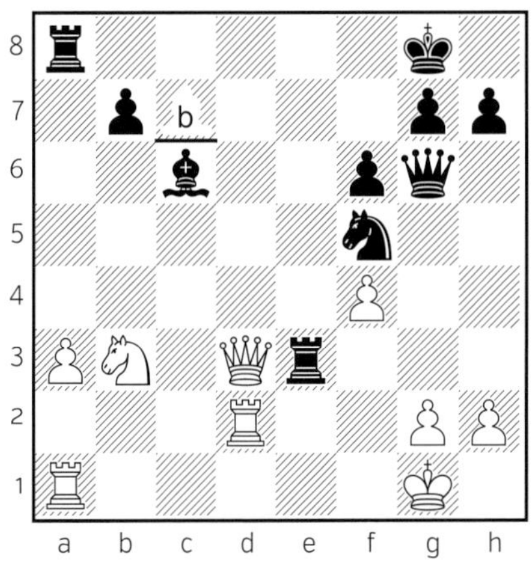

The center is fully open and Black's dominance is even more marked.

27.♕c4 ♔h8 28.♗b6 ♖ee8 29.♕f1 h5 30.♘d4 ♘d4 31.♗d4 ♖e4

The opposite-coloured bishops increase Black's dominance. The old rule teaches that opposite-coloured bishops don't prevent an attack, but on the contrary they make the defender's work even harder, because he cannot play against the bishop.

32.♖e1 ♖e1 33.♕e1 ♖a3 34.♔h1 ♖a8 35.♖e2 ♔h7 36.h3 ♖e8 37.♕f2 ♕g2 38.♕g2 ♖e2 0:1

White played the opening inaccurately and Botvinnik reached a serious advantage in development. White also continued inaccurately and ignored Black wishes for the opening of the center. With the excellent move 18...♕g5 Black provoked weaknesses around White's king and he later on exploited them instructively.

THE ATTACK ON THE KING

When the opponent has not yet castled it is best to open up the play as soon as possible. If our pieces are close to the opponent's king it will not be good for him. Then the play will be full of tactics, sacrifices happen often and the games usually end up on the short-list for chess beauty competitions.

1

▷ **Chebotarev**
▶ **Freidlin**
USSR 1948 (D39)

1.d4 ♘f6 2.c4 e6 3.♘f3 d5 4.♗g5 ♗b4 5.♘c3 dc4 6.e4 c5 7.e5 cd4 8.♕a4 ♘c6 9.0–0–0 ♗d7 10.♘e4 ♗e7 11.ef6 gf6 12.♗h4 ♖c8 13.♔b1 ♘a5 14.♕c2 e5

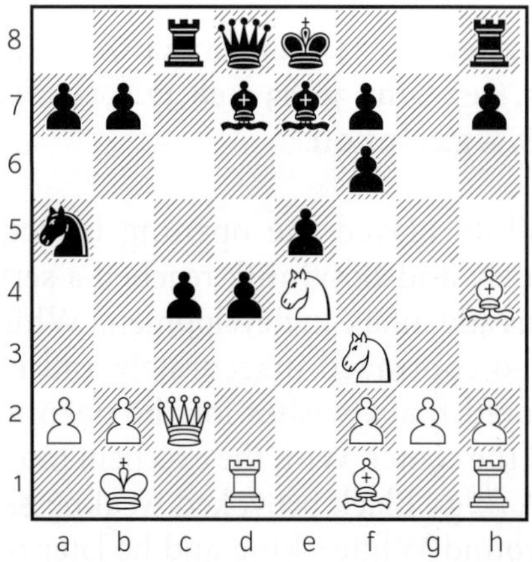

Black sacrificed the knight and in return received three pawns and a tremendous predominance in the center. White's decision to return the piece was not hard to make because of this. Especially when we consider the fact that Black's king has not yet moved.

15.♘d4! ed4 16.♖d4 ♕b6

16...0–0 17.♗f6! ♗f6 18.♖d7!

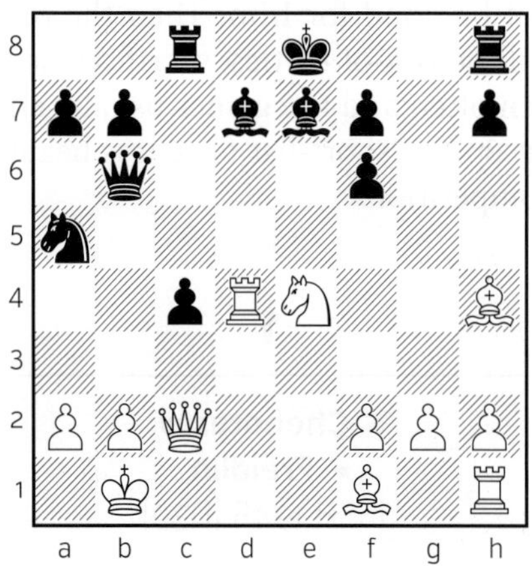

17.♖d6!

An excellent move, which points out all White's advantages and — conversely — all Black's disadvantages. The rook is untouchable: 17...♗d6 18.♘f6 and the queen is lost.

17...♖c6 18.♗f6 ♖g8 19.♗d4!

White firstly prevented Black from castling and now he frees the squares for attack with tempo; the bishop frees the square for the knight, which desperately wants to be placed on f6.

19...♕b5 20.♖c6 ♘c6 21.♗c5!

Removal of the defence — White attacks with great élan. An empty center offers a clean slate for fantasy and chess geometry.

21...♗f5 22.♗e7 ♘d4

Black banked on this counterstroke, but White calculated deeply and accurately:

23.♗c4!

Of course not 23.♗f6 ♕c6! (rather than 23...♘c2 24.♘f6! ♔e7 25.♘g8 and 26.♗b5).

23...♕c6 24.♘d6 ♔d7

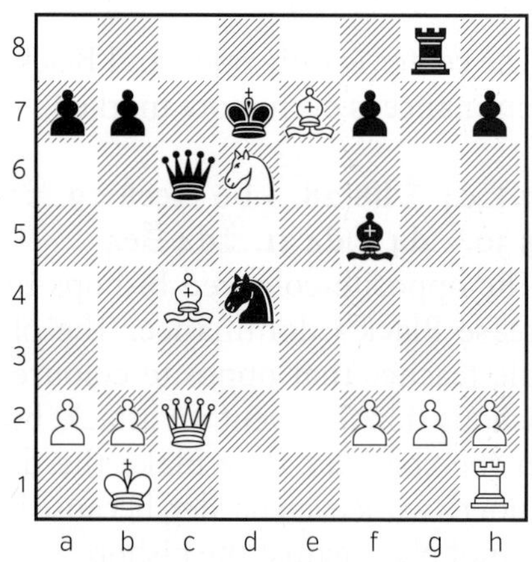

25.♘f5!

A magnificent queen sacrifice, which makes this game a beauty.

25...♘c2 26.♖d1 ♔c8

26...♔c7 27.♗b3.

27.♗f7 ♖g4

27...♖g2 28.♗d5 ♕d7 29.♗b7! or 27...♖h8 28.♖c1.

28.♘d6 ♔c7 29.♘e8 ♔b6 30.♖d6 1:0.

The most beautiful illustration of the attack on the short-castled king is the famous games between Tal and Smyslov from the Candidates tournament in Yugoslavia in 1959.

2

▷ **Tal**
▶ **Smyslov**
Yugoslavia 1959 (B10)

1.e4 c6 2.d3 d5 3.♘d2 e5 4.♘gf3 ♘d7

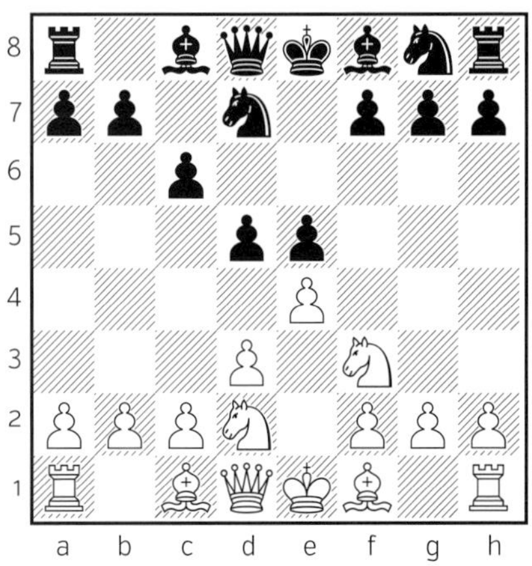

5.d4

An immediate invitation to an open fight and to clear the center! The pawns in the center cannot stand the mutual tension and it is only a matter of time before the center will unleash itself.

5...de4 6.♘e4 ed4 7.♕d4 ♘gf6 8.♗g5 ♗e7

White could exploit his initiative the most with a transposition to the endgame after 9.♘d6 ♗d6 10.♕d6 ♕e7 11.♕e7, where he would dominate with his pair of bishops. But young Tal thought differently: he was as a rule avoiding the exchange of queens and he adored attacks, even though he intentionally played some bad moves... we do not recommend you to play this way unless you have the abilities of Tal!

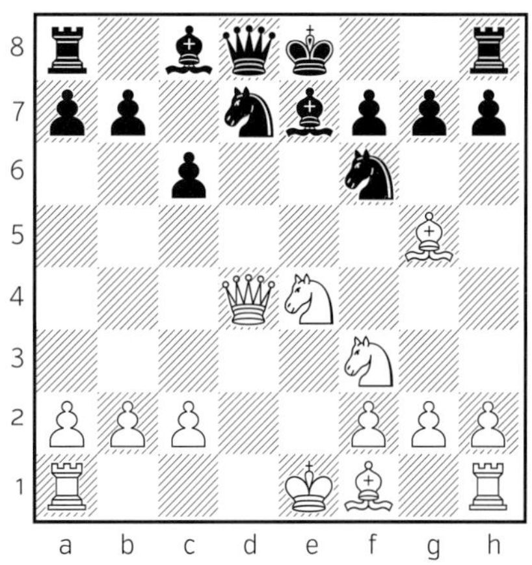

9.0–0–0?! 0–0 10.♘d6

The difference is obvious: Black's knight does not have to take anymore, because it is no longer check. A very good move for Black now would be 10...♘b6 and for example 11.♘c8 ♖c8 12.♕h4 ♘fd5! Did Smyslov want more?

10...♕a5 11.♗c4

White intentionally exposes himself to the attacks of Black's pawns and he will in the meantime play with his pieces in the center. Tal oriented himself in these circumstances very well.

11...b5

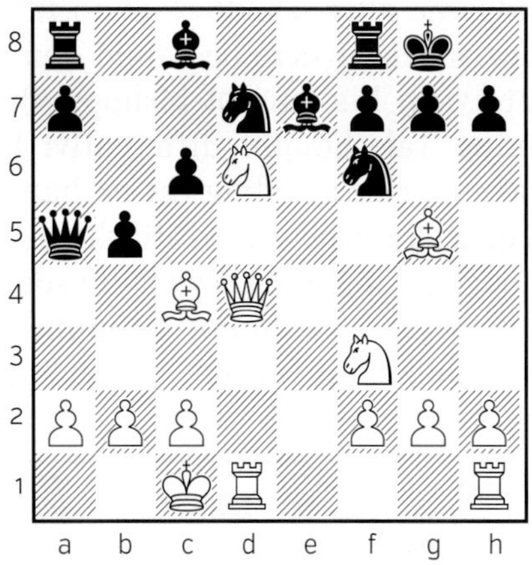

12.♗d2!

An excellent move! The bishop goes to the long diagonal, from where it will be a threat to Black's king, and also frees the g5-square for the queen from where she will threaten mate and more.

12...♕a6

The second possibility is 12...♕c7, whereupon Tal would definitely strike on f7: 13.♗f7 ♖f7 14.♘f7 ♔f7 15.♘g5 ♔g8 16.♖he1. Though we are taught from we are little that the two pieces are worth more than a rook and a pawn, and thus we usually do not strike in this way on the f7-square, Tal loved to prove things to the contrary. And he usually managed to prove it...

13.♘f5! ♗d8!

Both players are playing the best moves: White is already attacking wildly, while Black is defending himself accurately. After13...♗c5? Tal would let loose his imagination with 14.♕f4 bc4 15.♗c3 and Black would have no defence against many threats.

14.♕h4!

A classic intuitive sacrifice, the consequences of which were not possible to calculate during the game. The queen heads to g5.

14...bc4 15.♕g5

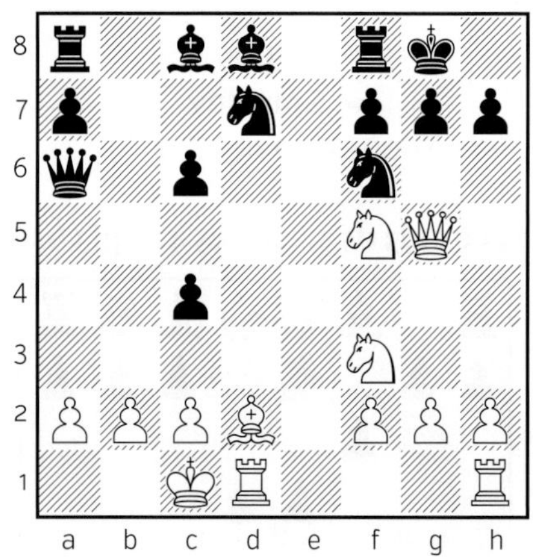

A famous position! Black has many possibilities for defence and the almighty computer, for example, proves that the game would end in a draw if the combatants had played the most accurate moves. But is this not true also after the first move 1.e2-e4?

15...♘h5!

One of Black's best possibilities.

16.♘h6 ♔h8 17.♕h5 ♕a2!

Even though the commentators half a century ago thought that this move was a decisive mistake, computer nowadays tell us that this is not true. After 17...♗f6 18.♘f7 White would have a strong attack, even though Tal intended to respond with the weaker: 18.♗c3? ♗c3 19.♘g5 ♗b2! 20.♔b2 ♕b5 21.♔c1 gh6 22.♕h6 ♕f5 and the critical h7-square is defended!

18.♗c3 ♘f6?

This really is a decisive mistake though — after 18...♗f6 or 18...♗c7 Black could probably defend himself. The first and the only mistake of Smyslov's in the game and — the immediate end!

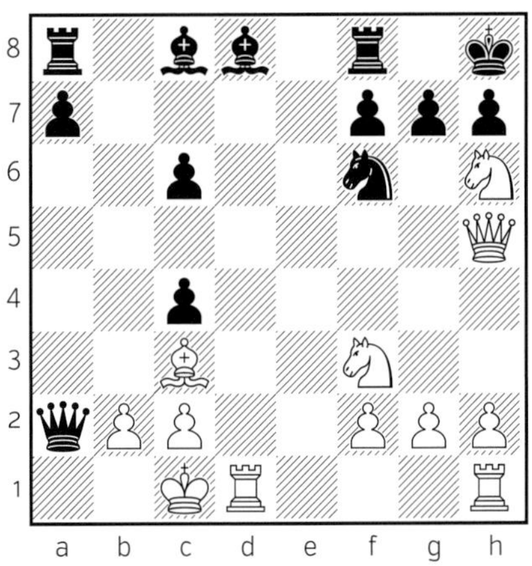

19.♕f7!

A lightning bolt from a clear sky!

19...♕a1

Or a smothered mate after 19...♖f7 20.♖d8 ♘g8 21.♘f7 or 19...♖e8 20.♕g8! and 21.♘f7 mate!

20.♔d2 ♖f7 21.♘f7 ♔g8 22.♖a1 ♔f7 23.♘e5 ♔e6 24.♘c6 ♘e4 25.♔e3 ♗b6 26.♗d4 1:0

THE DEFENCE OF THE OPEN CENTER

The placing of the pieces into an open center does not mean a decisive advantage, or even any advantage at all. It is very important to defend those pieces properly or to be prepared for the exchanges on which the opponent will rely heavily. What can a defender do? He cannot put up with the pressure from the centralized pieces and he needs to do everything within his power to remove them.

Because of this he basis of the defensive strategy is quite simple: manoeuvring with the goal of ridding himself of the opponent's centralized pieces.

1

▷ **Alekhine**
▶ **Euwe**
Netherlands 1935 (D17)

1.d4 d5 2.c4 c6 3.♘f3 ♘f6 4.♘c3 dc4 5.a4 ♗f5 6.♘e5 ♘bd7 7.♘c4 ♕c7 8.g3 e5 9.de5 ♘e5 10.♗f4 ♘fd7 11.♗g2 ♗e6

A very 'modern' variation in those days and especially during the two matches between the fourth and the fifth World Champions. Black has many moves to choose from now: 11...f6; 11...♖d8 and — nowadays the most popular — the wild 11...g5.

12.♘e5 ♘e5 13.0–0 ♗e7

Not the best move; theory recommends 13...f6.

14.♕c2!

White is already threatening 15.♘b5-d4 or 15.♘d5, a consequence of Black's careless play: two pieces are undefended — the queen on c7 and, indirectly, the centralized knight on e5 also.

14...♖d8 15.♖fd1 0–0 16.♘b5

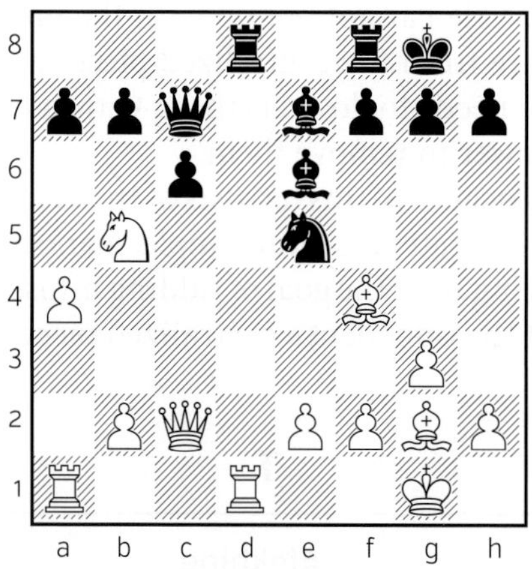

16...♖d1?

To figure out that this is a mistake it is not necessary to be a strong chess player. We do not give up the open lines without a fight, unless we are absolutely forced to by the opponent. With this exchange Black was preparing the move ...♕a5, which was not possible immediately: 16...♕a5 17.♖d8 ♖d8 18.♗e5 cb5 19.♗b7 ♖d2 20.♕c6±; but the idea is completely wrong. It would be correct to play 16...♕b8, strengthening the knight in the center.

17.♖d1 ♕a5 18.♘d4 ♗c8

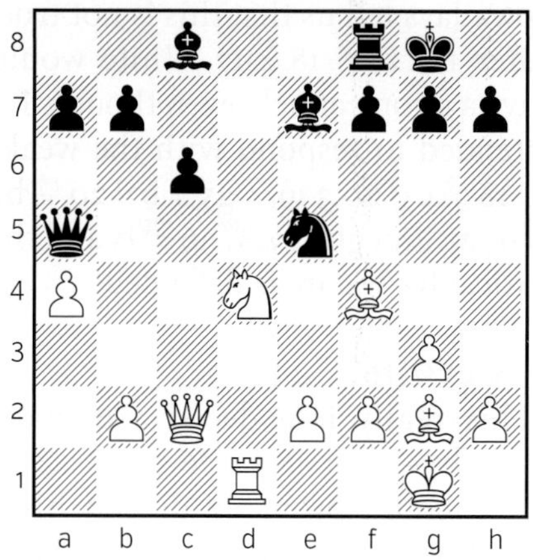

19.b4!

A marvellous wing stroke, which represents the end of White's play in the center. Black is fearful of the unstable placement of the knight on e5 and he cannot take the pawn: 19...♗b4 20.♘b3 ♕c7 21.♕e4 ♗c3 22.♖c1 ♗b2 23.♖c2 f5 24.♕b4+- and a piece is lost.

20.b5 c5 21.♘f5

The unfortunate knight on e5 is still calling for help, but by the next move, when Black strengthened its defence with the move ...f7-f6, it is already too late.

21...f6 22.♘e3 ♗e6

White plays the final part of the game flawlessly. The biggest hole in Black's camp is situated on the d5-square and that is why we need to remove its only defender first:

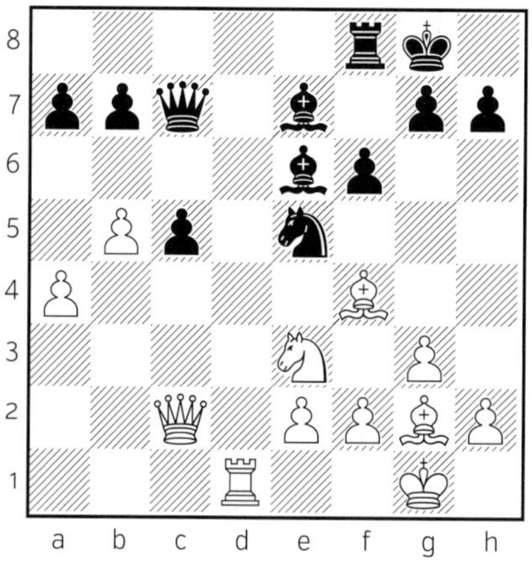

23.♗d5! ♗d5 24.♖d5 ♕a5

24...♖d8 25.♗e5 fe5 26.♕f5+- (Alekhine).

25.♘f5 ♕e1 26.♔g2 ♗d8 27.♗e5 fe5 28.♖d7!→ ♗f6 29.♘h6! ♔h8 30.♕c5 1:0

An instructive game which demonstrates the introductory words. Black's pieces in the center were unstable, not well-enough defended and White built his strategy upon this fact.

THE PLANNED OPENING OF THE PLAY

An example of the planned opening of the center was already seen in the game Tal–Smyslov (5.d4!). It was thought for a very long time that the quick opening of the center represented a draw offer. But this opinion is wrong: the player that masters this strategic element can confront the opponent with many troubles.

Usually the player decides to open the center when he notices that a free central square will be good for one of his pieces. Especially painful for the opponent is if we can place the queen there and the opponent is unable to get rid of it.

The World Champion Tigran Petrosian loved to show the following game on this theme to his students.

1

▹ **Suetin**
▸ **Petrosian**
USSR 1950 [C84]

1.e4 e5 2.♘f3 ♘c6 3.♗b5 a6 4.♗a4 ♘f6 5.0–0 ♗e7 6.d4 ed4 7.♖e1 0–0 8.e5 ♘d5

The theory of this variation was only then starting to develop- nowadays we know that the correct move is 8...♘e8. The knight on d5 offers White too many tempos for development.

9.♘d4 ♘d4 10.♕d4 ♘b6 11.♗b3 d5 12.ed6 ♕d6

A little bit better is 12...♗d6, though White is again better after 13.♗f4 ♕h4 14.g3 ♕g4 15.h3!

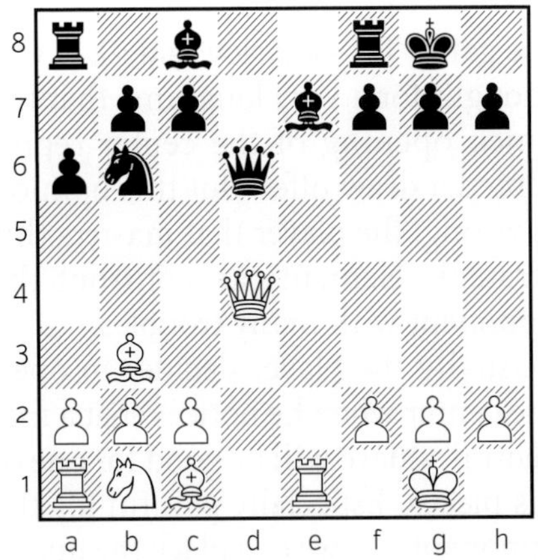

13.♕e4!

This is the kind of centralization that we are talking about. The queen on e4 controls practically all of the board and Black has no suitable piece with which to rid himself of it.

13...♗f6 14.♘c3 ♖b8 15.♗f4 ♕c5

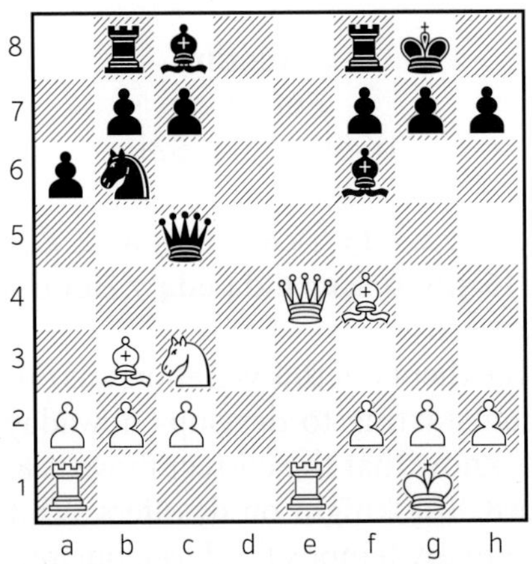

The next instructive moment! With his experienced manoeuvring White has forced Black to develop his pieces to bad squares and now he decides to exchange his pride and joy — the queen on e4! Why? Well, in particular because Black's strongholds were being defended only by his queen — after the exchange of the strongest pieces, Black's weaknesses will be seen only too clearly.

16.♕e3! ♕c6

A convincing variation is 16...♕e3 17.♖e3 ♗d8 18.♖d1 ♗d7 19.h3 and there is no defence against ♖ed3.

17.♕g3 ♗e6

Black sacrifices his pawn, heralding the beginning of the end. After 17...♗d8 18.♗e5 g6 19.♖ad1 ♗d7 20.♕f4 White would have a very strong attack.

18.♗c7 ♖bc8 19.♗e5 ♗b3 20.ab3 ♘d7 21.♗f6 ♘f6 22.♖ad1

And White easily realized his advantage.

22...♖fe8 23.h3 h6 24.♖e3 ♖e3 25.♕e3 ♕c7 26.♕g3 ♕g3 27.fg3 ♔f8 28.♔f2 ♔e7 29.♔e3 ♔e6 30.♖d4 ♘e8 31.♔d3 ♘d6 32.♘e2 g5 33.g4 f5 34.gf5 ♘f5 35.♖e4 ♔f6 36.♘d4 ♘d4 37.♖d4 ♖c7 38.♖d6 ♔f5 39.♖h6 ♔f4 40.c4 ♖d7 41.♔c3 ♖g7 42.g4 ♖e7 43.c5 ♔g3 44.b4 ♖e3 45.♔c4 ♖e4 46.♔b3 ♖e3 47.♔a4 ♖e2 48.♖h5 ♖b2 49.♖g5 ♔h3 50.♖g7 ♔h4 51.♖b7 ♔g4 52.♖f7 ♖a2 53.♔b3 ♖a1 54.♔c4 ♖c1 55.♔d5 ♖d1 56.♔c6 ♖b1 57.♔b6 ♖b4 58.♔a6 ♔g5 59.c6 ♔g6 60.♖f1 1:0.

Especially dangerous is a premature and unprepared opening of the center in the opening. Praxis shows that Black players often open the center prematurely and without preparation; they want to equalize and to take over the initiative. Let's have a look at two examples on this theme.

2

▷ **Boleslavsky**
► **Gurgenidze**
Rostov na Donu 1960 [B32]

1.e4 c5 2.♘f3 ♘c6 3.d4 d5?

A senseless experiment that will be abruptly refuted by White. Black will lag behind in his development and the opening of the center is in favour of the player that has the advantage in development, so...

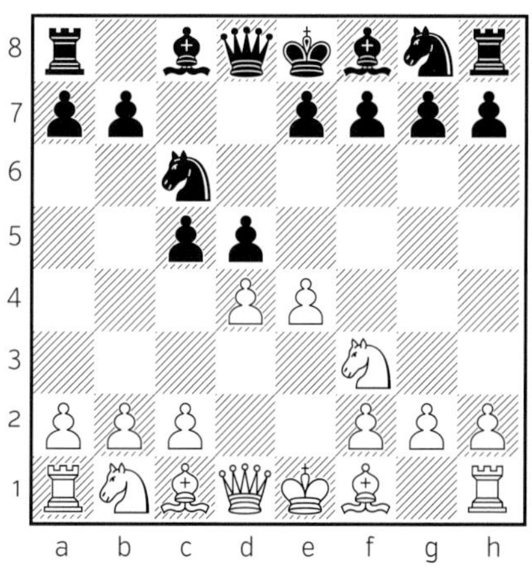

4.ed5 ♕d5 5.♘c3 ♕e6 6.♗e3 cd4 7.♘d4 ♕d7 8.♘db5! ♖b8 9.♕e2! f6 10.♖d1 ♕g4 11.f3 ♕h5 12.♗a7 ♘a7 13.♘d6 1:0.

3

▷ **Alekhine**
► **Eliskases**
Podebrady 1936 [C90]

1.e4 e5 2.♘f3 ♘c6 3.♗b5 a6 4.♗a4 ♘f6 5.0–0 ♗e7 6.♖e1 b5 7.♗b3 d6 8.c3 ♘a5 9.♗c2 c5 10.d3 ♘c6 11.♘bd2 0–0 12.♘f1 ♖e8 13.♘e3 d5 14.ed5 ♘d5 15.♘d5 ♕d5

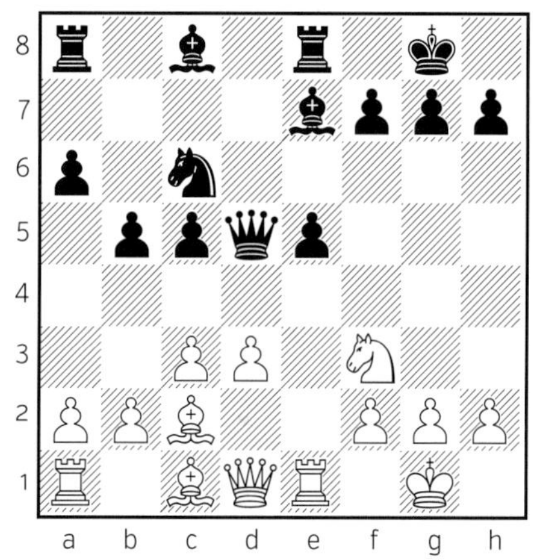

16.d4 ed4 17.♗e4 ♕d7 18.cd4 ♗f6 19.♗g5 ♖e4 20.♖e4 ♗d4 21.♘d4 ♘d4 22.♕h5 ♗b7 23.♖h4 ♕f5 24.♗e3 ♖d8 25.♖d4 1:0

THE CLOSED (BLOCKED) CENTER

We can talk about the closed or the blocked center when the central pawns of both players are blocked or when they are facing each other directly and are standing on squares of the opposite colors. Let us once more take a look at two characteristic pawn placements:

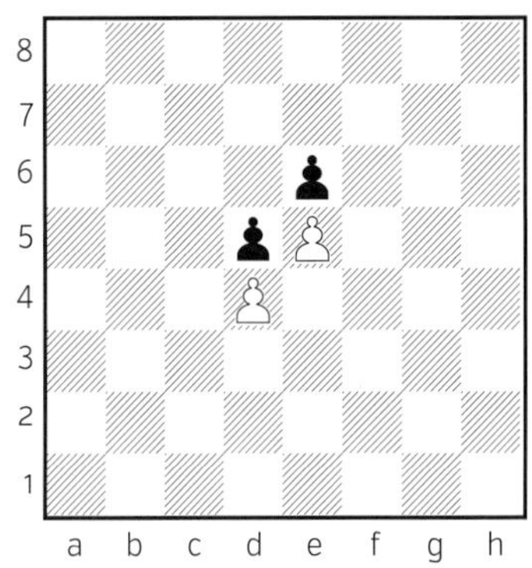

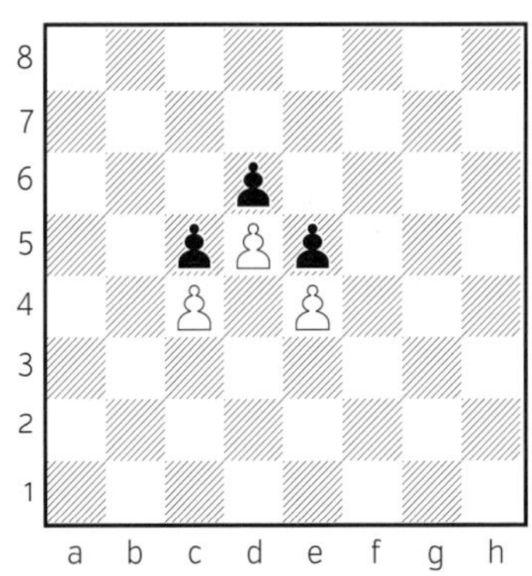

A fixed center makes our job easier when we are choosing our plans. When we use them in practice we aid ourselves with these known playing and strategic methods.

Simple logic, which can also be turned into a rule: where there is a closed center, the play must be moved to the wing. Usually one of the players attacks on the kingside and the other on the queenside. The position of the kings is very important: the attack on the king is usually more dangerous than the attack on the other wing. The price that we have to pay for a mistake is even higher there and we can often afford a sacrifice in order for the attack to be successful.

When there is a blocked center, a pawn wedge can occur. In the first diagram, White has a pawn wedge (pawns that are placed diagonally and that are linked) from the b2-square to the e5-square. If Black decides to exchange on d4 then the wedge becomes shorter (constructed from the d4 and e5 pawns). Black's wedge spreads out from the f7-square to the d5-square. If he would, instead of exchanging on d4, advance with ...c5-c4, then the wedge would become longer (from the f7-square to the c4-square).

Sometimes Black makes it even longer with the placement of his b-pawn on the b3-square. In the second case, White usually has a distinctive pawn wedge from g2 to d5 and Black from c7 to f4.

Aron Nimzowitsch spent a lot time on studying the wedge theory and he made a very important discovery: when we attack the opponent's wedge with the pawns, we always attack the last defended pawn!

In White's wedge from g2 to d5 the 'last defended pawn' is the pawn on f3 (he is defended by the g2-pawn). So Black's plan is simple: the advance of the g-pawn to the g4-square, which provokes White's reaction. He can let Black take on f3, which will leave the f3-pawn without pawn defence (if White takes g2xf3) or White's g-pawn would become weak and isolated (if White takes on g4). Something similar happens when White is playing against Black's wedge c7-d6. The pawn on d6 needs to be attacked and White can achieve that with the c4-c5 move. A similar rule can on principle be used in all attacks against pawn wedges.

When we attack the wedge with the pieces then we of course attack the last pawn in the wedge, but it is very hard to get to it without a contribution from our own pawns. That is why we often help ourselves with opening of adjacent files and so try to come around the wedge, especially when we try to attack with the rooks.

The defence is also connected with the logic or the actions that are trying to restrict the opponent's defensive techniques. When we know what the most suitable defensive plan is, we place our pieces so that they make the attacker's work very hard to accomplish. When we cannot prevent the plan from happening, we try to predict the consequences and then we set up the next defence.

When we use activity on the wings, we must keep the center blocked. Every change in the center's statics can be fatal.

1

▹ **Shishov**
▸ **Byvshev**
Riga 1954

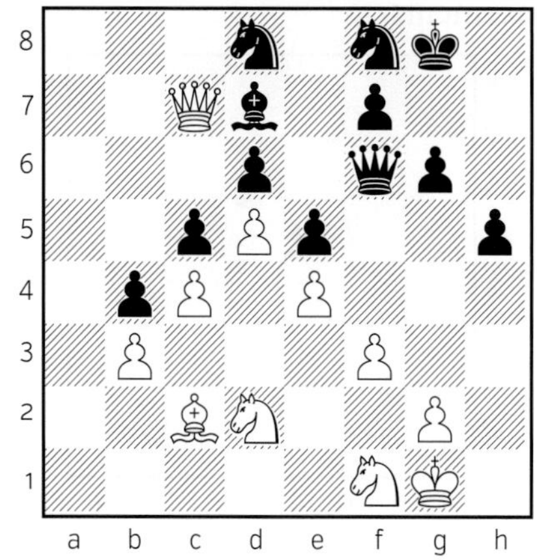

White's queen has managed to enter into the opponent's territory, but she will not be able to handle everything by herself. Black is a pawn up, has successfully blocked the queenside and- seemingly- also the center. If Black's pawn were on f4 then Black would surely win the game, because he would only need to correct the coordination of the pieces and then advance the pawns on the wing where he has the material advantage (here, the kingside). But as it stands, White saw a chance to break Black's center:

1.f4!

Suddenly Black is in trouble. White is threatening to take on e5 and the clumsy placement of the knight on d8 paralyzes Black's queen. It is only left to take with the pawn:

1...ef4 2.e5! de5 3.♘e4

The knight is now wide awake and the battle is immediately decided. Black's central pawns, which were only seconds ago still blocking the center, will fall.

3...♕h4 4.♕e5 ♘h7 5.♘c5 f3 6.♕g3 ♕d4 7.♕f2 ♕f2 8.♔f2

And White won quickly — **1:0.**

Similarly fatal can be an attack be on the 'wrong' side — the side where the player does not stand better. It is very important that we study similar positions: without understanding where the best place to attack is, it is pointless to learn the correct methods of attacking!

2

▷ **Opocensky**
▶ **Nimzowitsch**
Marienbad 1925 [E32]

1.d4 ♘f6 2.c4 e6 3.♘c3 ♗b4 4.♕c2 b6 5.e4 ♗b7 6.♗d3 ♘c6 7.♘f3 ♗e7 8.a3 d6 9.0–0 e5 10.d5 ♘b8 11.b4 ♘bd7

The diagram shows a classic position with a closed center.

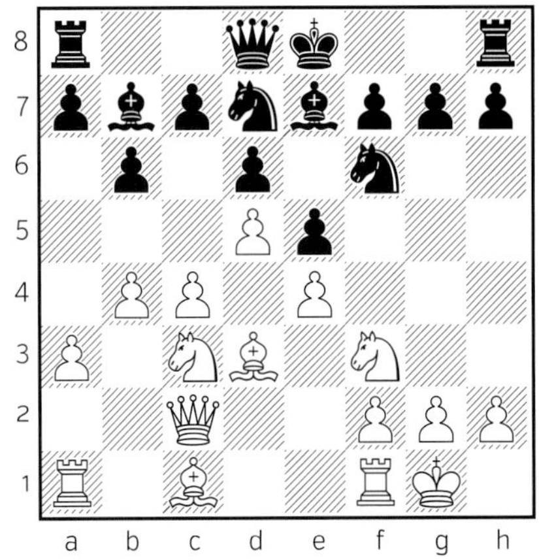

White's plan is not too hard to discern: Black is blocking the center with a pawn wedge from c7 to e5 and we already know that we need to attack this kind of wedge with the pawns and — more precisely — we need to attack the penultimate pawn. In our case that is the pawn on d6, which can be attacked with the c4-c5 move! Black will in the meantime prepare the ...f7-f5 move.

White's plan is clear: due to the c5-square being strongly defended, White first needs to prepare the move with his pieces. For example h3 (a defence against ...♘g4), ♗e3, ♘a4 etc. The Czech Grandmaster obviously did not understand the position and so he decided to attack on the other wing. On the wing where he has no advantage.

12.♗b2? 0–0 13.♘e2

Evaluating the following moves would be pointless, because White is following the chosen plan. The place for the pieces was on the queenside.

13...♘e8 14.♕d2 g6 15.g4 ♘g7 16.♘g3 c6!

Black first strengthened the kingside and now he is already active in the center: the rule teaches that the correct response to an action on the flank is to attack in the center. Of course, if that is possible.

17.♕h6 ♖c8 18.♖ac1 a6

Black waits with opening of the center, because he sees that White is weakening himself by preparing action on the kingside.

19.♖fd1 ♖c7 20.h4? cd5 21.cd5

After 21.ed5 Black would strike even further — 21...b5!

21...♖c1 22.♖c1 ♘f6 23.♘h2 ♔h8 24.♕e3 ♘d7 25.♘f3 ♘f6 26.♘h2 ♘g8 27.g5 f6

Black is already in counterattack mode and the game will be decided on the kingside, where White has placed all his hopes.

28.♘f3 fg5 29.hg5 ♗c8 30.♖c6 ♗d7 31.♗a6

Of course not 31.♖b6? ♖f3.

31...♗c6 32.dc6 ♕c7 33.b5 h6!

With this pawn sacrifice Black makes some room for the possible withdrawal of the king.

34.gh6 ♘e6 35.a4 ♗d8 36.♗a3 ♕f7 37.♘e5 de5 38.♗f8 ♕f8 39.a5 ♘h6 40.ab6 ♘g4 41.b7 ♘e3 42.b8♕ ♕f3 43.fe3 ♕g3 44.♔h1 ♕e3 45.♗c8 ♗c7 46.♕b7 ♘f4 47.♗h3 ♕h3 48.♔g1 ♕g2 0:1

White played the opening well, but then he completely missed the correct plan. His action on the kingside only weakened his position and Black exploited that instructively; firstly with action in the center and after that with the final attack on the kingside.

ATTACK THE BLOCKED CENTER WITH PAWNS

We have already said that we should attack the opponent's pawn wedge with pawns: we must try to break it, or loosen it, or we can try to weaken the last link of the chain — and in order to do that we aim our attack at the penultimate pawn. In the next legendary game we will see how the protagonists did not know all of these rules yet and therefore did not make completely accurate choices.

1

▷ **Chigorin**
▸ **Tarrasch**
St. Petersburg 1893 [C00]

1.e4 e6 2.♕e2 c5 3.g3 ♘c6 4.♘f3 ♗e7 5.♗g2 d5 6.d3 ♘f6 7.0–0 0–0 8.♘c3

We will come across these positions many times, where White develops his knight on the d2-square then blocks the center (with e4-e5) and later on he develops according to the system ♖e1, ♘f1, h4, ♗f4, ♘1h2, ♘g4 etc. and tries to attack Black's king. Meanwhile Black searches for an opportunity on the queenside, where no pieces are placed and so Black's pawns can progress without trouble. With the played move the father of the Russian chess school provoked Black into playing ...d5-d4.

8...a6 9.♗g5 h6

In positions in which we know that our opponent will attack us, we should rather not move the pawns in front of our king. A pawn movement in front of the castled position can result in weaknesses, which affords the attackers extra chances.

10.♗f4 b5 11.♖fe1

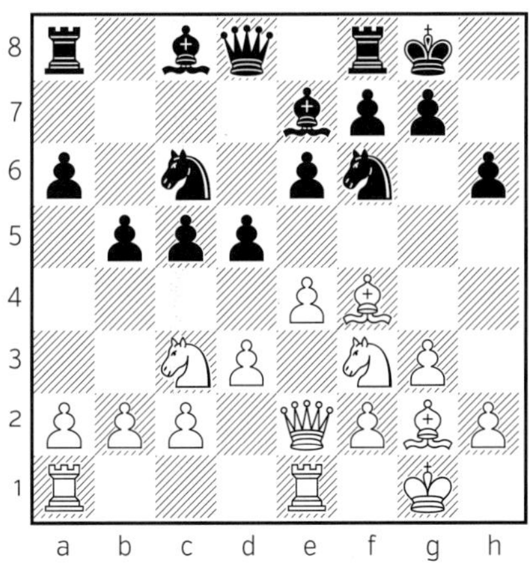

11...d4?

White wanted this to happen: the stable center will leave him with a free hand to attack on the kingside. Correct would be to maintain the tension with the move 11...♗b7.

12.♘d1 ♘d7 13.♔h1 ♖e8 14.♖g1 e5 15.♗d2 ♘f8 16.♘e1 ♘e6 17.f4 ♗b7 18.f5 ♘g5 19.♘f2 ♖c8

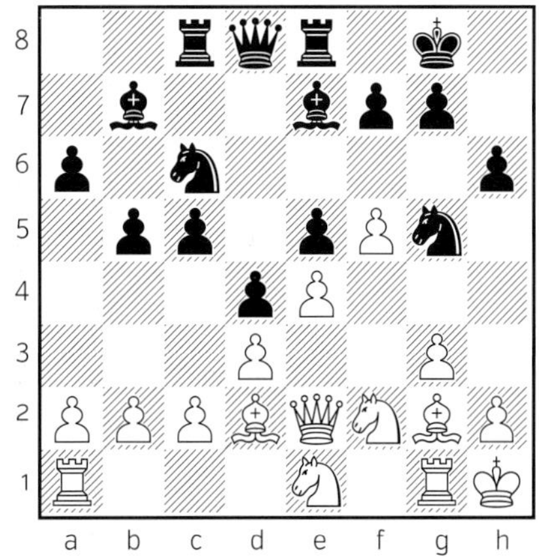

20.♕h5?

The beginning of the wrong plan. We already know that, when there is a blocked center, we attack with the pawns first and only afterwards with the pieces. Now the correct plan would be h4, and later ♘f3 and g3-g4-g5.

20...♘h7 21.♘f3 c4!

Black gets it: with the attack on the penultimate link of the wedge he will gain the best counterplay.

22.♗f1 cd3 23.cd3 ♘g5!

It is time for the blockade on the kingside — he is already dominant on the queenside. White's queen on h5 is causing himself problems because it blocks its own pieces.

24.♗g5 ♗g5 25.♘g4 ♔f8!

A preventative move which exploits the position of White's queen on h5.

White was threatening 26.h4 ♗f6 27.♘f6 ♕f6 28.g4 in 29.g5. After the move played the threat is gone: 26.h4 ♗f6 27.♘f6 ♕f6 28.g4 ♔e7! 29.g5 hg5 30.hg5 ♕d6 and Black controls the h-file with decisive threats.

26.♗e2 ♗f6!

Black starts to set up the defensive placement ♗f6, ♕d6, ♘e7-g8.

27.h4 ♕d6 28.♘fh2 ♘e7!

Black defends slyly: now White can't play 29.♘f6 ♕f6 30.♘g4 ♕f5!

29.♖af1 ♘g8 30.♗d1 ♖c7!

Black is passing over to the counter-attack.

31.♗b3 ♖ec8 32.♘f2 ♗d8 33.♕e2

The threat was 33...♘f6 so White had no choice but to admit that his choice of plan was wrong.

33...a5 34.♘f3 a4 35.♗d1 ♗c6!

This move hides the plan ...♗e8-f7-b3, with the exchange of the light-squared bishops. White's bishop prevents Black's rooks from entering the game and that is why Black wants to exchange it, even though his is 'officially' better. White can defend against Black's plans with the aid of an attack on the kingside, which has been in the making for at least 15 moves...

36.g4 f6 37.♘h3 ♗e8 38.♕h2 ♗f7 39.a3 ♗b3 40.♘f2 ♗d1 41.♘d1 ♖c2

Black has achieved all his little strategic goals and he will take over the decisive initiative on the queenside.

42.♕g3 b4 43.ab4 ♕a6 44.♘f2 ♖b2 45.g5 hg5 46.hg5 ♖cc2 47.♘g4 ♕d6

There is no obvious way that White can strengthen his attack and meanwhile Black has some serious threats on the second rank and also a passed a-pawn.

48.gf6 ♗f6 49.♕h3 a3 50.♘f6

Or 50.♕h8 (with a threat 51.♘h6) 50...g5!-+.

50...♕f6 51.♖g6

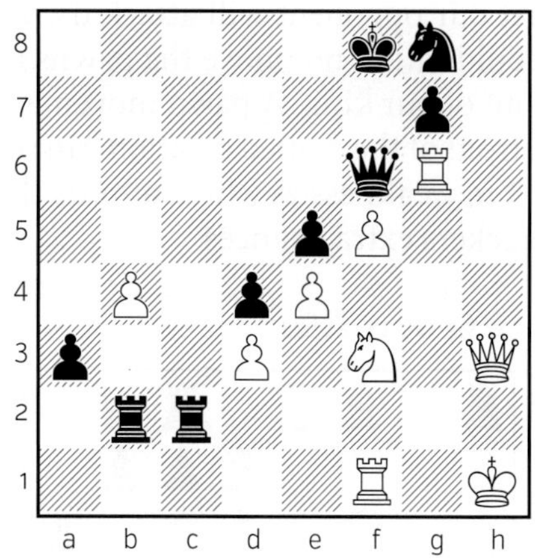

51...a2!

An elegant end to the game with a queen sacrifice.

52.♖f6 gf6 53.♖d1 ♖b1 54.♕f1 ♖cb2 55.♘d2 ♖d1 56.♕d1 ♖d2 57.♕c1 ♖d3 58.♔g2 ♖c3 59.♕a1 ♖c2 60.♔f3 d3 61.♕d1 ♖b2 62.♕a4 d2 0:1

We have seen how dangerous an incautious closing of the center can be: White could have gained an almost decisive advantage on move 20. But instead of the pawn advance he decided on an attack with the pieces, which was doomed from the start.

QUESTIONS ABOUT THE KING'S INDIAN DEFENCE

The attack with the pawns cannot be decisive by itself. The pawns do all that they can with their actions: they loosen the seemingly bulletproof pawn wedges, weaken the squares in their hinterland or around them and in doing so make room for their own pieces, so that they can finish the action off.

Positions from the classical Kings' Indian Defence are the most typical for questions about the closed center, and especially for the chapter about clearing the way for the pieces. Let's see in a little more detail the placement of the pawns in the Mar del Plata variation:

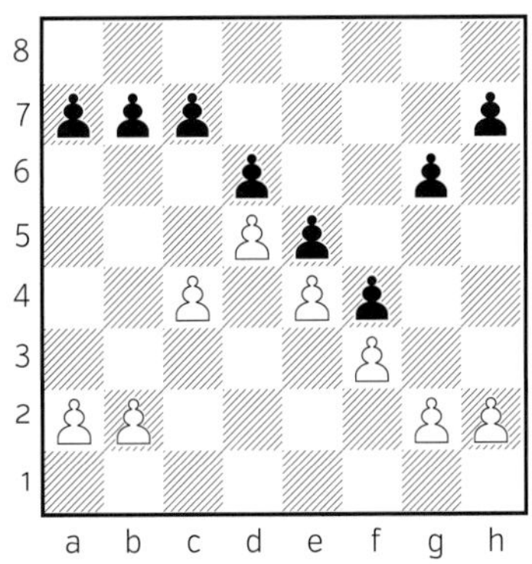

We can see that the position in the center is defined by the two pawn wedges: White's with the pawns from g2 to d5, and Black's with the pawns from c7 to f4. It is clear that it is very hard to get into the opponent's camp with the pieces without help from the pawns. Where should White attack in perspective? We already know that the correct plan is connected with the c4-c5 move.

After c5 Black will be faced with a question: he can swap on c5 and allow the c-file to open — from where White will attack the c7-pawn. He can also not react and instead allow White to make the choice. White usually takes on d6 and Black again needs to pick.

Taking with a piece leads to the previously described variations, with the backward c7-pawn and taking with the pawn leaves the d6-pawn without defence (the defender on c7 is gone) and at the same time White has opened the c-file where he will be able to prepare the penetration of the weak c7-pawn.

And Black? All his hopes are linked with the advance ...g6-g5-g4. If he achieves that, White will be facing similar questions as Black does after the c4-c5 move. White's job is a little more difficult due to his king being hidden behind the wedge — and of course he cannot allow the play to become open.

Does Black have the advantage? No, not even close. The placement of the wedges in the center offers White a space advantage and with it the possibility for him to complete his actions easily. Black must be patient: if he survives the first wave of attack and in the meantime prepares his own action, only then does he have a chance to take over the initiative.

1

▷ **Lilienthal**
▶ **Kan**
Moscow 1935 [E94]

1.d4 ♘f6 2.c4 d6 3.♘c3 ♘bd7 4.e4 e5 5.♘f3 g6 6.♗e2 ♗g7 7.0–0 0–0 8.d5

The 8.d5 move defines the following play because now two pawn wedges are formed. The playing plans are clear from the beginning: White will try to prepare the c4-c5 move, while Black firstly shoves ...f7-f5 and (after the possible f2-f3 move) usually the ...f5-f4 move and a further ...g6-g5-g4 with the attack on the f3-pawn.

8...♘c5 9.♕c2 a5 10.♗e3?!

This game is already old — but the players were facing this delicate position for the first time. Nowadays White would not allow Black the ...♘g4 move and the prevention is linked with certain digressions. Prevention with h2-h3 is not good, because the h3-pawn would become an ideal target for Black and his upcoming actions (the advance of the g-pawn). That is why White players usually move the knight from the f3-square and there are two realistic possibilities.

Whether to move to the e1-square (from where it wants to get to the d3-square and support the c5 stroke) or more optimistically to the d2-square from where it wants to go to the c4-square after c4-c5 has been played? More optimistic because in the second variation White believes that he will be able to play the c4-c5 move without the help of the knight.

The question of the knight's withdrawal square is one of the most important ones in the King's Indian Defence and depends on many other factors. It is similar on the other side, where Black needs to move his knight from f6 in order to play the ...f7-f5 move. Does he move it to the e8-square and defend the potentially weak c7-square? Or to the d7-square, where he is blocking the way of his light-squared bishop, but is also making it harder for White to play the c4-c5 stroke? Or perhaps aggressively to the h5-square from where it wants to get to the f4-square? There are no direct answers — everything depend on concrete factors at certain moments.

That is why it is so important to study these kinds of positions, and it is also useful as everyone will someday find themselves in similar structures. Attention: this structure can also be formed out of other openings, not only from the King's Indian Defence!

10...b6 11.♘d2 ♘e8 12.a3 f5 13.f3 f4 14.♗f2 ♘a6

With this move Black makes it more difficult for White to play the b2-b4 move, for which everything was prepared. Of course he cannot prevent it completely.

15.♖ab1

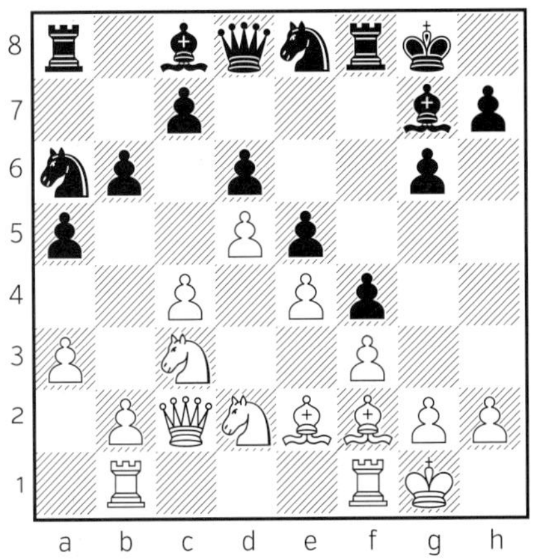

15...♕g5?

We already know that we must attack the pawn wedge with the pawns — here that means the g5-pawn and the h5 pawn. It is very hard to break through the defences with only the pieces.

16.♖fc1 h5 17.♔h1?!

If White was not scared after the previous move then this withdrawal is even harder to understand. Why not immediately 17.b4!

17...♕h6

Black understands that he can only get his counterplay with the advance of the g-pawn.

18.b4 ab4 19.ab4 g5 20.♘a4 ♗d7 21.c5

White gets his thrust in first and he will soon seriously weaken Black's position on the queenside. Can Black prepare something more serious on the other side of the board?

21...♘c5 22.♘c5 bc5 23.bc5 g4

We need to ask ourselves what each player is threatening? White has more plans: he definitely wants to get rid of Black's light-squared bishop, which defend some critical points, especially the one on c6. Black will also have a hard time attacking without the light-squared bishop — even now we cannot see any concrete threats. After 23...g4 he is threatening to open the g-file and to weaken the f3-pawn, but... he cannot really attack the f3-pawn and the opening of the g-file might just be more useful for White...

24.cd6 cd6 25.♘c4 gf3 26.gf3 ♗h3 27.♗f1 ♗f1

Black can't prevent the exchange because there would follow, after the withdrawal of the bishop to d7 or c8, 28.♘b6.

28.♖f1 h4 29.♖g1

Black plays heedlessly and White is now better on both wings, which is rare. Next follows the final part of the game and White will spice it up with a nice sacrifice.

29...♕h5 30.♘d2 ♔h8 31.♖g4 ♗f6 32.♖bg1 ♖d8 33.♕c6 ♕h7 34.♘c4 ♕e7

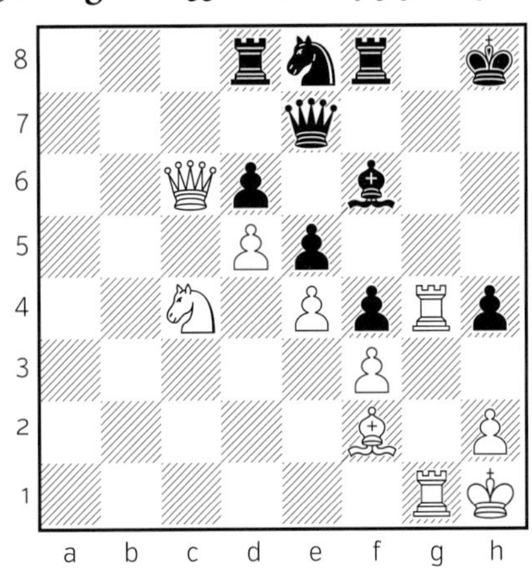

35.♗h4! ♖f7

After 35...♗h4 36.♘e5!

36.♖g8 ♔h7 37.♗f6 ♖f6 38.♕a4 ♖h6 39.♕a2 ♖c8 40.♕g2 1:0.

2

▷ **Illescas Cordoba**
▶ **Short**
Dos Hermanas 1997 [C66]

1.e4 e5 2.♘f3 ♘c6 3.♗b5 ♘f6 4.0–0 ♗e7 5.♖e1 d6 6.c3 0–0 7.d4 ♗d7 8.d5

The introduction into our positions with a blocked center.

8...♘b8 9.♗d7

The second possibility is 9.♗d3, keeping the light-squared bishops on the board. White clearly followed the basic rules about the evaluation of the bishops.

9...♘bd7 10.c4

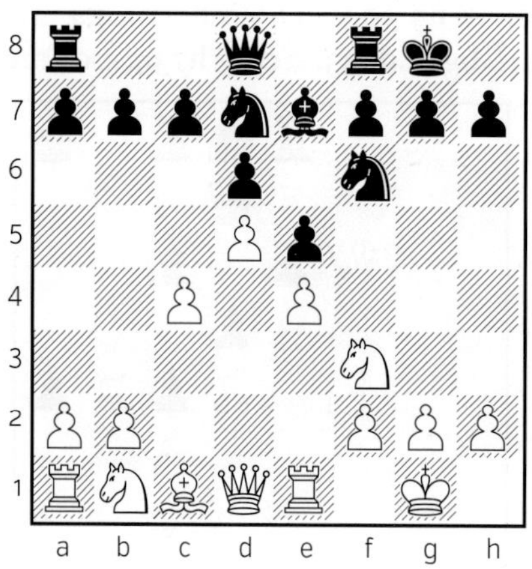

10...♘e8!?

Black was clear from the start: he wants to strike on the kingside. There is no need for moves like ...♘c5 or ...a5 in this position (with the ...a5-move Black strengthens the c5-square for his knight) because there is no bishop on c8, which needs to be unblocked.

11.♘c3 g6 12.♖b1?!

A strange, slow plan — what will the rook do on the b-file? For the preparation of the b2-b4 move better would be 12.♗h6 (or 12.b4 a5 13.♗h6 ♘g7 14.a3) 12...♘g7 13.♕d2 and further on b2-b4.

12...f5

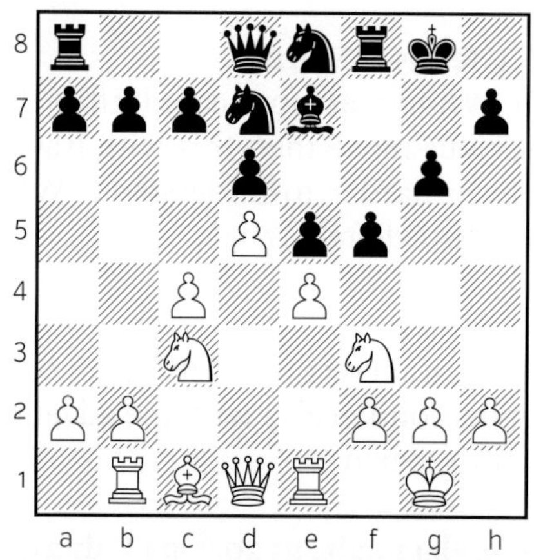

A position that needs to be studied carefully! It can be very dangerous to underestimate Black's actions, therefore White should take on f5. For example 13.ef5 gf5 (13...♖f5 14.♘e4) 14.♗h6 ♖f6! 15.♗g5 ♖g6 16.♗e7 ♕e7 17.g3, with unclear but approximately-equal play; there are chances for both sides. Worse is 13.♗h6!? ♖f7 14.b4?! f4! with play against the bishop on h6.

13.b4?! f4!

Black now has many nice possibilities for attacking on the kingside.

14.a4♖f7

Black could gain a tempo with the plan ...♔h8, ...♖g8, ...g5-g4 and ...♖g6. White's threats will not be serious for a long time so there is no need to place the rook on the second rank.

15.♗a3 g5 16.♘d2

16.h3 would weaken White's position even more: 16...h5 17.♘h2 ♘ef6 18.f3 ♖g7, with the movement of the queen to h6 and the placement of the other rook on g8.

16...♘ef6 17.f3♖g7 18.♔h1 g4 19.♕e2

Also after 19.fg4 ♘g4 20.♖e2 ♕e8 Black's attack would be strong.

19...♔h8 20.♖ec1

A pawn sacrifice after 20.c5?! would only be an exaggeration: 20...dc5 21.bc5 (21.♘c4 cb4 22.♗b4 ♗b4 23.♖b4 b6) 21...♗c5 22.♗c5 ♘c5 23.♘b3 ♕e7.

20...♖g6!

A very useful move — Black wants to place the heavy pieces on the g-file and the bishop on h6.

21.c5

White loses his nerve, even though he is already falling behind with his plan and there was nothing else left to do for him apart from this suicidal action. The slow attack 21.♘b3 ♕f8! 22.♘b5 (22.c5 ♕h6) 22...♕h6 23.♘c7 ♖ag8 24.♖c2 gf3 25.♕f3 (25.gf3 ♘h5–+) 25...♖g3 26.♕f1 ♘g4 27.♕g1 ♘e3–+ was sentenced to fail and the only serious alternative is 21.♘d1!? (Ftacnik) 21...♕g8 22.c5.

21...dc5! 22.bc5 ♗c5 23.♗c5 ♘c5 24.♘b5 b6

Black has taken the pawn and there is no visible substitute for White.

25.a5

After 25.♘b3 there would simply follow 25...gf3 26.gf3 ♘fd7!

25...♕e7 26.♘b3 gf3 27.gf3 ♘b3 28.♖b3

28.♖c7 ♘d4 –+.

28...♖ag8 29.♕f2

29.♘c7?? ♕c7 30.♖c7 ♖g1; 29.♖bb1 ♕g7 30.♘c7 ♖g2 31.♘e6 ♕g6 32.♘f8 ♖e2 33.♘g6 ♖g6–+.

29...♕g7 30.♖bb1

30.♘c7 ♖g2–+; 30.♖b2!? ♘d7 31.♘c7 ♘c5 32.♘e6 ♘e6 33.de6 ba5.

30...♖g2 31.♕h4

31.♕f1 ♖h2 32.♔h2 ♕g3.

31...♕g6

With the idea of ...♘e4.

32.♘c3

32.♘c7 ♘e4 33.♘e6 ♖h2! 34.♕h2 ♘f2 35.♕f2 ♕h5 36.♕h2 ♕f3.

32...b5! 33.♖e1 b4 34.♘e2 ♘e4 35.fe4 ♖g1! 0:1

THE ATTACK WITH BRUTE FORCE

With immovable centers and long pawn wedges we need to consider the possible sacrifices. The attacker usually sacrifices a piece for one or two pawns in the wedge and with it he frees his central pawns. Their advance without obstacles can often be the decisive factor. Many games were played in the past and even in the modern era that included such sacrifices — and their prevention.

Let us see how Tigran Petrosian, the ninth World Champion, handled the opponent's pawn wedge.

1

▷ **Petrosian**
▶ **Barcza**
Saltsjöbaden 1952 [C00]

1.e4 c5 2.♘f3 ♘c6 3.d3 e6 4.♘bd2

The development plan about which we discussed earlier, often referred to as the King's Indian Attack (KIA).

4...d5 5.g3 ♘f6 6.♗g2 ♗e7 7.0–0 0–0 8.♖e1 b6 9.e5 ♘e8

A pretty logical move is 9...♘d7, because the knight has many options from there: besides attacking, also defending with the withdrawal to f8 is possible.

10.♘f1 ♔h8 11.♗f4 f5 12.h4!

It is very important to learn how White will systematically build his wedge. First he prevents the possible counterplay with ...g7-g5 and then he prepares the c3 move and the d4 move.

12...♘c7 13.♘1d2 ♗b7

The move13...d4? would give White a chance to enter with his knight: ♘c4 ♘d5 15.♗g5! and Black can't go 15...b5? 16.♘d6 ♘e5, because of 17.♘e5 ♕d6 18.♗d5 and 19.♗e7+- (Petrosian)

14.c3 b5?

It was the last chance to play ...d5-d4.

15.♘b3! a5 16.♗g5

The c5-pawn is facing threats.

16...♘a6

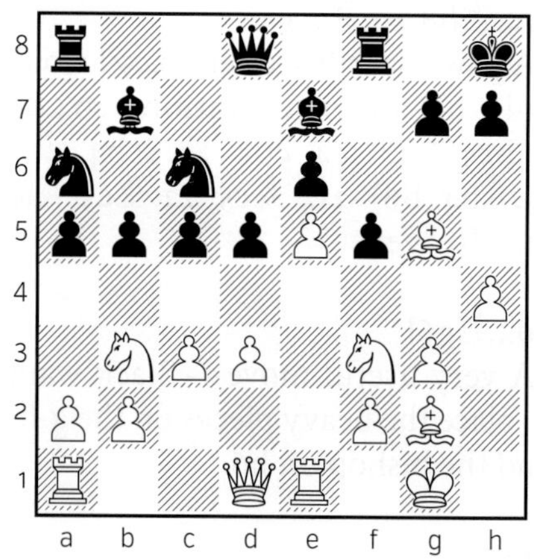

17.d4! c4

White is better because he will exchange the dark-squared bishops and his light-square bishop is more active than his opponent's (the strength of the bishops can easily be evaluated against the fixed pawns in the center: the one that is attacking the opponent's pawns is better and the one that is forced to defend its own pawns is weaker.

18.♘c1 ♘c7

It would be better to play 18...b4!? immediately, with the search for counterplay on the wing where Black holds the advantage.

19.♘e2 ♔g8 20.♘f4 ♕e8?

This move has no meaning. If Black had managed to foresee some moves, he would definitely move the rook from the long diagonal (20...♖b8) and so prevent White's tactical idea.

21.♗e7 ♕e7 22.♘g5 g6

The unpleasant 23.♕h5 was threatened.

23.a4! ♗a6?

After this move Black is immediately lost. White undermines Black's pawn wedge and he is already ready to make some sacrifices in the center (With the move 23.a4 he loosened the c4-pawn's defence). The only possibility was 23...b4, where White will choose from two different attractive continuations:

1) 24.♘fe6 ♘e6 25.♗d5 ♘cd8 26.♗c4 ♔g7 (26...♔h8) 27.♘e6 ♘e6 28.d5 ♘d8 29.♕d4 and White's central pawns become alive and gives him a large, almost decisive, advantage;

2) 24.b3 (positional, but a no-less-effective move) 24...bc3 (better is 24...cb3; Petrosian) 25.bc4 dc4 (25...♘b4 26.cd5 ♗d5 27.♗d5 ♘bd5 28.♘ge6!±) 26.d5 c2 27.♕c2 ♘b4 28.d6 ♘c2 29.de7 ♖fb8 30.♗b7 ♖b7 31.♖ed1!±. After the move played the game is immediately decided:

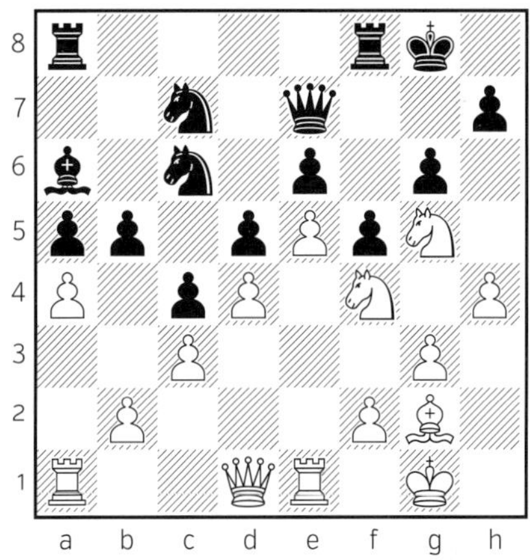

24.♘fe6!+- ♘e6 25.♗d5 ♖ad8

25...♘cd8 26.♗a8 — therefore 20...♖b8! was better!

26.♗e6 ♔g7 27.ab5 ♗b5 28.d5 f4 29.♕g4 h6 30.♘h3 1:0

THE STATIC CENTER

We can talk about a static center when the pawns are placed in some typical structure and are usually also in direct contact. But the pawns are more-or-less sentenced to wait, standing still, because every movement would be extremely delicate and could lead to decisive changes.

The positions that can be placed into 'static centers' are countless and we would need volumes of big books if we wanted to see them all or even study them. That is why we will concentrate on the two most typical structures and we will get to know them fleetingly and only with the basic plans. Both these structures are also so extensive that we could write a book based on each of them.

First we will get to know the positions with the isolated pawn, which are placed in the group of static centers. They belong there — until something happens with the isolated pawn: if he moves forward (d4-d5 or ...d5-d4), the center is as a rule transformed into an open center. When the exchanges occur on the adjacent file (c or e), there are hanging pawns and we will learn about them in the chapter about the 'dynamic center'. Positions with an isolated pawn can also be placed among the dynamic centers — the isolated pawn contains a lot of energy inside which it wants to explode while advancing. The fate of the whole game depends on whether the pawn managed to advance or not. Because of all this, it would be correct to place the positions with isolated pawns among a new group, let us name it the 'under-static' centers.

The second structure that we will get to know in this chapter is the 'Carlsbad' pawn structure. This structure can be formed out of many openings (The Queen's Gambit is the most common one) and it can be defined by various different strategic plans.

POSITIONS WITH AN ISOLATED PAWN

When we talk about the structure with the isolated pawn we have in mind positions where White has the isolated d4-pawn or Black has the isolani on d5-. We also talk about the isolated pawn when a player has a pawn that has no support of the pawns on the next files: with the isolated d-pawn the condition is that the player has no pawns on the e- or c- files.

This characteristic immediately defines the biggest **weakness** of the isolated pawn: we cannot defend it with another pawn and for this reason it is chronically weak — and thus a target of the opponent's attacks. Even worse than its own weakness are the weaknesses around the pawn and especially in front of it: the d5-square in front of the isolated d4-pawn is terribly weak because the opponent can make manoeuvres with his pieces there and it can become an outpost for his pieces. Isolated pawns are especially weak in the endgame where they can be easily attacked by the opponent's pieces, often without the chance of any counterplay.

Of course the position with the isolated pawn also has its **advantages.** Some chess players appreciate these types of positions so much that they even choose the openings which bring them to the isolated pawn positions. The advantages of the isolated pawn structures are especially shown in space. This space advantage makes possible a quick regrouping of the pieces over the board and, if needed, a quick change of plans. The attacker is dangerous when he is attacking the king — the d4 pawn creates an outpost for the pieces on the e5-square and in its hinterland the third rank is free for the penetration of the heavy pieces. Of course there are also at least two dangerous strategic plans: play on the c-file, or the d4-d5 stroke in the center, which brings many exchanges, after which the attacker is as a rule left with more active pieces.

I already mentioned that the positions with the isolated pawn can appear out of different openings. The most characteristic are different variations of The Queen's Gambit, The Nimzo- Indian Defence and these positions can also be formed out of the open or semi-open games, for example out of the Russian Defence, the Caro-Kann Defence or even out of the Sicilian Defence (The Alapin Variation).

PLAYING AGAINST THE ISOLATED PAWN

In the first match for the official World Championship title in 1886 the competitors were the big romantic, Johannes Zukertort, and the father of positional play, Wilhelm Steinitz. The starting points of each were clear: the first spoke in favour of the attack and the other for the defence. In the position with the isolated pawns their evaluations were diametrically opposed. Zukertort thought that the kinetic energy of the isolated pawn leaves White with the advantage, but Steinitz was against that and he thought that Black has the advantage if he manages to defend himself properly.

Steinitz was the better player and he won the match and became the first World Champion. His executions were so convincing that they convinced every doubter of that era. The positions with the isolated pawn were forgotten until Mikhail Botvinnik brought them back to life half a century later. Nowadays we know that there is no such thing as a united rule or evaluation: some prefer isolated pawns and others prefer to play against them.

1

▷ **Zukertort**
▶ **Steinitz**
New Orleans 1886 [D26]

1.d4 d5 2.c4 e6 3.♘c3 ♘f6 4.♘f3 dc4 5.e3 c5 6.♗c4 cd4 7.ed4 ♗e7 8.0–0 0–0

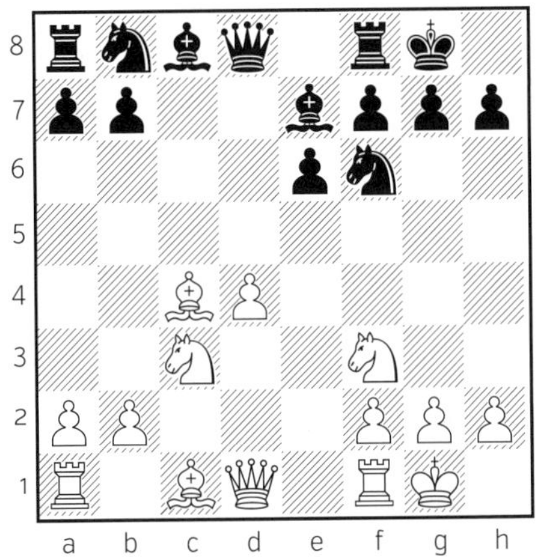

Steinitz was the first player who systematically thought about the classical position with the isolated pawn. The father of positional play understood that the isolated pawn in the center defines a special pawn structure and that is wise to play according to well-studied patterns when these structures arise.

9.♕e2 ♘bd7 10.♗b3

Zukertort trusted the White pieces, which at least seemingly offer more active play connected with the possible attack on the king. And that was all that the chess romantics wanted at that time. White could choose here 10.d5= with exchanges in the center and equal play.

10...♘b6 11.♗f4

Today we know that better plans include the development of the bishop to g5.

11...♘bd5 12.♗g3 ♕a5 13.♖ac1 ♗d7 14.♘e5 ♖fd8! 15.♕f3 ♗e8!

Steinitz had not only studied the position carefully but also understood it deeply. The technique that we use to place the pieces on the most suitable squares is very important when playing around pawn structures. We also need to know how many pieces we need for the attack and how many for the defence — the bishop on e8 does both jobs.

16.♖fe1 ♖ac8 17.♗h4

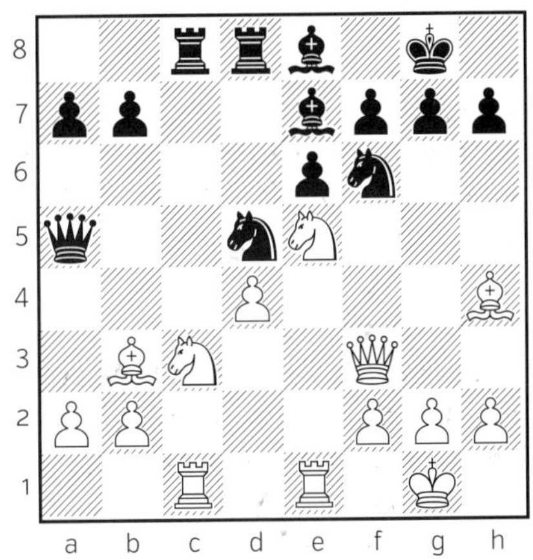

17...♘c3!

Nowadays many people know the ideas for the battle against the isolated pawn, but in 1886 it was virgin territory. Black first set up his bulletproof defence on the kingside and now he passes over to the counterattack in the center. He has changed the pawn structure, turning White's isolated pawn into a pair of hanging pawns. The d4-pawn is defended, but because of that White has a new weakness on the c3-square.

18.bc3 ♕c7

Nowadays many people would play 18...b5 and fix White's pawns, but Steinitz knew that the pawns would become even weaker if the pawn were to advance to c4. Black will not be against exchanges — this was also a consequence of his home preparation: when there are less pieces on the board it is harder to defend them...

19.♕d3 ♘d5

Yet another typical manoeuvre, which is now linked with the exchange of the pieces.

20.♗e7 ♕e7 21.♗d5?

Zukertort is doing what Steinitz wants him to do. He is only helping Black with this exchange.

21...♖d5 22.c4

Zukertort was in favour of active play and therefore he plays these overly-optimistic moves. The advance of the c-pawn will only loosen the center even more.

22...♖dd8 23.♖e3?

There is no attack here — Black's king is well-defended. It would be better to switch over to defence with the solid 23.♖ed1 and a slow preparation of the possible d4-d5 stroke.

23...♕d6 24.♖d1 f6 25.♖h3!? h6!

Black does not want to complicate matters with 25...fe5 26.♕h7 ♔f8 27.♖f3, with unclear play.

26.♘g4

26.♘g6 ♗g6 27.♕g6 ♖c4 28.♖h6 ♕d4! 29.♕h7 ♔f8 30.♕h8 ♔f7 31.♕d8 ♕d8!−+

26...♕f4!

The start of the counterattack, and one which was performed flawlessly by Black. The end of the game is not important for our theme, but let's have a look anyway at how the great master handled the situation!

27.♘e3 ♗a4! 28.♖f3 ♕d6 29.♖d2 ♗c6 30.♖g3

30.♖f6? gf6 31.♕g6 ♔f8 32.♕f6 ♔e8−+;

30.d5!? ♕e5! 31.♖g3 ed5 32.♕g6 ♖c7.

30...f5! 31.♖g6 ♗e4 32.♕b3 ♔h7! 33.c5 ♖c5 34.♖e6 ♖c1 35.♘d1 ♕f4 36.♕b2 ♖b1 37.♕c3 ♖c8 38.♖e4 ♕e4 0:1.

THE ATTACK ON THE KINGSIDE

The preliminary conditions for an attack on the kingside are fulfilled: White has an open e-file and a strong outpost on the e5-square, while Black is somewhat compressed and he has difficulties with his some of his pieces, which cannot join the defence. White can attack in two ways: with the pieces, where he intensively attacks one of Black's pawns in front of the king and is aided in this with some basic motifs — the transportation of the heavy pieces over the third rank or the battery on the b1-h7 diagonal. The second way of attacking is one in which the attacker additionally involves the pawns (usually with the f-pawn).

1

▷ **Botvinnik**
▶ **Vidmar**
Nottingham 1936 (D40)

1.c4 e6 2.♘f3 d5 3.d4 ♘f6 4.♗g5 ♗e7 5.♘c3 o-o 6.e3 ♘bd7 7.♗d3 c5 8.o-o cd4 9.ed4 dc4 10.♗c4 ♘b6 11.♗b3 ♗d7

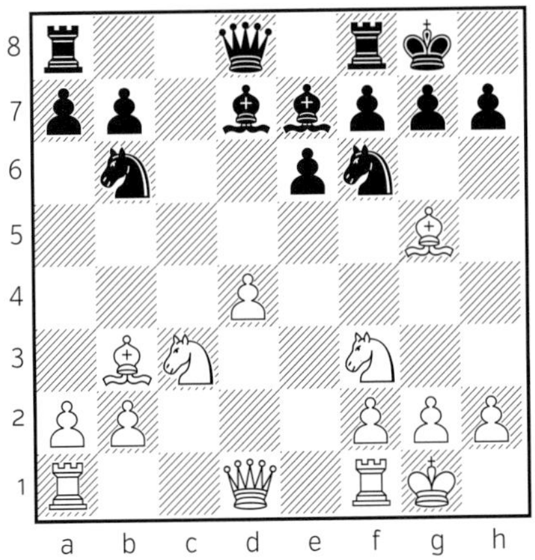

12.♕d3!

White doesn't clarify his plans for the attack yet with this move, but simply prepares the battery ♗c2-♕d3. All the preliminary conditions for an attack with the f-pawn are fulfilled: Black's knight is on b6 from where he is defending one of the really critical squares, the d5-square, but with that he allows White access to the e5-square and also to the d4-square.

12...♘bd5 13.♘e5 ♗c6 14.♖ad1! ♘b4 15.♕h3!

In positions with the isolated pawn, White's rook usually goes to d1 from where it defends the weak pawn. At the same time it supports the pawn's possible advance in the center.

15...♗d5 16.♘d5 ♘bd5?

A serious positional mistake — the right move is 16...♘fd5, where White has, after 17.♗c1 ♖c8, only a small advantage. But after the capture in the game White's hands are free to progress with the f-pawn that will decide the game in lightning-like fashion!

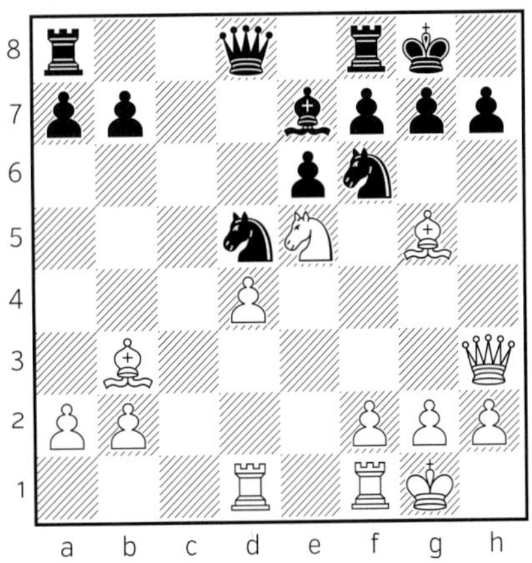

17.f4! ♖c8

There is no good defence against f5: 17...g6 18.♗h6 ♖e8 19.♗a4 +-. Or 17... ♘e4 18.♘f7! ♔f7 (18...♖f7 19.♕e6) 19.♖de1! with a decisive attack.

18.f5 ef5

Black would resist a little longer after 18...♕d6 19.fe6 fe6 20.♘c4 ♕c6 21.♖fe1, though his position would be fall apart sooner or later.

19.♖f5 ♕d6

Or 19...♖c7 20.♖fd1 ♘b6 21.♕h4 ♘bd5 22.♘f7 ♖f7 23.♗d5 ♘d5 24.♖f7 ♗g5 25.♕g5, with a mating attack.

20.♘f7! ♖f7 21.♗f6 ♗f6

21...♘f6 22.♖f6 ♗f6 23.♕c8 +-.

22.♖d5 ♕c6 23.♖d6 ♕e8 24.♖d7 1:0.

In positions with the isolated pawn, when White decides for active play on the kingside, the plans connected with piece-play must prevailing. Characteristic motifs occur, for example the battery ♕d3-♗c2, which forces Black to play ...g7-g6. White gradually places his rooks on d1 and e1: with one he defends the weak pawn (and supports its possible advance) and with the other he performs active operations on the semi-open file. The knight usually goes to e5, the bishop on g5...

2

▷ **Kamsky**
▶ **Short**
Linares, 1994 [E48]

1.d4 ♘f6 2.c4 e6 3.♘c3 ♗b4 4.e3 c5 5.♗d3 ♘c6 6.♘ge2 cd4 7.ed4 d5 8.cd5 ♘d5 9.0–0 ♗d6 10.♘e4

An unusual move. White has a hard time justifying the release of the pressure on the d5-square in such isolated pawn positions. The knight points at the kingside, where he will try to help with the attack on the king.

10...♗e7 11.a3! 0–0 12.♗c2! ♖e8 13.♕d3!

Remember the last three moves of White, because they are very characteristic: the a2-a3 move is prophylactic, because it defends the ♕d3-♗c2 battery from the ...♘b4-move. The battery provokes the weakness on g6 and White now has a clear plan of play and especially a free square to include his dark-squared bishop in the attack.

13...g6 14.♗h6 b6 15.♖ad1 ♗b7 16.♖fe1 ♖c8

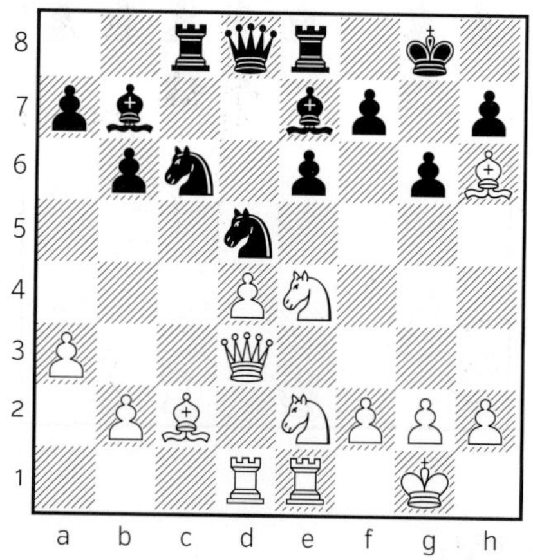

17.♗b3

The bishop has done everything that he could on the b1-h7 diagonal and now he moves back to his fundamental work place. The pressure on the d5-square is always useful and White can keep it with the help of his knight. An alternative is 17.♘2c3 ♘a5 18.♕g3 ♘c4 19.♗a4 ♗c6 20.♗b3 ♘c3 21.bc3 ♗e4 22.♖e4 ♘d6, but in the game Shirov : Psakhis, Klaipeda 1988, he did not achieve any advantage.

17...a6

A loss of tempo. It would be correct to move the rook to the d-file: 17...♖c7!? 18.♘2g3 ♖d7, with approximately equal play.

18.♘2g3 ♘b8?!

Yet another 'too-slow' move. Interesting is 18...♗h4! with the idea ...♘ce7-f5!

19.♕f3

White's queen bravely exposing herself on the long diagonal. Kamsky spotted the hole on the f6-square and now he directs his powers against it.

19...♖c7 20.♘h5! ♘d7

Black would lose quickly after 20...gh5? 21.♕g3 ♗g5 22.♗g5+-. Also bad is 20...f5 21.♘c3 and White has a big advantage.

21.h4! ♘7f6

White beautifully combines many different attacking motifs and Black already has no defence: 21...♗h4 22.♘d6 ♖e7 23.♘b7 ♖b7 24.g3 gh5 25.gh4+- or 21...b5 22.♘g5 ♘5f6 23.♘e6! fe6 24.♗e6 ♔h8 25.♗g7.

22.♘hf6 ♘f6

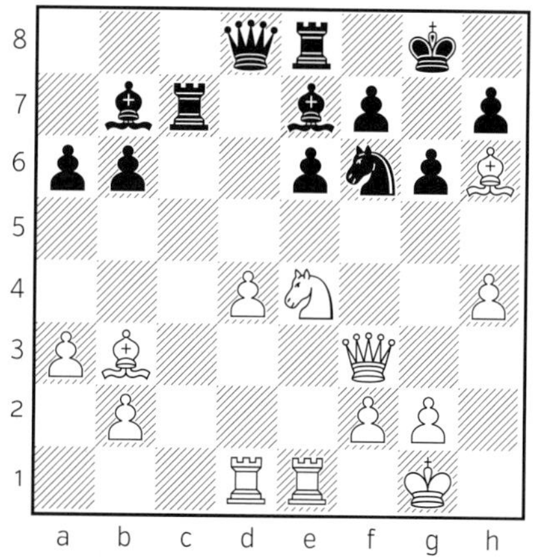

23.d5!

The final penetration, and one which completely breaks Black's defence.

23...♘e4

The capture on d5 would not save Black: 23...ed5 24.♘f6 ♗f6 25.♕f6!+- or 23...♘d5 24.♗d5 ♗d5 25.♖d5! ♕d5 (25...ed5 26.♘f6 ♗f6 27.♖e8 ♕e8 28.♕f6 ♕e1 29.♔h2+-) 26.♘f6 ♗f6 27.♕f6+-, and neither would the move 23...e5 24.d6+-

24.de6 f5 25.♖d8 ♖d8 26.♖d1 1:0.

THE d4-d5 BREAK

"The dynamic power of the isolated pawn is hidden in its energy, while it is progressing," said Aron Nimzowitsch. And really, the d4-d5 break in the center is one of the strongest weapons the player with the isolated pawn possesses. The move is usually very attractive because White strikes at the most defended square of the board.

The d4-d5 break contains many goals. The first one is the change in the pawn structure which will definitely occur. After the big exchanges (if they occur) White's pieces will move to a more active squares (the d5-square, which will be the place for White's pieces, is placed on the other half of the board). White usually achieves with this a space advantage, but this kind of stroke can be especially effective in the positions where Black has not yet castled. But the effect can also be strong when there is a castled king, particularly when it is connected with the motifs on the b1-h7 and the h4-d8 diagonals — and on the d-file, where White's rook and Black's queen are usually in 'x-ray' opposition.

1

▷ **Petrosian**
▶ **Balashov**
Moscow 1974 [E54]

1.c4 ♘f6 2.♘c3 e6 3.d4 ♗b4 4.e3 c5 5.♗d3 d5 6.♘f3 0-0 7.0-0 dc4 8.♗c4 ♘c6 9.♗d3 cd4 10.ed4 ♗e7 11.♖e1 b6 12.a3 ♗b7 13.♗c2 ♖c8 14.♕d3 ♖e8?

A position that was famous in the mid-70's and this move was also chosen in some games by the World Champion Anatoly Karpov. More cautious would be to close the dangerous diagonal with the ...g7-g6 move.

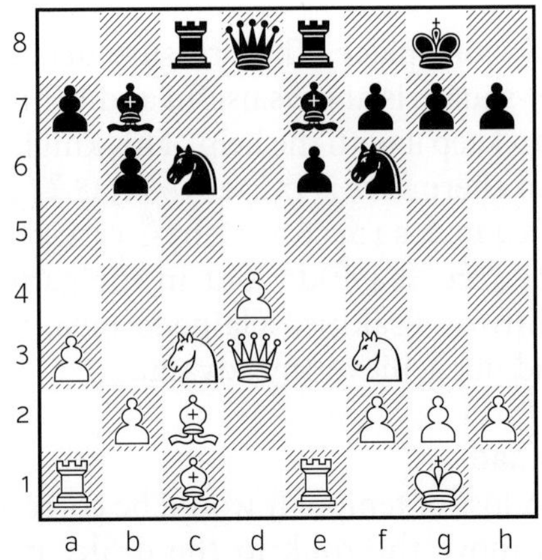

15.d5! ed5 16.♗g5!

This is the standard attacking mechanism which you should remember. It threatens 17.♗f6, and Black has no defence, e.g. 16...g6, due to 17.♖e7! ♕e7 18.♘d5.

16...♘e4 17.♘e4 de4 18.♕e4 g6 19.♕h4 ♕c7

The 20.♗b3 move is hanging in the air. White would continue in this way after 19...♖c7 as did Portisch against Karpov (Milano, 1975), who choose 19...h5. In both cases White's advantage is huge.

20.♗b3!

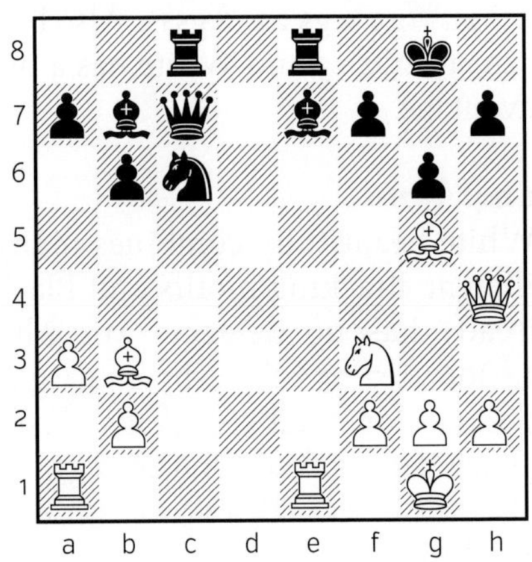

Black is already without a defence. 21.♗f7 is threatened and after 20...♗f8 21.♗f4 and 22.♘g5, or 20...♗d6 21.♗f6, with a quick decision.

20...h5 21.♕e4 ♔g7 22.♗f7! ♔f7 23.♗h6!
The point of White's attack.

23...♕d6
Or 23...♗d6 24.♘g5 ♔f6 25.♘h7 1:0, N. Garcia : Pomar, Salamanca 1975.

24.♕c4 ♔f6 25.♖ad1 ♘d4 26.♕d4 ♕d4 27.♖d4 1:0.

In most cases the d4-d5 stroke is not motivated by or connected to an attack on the king, but rather it is a positional move. White is not afraid of the "big" exchange in the center, because it usually leaves him with dominant endgame or middlegame, when there are enough pieces left on the board. One of the pioneers, a man who studied the d4-d5 break, was the universal player Akiba Rubinstein. Now let's see how Akiba performed this in practice!

2

▷ **Rubinstein**
▶ **Tartakower**
Marienbad 1925 [D27]

1.c4 e6 2.♘f3 d5 3.d4 ♘f6 4.♘c3 dc4 5.e3 a6 6.a4
The move has both good and bad sides: White prevents the ...b7-b5 move but at the same time gives up the b4-square, which will be available for Black's knight.

6...c5 7.♗c4 ♘c6 8.0-0 cd4 9.♘d4
It seems more logical to take with the knight, with a transposition to the known positions.

9...♘d4?!
After 9...♗d7 the position would be almost equal.

10.ed4 ♗e7

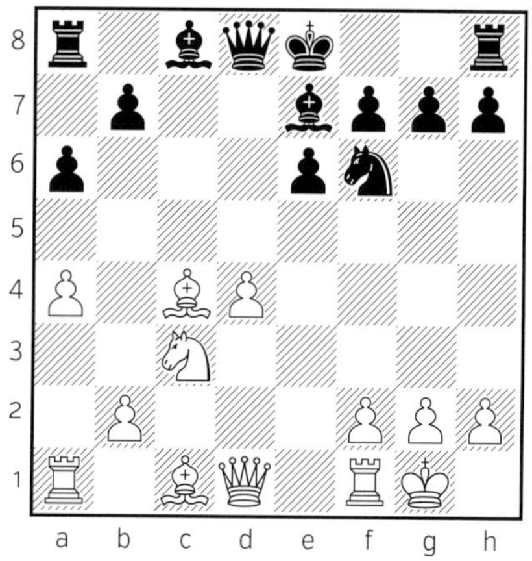

11.d5
The classical break. White provokes the exchanges in the center due to him being better in any endgame.

11...ed5 12.♘d5 ♘d5 13.♗d5 0-0 14.♕f3
After this move, the capture with the knight on the ninth move makes sense — White's queen is marvellously placed on f3 and does many things at the same time: it attacks b7, has an eye on f7 and it has also in the meantime freed the d1-square for the rook.

14...♗d6 15.♖e1

Black indirectly defended his pawn: 15.♗b7? ♗h2! 16.♔h2 ♕c7. We need to remember this kind of defence.

15...♕h4 16.h3 ♕b4 17.♖d1

On the attractive-looking 17.♖e8 move, Black defends himself with 17... ♗e6!, with a counter-threat of mate on e1.

17...♖b8

Black has managed to defend the b7-square, but White is still well-placed and is making new threats with every move.

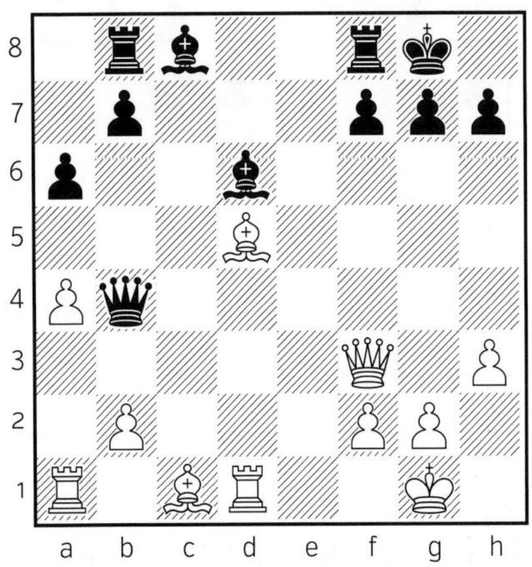

18.b3! ♗e6!

Black defends thoughtfully and is willing to sacrifice a pawn for attractive counterplay.

19.♗e6 fe6 20.♕e2 ♗c5!

Counterplay at any cost!

21.♕e6 ♔h8 22.♗a3!

A marvellous move, which needed to be seen by Rubinstein earlier, and that is connected to deep calculations. The analyses show that White keeps his advantage in every variation!

22...♕a5

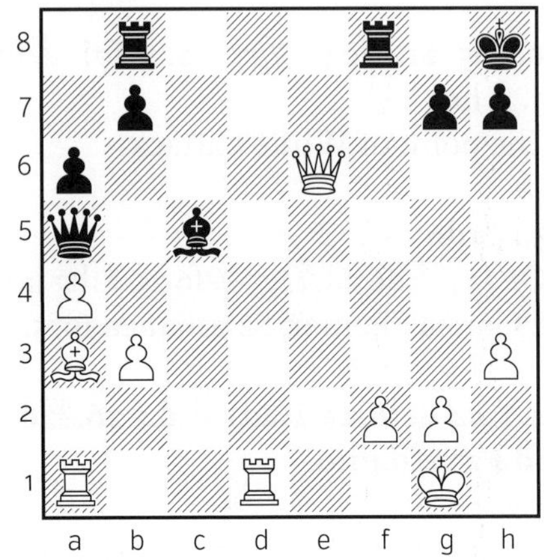

23.♖d5!

The point of the previous move. White returns the pawn and offers a transition to the endgame in which he will definitely be better. His work would be harder with the transition to the endgame with the heavy pieces, even though he would be a pawn up: 23.♗c5 ♕c5 and Black's active play would cause him problems.

23...♗f2 24.♔h1 ♕c3 25.♖c1 ♕f6

25...♕e3? 26.♖e5+-.

26.♕f6 ♖f6 27.♖d7

Even though there is not much material left on the board, White's advantage is huge. Many things are threatened: ♖b7, ♗b2 or ♖cc7.

27...♗e3 28.♖b7! ♖b6 29.♖b6 ♗b6 30.♖c6!

White has won a pawn and there was never any doubt in Rubinstein's technique. The rest of the game requires no comments.

30...h5 31.♗d6 ♖b7 32.b4 a5 33.b5 ♔h7 34.g4 hg4 35.hg4 ♔g8 36.♔g2 ♔f7 37.♔f3 ♗d8 38.♔e4 ♔e8 39.♔d5 g5 40.♔e6 ♗b6 41.♖c8 ♗d8 42.♗c5 ♖b8 43.♖c6 ♖b7 44.b6 ♖b8 45.♖c7 ♗c7 46.bc7 ♖c8 47.♗b6 ♖a8 48.♗a7 1:0.

THE ATTACK ON THE QUEENSIDE

In modern chess the level of defensive play has risen. Even more, defenders are preventing any thoughts of an attack on the king with positional play, and therefore the attackers are turning to other plans. The situation is the same with positions involving isolated pawns. One of them — the preparation and the execution of the d4-d5 break — was shown in the previous chapter. Now let us see what White can do when the d5-square is well defended (and is thus preventing this stroke).

We already know that the player with the isolated pawn needs to maintain the initiative. His actively placed pieces make that possible, and now only the objects of the attack need to be found. When Black successfully prevents the attack on the king, and also the d4-d5 stroke in the center, he usually needs to pay for that with a weakness on the queenside.

The battle in most cases revolves around the c-file and around the bad pawns in Black's camp. If White manages to occupy the file and also create an outpost (usually on the c5 or c6 squares) or even penetrate to the seventh rank, then his advantage would be unquestionable.

White's work would be made easier if Black were to move a pawn on the queenside. Due to him being incautious or due to development problems he may have no defenders available to defend the weak squares. In the structure a6-b7 the dark-squares are weak and it is even worse when the structure is a7-b6, if White manages to exchange the light-squared bishops, as happened in the next game...

1

▹ **Karpov**
▸ **Geller**
Moscow 1981 [D58]

1.d4 d5 2.c4 e6 3.♘c3 ♗e7 4.♘f3 ♘f6 5.♗g5 h6 6.♗h4 0-0 7.e3 b6 8.♖c1 ♗b7 9.♗d3 ♘bd7 10.0-0 c5 11.♕e2 ♖c8 12.♗g3 cd4 13.ed4 dc4 14.♗c4 ♗f3?!

Better is 14...♘h5!? 15.♖fd1 (or 15.♗a6 ♘g3 16.hg3 ♗a6 17.♕a6 ♖c7, Naidorf : Horth, Lugano1968) 15... ♘g3 16.hg3 ♘f6 17.♘e5 ♗b4! 18.♗a6 ♕e7, Gurevich : Beliavsky, Reggio Emilia 1989, in both cases with approximately equal play.

15.gf3 ♘h5

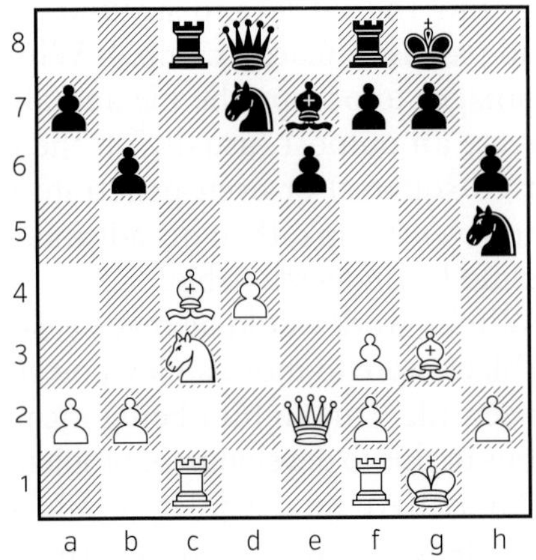

Black has given up his important bishop in exchange for nothing: he will have to make the position of White's pieces better by taking on g3 or he will lose the rook. And without the light-squared bishop his queenside is desperately weak: in the structure a7-b6 keeping the light-squared bishop is obligatory!

16.♗a6!

White immediately exploits his advantages.

16...♘g3

The only move — after 16...♖a8 or 16...♖c6 then 17.♗b7.

17.hg3 ♖c7

After 17...♖c6 18.♖fd1 ♘f6 19.♔g2! White is clearly better and he has also prepared a trick: 19...♕b8? 20.♘d5!±. The withdrawal of the rook to a8 — 17...♖a8 allows a penetration in the center to happen: 18.♖fd1 ♘f6 19.d5! ed5 20.♗b7 and White is too strong.

18.♖fd1!

There is nothing after 18.♘b5 ♖c1 19.♖c1 ♘b8! 20.♘a7 ♕d4.

18...♘f6

Black is of course angry about the bishop on a6, but he cannot get rid of him with 18...♘b8 because the knight needs to control the d5-square. After 19.♗c4, and a further d4-d5, White would be a lot better.

19.♘b5!

Now it is time to attack Black's pawns on the queenside.

19...♖c1 20.♖c1 ♘d5

20...♕b8 21.♖c7 ♘d5 22.♖a7± or 20...♕d5 21.a3, also with a big advantage.

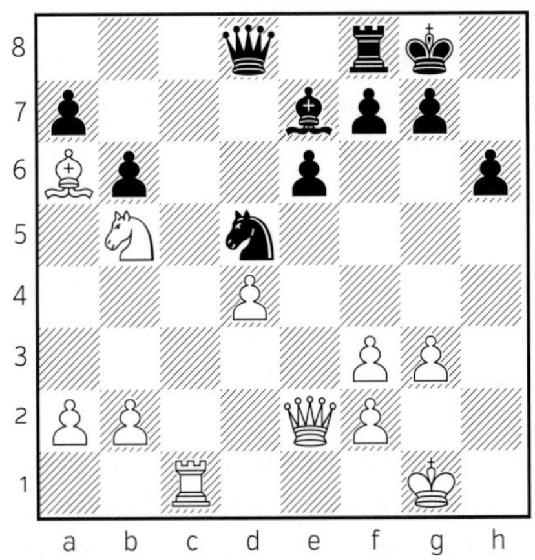

21.♘a7!

Everything looks a little odd, but Karpov calculated well and evaluated the consequences even better. Here Black cannot exploit the fact that White's pieces are a bit lost.

21...♘b4 22.a3! ♕a8!?
22...♘a6 23.♘c6! ♕d7 24.♕a6±.

23.♖c7!
White plays like a machine and sees everything: 23.♘c8? ♗g5!−+.

23...♘d5 24.♖b7!
Black defends himself thoughtfully: 24.♖d7 ♖d8! 25.♖d8 ♗d8 26.♕b5 ♗f6, but White has an answer to everything. The game is decided.

24...♗f6 25.♘c6 ♖c8 26.♘e5 ♗e5 27.de5 ♖c1

28.♔g2! ♕d8 29.♗d3 ♖a1
29...g6 30.♕d2 ♖a1 31.♕h6+-; 29...♖c7 30.♖c7 ♕c7±.

30.♕e4 g6 31.♖f7!+- ♔f7 32.♕g6 ♔f8 33.♕h6 1:0.

THE BATTLE AGAINST THE C-PAWN

This special chapter deals with isolated pawn positions in which the opponent is fighting with the c-pawn (instead of the e-pawn). These kinds of positions usually arise from the Queen's Gambit and in modern chess also out of some variations of the Russian (Petroff) Defence. Let's see some characteristic examples!

1

▷ **Farago**
► **Velikov**
Albena 1983 [D68]

1.d4 d5 2.c4 c6 3.♘c3 ♘f6 4.♘f3 e6 5.♗g5 ♗e7 6.e3 ♘bd7 7.♖c1 0-0 8.♗d3 dc4 9.♗c4 ♘d5 10.♗e7 ♕e7 11.0-0 ♘c3 12.♖c3 e5 13.♕c2 ed4 14.ed4 ♕d6

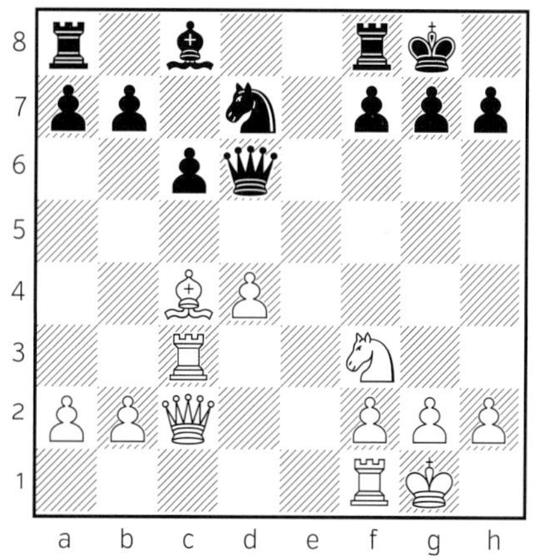

We need to stop and look for a minute at this position. White has the advantage in development and has already mobilized his pieces. The rook on c3 can easily move to the kingside, the queen and the bishop are already looking in that direction, and the knight only needs a single move to jump to e5 or g5. Black has not finished his development and his biggest problem is that he will not be able to cover the a2-g8 diagonal with his knight, a diagonal that White's light-squared bishop is dominating. Black doesn't have enough pieces to defend the king and therefore White goes straight in action.

15.♘g5!

The best square for the knight, from where he attacks both h7 and f7.

15...♘f6

An instructive mistake is 15...g6: 16.♘f7! ♖f7 17.♖f3 ♘f6 18.♕b3 ♕e7 19.♗f7 ♕f7 20.♖f6.

The defence with 15...♕g6 would also be bad due to the transposition to the endgame: 16.♕g6 hg6 17.♖e1 and the game would be decided by the penetration of White's rook on the e7-square.

16.♖f3 g6 17.♕b3 ♘d5

After 17...♕e7 there follows the already-known 18.♘f7! ♖f7 19.♗f7 ♕f7 20.♖f6.

18.♘e4 ♕d8 19.♗d5 cd5

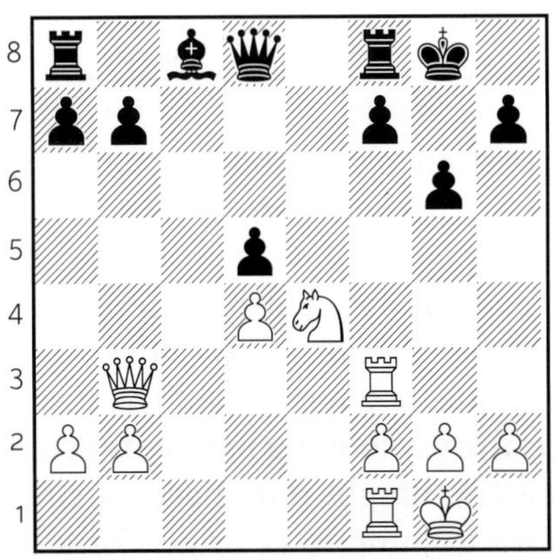

Next follows an effective mating attack, a demonstration of the strong knight against the bad bishop and at the same time a demonstration of the power of the developed pieces against ones that are not.

20.♘f6 ♔g7 21.♕e3! h5 22.♕e5 ♔h6 23.♘h5! ♗g4 24.♕g7 ♔g5

24...♔h5 25.♕h7 ♔g5 26.h4 mate!

25.♖g3 1:0

The next game that we will see is very similar to the previous game — the differences will be small, but important!

2

▷ **Lputian**
▶ **Balashov**
Erevan 1986 [D68]

1.d4 ♘f6 2.c4 e6 3.♘f3 d5 4.♘c3 ♗e7 5.♗g5 0–0 6.e3 ♘bd7 7.♖c1 c6 8.♗d3 dc4 9.♗c4 ♘d5 10.♗e7 ♕e7 11.0–0 ♘c3 12.♖c3 e5 13.♕c2 ed4 14.ed4 ♘f6 15.♖e1 ♕d8

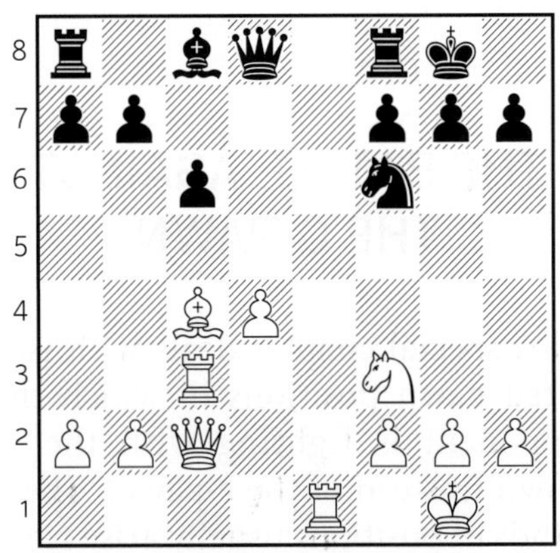

The position in the diagram is almost identical to the previous one after Black's fourteenth move. The pawn structure is the same, only here White's rook is placed on e1, Black's queen on d8 and — the most important thing — Black's knight is already placed on f6, from where it is able to cover the dangerous diagonal with the ...♘d5 move.

For this reason White cannot count on a direct attack; he needs to prepare it first. What is Black's biggest problem? His undeveloped bishop, of course! Because Black already wants to play ...♗c8-g4, White's response is clear:

16.h3!

The mastery of the positional play is hidden in prevention of the opponent's plans.

16...♘d5 17.♗d5!

The next instructive moment. Black needed to jump into d5 due to the threat of 17.♖ce3 and the penetration of the rook to the seventh rank. After the swap on d5 Black again has no choice: after 17...cd5 18.♖c7 White is completely in control.

17...♕d5 18.♖e5!

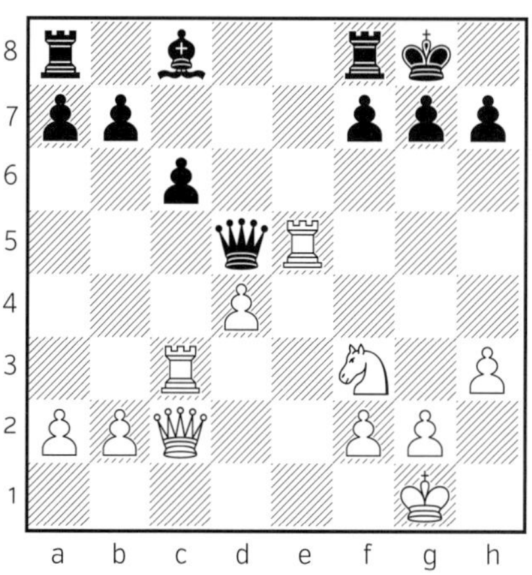

After the exchange of the knight, Black's king is left with no defenders. It is time for action on the kingside again, where all White's pieces will be in a couple of moves.

18...♕d6

Of course not 18...♕a2? 19.♖a3 and the queen is captured.

19.♘g5 g6

19...♕g6 20.♕b3.

20.♖f3 f6

Black is already lost, but the chosen move is linked with a great end.

Also dangerous is 20...♕d4 21.♖e4 ♕d5 22.♘f7 ♖f7 23.♖e8 ♔g7 24.♕c3 ♔h6 25.♕e3 ♔g7 26.♖f7 ♕f7 27.♖e7.

After 20...♗f5 direct play is decisive: 21.♖f5! gf5 22.♖g3 ♔h8 23.♕f5 ♕g6 24.♕f4 f5 25.♘h7.

21.♕b3 ♔g7

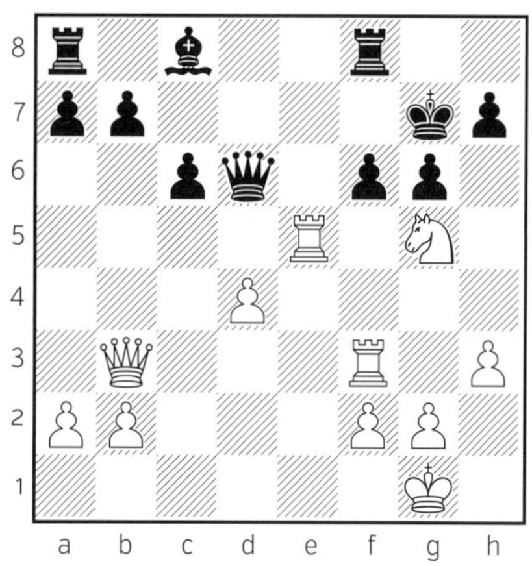

22.♖e8! a5

After 22...♖e8 mate is forced for White: 23.♕f7 ♔h6 24.♕h7 ♔g5 25.h4 ♔g4 26.♕g6 ♔h4 27.g3.

23.♖c8 1:0.

In both cases the same amount of pieces was left on the board and the exchanges were forced by White in his favour. Similar structures can also appear when all the pieces are still on the board, but there is no less danger in the position — except that these tend to be more positional, because it is harder to attack the king.

3

▷ **Vaganian**
▶ **Hübner**
Tilburg 1983 [C42]

1.d4 d5 2.c4 dc4 3.♘c3 e5 4.e3 ed4 5.ed4 ♘f6 6.♗c4 ♗e7 7.♘f3 0–0 8.0–0 ♘bd7 9.♖e1 ♘b6 10.♗b3 c6 11.♗g5 ♗g4

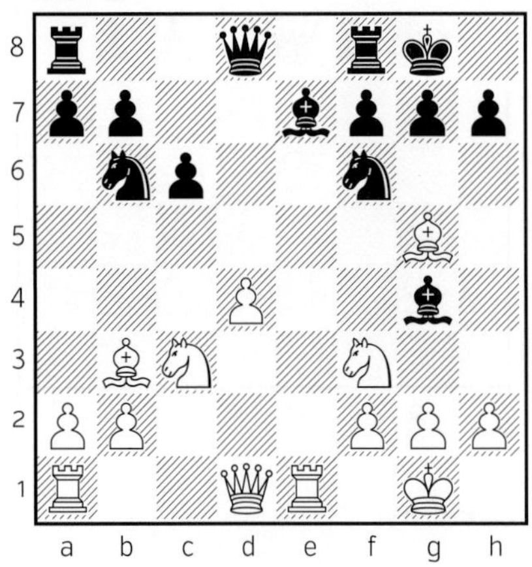

White is more active due to his control over the e-file. With the next move he will get rid of the pin and will then be threatening to jump into e5 and therefore Black needs to take.

12.♕d3! ♗f3 13.♕f3 ♘fd5 14.♗e7
White cannot exploit the pin even more, because 14.♖e7 doesn't quite work after 14...♘e7 15.♖e1 ♘bc8 16.♕e2 ♖e8 17.♗f7 ♔f7 18.♕e6 ♔f8 19.♖e3 ♘d6 20.♖f3 ♘ef5! and Black is saved thanks to White's weaknesses on the first rank.

14...♘e7

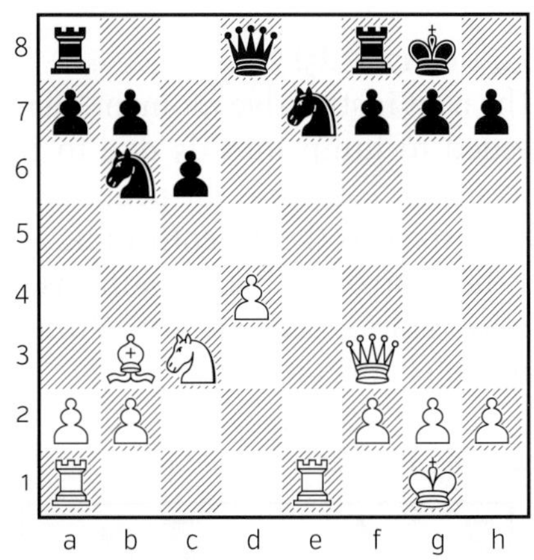

15.♖e5!
And once again this instructive manoeuvre with the rook on the fifth rank. The rook on e5 has many functions: it is threatening to move to the kingside, it is preparing a doubling on the e-file and it is also controlling the d5-square. Therefore Black's knight needs to chase it away in exchange for its modest position on the g6-square.

15...♘g6 16.♖e4 ♘d7 17.♖d1 ♕a5

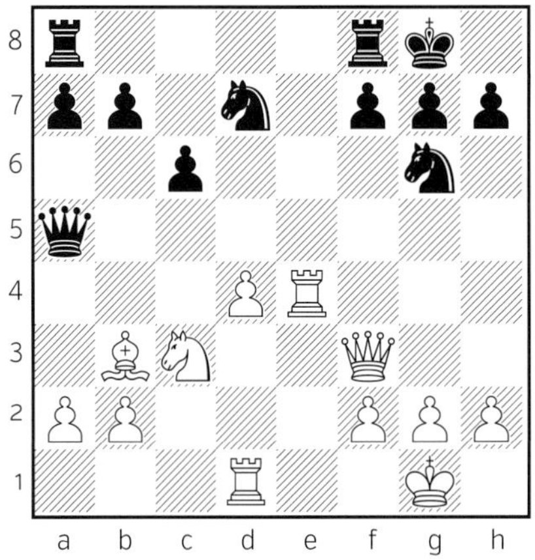

18.♖e3!

Freeing the square for the knight.

18...♖ad8 19.♘e4 ♕c7 20.h4!

When there is a knight on g6 (b6) we need to be afraid of the attack with the rooks pawn — this rule goes for all the positions, not only for the ones with an isolated pawn.

20...h6

White exploited the right moment, because black can't go 20...♘h4 due to 21.♕h5 ♘g6 22.♖h3 h6 23.♕g6.

21.♕g4 ♔h8 22.h5 ♘f4 23.♖g3 g5 24.hg6 fg6 25.♖e1 ♖de8 26.♖ge3 ♘b6 27.♘c5 ♕c8 28.♕f4 1:0.

THE CARLSBAD STRUCTURE

This characteristic pawn placement got its name after the international tournament in Carlsbad in 1923. At that time a very popular variation was the Cambridge-Springs in the Queen's Gambit:

1.d4 d5 2.c4 e6 3.♘c3 ♘f6 4.♗g5 c6 5.e3 ♘bd7 6.♘f3 ♕a5, against which White players did not know how to achieve the advantage. For this reason many players decided on the quick exchange in the center: **6.cd5 ed5**, with a transposition to our pawn structure. Nowadays the Carlsbad structure usually arises out of the Queen's Gambit and White usually chooses it a move or two earlier with the exchange on d5. These kinds of positions with this structure were seen even earlier, but White players did not plan this kind of play in these positions, they were more-or-less coincidental.

White decides for the Carlsbad structure with the exchange on d5 and he also has the advantage in choosing one of the typical game plans first. We will get to know two of them: the minority attack with the pawns on the queenside: b2-b4-b5-c6, with which White wants to change the pawn structure and weaken the pawns on Black's queenside. The second characteristic plan is linked with the preparation of the e3-e4 move in the center, which will also bring important differences to the pawn structure.

Black needs to wait and decide on his counterplay based on White's plan. It is logical that he will respond to White's action on the queenside with action on the other side of the board — he will prepare an attack on

White's king. He can use his pawns or attack just with the pieces. He can make White's plans with the minority attack harder using some positional methods, for example with the strengthened defence of the b5-square (where White is supposed to advance his b-pawn) or with the strengthening of the possible outpost on c4.

If White is preparing the play in the center (the plan e3-e4) then Black also needs to be well-prepared. He can do that with action on the wing and it would be even better if he could, only temporarily, leave control of the center to White and later attack it very quickly.

THE MINORITY ATTACK

We already stated that with this name we are talking about a simple plan. White will advance with the b-pawn and he will try to loosen Black's strong pawn wedge on the queenside. If we imagine, in a basic Carlsbad structure, a white pawn on b5 then Black has a hard time deciding what to do. If he leaves the move to White, he will take on c6 and weaken the c6 pawn (if Black takes bc6) or he will weaken the d5 pawn, if Black takes with a piece. It is similar if Black takes on b5 or if he plays the ...c6-c5 move — in both cases the d5 pawn is left weak.

But the worst thing that he can do is to wait. If Black just waits, White will make the c6 pawn weak and later arrange suitable exchanges and transpose into an endgame, where he will try to exploit his advantage.

1

▷ **Petrosian**
▶ **Krogius**
Tbilisi, 1959 [D91]

1.d4 ♘f6 2.♘f3 g6 3.c4 ♗g7 4.♘c3 d5 5.♗g5 ♘e4 6.cd5

The transposition to the Carlsbad structure for which White is ready to give up his dark-squared bishop.

6...♘g5 7.♘g5 e6 8.♘f3 ed5 9.e3 0–0 10.♗d3 ♘c6

An immediate transposition to the Carlsbad structure would occur after 10...c6.

11.0–0 ♘e7 12.b4 ♗f5

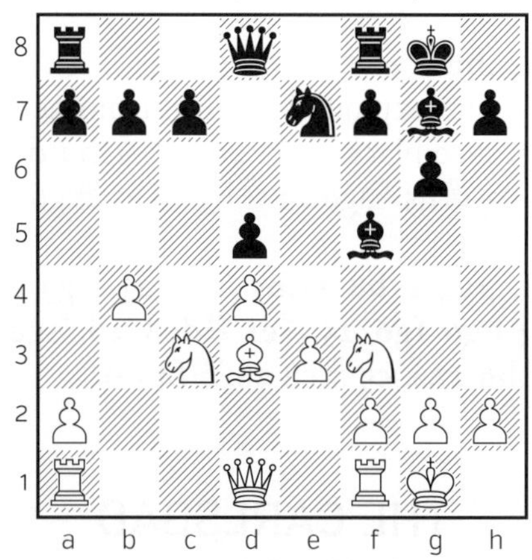

The swap of the light-squared bishops is Black's first thought in these structures, but in our position better would be 12...♗g4, because Black will obtain his counterplay more easily with the pin. But now he has freed White's hand and Petrosian will use that for an immediate attack on the queenside.

13.♗f5 ♘f5 14.b5 ♕d6 15.♕b3 ♘e7 16.♖fc1 ♔h8 17.♖c2 h6 18.♖ac1 c6

Black hesitates and has not made any threats on the kingside yet. In the meantime White had gradually improved his position and placed his pieces ideally. Black is in trouble: after ...c6-b5 he would retain a stable d-pawn but White's rooks would control the c-file. And if he does not take, White will sooner or later.

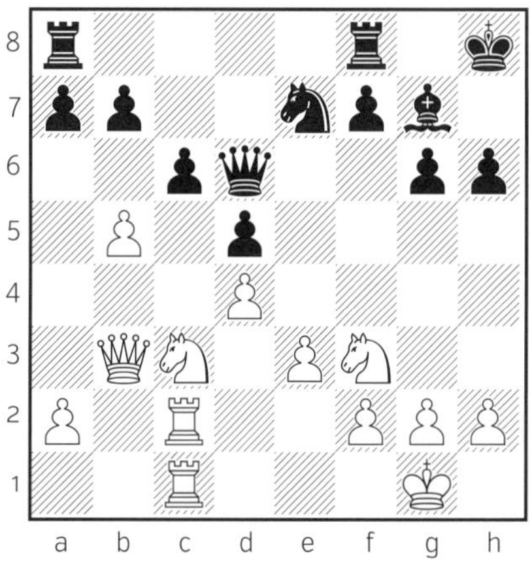

19.♘a4!

Petrosian plays very accurately. After 19.bc6 bc6 20.♘a4 ♖ab8 there would be no squares for the queen to move to. For this reason White waits before taking on d5, because it will certainly wait for him.

19...♖ab8 20.g3!

Yet another marvellous, preventive move. With 20.g3 White avoids the possible counterplay for Black (...f7-f5-f4).

20...♔h7 21.♘c5 ♖fd8

After this move the pawn is lost by force.

22.bc6 bc6 23.♕a4

Black has, besides the weakness on c6, a weakness on a7 also. This is a very important moment! If Black fights against White's advance b4-b5 with the ...a6 move (this move does not prevent the thrust b5 because White would play a2-a4), he would only have one weakness (on the c6-square).

23...♕f6 24.♔g2 ♖a8 25.♘b7 ♖e8 26.♘a5

The c6 pawn is sentenced to death and that is the end of the story.

26...g5 27.h3 ♕f5 28.♘c6 ♕e4 29.♖c5 f5 30.♕c2 ♘c6 31.♖c6 f4 32.ef4 gf4 33.g4 ♗d4 34.♕d2 ♗g7 35.♖e1 ♕a4 36.♕d5 ♖e1 37.♘e1 ♖f8 38.♘f3 ♔h8 39.♖c7 a6 40.♕b7 ♖g8 41.♘h4 1:0

We can learn a lot of things from this instructive game. Above all it is glorious to see how carefully and uncompromisingly Petrosian built the game. The advance with the b-pawn at the right moment, while being careful all the time to not allow the ...c6-c5 move. A very important conclusion is that White's dark-squared bishop does not have an important role within the minority attack strategy — White needs to attack the c6-

square with the light-squared bishop, with the knights and with the heavy pieces. Black in the meantime had not taken care of his counterplay: when White gets to play the b4-b5 move, Black must be ready to respond in the center or on the kingside.

2

▹ **Smyslov**
▸ **Keres**
Haag 1948 (D36)

1.d4 d5 2.c4 e6 3.♘c3 ♘f6 4.♗g5 c6 5.e3 ♘bd7 6.cd5 ed5 7.♗d3 ♗e7 8.♘f3 0–0 9.♕c2 ♖e8 10.0–0 ♘f8

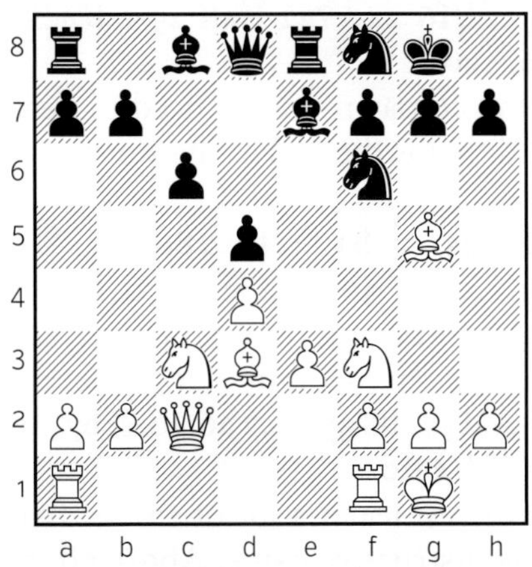

The classical position, one of the basic ones in positions with the Carlsbad structure. Black wants to unburden himself with the ...♘f6-e4 move, which did not work immediately: 10...♘e4? 11.♗e4 ♗g5 (11...de4 12.♘e4) 12.♗h7. Therefore Black needs to defend the h7-square first and only then carry out the relieving manoeuvre, one which White cannot prevent.

11.♖ab1

The beginning of the minority attack — White's intentions are not hidden.

11...♘g6

Black restricts the bishop on g5 by taking away his squares. We already know that White wants to swap it and that he is not upset by the plans of Black.

12.b4 ♗d6

Better is 12...a6!, with which Black gets rid of the weak pawn on the a-file for good.

13.b5 ♗d7?!

For some unknown reason Black did not proceed with the plan to play against the dark-squared-bishop — 13...h6. In truth White would display new motifs in the center: 14.♗f6 ♕f6 15.e4 (worse is 15.bc6 bc6 16.e4?! ♘f4!), where the play after 15...♘f4! 16.e5 ♕e6 is not yet decided due to Black's threats on the kingside, for example 17.ed6 ♕g4 18.♘e1 ♖e1.

14.bc6 ♗c6?

A mistake. Better is 14...bc6, because White would have fewer attacking plans.

15.♕b3±

White is clearly better: he is threatening the d5-pawn and is preparing a marvellous positional operation ...

15...♗e7 16.♗f6 ♗f6

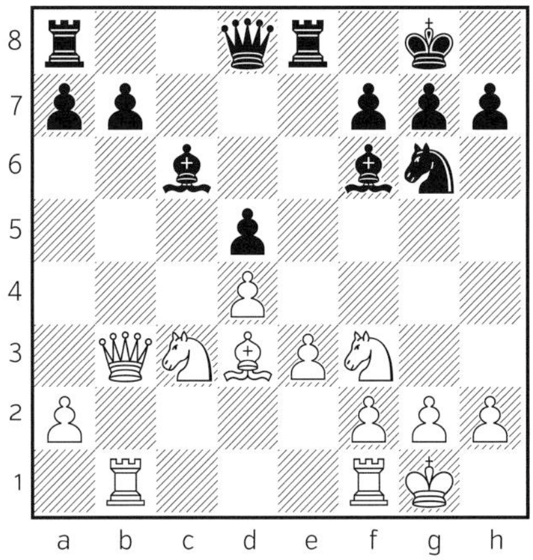

17.♗b5!

A very logical removal of Black's defensive piece. Black's dark-squared bishop is a bad piece for the endgame, but is taking care of Black's holes in the middlegame.

17...♕d6 18.♖fc1 h5

Black is searching for some counterplay. A possible — and perhaps even better — move is ...♘h4 (or even 18...♘e7) with the idea of ...g7-g5.

19.♘e2 h4 20.♗c6 bc6 21.♕a4 ♘e7

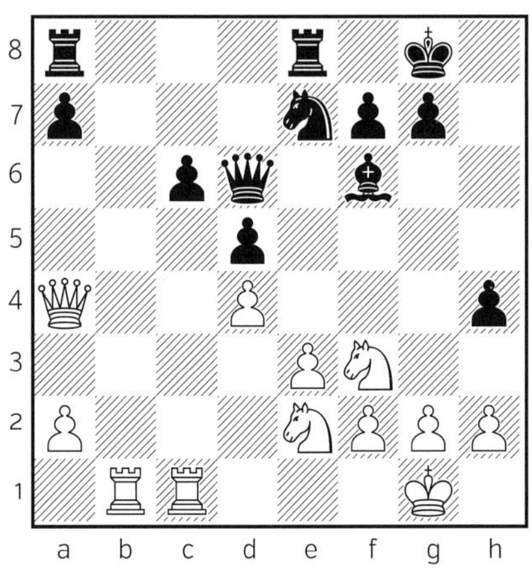

White has reached his ideal position with the queenside attack. Black's pieces are forced to stay put because they need to defend the pawns or the entrance squares in their hinterland. There is no counterplay to be seen and White's best move is 22.♕a6!, with which he paralyses the queenside even more. Smyslov, who was most-likely sure that the game is already won, continued even more ambitiously.

22.♖b7 a5 23.h3

After 23.♖cb1 ♖eb8 big exchanges occurs on the b-file — and as a rule, exchanges in 'compressed' positions are good for the defender.

23...♖eb8 24.♖cb1 ♖b7 25.♖b7 c5!

Keres is playing excellently and saves his biggest weaknesses.

26.♖b5!

Smyslov directs the attack towards Black's pawns on the queenside.

26...cd4 27.♘ed4 ♖c8

After 27...♕c7 28.♘b3 ♕c6 29.♘c5 White is better. If 29...♕c7, then 30.♕g4, and if 29...♗c3 30.♘h4 d4 31.♘f5! ♘f5 32.♖b8 White wins the queen.

28.♘b3 ♗c3

One of Black's pawns will fall and Keres preferred to give up the pawns on the kingside. White's strategy turned out to be too strong.

29.♕h4 ♖c4 30.g4! a4

30...♖a4 31.♘g5, with a strong attack.

31.♘bd4 ♗d4 32.♘d4 ♕e5

After 32...♘c6 33.♘c6 (33.♖b6? ♘d4!) 33...♖c6 34.♖a5.

33.♘f3 ♕d6 34.♖a5 ♖c8 35.♖a4 ♘g6 36.♕h5 ♕f6 37.♕f5 ♕c6 38.♖a7 ♖f8 39.♖d7 d4 40.♖d4 ♖a8 41.a4 1:0.

We already stated that Black cannot just sit and wait. For a while it was thought that the only suitable counterplay was the attack with the pawns on White's king. Let's see a game on this theme.

3

▷ **Bogoliubow**
▶ **Rubinstein**
San Remo 1930 [D65]

1.d4 d5 2.♘f3 ♘f6 3.c4 e6 4.♗g5 ♘bd7 5.e3 ♗e7 6.♘c3 0–0 7.♖c1 ♖e8 8.a3 a6 9.cd5

White decides on the transposition into the Carlsbad structure, which is doubtful. The trouble lies in the fact that he already played ♖c1 — with the minority attack the rook must be placed on b1 and for the execution of the plan e3-e4 it needs to be on the e1-square. The moves a3 and a6 are in Black's favour: Black's move is a part of his defensive system while White's move simply equates to a loss of tempo...

9...ed5 10.♗d3 c6 11.0–0 ♘f8 12.♕c2 ♘h5

Tournament practice later showed that there are two better move, which we already know: 12...♘e4 or 12...♘g6.

13.♗e7 ♕e7 14.b4 ♗e6 15.♕b2 ♖ad8 16.a4

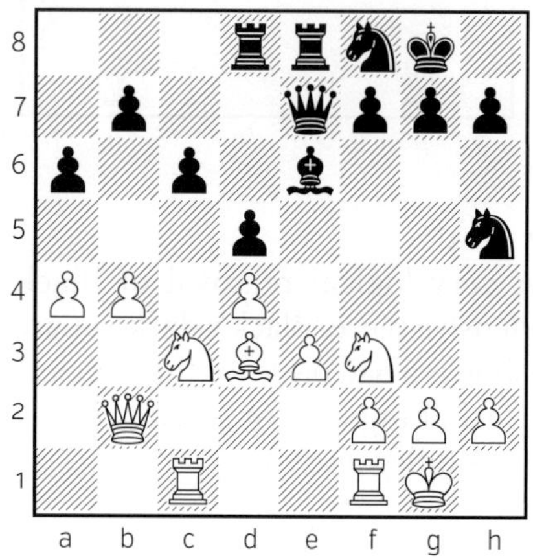

16...g5

Rubinstein shows his cards and there will be a huge battle across both wings.

17.b5 ab5 18.ab5 g4 19.♘d2 ♗c8 20.♖fe1 f5

The unpleasant e3-e4 was threatened.

21.♘a2!

The beginning of the siege of the weak c6-pawn. It appears as though we have seen this before–Black is not threatening anything and meanwhile White is already attacking.

21...♖d6 22.bc6 bc6 23.♕b6 ♗d7 24.♘b4 ♘f6

The c6-pawn is not directly threatened: 25.♘c6? ♕e6 26.♗b5 ♖c8 –+.

25.♖c2 ♘e4 26.♗e4

A typical capture for this kind of position: Black's bishop is helpless in comparison to the knights. Of course the capture opens the f-file, where Black will be searching for his counterplay and he will be combining the defence of his only weakness with a chance for counterplay.

26...fe4 27.♖ec1 ♕f6 28.♕b7 ♖e7 29.♕a8 ♖f7 30.♘f1 h5 31.♘g3 h4 32.♘h5 ♕g5

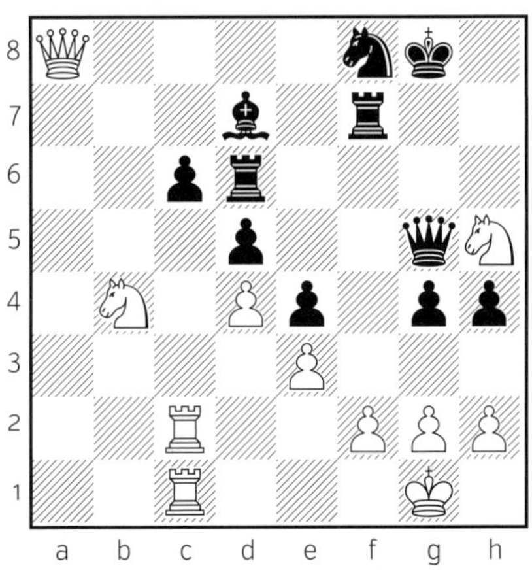

33.♕b8!

An excellent in-between move, which decides the game. Unnecessary complications would occur after 33.♘f4 ♖f4 etc.

33...♖h6 34.♘f4 g3 35.♘c6 gf2 36.♔f2 ♗c6 37.♖c6 ♖c6 38.♖c6

And White patiently won the endgame on the 77th move — **1:0**

After this game a new crisis appeared: many people believed that this meant the end of the Carlsbad structure. Only in the Russian chess school did players understand that Black needed to search for counterplay — the attack on the white king — with the help of the pieces.

4

▷ **Furman**
▸ **Klovans**
USSR 1964 [D36]

1.c4 ♘f6 2.d4 e6 3.♘c3 d5 4.cd5 ed5 5.♗g5 ♗e7 6.e3 0–0 7.♗d3 ♘bd7 8.♘f3 c6 9.♕c2 ♖e8 10.0–0 ♘f8 11.♖ab1 ♘g6 12.b4 ♘e4 13.♗e7 ♕e7

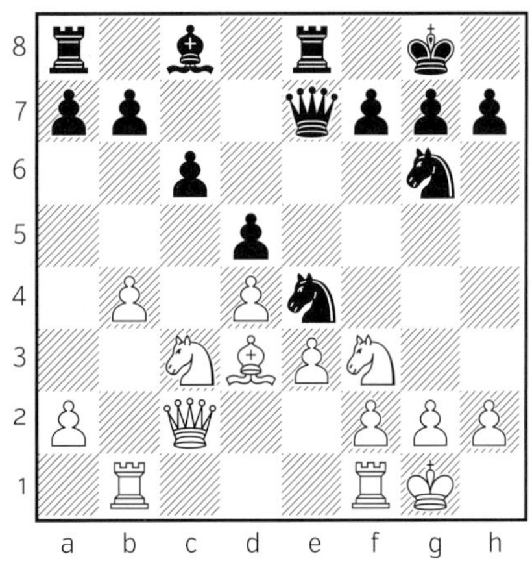

14.♖fe1

This move is not a part of a suitable plan. Correct and principled it would be 14.♗e4!. As practice has shown, Black has a hard time attacking in this structure.

14...♘c3 15.♕c3 ♗g4 16.♘d2 ♖ac8

Black decides on a preventive move, which temporarily stops White's b4-b5 action. The following moves will be clear: the pieces will head to more aggressive positions and White needs to seriously think about his defensive plan and defensive placement.

17.♖bc1 ♘h4 18.♗f1 ♕g5 19.♔h1 ♖e6

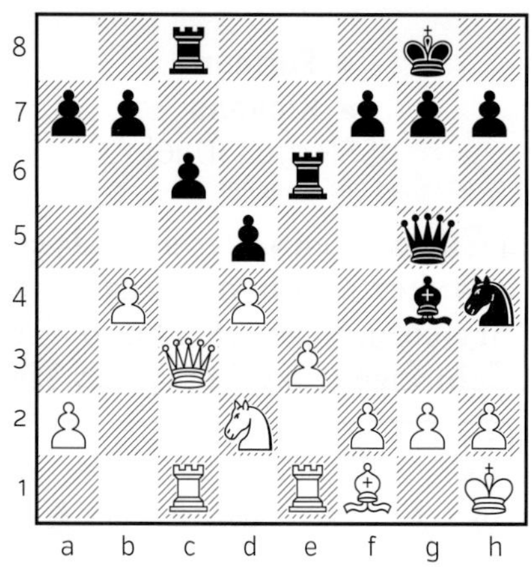

20.e4

White seeks a solution in the center.

20...de4 21.♘e4?

After this move White will have a hard time defending. After 21.♖e4 big exchanges would occur on the e-file and also a possible draw.

21...♕f4 22.♘c5 ♘f3!

From now on everything is forced.

23.g3 ♖h6 24.h3 ♖h3 25.♗h3 ♕h6 0:1

It is clear that White made some mistakes and thereby made it possible for Black to end things efficiently. Later on the theoreticians made some improvements in White's defence, practically everything is based on the capture of the knight with the ♗e4 move.

The Russian chess school kept on working. Later on they discovered that Black can also use positional motifs and not only tactical ones. The plans, with a quick exchange of the light-squared bishops and a later placement of the pawns in the triangle b5-c6-d5 -and with a jump into the e4-square — became modern. This plan completely upturned the flow of the play due to White being stopped on the queenside forever.

5

▹ **Polugajevsky**
▸ **Spassky**
USSR 1963 [D36]

1.c4 ♘f6 2.♘c3 e6 3.♘f3 d5 4.d4 ♗e7 5.cd5 ed5 6.♗g5 c6 7.♕c2

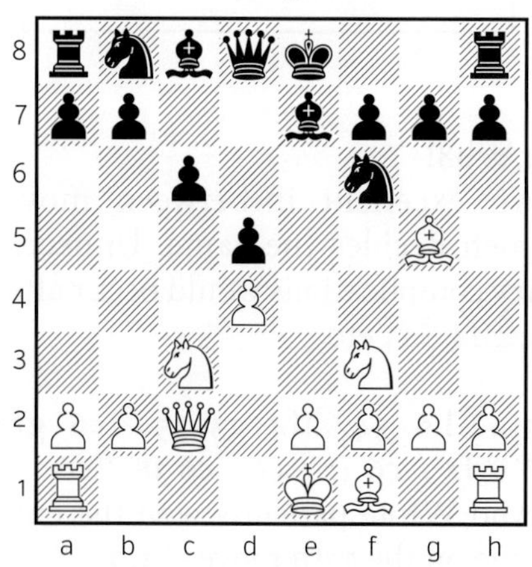

7...g6!

An instructive manoeuvre, with which Black solves the troubles faced by his light-squared bishop. In the positions where White manages to set up the ♕c2-♗g6 battery (and so prevents Black from playing ♗f5) Black helps himself with a long but effective plan: ...♘b8-d7-f8-e6-g7! and there is once again no defence against ♗f5!

8.e3 ♗f5 9.♗d3 ♗d3 10.♕d3 0–0 11.♗f6 ♗f6 12.b4

White is not feeling sorry for his bishops' departures and he is playing on the time gained — the b2-b4 move was performed without losing time with preparatory moves.

12...♘d7 13.0–0?

This move is inconsistent. When you say a, then you also need to say b ...

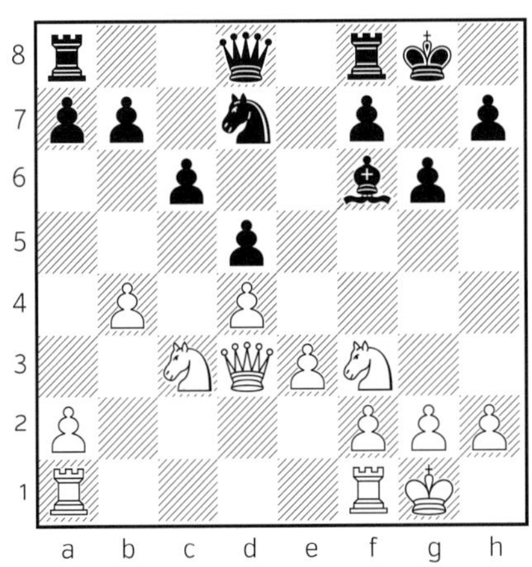

13...b5!

An exclamation mark for courage! Black has already succeeded in doing many things in this game: he swapped the "bad" light-squared bishop and he blocked White's b-pawn, which can now forget about advancing. If Black manages to put his knight on c4, then he will be able to think about taking over the initiative.

14.a4! a6 15.a5!

Polugajevsky also knew what we described previously and therefore he decided on a manoeuvre which does not allow Black's knight come to b6 or c4. .

15...♖e8 16.♘e2 ♗e7 17.♕b3 ♗d6 18.♘c1 g5

Black has only one weakness — the c6-paw — which cannot be attacked easily by White. Black has a free hand on the kingside and besides that the bishop on d6 is looking at the b4-square, where the passed pawn stands.

19.♘d3 g4 20.♘d2 ♖e6 21.♖fc1 ♕g5

Black will not easily land mate and it is hard to see how White can improve his position. They will both use all their forces and the most logical result was seen after a few more moves...

22.♖a2 ♖ae8 23.♖ac2 ♕h6 24.♘f1 ♗b8 25.♘c5 ♘c5 26.♖c5 ♖g6 27.♕c2 ♖ee6 28.g3 ♔g7 29.♕f5 draw.

Garry Kasparov confused things even more when he brought back to life an old and forgotten plan for the defence, one which he improved towards the end of the 20th century.

6

▷ **Portisch**
▶ **Kasparov**
Skelleftea 1989 [D36]

1.d4 d5 2.♘f3 ♘f6 3.c4 e6 4.cd5 ed5 5.♘c3 c6 6.♕c2 ♘a6

Kasparov is not interested (yet) in the exchange of the light-squared bishops due to being afraid of a draw. Therefore he first takes care of the knight — a manoeuvre which hides an interesting plan — and prevents the placement of the ♗d3-♕c2 battery due to the ...♘b4 move.

7.a3 ♘c7

An elastic square for the knight, from where it controls the b5 square and from where it can also quickly move to the kingside.

8.♗g5 g6

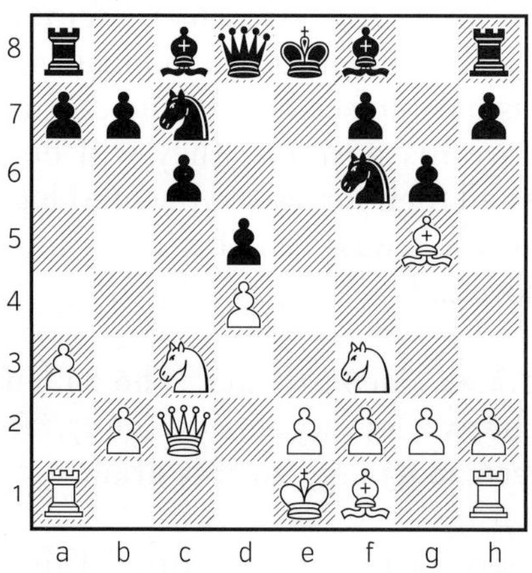

9.e3

9. e4 is a risky move, because Black controls the d5 square. If White continues with the thrust, he will be left in a bad endgame. For example: 9.e4 de4 10.♘e4 ♗g7 11.0–0–0 0–0 12.h4 ♗f5 13.♗f6 ♗f6 14.h5 ♖e8 15.♗d3 ♗g7! and White has no serious threats.

9...♗f5 10.♗d3

Theory recommends 10.♕b3 ♖b8, with approximately equal play. The swap of the light-squared bishop is good for Black.

10...♗d3 11.♕d3 ♗e7 12.0–0 0–0 13.b4 ♘e4!

The classic relieving manoeuvre. Black is offering the transitions to outcomes which favour him.

14.♗f4

The exchange on the e7-square is more logical because White cannot escape it in any event.

14...♘c3 15.♕c3 ♗d6! 16.♗d6 ♘b5! 17.♕b3 ♘d6

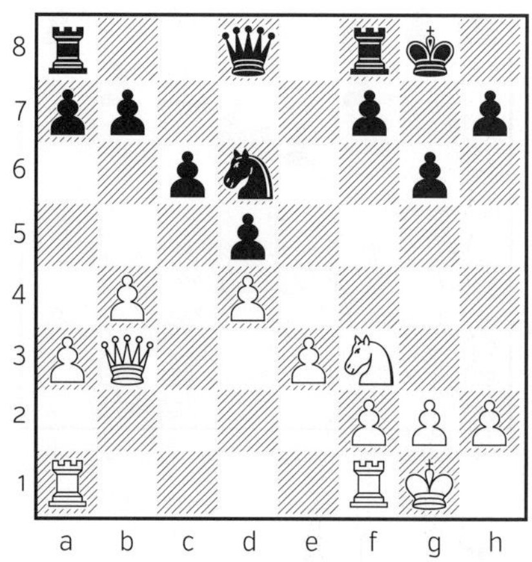

Black wanted this exact position! He exchanged all the pieces that he wanted to and the d6 knight dominates the board. White is left without an active plan: he can forget about the b4-b5 move and also the e3-e4 stroke in the center. He can nothing but wait., but Black will in the meantime improve the position of his pieces and start to advance his pawns on the kingside.

18.a4 a6 19.♘e5 ♖e8 20.♖fe1 ♕g5 21.h3 ♔g7 22.♕c2 ♖e6 23.♖ac1 ♖ae8 24.♕b1 ♕h5 25.♕b3 f6 26.♘d3 g5

Kasparov's technique is fantastic. White's knight can jump to c5, but the rook on e7 is able to deal with its threats. Portisch wants to somehow swap the knight, but there is no obvious way to do so.

27.♕d1 ♕g6 28.♕c2 ♖6e7 29.♖ed1 h5 30.♕b1 h4 31.♕c2 g4

Kasparov opens an attack on the king. White is faced with a sad choice: whether to allow the attack or to transpose to an endgame that is bad for him. He chose the second possibility.

32.♘f4 ♕c2 33.♖c2 g3!

The point of Black's 31st move: the game will be decided by the weak e3 pawn.

34.♖d3 ♔h6 35.♔f1 ♔g5 36.♘e2 ♘c4! 37.♖cc3 ♘b2!

The first achievement of Black's strategy is the a4 pawn.

38.♖d2 ♘a4 39.♖b3 ♘b6 40.♘g1 ♘c4 41.♘f3 ♔h5 42.♖dd3 a5! 43.ba5 ♖a8!

Black's technique is excellent. Now let us observe how he finished his work systematically.

44.♖d1 ♖a5 45.♖e1 b5 46.♖e2 ♖a1 47.♖e1 ♖ea7 48.fg3 ♖e1 49.♔e1 ♖a1 50.♔e2 hg3 51.♘e1 ♖a2 52.♔d1 ♖d2 53.♔c1 ♖e2 54.♔d1 ♖e3 55.♖e3 ♘e3 56.♔e2 ♘f5 57.♘c2 ♘h4 58.♘b4 ♘g2 59.♔f3 ♘h4 60.♔g3 ♘f5 61.♔f4 ♘d4 62.♔e3 ♘f5 0:1

Kasparov had yet another ace up his sleeve, but he never used it in the game. Magnus Carlsen, Kasparov's one-time student, is making sure that the variation will not be forgotten.

7

▷ **Van Wely**
▶ **Carlsen**
Wijk aan Zee 2010 [D36]

1.♘f3 ♘f6 2.c4 e6 3.♘c3 d5 4.d4 ♘bd7 5.cd5 ed5 6.♗g5 ♗e7 7.e3 c6 8.♕c2 0–0 9.♗d3 ♖e8 10.h3

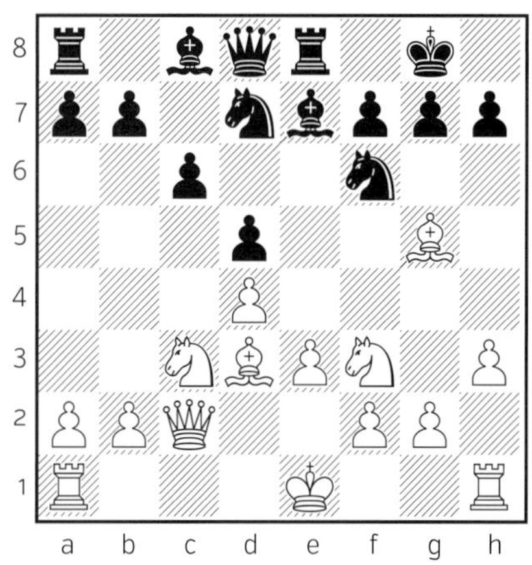

Similar positions have been known for decades. Black players automatically play: 10...♘f8 (with the idea 11...♘e4). Carlsen (Kasparov) did not hesitate:

10...♘e4!?

Unbelievable: every school boy knows that this does not work due to:

11.♗e4 de4

11...♗g5 12.♗h7! — for this reason Black players usually defend the h7-square.

12.♘e4

And White is a pawn up. But:

12...♕a5! 13.♔f1 ♗f8 14.♗f4?!

The Dutchman is confused. It would be better to avoid the pin on the b1-h7 diagonal, for example with the 14.♘c3 retreat.

14...♕f5!

Black's threats are becoming more and more real.

15.♘fd2 ♘b6 16.♖c1

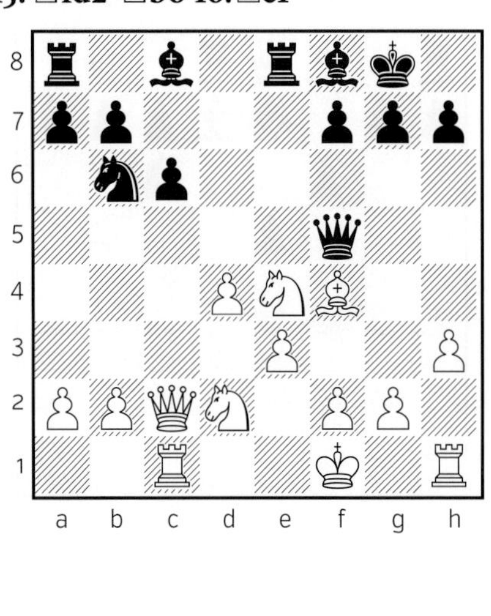

16...♘d5!

Black has more than enough compensation and is not scared of exchanges.

17.g4 ♕g6 18.♘d6 ♖d8 19.♕g6

A tough decision. The computer suggests a similar continuation for White, but with the queens still on the board: 19.♘c8 ♘f4 20.ef4 ♖d4! 21.f5 ♕b6 22.♘f3, with unclear play. The main game follows the same motif.

19...hg6 20.♘c8 ♘f4 21.ef4 ♖d4 22.♘b3 ♖b4 23.♔g2

After 23.♘a7 ♖a7 the a2 pawn is lost.

23...♖c8 24.♖hd1!

Van Wely is playing thoughtfully. In two moves he has managed to turn the position upside-down: instead of being a pawn up he transpose into a position a pawn down but with compensation.

24...♖f4 25.♖d7 ♖b4 26.♖c2 ♖e8 27.♖cd2 ♗e7

The bishop heads to the more active f6-square.

28.♖c7 ♗f6 29.♖dd7 b6 30.♖a7 g5 31.♖d2

Better would be 31.♖f7, though Black defends the seventh rank well.

31...c5 32.♖a6 c4 33.♘d4 ♗d4 34.♖d4 ♖b2

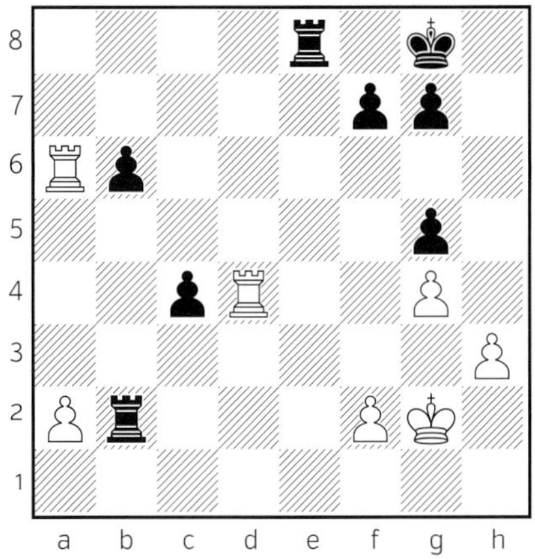

35.♖d7?

This loses immediately. After 35.♖c4! ♖ee2 36.♔g3 ♖f2 37.♖b6! it is true that Black is better: 37...♖g2 38.♔f3 ♖bf2 39.♔e4 ♖f4 40.♔d5 ♖d2 41.♔c5 ♖a2, but the position looks like a draw! But now the pawn escapes:

35...c3 36.♖aa7 ♖f8 37.♖dc7 c2 38.♔g3 ♖d8 39.♖f7 ♖d3 40.♔g2 c1♕ 0:1

The minority attack was always White's secret weapon in the Carlsbad structure. Even nowadays it is believed to be a strong weapon, though Black players have found some suitable possibilities for a counterplay.

THE ADVANCE IN THE CENTER

Practice has shown that White has good chances to achieve the advantage with the e3-e4 plan. Especially effective is the plan that was devised by Mikhail Botvinnik: a normal development of the pieces, only the knight is placed on e2 instead on f3. And with this he already announces that his plan will include the e3-e4 move, but that does not make Black's job any easier. The rook goes to e1, the pawn to f3, the knight — if needed — on g3 and the e3-e4 stroke is prepared. Black needs to be well prepared and usually after the exchange on e4 he starts to put pressure on the center, specifically on the new and unstable White's e4-d4 pawn pair.

Tigran Petrosian was a deep thinker who discovered Black can prevent White's placement with a small change in the order of the moves. Namely, after

1.d4 d5 2.c4 e6 3.♘c3 ♗e7!

White has nothing wiser than the ♘f3 move...

Later on some positions were discovered where the e3-e4 move can be played without preparations. After the exchange he places a piece on e4 (a knight, a bishop or even a rook) and then makes threats with it on both sides of the board.

In our introduction we got to know the game Botvinnik : Capablanca, where Black did not take White's threats seriously and made a mistake when he took a pawn on the other side of the board. Now let us see yet another game of Botvinnik's, where he systematically prepares the e3-e4 move and Black did not exactly know how to defend against the dangers aimed at his king...

1

▷ **Botvinnik**
► **Keres**
USSR 1952 [D36]

1.d4 ♘f6 2.c4 e6 3.♘c3 d5 4.cd5 ed5 5.♗g5 ♗e7 6.e3 0–0 7.♗d3 ♘bd7 8.♕c2 ♖e8 9.♘ge2 ♘f8 10.0–0 c6

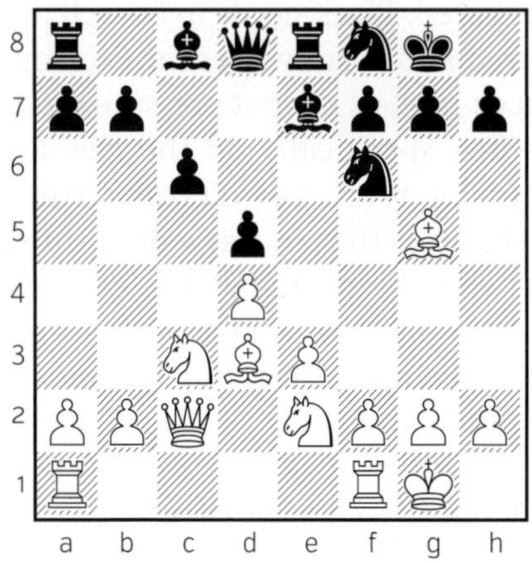

We have a classic position in front of us, one where Botvinnik unexpectedly decided upon a game of hide and seek: with the next move he announced the minority attack.

11.♖ab1!? ♗d6?!

Black is threatening ...♗h2 and ...♘g4. White of course saw this and he quickly underlined the weaknesses of Black's bishop on d6. Theory nowadays recommends the move 11...♘h5 or 11...♘e4, in both cases with approximately equal play.

12.♔h1 ♘g6 13.f3!

White is already threatening the e3-e4 push and Black's pieces will face a threat (the fork e4-e5 looms). Therefore Keres was forced to admit his mistake and return with his bishop.

13...♗e7 14.♖be1!

White is also prepared to give up a tempo to place his rook on its natural spot. Black commonly fights against the e3-e4 plan with the ...c6-c5 stroke, which however does not work in our position: 14...c5? 15.dc5 ♗c5 16.♗f6 gf6 17.♘d4. The pawn on e3 is weak, but there is no clear way for Black to attack it additionally. Therefore Black's kingside is fatally and irreparably damaged.

14...♘d7 15.♗e7 ♖e7 16.♘g3 ♘f6 17.♕f2!

The position plays itself. White places his pieces on suitable squares and prepares the advance in the center. Of course the defence of the d4-square must be strengthened first. The queen on f2 is ideally placed: it defends the d4 pawn and at the same time prepares itself for the opening of the f-file (after e4-de4-fe4), after which it will as quickly as possible start to put pressure on the f7-square.

17...♗e6 18.♘f5 ♗f5?!

A tough, and wrong, choice. Without the light-squared bishop Black's defence will collapse. Better was 18...♖d7 with a passive, but still strong defence.

19.♗f5 ♕b6

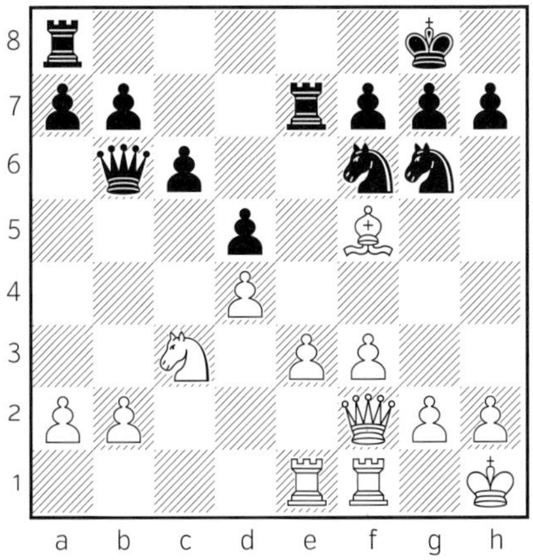

20.e4!

A systematic move, after which White takes over the initiative.

20...de4

If Black waits White will play e4-e5, return his bishop to d3 and advance the f pawn to f5, with strong pressure.

21.fe4 ♖d8 22.e5 ♘d5 23.♘e4 ♘f8 24.♘d6

White's pressure on the f-file will be decisive and the f7-square is especially vulnerable.

24...♕c7 25.♗e4 ♘e6

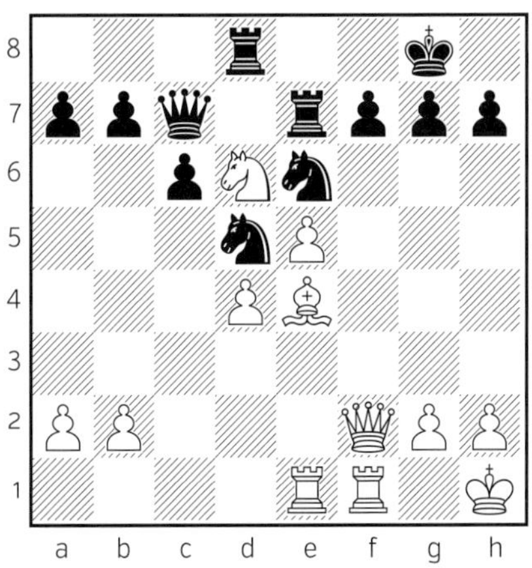

26.♕h4!

The final precise move, with which White will provoke new weaknesses in front of Black's king. Botvinnik finished the game with energetic and technical play.

26...g6 27.♗d5 cd5 28.♖c1 ♕d7 29.♖c3 ♖f8 30.♘f5! ♖fe8 31.♘h6!

The knight will play a big part in the final mating attack and is definitely worth more than a rook.

31...♔f8 32.♕f6 ♘g7 33.♖cf3 ♖c8 34.♘f7 ♖e6 35.♕g5 ♘f5 36.♘h6 ♕g7 37.g4 1:0

Let us have a look at yet another game on this theme, and what happens if Black just waits.

2

▷ **Karpov**
▶ **Kasparov**
London/Leningrad 1986 [D31]

1.d4 d5 2.c4 e6 3.♘c3 ♗e7

With the chosen move-order Black has achieved something: White needs to somehow decide at this moment whether he will chose the familiar systems with ♘f3 (and give up the dangerous placement ♗d3-♕c2-♘ge2) or if he will develop his bishop on the seemingly more modest f4-square.

4.cd5 ed5 5.♗f4

After ♗f4 White gives up the standard pressure on the d5 square and the play is now completely fresh. It is clear that White will be playing on the kingside and Black will search for his opportunities on the queenside or in the center.

5...c6 6.♕c2 g6

We already know this idea: Black wants to swap the dark-squared bishops with the ♗f5 move. The second possibility is the provocative 6...♗g4, where Black surrenders the space advantage in the center to White: 7.f3 ♗h5 8.e4 ♗g6 9.♗d3 ♘f6, but thereby places huge pressure on White's center with his well-developed pieces.

7.e3 ♗f5

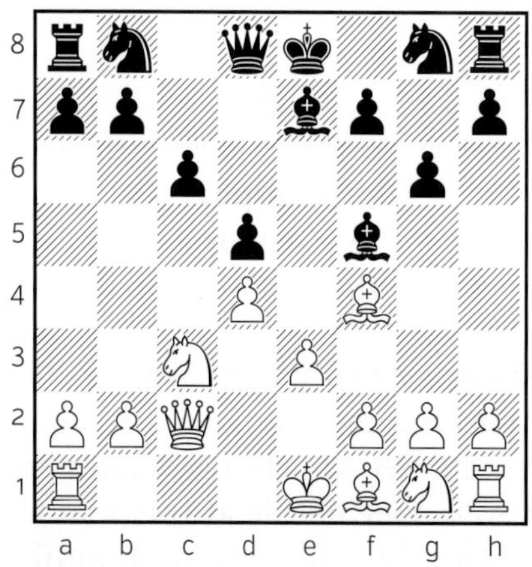

8.♕d2!

A loss of tempo, but it is not detrimental due to the closed position. Black's f5 bishop will be the target of White's pawns (e4 or g4), with which White will easily win back his lost tempo. An additional problem for Black is hidden in the g6 pawn, which takes away a good square for the possible withdrawal of the bishop.

8...♘d7

Black is pressed for space and he needs to think deeply about where he will develop his pieces. White's f3 or g4 (or e4) action is unstoppable and Black needs to find suitable squares for his pieces.

9.f3 ♘b6

Freeing the d7-square for the other knight.

10.e4 ♗e6 11.e5!

White makes it even more difficult for Black to finish his development. The e5 pawn is very unpleasant, because it is compressing Black. How can Kasparov finish his development?

11...h5

One of the possibilities, but not the best one. The old rule states that we need to move as few pawns as possible on the side where we are weaker and where the opponent is planning his actions. Black could strike in the center — 11...f5!? Or he could think about developing his knight to e7 (after the withdrawal of the bishop from e7 to d8 once the queen moves). But absolutely not 11...♘c4? 12.♗c4 dc4 13.♘e4 and White penetrates through one of the weak Black's squares (d6 or f6).

12.♗d3 ♕d7 13.b3!

Karpov is a master of prophylactic play — this move takes away the possibility for Black to jump into c4.

13...♗h4? 14.g3 ♗e7

The reason for this manoeuvre is not completely clear. Kasparov passes the move to White but the g2-g3 move is not weak at all.

15.♔f2 ♗f5

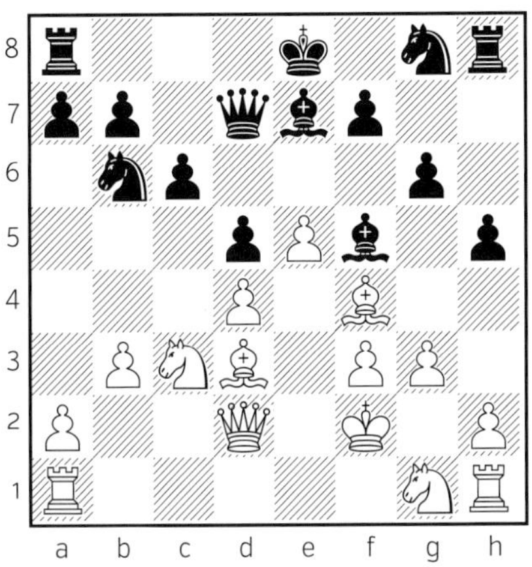

16.♗f1!

An excellent move! The player with the space advantage should not exchange pieces, because the opponent would then be able to defend more easily—a classic chess rule. White's pawns will advance and nothing will stop them (h3 and g4), they will push Black's bishop back and later White's light-squared bishop will return to d3 (or somewhere else) victoriously.

16...♔f8 17.♔g2 a5 18.a3?!

A completely unnecessary jump to the other wing, because White needs to play on the kingside, where he is a lot better. The plan is clear and simple: h3 and g4.

18...♕d8 19.♘h3!

Threatening the unpleasant ♘g5 so Black has no choice but to take.

19...♗h3 20.♔h3 ♔g7 21.♔g2 ♘d7!

Kasparov immediately senses his opportunity: the knight goes to e6, from where it will attack the d4 and the f4 squares and at the same time prepare the ...c6-c5 thrust.

22.♗d3 ♘f8 23.♗e3 ♘e6 24.♘e2 ♘h6

Even though Black is trying really hard, his prospects are not good. There is no counterplay in sight—his only chance is hidden in the ...c5 shove. White can in the meantime prepare the advance with his pawns, pushing Black's pieces even deeper into defence and then open the play and take care of the Black monarch.

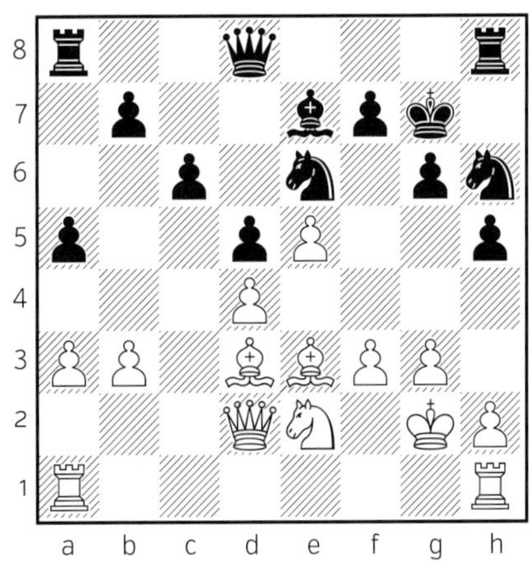

25.b4?!

White's tendency towards preventing Black's ...c6-c5 break can be understood, but the pawn movement on the wing where he is weaker can only be useful for Black.

25...♕b6 26.b5?

A serious mistake. After 26.♖ab1 Black would gain the a-file (after the exchange on b4), but at least for now he cannot do so. For example: 26.♖ab1 ab4 27.ab4 ♖a3 28.♖hc1, with the preparation of the b4-b5 move and delaying the counter attack ...c6-c5. But like this...

26...c5!

Black succeeds and his counterplay arrives! White was the master of his fate — only a few moves ago the pawns were still on a3 and b3 and Black could only dream about such counterplay. But this is a result of not following basic principles and playing on the wing where we have no advantage.

27.♘c3 cd4 28.♗h6 ♖h6 29.♘d5 ♕d8 30.♗e4 h4 31.♖hf1?!

White needs to think about equalizing and that was offered by the 31.♖hc1 move. But now Black has the initiative.

31...hg3 32.hg3 ♖c8 33.♖h1 ♖h1?!

A waste of time, and correct is 33...♗g5 34.f4 ♖c5! when Black has a strong initiative. The game ended in a draw.

34.♖h1 ♗g5 35.f4 ♖c5 36.fg5 ♖d5 37.♗d5 ♕d5 38.♔h2 ♕e5 39.♖f1 ♕b5 40.♕f2 ♘g5 41.♕d4 draw.

After long years of study, Black players came up with a suitable method as to how we are supposed to face the dangers in the center, ideas which are connected with the e4 and d4 pawn pair.

3

▹ **Kasparov**
▸ **Barua**
Internet 2000 [D36]

1.d4 d5 2.c4 e6 3.♘c3 ♘f6 4.cd5 ed5 5.♗g5 c6 6.♕c2 ♗e7 7.e3 ♘bd7 8.♗d3 0–0 9.♘ge2 ♖e8 10.0–0 ♘f8 11.f3 ♘g6 12.♖ad1 h6

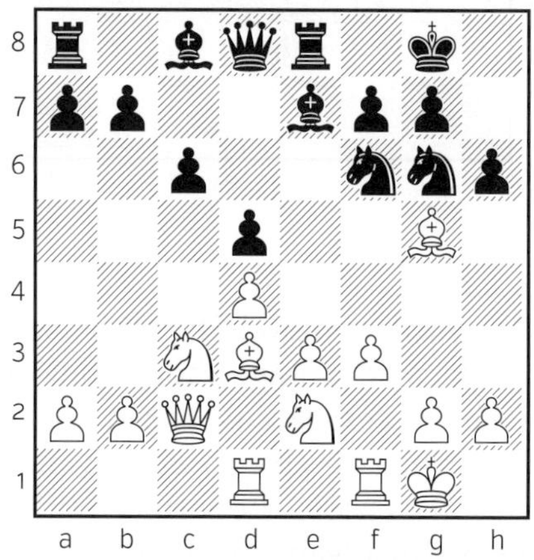

Black is paying no attention to White's plans in our game. Kasparov was Botvinnik's student and he of course taught him his system well. The Indian's attempt was new at the time, until then 12...♗e6 was played, with great success, for example: 13.♔h1 (better would be 13.♘g3! ♖c8 14.♗f5 ♗f5 15.♘f5 h6 16.♗f6 ♗f6 17.e4, where White's advantage is also only symbolic) 13...♖c8 14.e4 (premature!) 14...de4 15.fe4 ♘g4! 16.♗c1 c5! and Black attacked White's central pawns at the right moment. No good is 17.d5, due to 17...♗d7 and 18...♗d6, with the idea ♕h4. In the game Gulko : Sturua, Elista 1998, there followed 17.♗b5 ♕c7 18.♘f4 cd4 19.♗e8 dc3 20.♗b5 cb2 21.♕b2 ♘f4 22.♗f4 ♕c2 23.♕c2 ♖c2 24.♖d2 ♖d2 25.♗d2 ♗c5, with the advantage for Black. Popular, but worse, is 12...♘h5 13.♗e7 ♕e7 14.e4 de4 15.fe4 ♗e6 16.e5 c5 17.d5 ♗g4 18.e6→ as in the game Yakovitsch : Ahlander, Stockholm 1999.

13.♗f6

The complications after13.♗h6 gh6 14.♗g6 fg6 15.♕g6 ♔h8 16.♘f4 ♗f8 17.e4 are completely unnecessary as now the position is unclear.

13...♗f6 14.♗g6 fg6 15.e4 g5 16.e5

White has no advantage after 16.a4 ♗e6 17.a5 ♗e7 18.f4 gf4 19.♘f4 ♗g5.

16...♗e7 17.f4 gf4 18.♘f4 ♖f8 19.♘g6 ♖f1 20.♖f1 ♗e6 21.♘e2

A rare case where in an open position the pair of knights is better than a pair of bishops.

21...♕d7 22.h4 ♖e8 23.♘g3 ♗f7?!

Better is 23...♗d8!?, because Black will have a hard time without his dark-squared bishop — the d6 square is too weak. At the same time the bishop would be threatening to transfer to the b6-square with an attack on the d4 pawn, the only weak point in White's camp.

24.♘e7 ♖e7 25.♘f5± ♖e6 26.♘d6

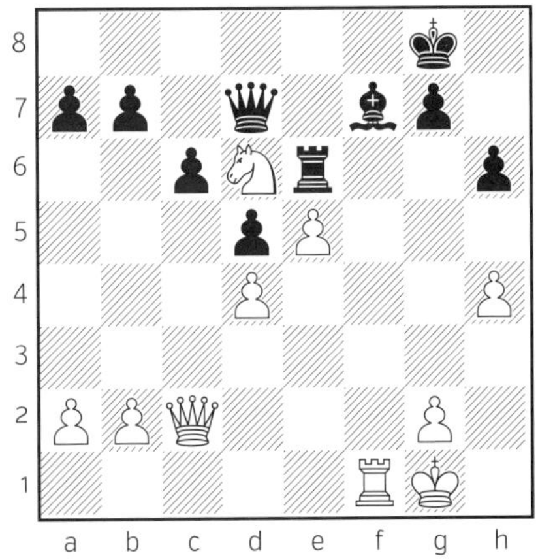

The rest of the game is like the play between a cat and a mouse — the knight on d6 will paralyze Black, and the light-squared bishop is completely helpless against it.

26...♗g6 27.♕c3 ♖d6

Black can no longer tolerate the knight's dominance, but even an exchange sacrifice cannot save him. The rest is a purely technical part of the game:

28.ed6 ♕d6 29.♕a3 ♕b8 30.♕e7 ♕g3 31.♖f3

White makes his work harder — after 31.♖f8 ♔h7 32.♕d8!+- ♗e4 33.♖h8 ♔g6 34.♕e8 ♔f5 35.♕f7 ♔g4 36.♕g7 his path to victory would be a lot quicker.

31...♕g4 32.♕f8 ♔h7 33.♕f4 ♕d7 34.♖g3 ♗e4 35.♕e5 ♕f7 36.h5 ♕d7 37.b4 a6 38.a4 ♔g8 39.a5 ♔h7 40.♔f2 ♔g8 41.♕b8 ♔h7 42.♕f8 ♗c2 43.♕f4 ♗e4 44.♕e5 ♔g8 45.♔e3 ♔h7 46.♔e2 ♔g8 47.♕b8 ♔h7 48.♕f8 ♗c2 49.♔d2 ♗e4 50.♔c1 ♕c7 51.♖g4 ♕d7 52.♖f4 ♗g2 53.♕f5 ♕f5 54.♖f5 ♔g8 55.♔d2 ♗h3

56.♖f4 ♗e6 57.♔e3 ♗f7 58.♖f5 ♔f8 59.♖e5 ♗e8 60.♔f4 ♗f7 61.♔g4 ♗e8 62.♔g3 ♗f7 63.♔f4 ♗e8 64.♔f5 ♗h5 65.♔e6 ♗g6 66.♖e3 ♗c2 67.♖f3 ♔g8 68.b5 cb5 69.♔d5 b4 70.♔c4 b3 71.♔c3 g5 72.d5 g4 73.♖f4 h5 74.d6 1:0

In the Carlsbad structure there also exist plans where White plays the e4 move without the support of the f3 pawn. In these cases he wants to recapture on e4 with a piece (after e4-de4) and he to play for the initiative with the pieces in the center, or he wants to attack the opponent's king very quickly.

4

▹ **Marshall**
▸ **Rubinstein**
Moscow 1925 [D36]

1.d4 d5 2.c4 e6 3.♘c3 ♘f6 4.♗g5 ♘bd7 5.e3 ♗e7 6.♘f3 0–0 7.cd5 ed5 8.♗d3 ♖e8 9.0–0 c6 10.♕c2 ♘f8

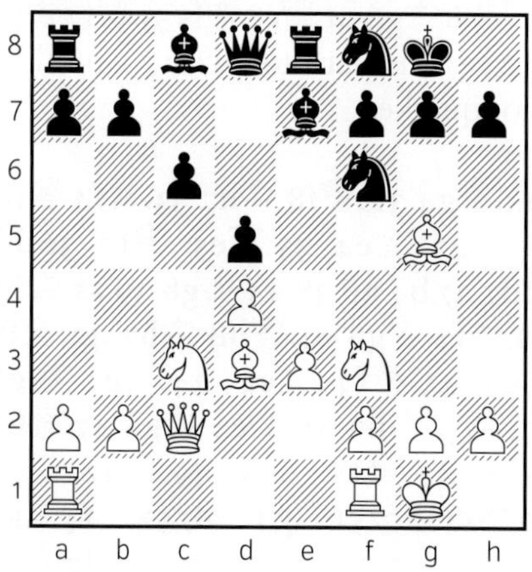

11.♖ae1

White shows his cards immediately — he wants to play the e3-e4 move. For now Black is defending the e4 square very well and we can't see how White can succeed.

11...♘e4 12.♗e7 ♕e7 13.♗e4 de4 14.♘d2

White's plan is now becoming clear: to provoke the ...f7-f5 move, because 14...♗f5 is not playable due to 15.f3. White will, after ...f7-f5, open the center and hope for the advantage thanks to the initiative.

14...f5 15.f3! ef3 16.♘f3 ♗e6 17.e4! fe4 18.♖e4 ♖ad8

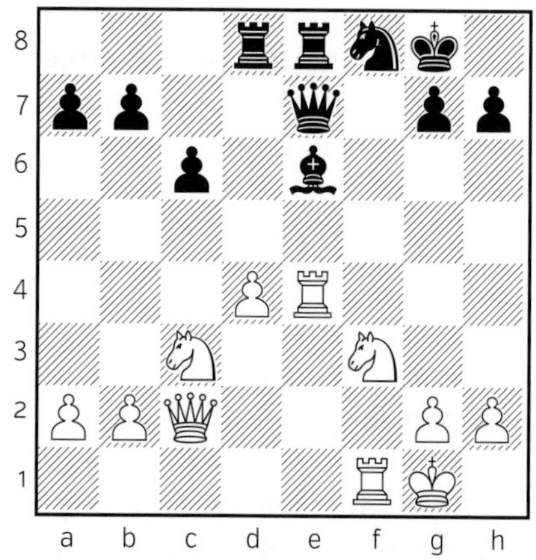

A critical position, which can be seen in many games.

Let us see one example of the same scene, only half a century later:

19.♖fe1 h6 20.♖e5 ♕f7 21.♕e4 ♖d6 22.♕e3 ♘d7 23.♖a5 ♘f6 24.♕f4 ♖ed8 25.♖a7 ♕d7 26.♘a4 ♘d5 27.♕g3 ♕c7 28.♘c5 ♗c8 29.♘e5 ♖f6 30.♘e4 ♖f4 31.♘g6 ♕b6 32.♘f4 ♕a7 33.♘d5?

From this moment on White's play was fantastic and he almost achieved a decisive advantage due to the constant maintenance of the initiative, which would be retained after 33.♘h5! ♕d4 34.♔h1 ♔h8 35.♘ef6 g5 36.♘d5.) 33...♕d4 34.♕e3 draw, Tal : Vaganian, Moscow 1975.

19.♖e5 h6 20.♘e4 ♕b4?

It is correct to play 20...♕c7 and ...♗e6-d5. Marshall quickly finished the game in his own typical 'gunman' style.

21.a3! ♕c4 22.♕f2 ♗f7

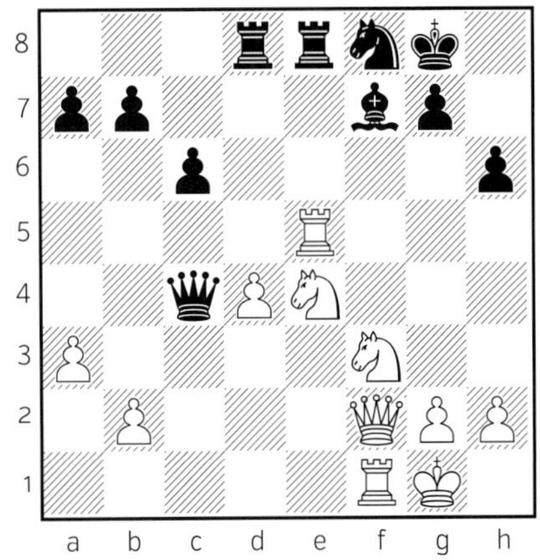

23.b3! ♕b3 24.♘fd2 ♕a2 25.♘c3 1:0

THE DYNAMIC CENTER

Positions with as yet undetermined pawn structures in the center are more common in chess. We can talk about these positions when the central pawns are not in direct contact. They contain a lot of traps and demand a lot of knowledge, because these positions can transform into all the previously described structures, so it is important to know them well first — and only after that do we need to start learning about the dynamic center. But of course these kinds of positions, with this type of center, are hard to play: there are no clear plans and we always need to be careful and constantly evaluate the possible consequences of the transitions.

The active side will try to maintain his dominance of the center and the attacker will always be threatening with a transition into whichever central pawn structure is good for him. And he will achieve more easily if he advances the pawns as far as possible, at least across the center of the board (with White's pawns at least to the fifth rank and to the fourth rank with Black's pawns). He can start to perform actions on the wing only after the outcome has been clarified in the center, but before that one needs to be careful about the attack with the pawns on the wing. You need to keep in mind the possibility of a counterattack in the center!

The defender needs to delay the outcome in the center for as long as possible and to support the pawn tension in the center. This will be the easiest way for him to defend himself against attacks: but if it occurs, almost certainly a chance for counterattack will appear. If the defender starts to sense the attacker's wing action, then he needs to prepare the counterattack in the center immediately: success is almost assured!

The most appropriate openings for studying the dynamic center are the Sicilian openings: we come across a lot of positions like that in modern chess, but every single one of them has its traps. Therefore we will only get to know a few of them and we will try to give you some basic advice.

ACTIVE PLAY IN THE CENTER: THE ADVANCE OF THE PAWNS!

1

▹ **Tal**
▸ **Olafsson**
Bled 1961 [B82]

1.e4 c5 2.♘f3 ♘c6 3.d4 cd4 4.♘d4 e6 5.♘c3 ♕c7 6.♗e3 a6 7.a3?! ♘f6 8.f4 d6

The acceptance of the pawn sacrifice by 8...♘d4 9.♗d4! ♕f4 10.g3 ♕c7 11.e5 would be risky. Olafsson instead chooses a transposition to some kind of Scheveningen version of the Sicilian Defence, where White has saved a move and already developed his bishop to the active d3 square (usually the bishop firstly goes to e2).

9.♕f3 ♗e7 10.♗d3 0–0 11.0–0 ♗d7?!

A novelty, but still a worse move than the -until that time known — 11...♘d4!? 12.♗d4 e5 13.♗e3 (13.fe5 de5 14.♕g3 ♗c5!=) 13...ef4 14.♗f4 (14.♕f4! — Boleslavsky) 14...♗e6=.

12.♖ae1 b5 13.♕g3 ♔h8 14.♘c6 ♗c6

White has completed his centralization of the pieces and decides to define the position of his pawns in the center.

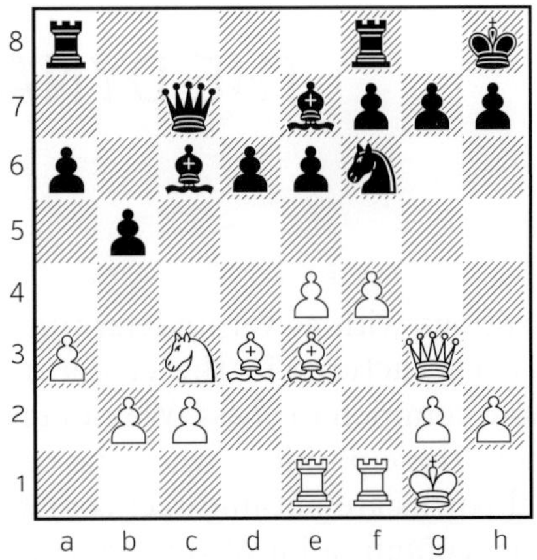

15.e5! ♘g8

Tal suggested in his comments the move 15...♘e8!?, where White is better after 16.♕h3 g6 17.f5 ef5 18.♖f5 ♗d7 19.♖ef1. Also the capture 15...de5 is not advisable: 16.fe5 ♘h5 17.♕h3 ♕e5 18.♔h1± or 18.g4!? g6 19.gh5 gh5 20.♔f2±.

16.♕h3 ♘h6 17.f5!

According to his plans, but in Tal's style — a little impatiently! After 17.♔h1 or 17.♗d4 White's advantage would be clearer.

17...♘f5 18.♖f5 ef5 19.♗f5 g6 20.♗d4 ♔g8?

Olafsson played this move without thinking. The real challenge for the attacker, the pirate from Riga, would be the move 20...♕d8!

After 21.ed6! Tal saw that it would be bad to play 21.♕h6? de5 22.♗e5 ♗f6 23.♖e3 ♖g8! and also 21.e6? ♗f6 22.♕h4 fe6 23.♖e6 ♗e5!–+ 24.♗e5 de5 25.♕d8 ♖ad8, but he recommended 21.♗e4! and continued the analysis: 21...♗e4 (21...♖c8 22.♖f1

♗e4 23.e6 ♔g8 24.♕h6 f6 25.♖f4! g5 (25...♕c7 26.♖e4 and 27.♘d5!) 26.♘e4! or 21...d5 22.♗d3) 22.♘e4 de4 23.♗e5 f6 24.♘g5 h5 25.♘e6 and 26.♕e3!.

Even more interesting are the variations after 21.ed6!? ♗f6 22.♕h4 ♔g7 (22...♗d4 23.♕d4 ♔g8 (23... f6 24.♖e7!) 24.♗e4 ♖e8 25.♖d1±) 23.♗d7!! (with the threat ♖e7!) 23... ♗d7 24.♘d5 ♗d4 25.♕d4 ♔h6 (25... f6 26.♖e7 ♔g8 27.♕h4 ♖f7 28.♘f6+-) 26.♖e4 f6 27.♖e7, but the variation was turned upside down by Fritz, with the move 26...g5!−+

21.e6 ♗g5

Let's see the final attack by Tal and the transition into the won endgame: an elegant solution, with which many Sicilian battles end...

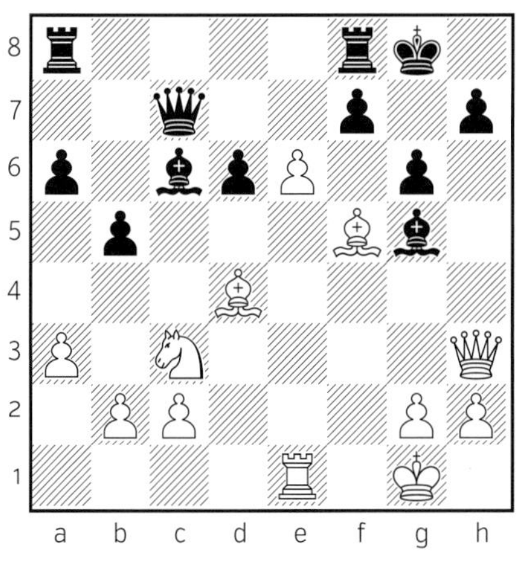

22.ef7! ♖f7 23.♗g6! ♖g7 24.♕e6 ♔h8 25.♗e8! h6 26.♗c6 ♕c6 27.♘e4 ♖e8 28.♕g6 ♖ee7 29.h4 ♕d5 30.♗g7 ♖g7 31.♕d6 ♕d6 32.♘d6 ♗h4 33.♖e8 ♖g8 34.♘f7 ♔g7 35.♖g8 ♔g8 36.♘h6 ♔h7 37.♘f5 ♗g5 38.b3 1:0.

There is no room for attacks on the wing in positions with a dynamic center. Mikhail Botvinnik showed this in his next classic game.

2

▷ **Alekhine**
▶ **Botvinnik**
Nottingham 1936 [B72]

1.e4 c5 2.♘f3 d6 3.d4 cd4 4.♘d4 ♘f6 5.♘c3 g6 6.♗e2 ♗g7 7.♗e3 ♘c6 8.♘b3 ♗e6 9.f4 0-0

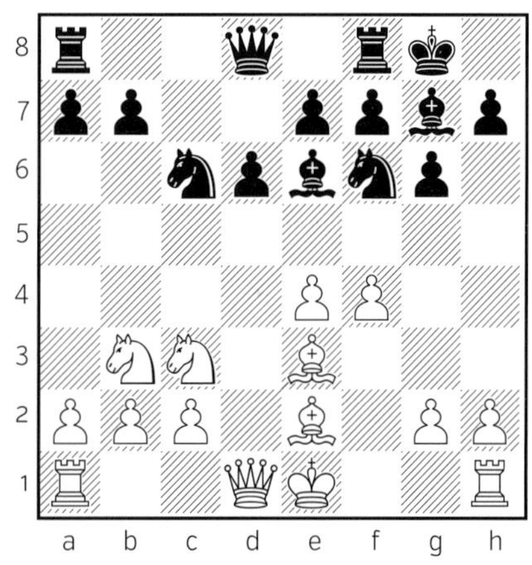

A famous position in chess history! Alexander Alekhine, who lost his World Champion title a year previously, wanted to prove in this tournament that he was still the best. Before the game, he was sure that he would defeat the young Russian and the next move shows that he wanted to blow him off the board:

10.g4 d5!

Mikhail Botvinnik is a chess player with a classical education, which teaches you the basic and strong rules: **against a quick action on the wing, we need to strike in the center**! Every delay will only bring trouble:

10...♘a5 11.g5 ♘d7 12.♗d4.

11.f5

Or 11.e5 d4 12.♘d4 ♘d4 13.♗d4 ♘g4.

11...♗c8 12.ed5

A little better would be 12.fg6 hg6 13.ed5 ♘b4 14.♗f3.

12...♘b4 13.d6 ♕d6 14.♗c5 ♕f4! 15.♖f1 ♕h2 16.♗b4 ♘g4

The next sacrifice, which brought Black a draw. No good was 16...♕g3 17.♖f2 ♘g4 18.♘e4!

17.♗g4 ♕g3 18.♖f2 ♕g1 19.♖f1 ♕g3 20.♖f2 ♕g1 draw

Let us put aside the complicated Sicilian dynamic structures and let us get to know the so called "Hedgehog structure". The structure got its name after the typical placement of Black's pawns — in a line on a6, b6, d6 and e6 these pawns look like a hedgehog and they are practically untouchable. The pawns are placed along the sixth rank and Black's pieces are wait behind them, but that does not mean that Black is performing his operations in a completely restricted area (on the last three ranks). He is intentionally leaving the space advantage to White: and although White cannot place his pieces and pawns on the fifth rank (it is controlled by Black's quills), there are still four ranks left for him on his side of the board.

White usually places his pawns in the center, at least on e4 and c4 (White's d4 pawn and Black's c5 pawn leave the board quickly) and he has, at least, a theoretical advantage on this part of the board. But Black concentrates on the center and he waits for the perfect moment to make a strike on the wing (...b6-b5) and to attack the c4 pawn (if the c4 pawn is out of the picture, White's pressure in the center will be weaker). But when the right moment comes, Black attacks right in the center: the ...d6-d5 move, if played at the right time, as a rules solves all his problems and often leaves him with an advantage. The freed pieces, which were sitting behind the quills, double their power.

In these positions White usually manoeuvres and strengthens the pressure on the weak Black pawns on b6 — and especially on d6. He must at all times be prepared for the strikes of Black and he himself want to play the f4-f5 move, hoping to force Black to take on f5, or to play ...e6-e5. After the movement of the e pawn he gains control over the d5-square, where he will later place a piece (usually the knight) and control the board with it.

The second plan is active play on the queenside, something similar to that which the Indian champion Viswanathan Anand achieved to in the following game.

3

▷ **Anand**
▸ **Illescas Cordoba**
Linares 1992 [B44]

1.e4 c5 2.♘f3 e6 3.d4 cd4 4.♘d4 ♘c6 5.♘b5 d6 6.c4 ♘f6 7.♘1c3 a6 8.♘a3 b6 9.♗e2 ♗b7

10.0–0 ♘b8

The other serious possibility is connected with the manoeuvre of the knight to the-d7 square, via the e5-square: 10...♗e7 11.♗e3 ♘e5!

The knight is better placed on e5, because he looks towards the c4-square where the poorly-defended pawn stands. For this reason White has troubles with the rescue of his knight from the a3-square, which he wants to place on d4 or on e3.

One continuation might look like this:

12.f3 (12.f4 ♘g6 or 12.♗f3 ♘h4) 12...0–0 13.♕d2 ♕c7 14.♖fd1 ♖ac8 15.♖ac1 (15.♔h1 d5!) 15...♕b8, with approximately equal play.

11.f3 ♗e7 12.♗e3 ♘bd7 13.♕d2

Akopian showed a better move: 13.♘c2! 0–0 14.♕d2 ♕c7 15.♖fd1 (later we will see why the position of the rook on d1 is so important) 15...♖ac8 16.♗f2 ♖fe8 17.♗f1 ♕b8 18.♘e3!

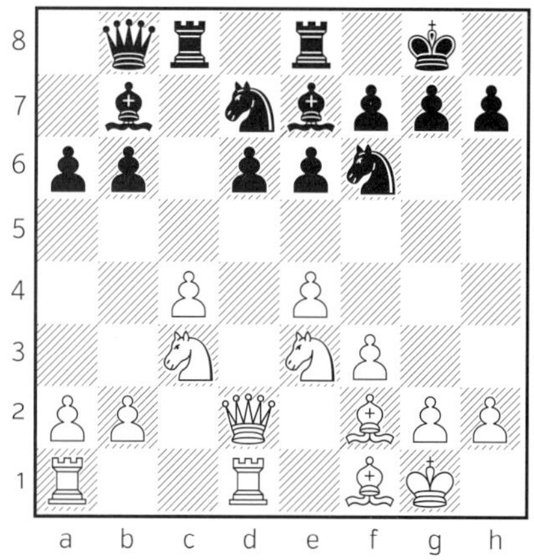

The diagram shows an important position — and an ideal one for White for many reasons: the queen and the rook on the d-file pressurise the d6 pawn and Black does not have his standard plan ♗d8-c7 available; the knight on e3 controls the c4 and the d5 squares; the rook on the a-line will support the advance of the a-pawn to the a5-square.

13...0–0 14.♖fd1 ♕c7 15.♖ac1 ♖ac8 16.♗f1

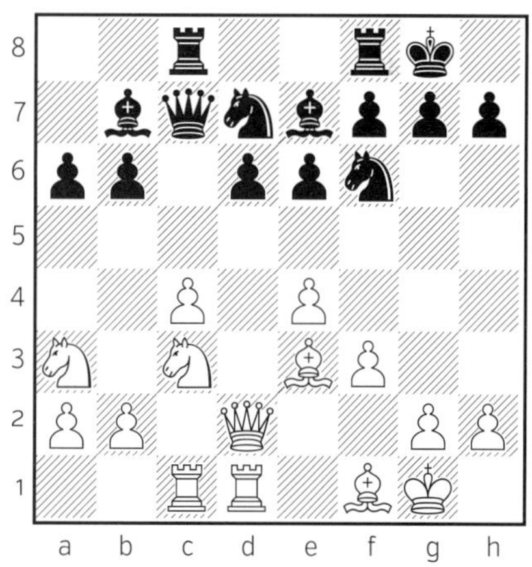

The second critical position occurs after 16.♔h1 ♕b8 17.♗f1 ♔h8 18.♘c2! (Incorrect is 18.♕f2 ♗d8! — the queen needs to be on the d-file, restricting the bishop.)18...♖g8 19.b3 ♗c6 20.♗g1 g5 21.♖e1! (Defence of the e-pawn, after ...g5-g4 would follow f3-f4.) ♖g6 22.♘d5! and White had a huge advantage in the game Anand : Z. Polgar, New Delhi 1990.

16...♖fe8 17.♔h1 ♕b8 18.♘c2 ♘e5

After the standard 18...♗d8!? 19.♗f4 ♘e5 20.b3 ♗c7 21.♗g5 White has the advantage.

19.b3 ♗a8 20.♗g1 ♖ed8?!

We already know the defence against the 20...♔h8 plan: 21.♖e1! ♖g8 22.♘d4 and White is prepared for ...g7-g5 with the f3-f4 move!

21.♘d4 ♗f8?

A mistake, and from now on the b6 pawn will be left with no defence. It would be better to admit the mistake with 21...♖e8.

22.♖e1 ♘ed7?

A new mistake, better is 22...g6.

23.a3 ♗b7

And not 23...d5 24.cd5 ♗a3 25.♖c2 ed5 26.♗a6 ♗b7 27.♗b7 ♕b7 28.e5±.

24.b4±

Black released the pressure on the c4 pawn and White exploited it. Next follows some classic activity on the queenside.

24...♖c7 25.♘b3 ♗a8 26.♘a4! ♗c6 27.♘b2! ♗a8 28.♗d4 ♖dc8 29.♖ed1

Black is helpless without the counterplay linked to the ...b6-b5 or ...d6-d5 strokes.

29...♗e7

After 29...b5 White would easily keep his advantage: 30.♘a5! bc4 31.♖c4 ♖c4 32.♗c4±.

30.♕f2 ♕b7? 31.♘a4+- ♖b8

Next follows a nice final combination:

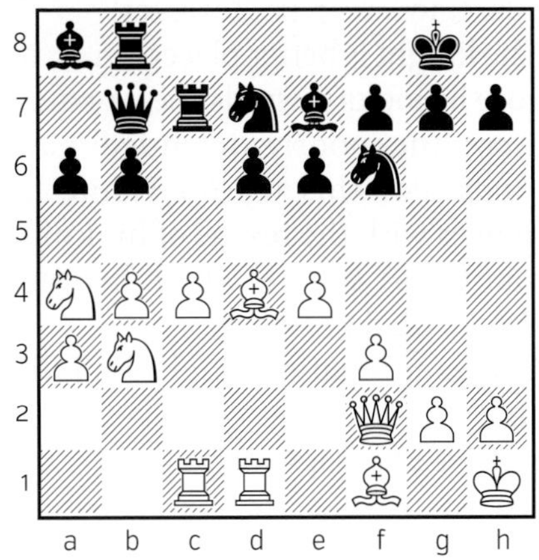

32.♘b6! ♘b6 33.♘a5 ♕a7 34.c5 dc5 35.bc5 ♘c8 36.c6 ♖b6 37.♖b1 ♖b1 38.♖b1 1:0.

Of course the Hedgehog structures are not a one-way street, like we just saw in the previous game. Let's see what can White expect if he is incautious, even though he is famous...

4

▷ **Polugajevsky**
▶ **Ftacnik**
Luzern 1982 [A30]

1.♘f3 ♘f6 2.c4 c5
Our typical placements can be formed out of the English opening.

3.♘c3 e6 4.g3 b6 5.♗g2 ♗b7 6.0–0 ♗e7 7.d4 cd4 8.♕d4 d6 9.♖d1
Now White has many plans but Polugaievsky chooses the most common one.

9...a6 10.b3 ♘bd7 11.e4 ♕b8 12.♗b2 0–0 13.♘d2 ♖d8!
An excellent understanding of the position — when the bishop is on b2, the rook needs to be on d8.

14.a4 ♕c7 15.♕e3 ♖ac8 16.♕e2 ♘e5 17.h3?!
White weakens his kingside for no good reason. Better would be 17.♔h1, with complicated play.

17...h5!
A typical idea. Black wants to attack the g3 pawn and also to weaken the pawns on the kingside.

18.f4 ♘g6 19.♘f3
After 19.h4, which prevents the ...h5-h4 push, White weakens his g4-square: 19...♘g4 20.♖f1 ♕c5 21.♔h1 ♕e3 and now White has many weaknesses.

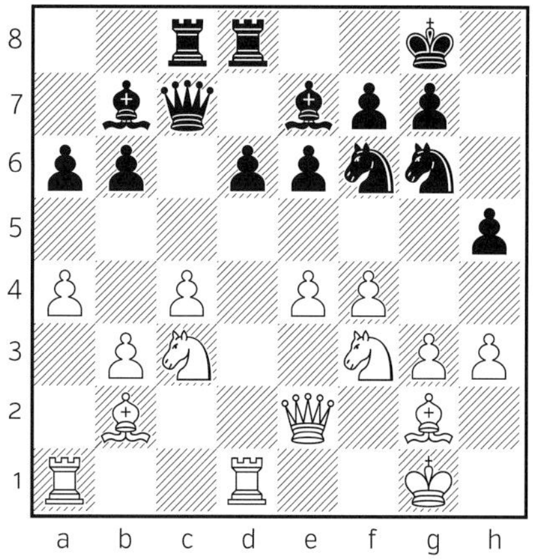

19...d5!!
Shockingly!

20.cd5?
White — logically — lost his nerves. This kind of strike always shocks the player and Polugaievsky obviously wanted to simplify the position with exchanges. An improvement would be 20.e5.

20...h4!
The main point of Black's combination.

21.♘h4 ♘h4 22.gh4 ♕f4 23.de6 fe6 24.e5?!
Black's strong attack will endure even after the more resistant 24.♖d8 ♖d8 25.♖d1 ♖d1 26.♕d1 ♕e3 27.♔h2 ♕f2, with many threats.

24...♗c5 25.♔h1 ♘h5 26.♕h5 ♕g3 27.♘d5 ♖d5 28.♖f1 ♕g2 29.♔g2 ♖d2 0:1.

DYNAMICS OF THE CENTER

by Adrian Mikhalchishin

In the first part of our book we have already learned about the importance of the center on the chess board. We know about the importance of pawns and arising structures. In the second part of our book we will focus more on the pieces which occupy the squares, on the cooperation between pawns and pieces, and on the power of pieces on central squares. Mostly these are bishops and knights, but they are supported in many cases by the heavy pieces on the central (and not central) files. But in many cases young and experienced players wrongly evaluate different changes to the structure in the center and it is one of the most important and difficult subjects of chess strategy.

There are many forms of co-ordination of the pawns and pieces in the center, in many cases a central strategy is supported by flank measures. The center is the most important part of the chess board, as pawns placed there control the most important part of this space, plus they limit the possibilities of the opponent's pieces. At the same time the central position of the pieces allows them to achieve maximum activity, and such positions allow them to attack both flanks, or to be transferred quickly to either flank. We will consider two kinds of the center.

In principle we will consider two kinds of center — closed and opened. Some specialists believe in semi-opened centers and in positions without a center. But in most cases the fight is for the opening of the center or the closing of it. Here again, both young and experienced players conduct a lot of wrong decisions.

In the following chapters we will exam the subjects as:

— the power of the center and how to exploit it.
— the power of pieces in the center.
— Passed pawn in the center.
— Flank actions against the center.
— Destroying the opponents center with piece or pawn activity.
— Closing the center and blocking the center.
— Doubled pawns in the center, the weakness and power of them.
— Different changes to the central structures.

Adrian Mikhalchishin

POWER OF THE CENTER

We talk a lot about it, but it is necessary to understand practically how we use the space which is created by the powerful center, and also how to prepare the expansion of the pieces which are placed behind the pawns. It is always necessary to conduct a central breakthrough, which will stretch the opponents pieces to the maximum. Let's see immediately how it was performed by legendary champions of the game.

1

▷ **Rubinstein**
▶ **Schlechter**
Berlin 1918 [D25]

1.d4 d5 2.♘f3 ♘f6 3.c4 c6 4.♘c3 dc4 5.e3 ♗g4 6.♗c4 e6 7.0–0 ♘bd7 8.h3 ♗f3 9.♕f3 ♗e7

Modern chess players would create immediate counterplay in the center: 9...♗d6 10.♖d1 ♕e7 11.e4 e5.

10.♖d1 0–0 11.e4 ♖e8 12.♗f4 ♘f8

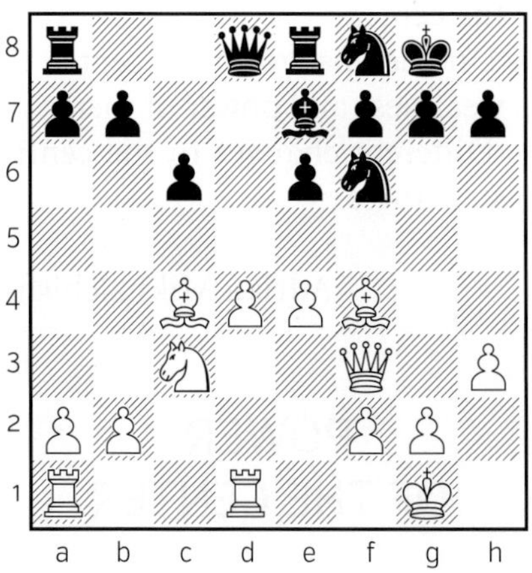

White has created strong center and as a result, obtained powerful positions for his pieces plus a serious space advantage. But to realize this advantage it is necessary to open the center and only in this case will it be possible to exploit effectively the better positioning of the White pieces.

Rule number one for the powerful center — open it!

13.d5! ed5 14.ed5 ♕b6

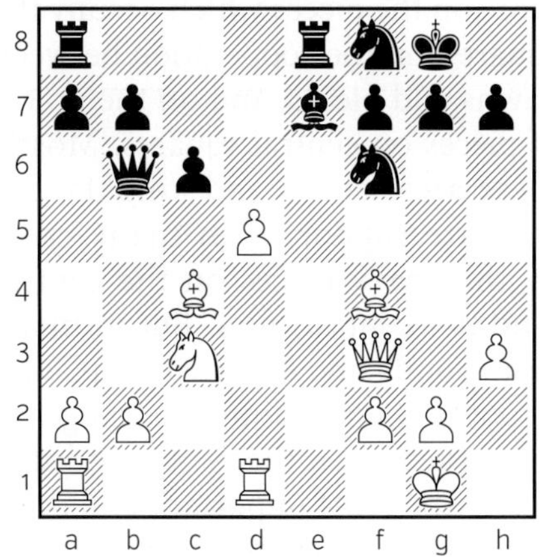

14...cd5 15.♘d5 ♘d5 16.♗d5 is very unpleasant for Black, as too many pawns are under attack.

15.d6!

Another transition — a powerful central passed pawn appears, which will cut down the available space for the opponents pieces.

15... ♗d8 16.g4!

Now a flank attack to remove the opponent's knight from the center.

16...♘e6

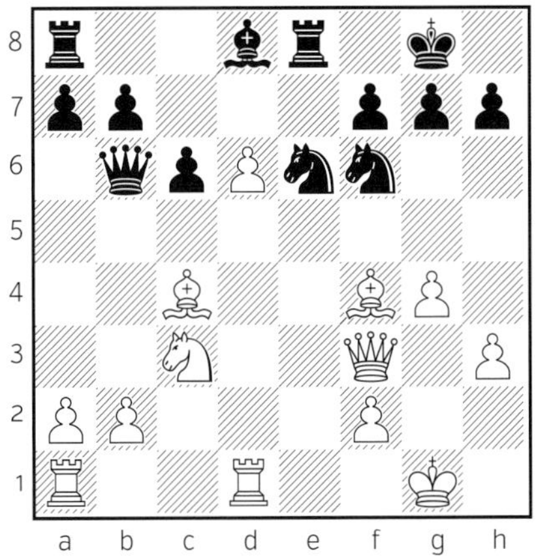

17.d7!

The powerful positions of the white pieces allows them to start a forcing attack on the King. 17.♖d2.

17...♖e7 18.♗d6 ♖d7

18...♘g5 19.♕f5 ♘h3 20.♔g2 ♘f2 21.♕f2 ♕f2 22.♔f2 ♖d7 23.♔f3.

19.♗e6 fe6 20.g5

Now the knight is lost, so Schlechter aims for some tactical complications.

20...♖d6 21.♖d6 ♕c5

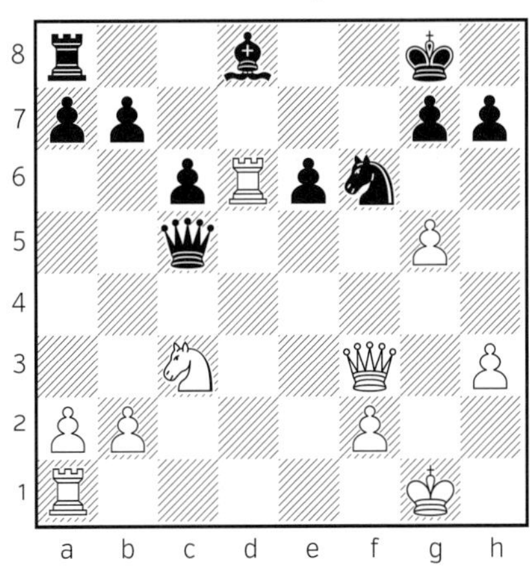

22.♖d8!

The simplest way to realize the advantage.

22...♖d8 23.gf6 ♕g5 24.♕g4 ♕f6 25.♖e1 e5 26.♕g3 ♖e8 27.♘e4

Extra pieces will add power to White's attack.

27...♕e7 28.♖d1!

Instructive manoeuvres by White's rook — firstly attacking the pawn, then exploiting the open file.

28...♖f8 29.♖d6 ♔h8 30.♕g4 ♖d8 31.♖e6 ♕b4 32.♕g5 ♕e1 33.♔h2 ♖f8 34.♖e7 ♖f2 35.♘f2 ♕f2 36.♕g2 ♕f4 37.♔h1 ♕c1 38.♕g1 1:0.

And there are no more checks — White's king and queen decentralized Black's queen in an instructive way.

2

▷ **Polugajevsky**
▶ **Dorfman**
USSR 1978 [D85]

1.d4 d5 2.♘f3 ♘f6 3.c4 g6 4.cd5 ♘d5 5.e4 ♘b6 6.h3!

An important prophylactic move, as now the knight can't be attacked and White's center will be much more stable.

6...♗g7 7.♘c3 0–0 8.♗e2

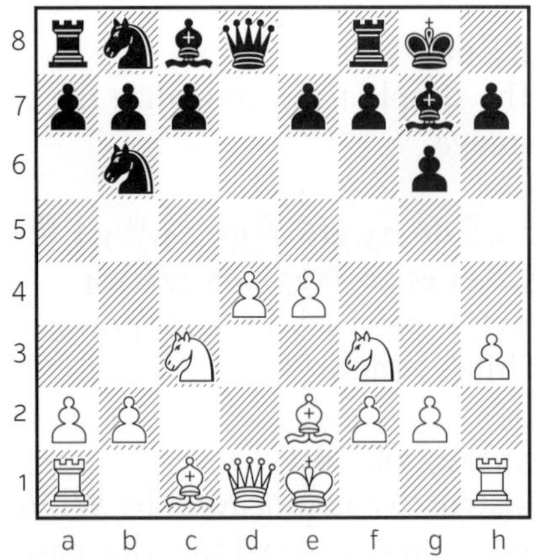

8...♗e6?!

Another plan was 8...c6 and then ...♘bd7, intending to attack the center with ...e7–e5. It seems that this idea was more sound, but Dorfman decides to exchange bishops first, with the idea of reducing White's space advantage.

9.0–0

9.d5 ♗d7 10.0–0 c6 11.♗e3 cd5 12.ed5 ♘a6.

9...♗c4? 10.♗c4 ♘c4 11.♕e2 ♘b6 12.♖d1

With this rook, as the other one will be used for operations on the c-file.

12...♘8d7 13.♗g5 c6 14.a4! ♕e8

14...a5 15.♖ab1 ♖e8 16.b4 ab4 17.♖b4 ♕c7 18.♖b3 (18.♖db1).

15.a5 ♘c8

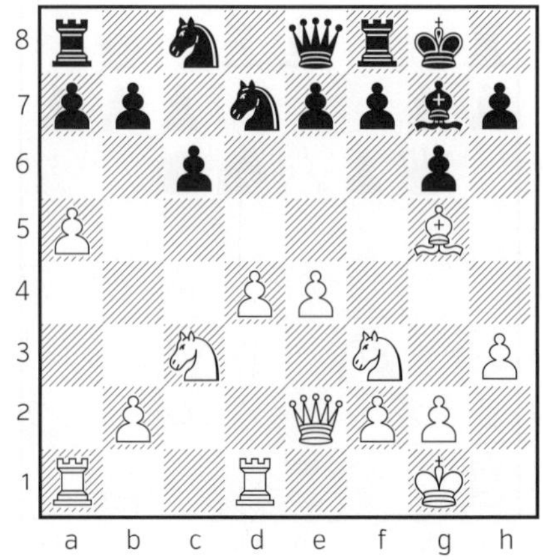

16.d5!

As White has achieved a huge space advantage and much better positions for all pieces, it is necessary (and very typical) to open central files to exploit the power of his well-developed forces.

16...a6 17.e5!±

Increasing the space advantage and usefully reducing the power of the bishop on g7.

17...h6 18.♗h4 e6

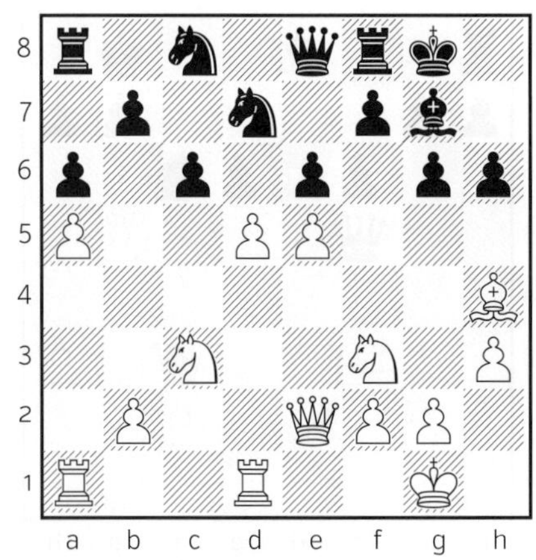

18...cd5 19.♖d5 (19.♘d5).

19.d6

Another possibility was to create a weakness on c6, and then attack it: 19.dc6 bc6 20.♘e4 g5 21.♗g3 ♘e7 22.♘d6.

19...g5 20.♗g3 f5

Black tries to free himself, but in vain. After 20...♘a7 21.♖a4 there appears the terrible threat h2–h4.

21.ef6

21.♖a4 f4 22.♗h2 ♖f5.

21...♖f6

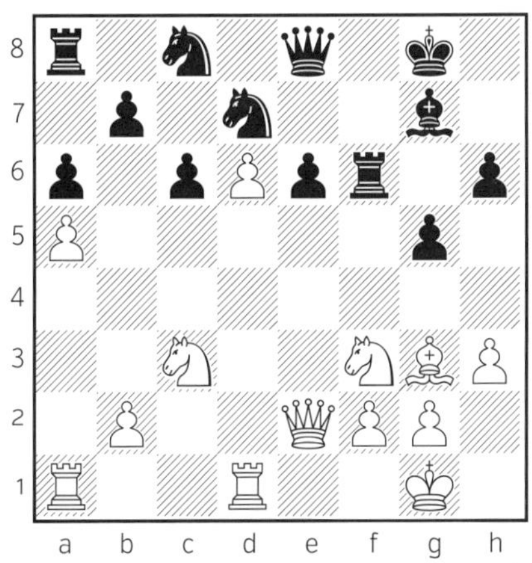

Another capture gives White the possibility of opening the kingside immediately 21...♗f6 22.h4 gh4 23.♗h4.

22.♖a4!

White adds an important piece to the attack. 22.h4 was possible immediately: 22.♘e5 ♘a7 23.♘d7 ♕d7 24.♘e4 ♖f5 25.♕c2.

22...♘a7

A bit more stubborn would be 22... e5 23.♘e4 ♖g6 24.♕c2 ♕f7 25.♖b4.

23.h4!

This is the start of a powerful final attack.

23...gh4 24.♖h4

Capturing with tempo is very strong: 24.♗h4 ♖f5 25.♖e4 e5 26.♘a4.

24...♘b5

Finally Black creates some threat to exchange some bad pieces, but it is too late.

25.♗e5 ♖g6

The attack against e5 doesn't help: 25...♘e5 26.♘e5 ♖f5 27.d7 ♕d8 28.♖h5 ♖h5 29.♕h5 ♗e5 30.♕e5 ♕e7 31.♘e4 ♖d8 32.♘c5 ♔f7 33.♖d3.

26.♗g7 ♔g7 27.♘e5

Exchanging off the blockading piece is always a successful strategy for the attacking player.

27...♘c3 28.bc3 ♖g5

Another possibility is very similar: 28...♘e5 29.♕e5 ♔h7 30.d7 ♕e7 31.♕c7 ♖d8 32.♖b4 ♕g5 33.g3 and Black's threats are over.

29.f4 ♖f5 30.♕g4+– ♔h7 31.♕h3 ♖f6 32.♘g4

Every move is attacking and creating unpleasant threats.

32...♕f8 33.♘f6 ♕f6 34.♖e1 ♘f8 35.♖e5 ♔g7 36.♖eh5 1:0.

3

▹ **Rubinstein**
▸ **Duras**
San Sebastian 1912 [D26]

1.d4 d5 2.♘f3 ♘f6 3.c4 dc4 4.e3 e6 5.♗c4 c5 6.0–0 ♘c6 7.♕e2 cd4 8.♖d1 a6 9.ed4 ♗e7 10.♘c3 0–0

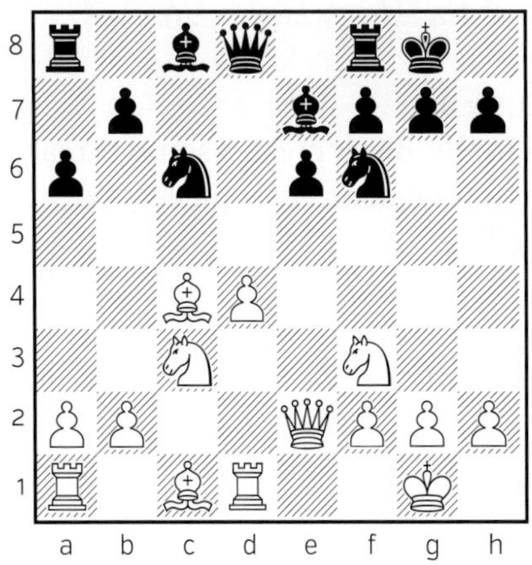

11.d5!

The aim of such moves is to open a file in the center, plus to obtain very centralised squares for the pieces -in this case for the bishop.

11...ed5 12.♘d5 ♘d5 13.♗d5 ♕c7 14.♗g5

An extremely interesting option would be the attacking (c6 and h7) and preventive (♗f5) move 14.♕e4! but it was very difficult to find. The move played by Rubinstein has its own real logic — development and preparation of an attack on the kingside.

14...♗g5?

The main rule of defence is: don't help your opponent to improve his pieces! Correct was development with a pin, which is always useful. 14...♗g4.

15.♘g5 ♗f5

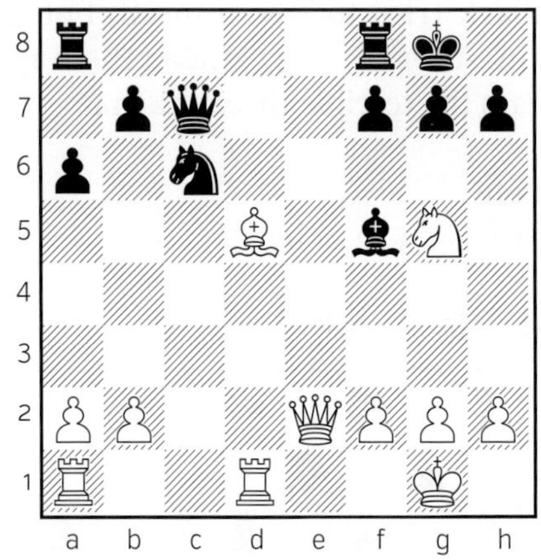

White would obtain too big an advantage in development after the queen swap 15...♕e5 16.♕e5 ♘e5 17.♖ac1.

16.♕f3

It was possible to complete development, with a threat to create weakness on c6: 16.♖ac1.

16...♗g6 17.h4!

Adding new resources — the pawn h2 can attack the bishop's position on the kingside.

17...♘e5?

The principled counterstrike 17...h6 leads to a very unclear game: 18.h5 ♘e5 19.♕h3 hg5 20.♖ac1 ♗c2 21.♖d2 ♕a5 22.♖cc2 ♖ad8.

18.♕g3

Slightly better would be to centralize the pieces and to transfer into an endgame with 18.♕f4 ♖ae8 19.♖ac1 ♕b6 20.♕d4 ♕d4 21.♖d4.

18...♖ae8

Better was to protect the queen by 18...♖ac8.

19.♖e1!

Now the unpleasant pin will force Black to weaken his position.

19...♕b8 20.♖e3!

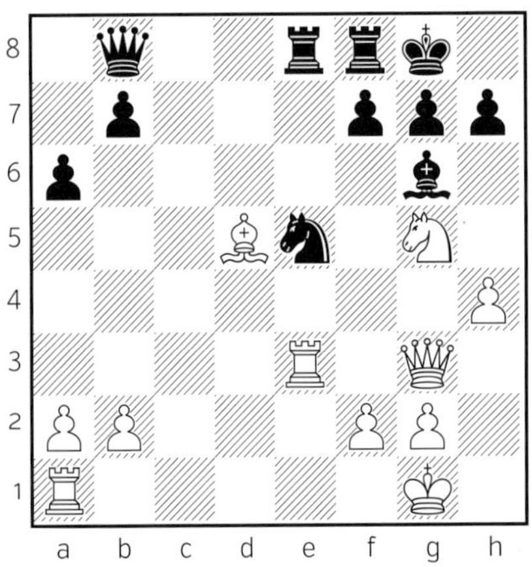

Controlling the d3 square and preparing a doubling on the file.

20...b5

A very nice tactic lies in wait for the direct 20...h6: 21.♘e6 fe6 22.♗b3!

21.♖ae1 ♘d3?

A clear mistake, but the endgame was not easy to hold either: 21...♘c4 22.♖e8 ♖e8 23.♕b8 ♖b8 24.♖e7 ♖f8 25.b3 ♘b6 26.♗e4.

22.♖e8 ♕g3

Another losing variation is 22...♖e8 23.♖e8 ♕e8 24.h5.

23.fg3 ♘e1 24.♖e1 h6 25.♘h3 ♖c8 26.♘f4 ♔h7 27.h5 1:0.

But not always opening of the Center works so powerfully — there happens premature and wrong openings of the Center.

4

▹ Reshevsky
▸ Ghitescu
Tel Aviv 1964 [D32]

1.d4 d5 2.c4 e6 3.♘c3 c5 4.e3 ♘c6 5.♘f3 ♘f6 6.cd5 ed5 7.♗e2 ♗e7 8.dc5 ♗c5 9.0–0 0–0 10.b3 a6 11.♗b2 ♗a7 12.♖c1

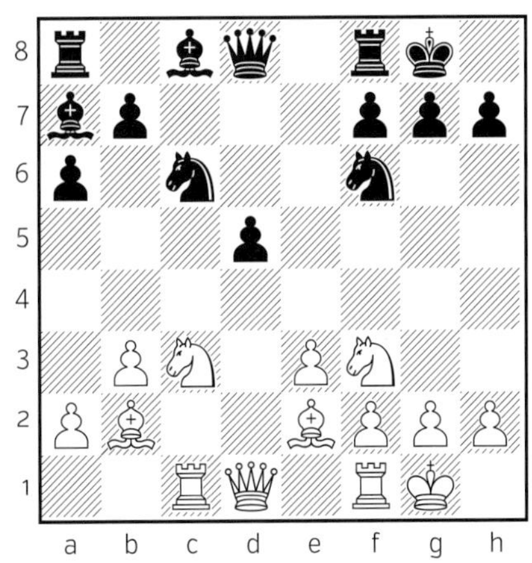

A typical structure with an isolated pawn and Black has a few classical, solid plans.

12...d4?

It looks strong and logical to get rid of the weak pawn, but correct were other set-ups here such as: 12...♗g4 or 12...♗e6. But on first look it is not clear why the classical break is wrong.

13.ed4 ♘d4 14.♘d4 ♕d4

A different capture is no better 14...♗d4 15.♗f3 ♗f5 (passive defence leads to a very uncomfortable ending: 15...♖b8 16.♗a3 ♖e8 17.♘d5 ♗e5 18.♘e7 ♔h8 19.♕d8 ♖d8 20.♖fe1) 16.♗a3 ♖e8 17.♗b7 ♗g4 18.♗f3.

15.♕d4

It was possible to try to achieve a very comfortable endgame with 15.♗f3 ♕d1 16.♖fd1 ♗g4 17.♘d5 ♘d5 18.♗g4 ♖fd8 19.♗d4 ♗d4 20.♖d4 ♘e7 21.♖d8 ♖d8 22.♖c7.

15...♗d4 16.♖fd1 ♗a7

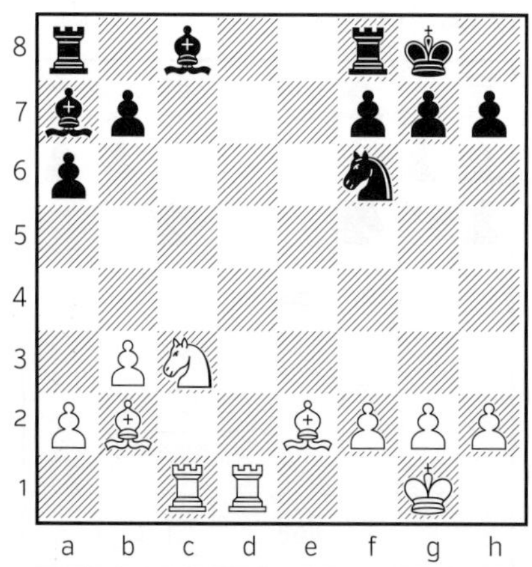

Clearly better is to keep the bishop in the center and try to reduce White's development advantage, so 16...♗e5.

17.h3!

A very important prophylactic move which eliminates any possibility to come to g4 with the bishop or knight.

17...♗f5 18.♗f3 ♖ab8

The black pieces are passively placed and White increases his space advantage.

19.g4! ♗g6 20.g5 ♘h5 21.♘d5

The idea of the flank manoeuvre g2–g4–g5 is to obtain a strong knight on d5, which decides the fate of the game.

21...♖fe8 22.♖c7

Every white piece is better placed than the opponent's.

22...♔h8 23.♘e7 ♘f4 24.♘g6 hg6 25.♖f7 ♘h3 26.♔g2 ♘f2 27.♖dd7 1:0.

At the end White's pieces are terribly active, especially the rooks on the 7th rank and mating threats are unavoidable.

Of course, the power of the center is not always demonstrated by the opening of it — in many cases a strong center reduces the opponent's pieces to passivity and the pawns structure does not allow him to improve their positions.

5

▷ **Pavasovic**
▶ **Franic**
Medulin 2002 [B22]

1.e4 c5 2.c3 b6 3.d4 ♗b7 4.♗d3 ♘f6 5.♘d2 cd4 6.cd4 ♘c6 7.♘e2 e6 8.0–0 ♗e7 9.a3

Black has allowed White to create a strong center. This move has the idea not just of stopping counterplay with ...♘b4, but to start additional space-gaining activity on the queen's flank. Control over a strong center alone is not sufficient to play for a win — other elements have to be improved also.

9...0–0 10.b4

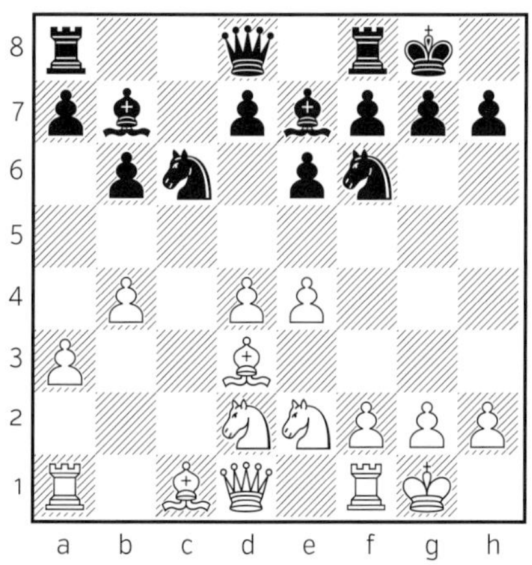

10...♖c8

Other slow play allows White to create a space initiative everywhere: 10... d6 11.♗b2 a6 12.h3 preparing f2–f4.

11.♗b2 d6 12.♘g3

Still the same set-up looks dangerous 12.h3 and f2–f4–f5.

12...g6 13.f4 d5

Sooner or later it is necessary to fix White's structure against the threat f4–f5.

14.e5 ♘e8

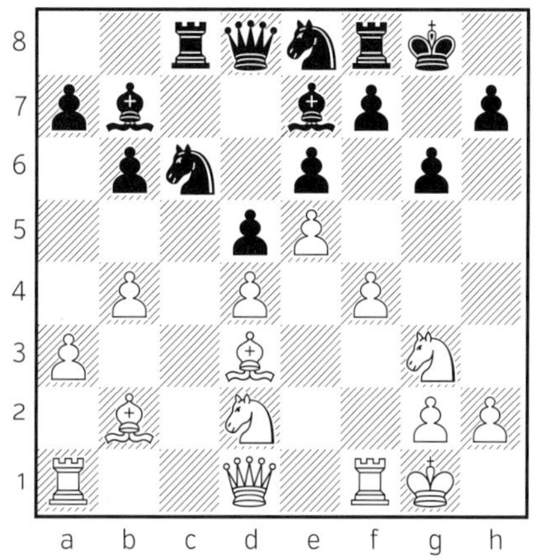

15.♘h1!

White must make way for his g-pawn otherwise it will be impossible to open the position.

15...♕d7

15...f5! Much better was to play this immediately: 16.ef6 ♗f6 17.♘f3 ♘d6 and White will have his own problems with the squares c4 and e4.

16.♕e2 ♘g7 17.♘f3 ♘b8 18.b5!

A nice move, which eliminates any activity on the queen's flank.

18...♖c7 19.g4 f5

It is necessary to stop ♘h1–g3 and the break f4–f5. But on the other hand, now White gets a strong knight on e5, plus the pawn on e6 is weakened.

20.ef6 ♖f6 21.♘e5 ♕e8 22.♘g3 ♘d7

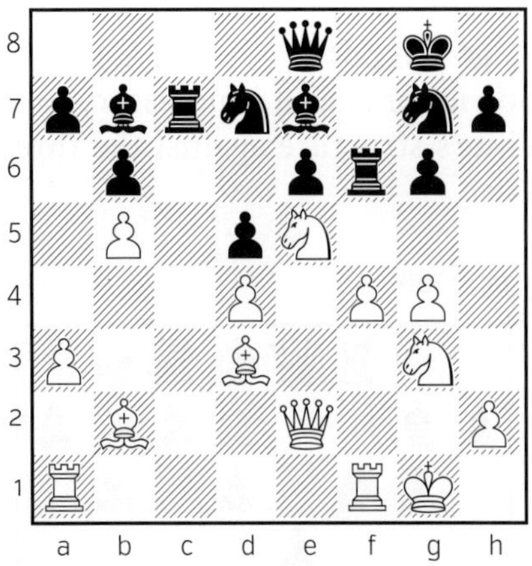

23.f5?!

It is possible to delay the break and slowly improve his position as the black pieces are very passive: 23.♕e3 ♖f8 24.♘e2.

23...gf5 24.gf5 ♘e5 25.de5 ♗c5 26.♔h1 ♖f5 27.♘f5 ef5 28.♖f4 d4

A very unpleasant trick is 28...♗e3!

29.♔g1 ♕g6 30.♔f1 ♕h6 31.♕f2 ♕h3 32.♔e2

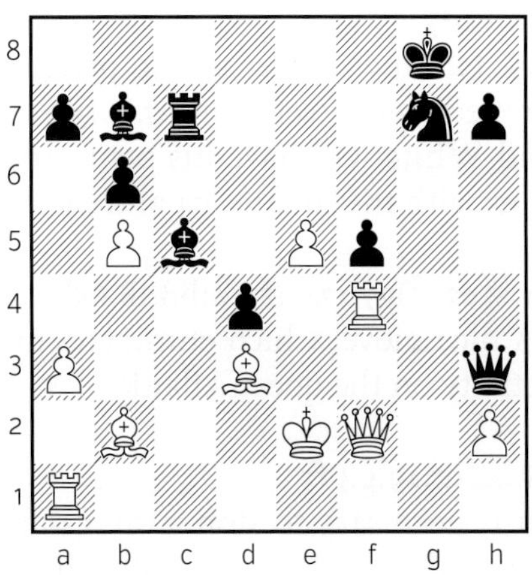

32...♖e7?

A better chance to save the game is 32...♗e4.

33.♖g1

And a technical solution is to exchange queens: 33.♖h4 ♖e5 34.♔d2 ♕f3 35.♕f3 ♗f3 36.♗d4.

33...♖e5 34.♔d2 ♔f8

Once more, it is necessary to exchange bishops 34...♗e4.

35.♗d4 ♗d4 36.♕d4 ♕h2 37.♔c1 ♘e6 38.♕d6 ♔f7 39.♖f5 1:0.

6

▹ **Beliavsky**
▸ **Borisek**
Bled 2016 (D79)

1.d4 ♘f6 2.c4 g6 3.g3 c6 4.♘f3 ♗g7 5.♗g2 d5 6.cd5 cd5 7.0–0 0–0 8.♘e5 ♗f5

The most complicated way — theory promises Black no problems after 8...e6 or 8...♘g4.

9.♘c3 ♘e4

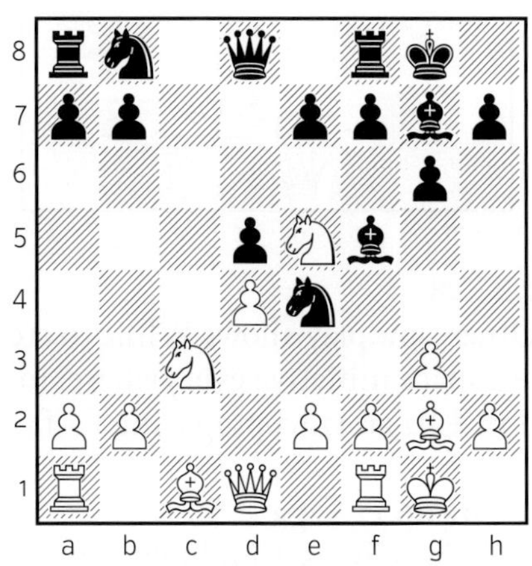

10.g4!?

Beliavsky's style — a direct attack on the center from the flank. But it is not a novelty at all! More usual here are two options: 10.♗f4 or 10.♕b3.

10...♘c3 11.bc3 ♗e6

If Black wants to avoid f2–f4–f5 then preferable is 11...♗c8 12.h3 ♘c6 13.♘c6 bc6 14.♗a3 f5 15.e3 ♕d7 16.f3 ♗a6 17.♖f2, draw, Pribyl : Novak, Stary Smokovec 1976.

12.f4

A direct conduct of the plan. Here there are two other options:

12.h3 ♘d7 13.f4 ♘b6 14.f5 ♗d7 15.e4 ♗b5 16.♖e1 de4 17.♗e4 ♖c8 18.a4 ♗c6 19.♘c6 bc6 20.♗a3 ♗f6 21.♔h1, with attacking chances (Skoberne : Antal, Austria 2015).

The direct central attack is logical too:

12.e4 de4 13.♗e4 ♘c6 14.♘c6 bc6 15.♗a3 ♕d7 16.g5 ♗d5 17.♕e2 ♖fe8 18.f4 ♗f8 19.♖ae1 e5!, with very good counterplay (Terentiev : Mirumian, Decin 1998).

12...♘c6

Very serious consideration should be given to:

12...f6 13.♘d3 ♗g4 14.f5?! (14.♕b3 ♗e2 15.♗d5 ♔h8 16.♘c5 ♗f1 17.♘e6) 14...♗f5 15.♖f5 gf5 16.♘f4 ♔h8 and the position is very sharp, Delchev : Stevic, Pula 2000.

13.f5 ♗c8 14.♘c6 bc6

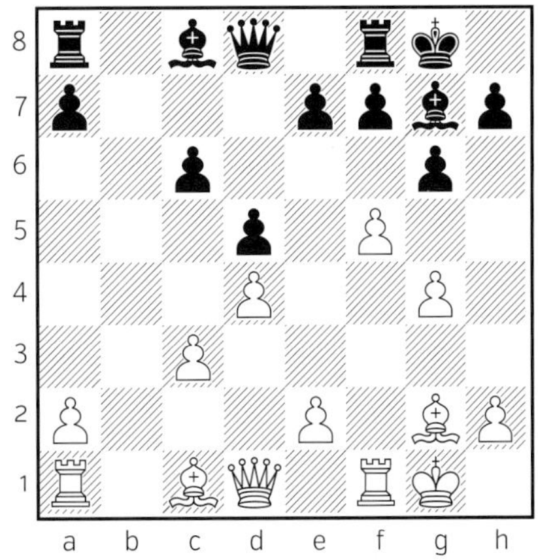

15.♗g5!?

The central attack 15.e4 seems very logical.

15...♗a6 16.♕d2 ♕d6

More logical is to stop White's aggression with 16...f6 17.♗h6 e5 18.de5 fe5 19.♖f2 e4.

17.♖f2 f6 18.♗h4 e5 19.♗g3 gf5 20.gf5

Beliavsky decides to go for an attack on the g-file, but no less logical is to continue the central assault with 20.♖f5 ♖ae8 21.e4.

20...♗c4 21.e4

A direct preparation of the g-file attack with 21.♔h1 is possible.

21...♖ad8 22.ed5

A completely different game arises after the very tempting 22.de5 fe5 23.♕g5.

22...cd5

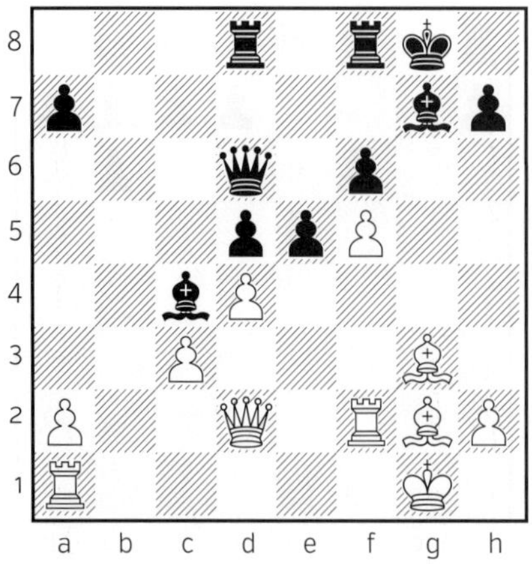

23.♔h1! 23...♕c6

In such cases, preferable is preparation of the defence on the same file: 23...♔h8 24.♖g1 ♖g8.

s24.♖g1 e4?

An incorrect closing of the center — much better is 24...♔h8.

25.♗f4! ♖f7 26.♗h3 ♔h8 27.♖fg2 ♗d3 28.♗g4 ♖e7 29.♖g3

It is possible to begin with 29.♗d1.

29...♕d7 30.♗e3 ♖b8 31.♕g2!

Tripling on the attacking file!

31...♖g8 32.♗d1 ♖ee8 33.♗a4 1:0.

7

▷ **Vallejo Pons**
▶ **Arvind**
Pattaya 2011 [B20]

1.e4 c5 2.♘e2 d6 3.g3 g6 4.♗g2 ♗g7 5.c3 e6?!

Black plays too passively and shy in the center. Much better is to develop first and then to prepare a counterstrike in the center: 5...♘f6 6.d4 0–0 7.0–0 ♘c6 8.h3 e5 9.♗e3 cd4 10.cd4

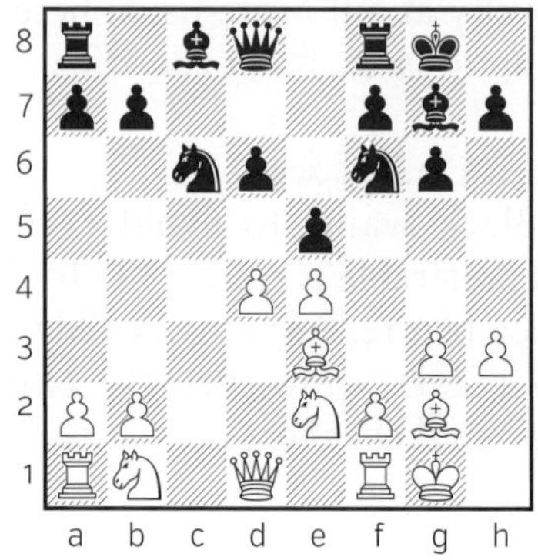

10...d5.

6.d4 cd4 7.cd4 ♘e7 8.♘bc3 0–0

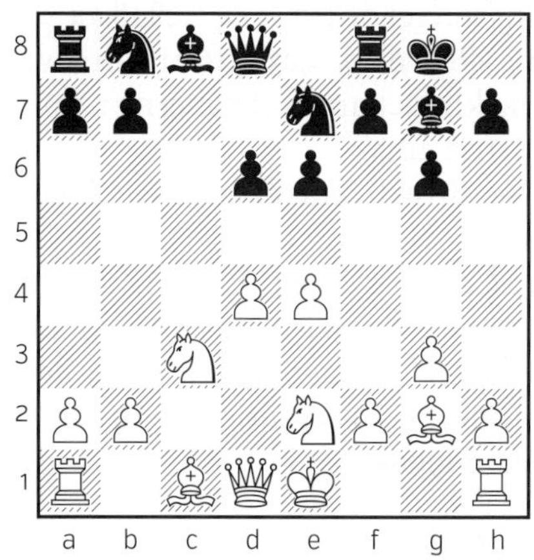

9.h4!?

A very interesting decision — using his strong center, White wants to create directly some weaknesses in his opponent's position.

9...h6

It is better to fix — and then start to pressure — this kind of the center. 9...d5 10.e5 ♘f5 11.h5 ♘c6. Another central counterstrike looks too risky: 9...f5 10.h5 fe4 11.hg6 hg6 12.♗e4.

10.♗e3 ♘bc6 11.♕d2 ♔h7 12.h5 g5 13.f4!

Of course, it is necessary to open the opponent's king position first.

13...gf4 14.gf4

White prefers to keep a strong center, as attacking attempts would be met by a central counterstrike.

14.♘f4 e5.

14...♖g8 15.♖g1 d5 16.♗f2

It is possible to castle, but in reality the white king is much safer in the center than on the wing!

16...f5

Black has to open the center, despite the fact that it looks a bit ugly with such weaknesses on e5 and d5. 16...de4 17.♗e4 f5 18.♗f3. Now White closes the center and keeps his huge space advantage.

17.e5 ♗d7 18.♗h4 b5?!

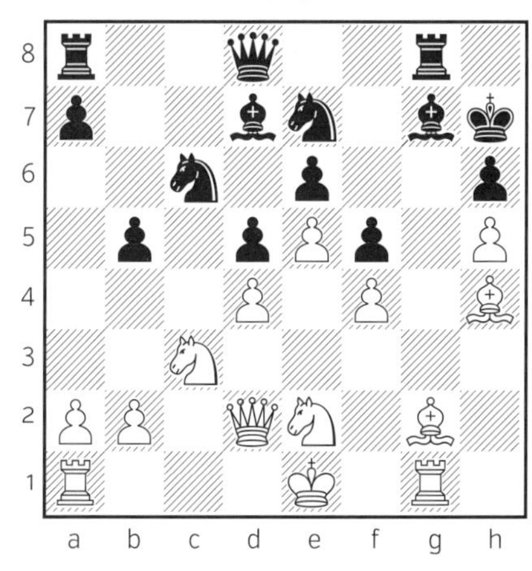

Black tries urgently to change the course of the game, even sacrificing a pawn. But a more normal way was preferable: 18...♖c8.

There are two good options: 19.♘b5 and the much more concrete 19.♘d5! ed5 20.♗d5 ♖f8 (20...♘d5 21.♗d8 ♖ad8 22.0–0–0) 21.♗f3, with d4-d5 next leading to complete White control in the center.

19.♗f3 ♕b6 20.♔f2!

Now it's time to connect the rooks.

20...♗h8 21.♖gc1!

Avoiding exchanges, as this would reduce White's space advantage.

21...a6 22.♘d1 ♖gc8 23.♘e3 ♗g7 24.♖g1

White returns to the g-file, and with such a space advantage it is a luxury he can allow himself. Black has no counterplay and now should return back to g8 with his rook.

24...♖c7?! 25.♖g3 ♖f8 26.♖ag1 ♖f7 27.♖g6!

These typical, small tactics allow White to demonstrate the power of doubled rooks.

27...♘g8

After a few preparatory moves, White will destroy his opponent's strongholds in the center with a decisive attack 27...♕b8 28.♘c3 ♖c8 29.♘ed5! ed5 30.♗d5 ♘d5 31.♘d5.

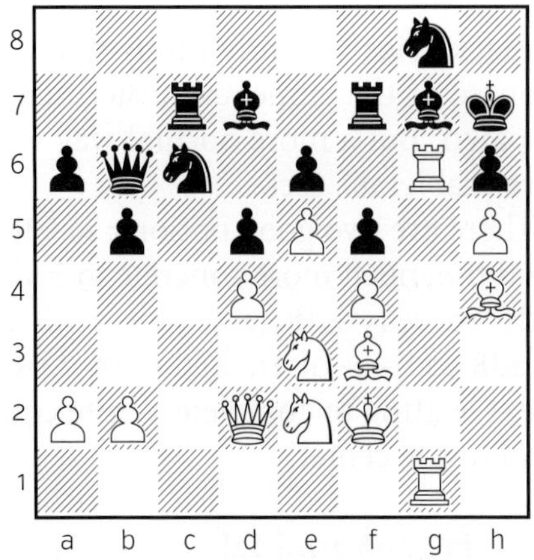

28.♗d5!

White was also ready to sacrifice on d5 in a different manner, again with a decisive attack. 28.♘d5 ed5 29.♗d5.

28...ed5 29.♘d5 ♕a7 30.♘c7 ♕c7 31.e6 ♗e6 32.♖e6 ♗f6 33.♗f6 ♘f6 34.♕c2 1:0.

CONTROL OF THE CENTER WITH THE PIECES

Completely different cases occur when there are strong squares in the center (we say weak squares of the other side!) which can be controlled by powerful pieces. Such pieces conduct strong pressure on the opponents position and help coordinate attacks together with other pieces. First of all let us see examples of total control over the d5(d4) squares, which are extremely important strategical strongholds.

1

▹ **Fischer**
▸ **Bolbochan**
Stockholm 1962 [B90]

1.e4 c5 2.♘f3 d6 3.d4 cd4 4.♘d4 ♘f6 5.♘c3 a6 6.h3 ♘c6 7.g4 ♘d4 8.♕d4 e5 9.♕d3 ♗e7 10.g5!

One of the most important characteristics of this move is that it is not an attack on the king, but rather remove knight from the center — thus allowing White to increase his control over the important d5 square.

10...♘d7

The knight has to stay in the center, as on the edge it is in danger: 10...♘h5 11.h4± and ♘e2. **11.♗e3**

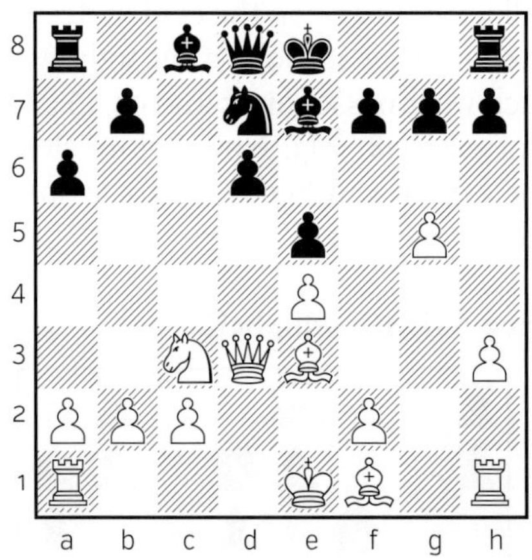

11...♘c5?

It is possible to try some exchanges, but White keeps the advantage: 11...♗g5 12.♗g5 ♕g5 13.♕d6 ♕e7 14.♕e7 ♔e7 15.♘d5 ♔f8 16.0–0–0 g6. (Kotov)

12.♕d2 ♗e6 13.0–0–0 0–0 14.f3 ♖c8

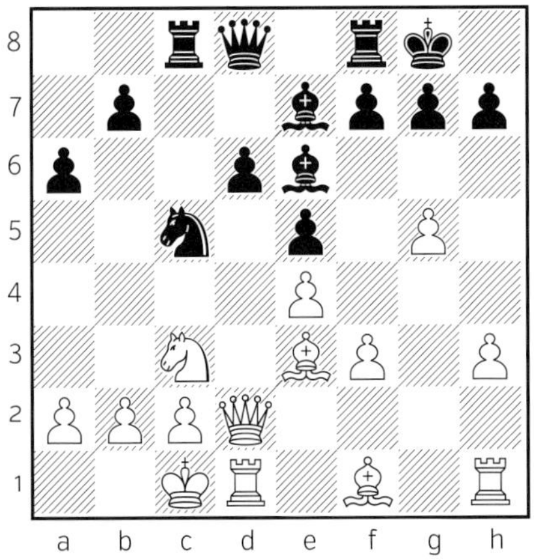

15.♔b1

A typical move, but it is also possible to start play on the kingside with 15.h4.

15...♘d7

A very interesting try is to start counterplay on the kingside, despite the inherent dangers there: 15...f5 16.gf6 ♖f6 17.♖g1 ♖f7.

16.h4 b5 17.♗h3

An interesting idea, but quite playable is the direct occupation of the central square — 17.♘d5.

17...♗h3

17...♘b6 simply leads to the loss of a pawn: 18.♗b6 ♕b6 19.♘d5 ♕d8 (19...♗d5? 20.♗c8) 20.♘e7 ♕e7 21.♕d6.

18.♖h3 ♘b6 19.♗b6!

The bishop is not important — more important is control of d5.

19...♕b6 20.♘d5 ♕d8

A better try is 20...♕b7 21.♖g3 f5 22.gf6 ♗f6 23.h5.

21.f4

Fischer does not fall into the trap 21.♘e7? ♕e7 22.♕d6?? ♖fd8–+.

21...ef4 22.♕f4 ♕d7 23.♕f5

A very strong move, driving the queen from the center.

23...♖cd8

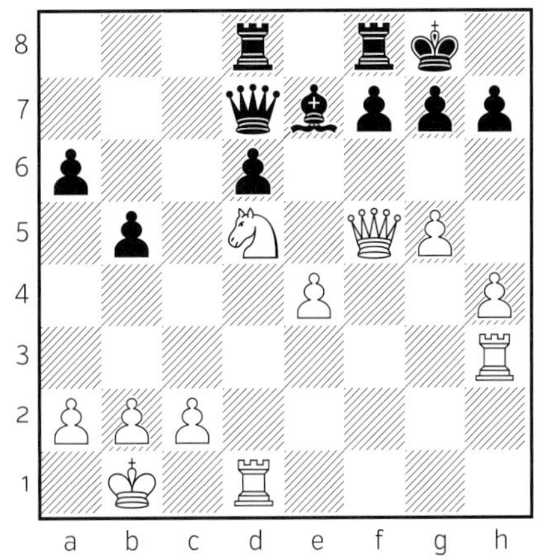

A very bad position arises after 23...♕b7 24.h5 ♗d8 25.h6 g6 26.♕f4.

24.♖a3!

A strong move deflecting the opponent's queen.

24...♕a7 25.♖c3

Possible, but not best is the direct attack with 25.♘f6!? ♗f6 (25...gf6? 26.gf6 ♔h8 27.♕g5 ♖g8 28.fe7!) 26.gf6 g6 27.♕g5 ♕f2. 25.h5 is also playable and logical.

25...g6!

The best defence, but it does not help much. 25...♕d7? 26.♖c7+-. 25...♖d7? 26.♘f6! ♗f6 (26...gf6 27.gf6 ♔h8 28.fe7+-) 27.gf6 g6 28.♕g5 ♔h8 29.♕h6 ♖g8 30.♖c8!+-.

26.♕g4 ♕d7 27.♕f3 ♕e6

Not 27...♖c8? 28.♖c8 ♖c8 29.♘b6.

28.♖c7 ♖de8

Other possibilities are 28...♖d7 29.♘f4+- or 28...♖fe8 29.♖f1 or 28...♖c8 29.♖a7 ♖a8 30.♖a8 ♖a8 31.♘c7.

29.♘f4 ♕e5 30.♖d5 ♕h8

Yes, a queen in the corner is the result of Black's unlucky strategy and White's total control of d5 square.

31.a3 h6

Losing even more quickly is the opening of the position with 31...f6 32.♕b3 ♖f7 33.♖d6 fg5 34.hg5 ♕e5 35.♖f6! ♖ef8 36.♖f7 ♖f7 37.♖c8 ♗f8 38.♘e6+-.

32.gh6 ♕h6

Another way to lose immediately is 32...♗h4? 33.♕g4 ♕h6 34.♖h5.

33.h5 ♗g5

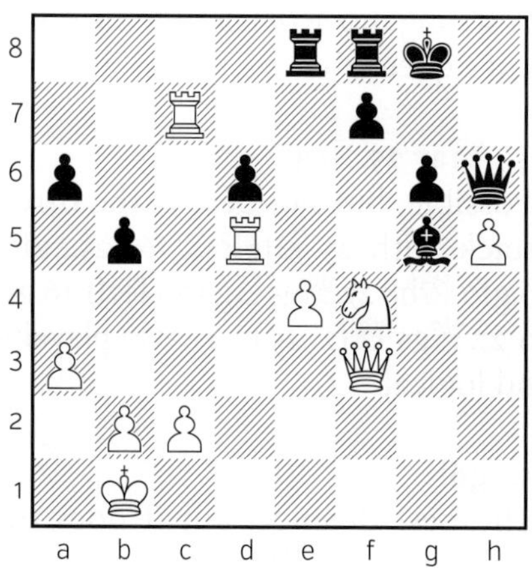

Or 33...g5 34.♘h3 ♔h8 35.♖a7.

34.hg6! fg6

This capture was calculated by Fischer very quickly: 34...♗f4 35.gf7 ♖f7 36.♖f7 ♔f7 37.♖h5!+-

35.♕b3!

With this piece sacrifice White conducts a mating attack.

35...♖f4

35...♔h8 36.♘g6 ♕g6 37.♖g5 ♖f1 (37...♕g5 38.♕h3+-) 38.♔a2 ♕g5 39.♕h3 ♔g8 40.♕f1+-; 35...♗f4 36.♖h5.

36.♖e5 ♔f8 37.♖e8 ♔e8 38.♕e6 ♔f8 39.♕c8 1:0.

2

▷ **Botvinnik**
▶ **Kan**
Moscow 1953 [B59]

1.e4 c5 2.♘f3 ♘c6 3.d4 cd4 4.♘d4 ♘f6 5.♘c3 d6 6.♗e2 e5 7.♘b3 ♗e7 8.0–0 0–0

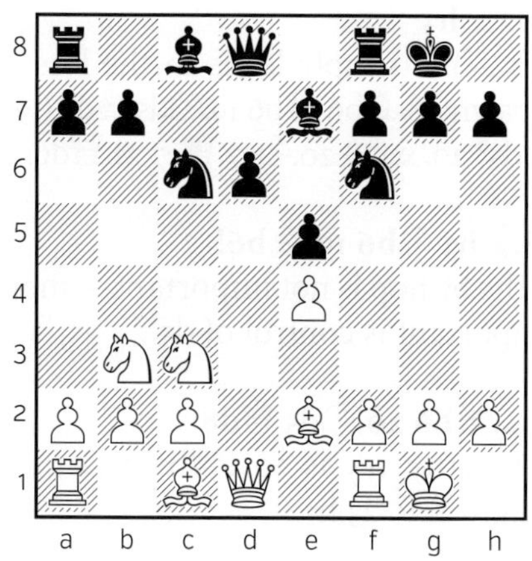

9.♗f3

An old-fashioned method of control over the d5 square, modern players preferring more natural set-ups starting with 9.f4 or 9.♗e3.

9...♘a5?!

It seems a bit strange to exchange off the unimportant knight on b3, but the fact that Black has some space problems — and therefore exchanges are welcomed — makes this move not so bad.

Modern methods of handling such situations include the active 9... a5. Later a method was developed for how to fight for control over d5 square:

10.a4 ♘b4 and then ...♗e6 and Black will be perfectly ready for d6-d5.

10.♘a5

The same position arises after 10.♕d3 ♗e6 11.♘a5.

10...♕a5 11.♗g5

Continuing the fight for control over d5.

11...♗e6 12.a3 ♕c5 13.h3 ♖fd8 14.♕d2 h6 15.♗f6

It's a shame to give up the bishop, but this exchange is forced.

15...♗f6 16.♖fd1 ♖ac8

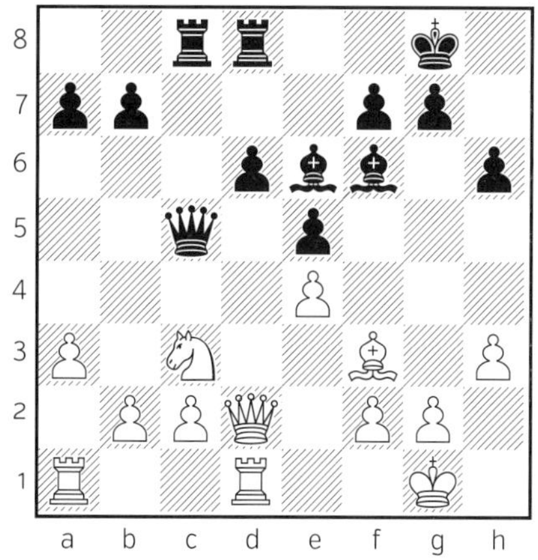

17.♗g4!

This is the correct method — White dreams of exchanging off the white-squared bishops, but sometimes it is even possible to exchange on e6, creating some weaknesses on the kingside.

17...♔f8 18.♕e2 a6

Black's dream is to conduct activity on the other side with ...b7-b5 and ...a6-a5, intending to attack the knight c3 and to drive it far away from d5.

19.♕f3

Now the first threat appears — ♘d5.

19...♖c6 20.h4!

Exploiting the current pin, White starts to control Black squares, as he has no bishop of this colour.

20...♔e7 21.g3 b5 22.♖ac1 ♕c4 23.♖d3 b4

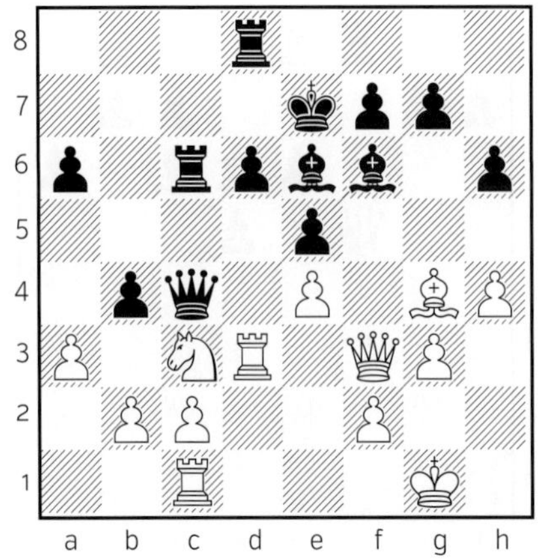

The natural 23...a5 was not possible because of tactics: 24.♗e6 fe6 25.♘d5 ed5 26.♖c3.

24.b3! ♕c5 25.♘d5 ♗d5 26.♖d5

Finally White's control over d5 becomes real and now it is necessary to use the power of his active pieces.

26...♕b6 27.ab4 ♕b4 28.♕e2 ♕c3

Another option is 28...a5 29.♖a1 ♖a8 30.♖b5 ♕c3 31.♖a2 ♔f8 32.♕d1 trying to reach d5 with the queen.

29.♕d1 ♖b8 30.♗e2!

A very important moment — the bishop changes direction as the most important square now is c4.

30...a5 31.♗c4 a4 32.♖a1 ♖b4 33.♖d3 ♕b2 34.c3!

Forcing Black into some sacrifices.

34...♖bc4 35.bc4 a3 36.♖b1 ♕a2 37.♖b4

Closing the escape route for the queen.

37...♖a6 38.c5!

There is always room for natural moves which are sometimes serious mistakes. 38.♖d2 ♕d2 39.♕d2 a2.

38...dc5 39.♖d7 1:0.

3

▹ **Ivacic**
▸ **Mikhalchishin**
Slovenia 1993 [A07]

1.c4 ♘f6 2.g3 e5 3.♗g2 d5 4.cd5 ♘d5 5.♘f3 ♘c6 6.d3 ♗e7 7.0–0 0–0 8.a3 a5 9.♘c3 ♗e6 10.♘d5 ♗d5

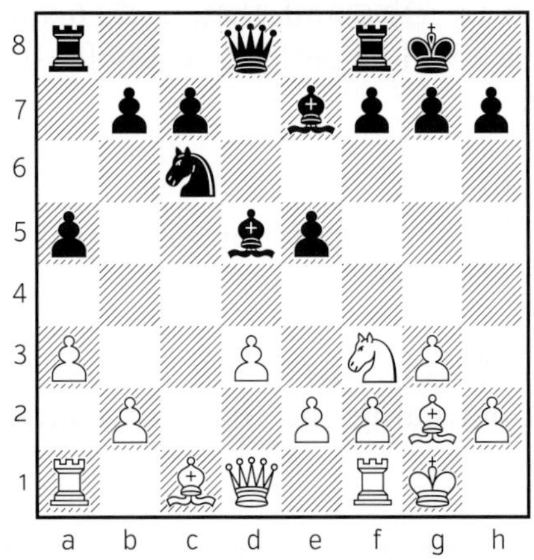

11.e4!?

Such a plan has its own logic — White drives the black bishop away from the center and starts to prepare d3-d4, after which White will obtain an extra pawn in the center. The danger is clear also — at the moment the weakness on d4 can be exploited by the opponent.

11...♗e6 12.♗e3

Too slow is 12.h3 ♕d7 13.♔h2 ♖fd8. Now White prepares d3-d4 and Black has to stop it immediately.

12...♗f6 13.b3

It is clear that White does not like ...a5-a4, which will seriously weaken the square b3.

13...♕d7 14.♕c2 ♖fd8 15.♖fd1 ♗g4

This move increases pressure on d4, additionally creating an unpleasant pin.

16.♖d2

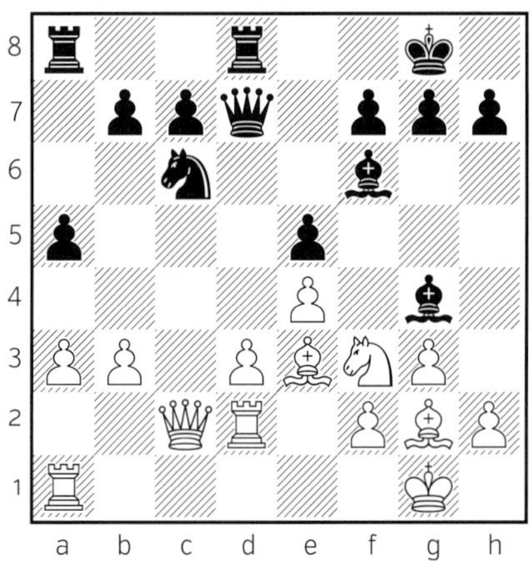

16...h6

A direct option to occupy the d4 square is possible: 16...♗f3 17.♗f3 ♘d4 18.♗d4 ♕d4 19.♖b1 c6, but the presence of opposite-colour bishops will give White some additional chances for a draw. So, Black's plan is created by Botvinnik — here it is necessary to exchange dark-squared bishops, then control over d4 will absolute.

17.♖c1 ♗f3 18.♗f3 ♗g5 19.♗d1

White activity would just help Black to launch a few positional/tactical blows: 19.♕c4 ♘d4 20.♗h5 b5 21.♕c3 c5!

19...♕d6

It is possible to create a weakness on e3 and then try to launch an attack against the king 19...♗e3 20.fe3 ♕e7 21.♕c5 ♕g5 22.♔f2 h5.

20.♕b2 ♕g6

Black still has in mind ...h6-h5-h4.

21.♗g5 ♕g5!

Just so, as Black will need to have the ...h5-h4 attack. Additionally, doubled pawns are very limited during any attack. Of course, it is the only active possibility for White.

22.b4 ab4 23.ab4 ♖d4!

The simple option is to protect the c7 pawn: 23...♖d7, but the move in the game is much more active.

24.♖c4

Possible is 24.♗b3 ♖b4?, provoking premature tactics: 25.♖c6 bc6 26.♗f7 ♔f7 27.♕b4±.

24...♖ad8 25.h4 ♕e7

Also possible is the sharper 25...♕d2 26.♕d2 ♖c4 27.b5 ♘b4.

26.b5 ♖c4 27.dc4 ♘d4

Finally Black obtains his ideal position with the knight on d4.

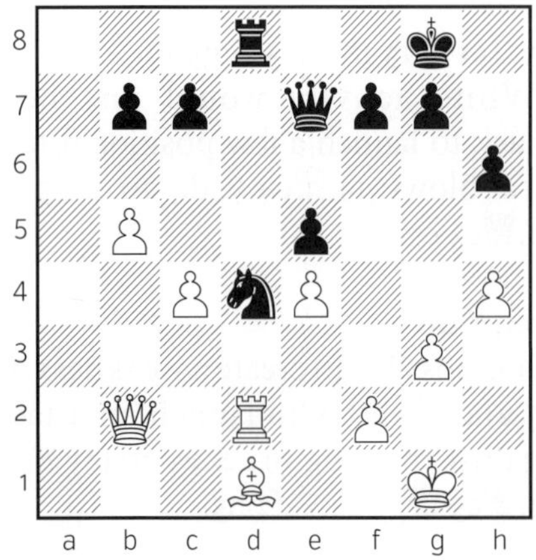

28.♕a2 ♕f8!

As Black has to create new weaknesses in his opponent's position, it is useful to have a file for his own rook.

29.♔g2 ♖a8 30.♕b1 ♕a3

Now all Black's pieces start a tremendous space expansion.

31.♗e2 b6 32.♗g4 ♖a4

The target is clear — the pawn c4.

33.♖d3 ♕c5 34.♗d1 ♖c4 35.♕a2 ♖c1 36.♕a8 ♔h7 37.♕e8 37...♕b5 0:1.

WEAK SQUARES IN THE OPPONENTS CAMP

Now we will see a beautiful example of the technique required to conduct a plan of weakening the square d6, then controlling it fully and finally, how to use it for the decisive attack.

1

▷ **Geller**
▶ **Ree**
Wijk aan Zee 1969 [B07]

1.♘f3 g6 2.e4 ♗g7 3.d4 d6 4.c3! c6 5.♘bd2 ♘f6 6.♗e2 0–0 7.0–0 ♘bd7 8.♖e1 ♕c7 9.♗f1! e5 10.a4 ♖e8?!

10...a5. In similar situations it is always necessary to stop the opponent's space expansion.

11.a5 ♖b8

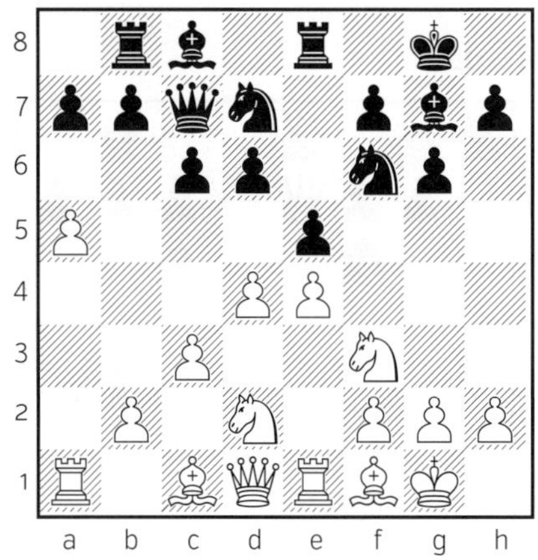

12.♘c4!

With this move Geller shows his intention to occupy square d6.

12...b5

A forced variation was calculated by Geller to support his plan: 12...ed4 13.♗f4! ♘e5 14.cd4 ♘c4 15.♗c4 ♖e4 (15...♘e4 16.♘g5) 16.♖e4 ♘e4 17.♕e2! ♘f6 18.♘g5 ♘d5 19.♗d5 cd5 20.♕e8 ♗f8 21.♗d6!+-, but sometimes retreat is not shameful, but the best solution — 12...♗f8.

13.ab6 ab6 14.de5 de5 15.♕d6

In order to control this important square it is preferable to exchange queens, which is not very favourable for Black.

15...♕b7

15...♕d6 16.♘d6 ♖e6 17.♘c8 ♖c8 18.♖a7 with a big advantage. It is always this way if a rook is able to penetrate to the 7th rank.

16.♕a3!

Now is time for the knight.

16...♕c7

After the possible 16...♗f8 17.♘d6 ♗d6 18.♕d6 b5 19.b4 White's advantage has increased.

17.♘d6 ♖f8 18.♗c4

Every move is an improvement of the piece positions and the creation of new threats. The knight's function on d6 is not just to cause problems for the black pieces, especially the rooks, but also to help in the co-ordination of an attack on f7.

18...b5

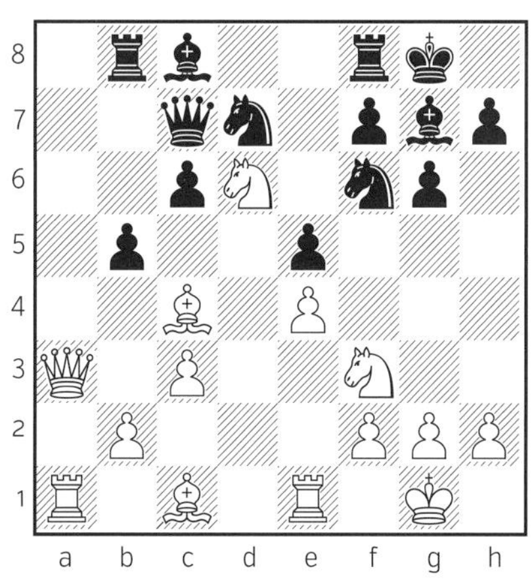

White is ready for tactics in the case of 18...♘c5 19.♘f7! ♖f7 20.♘g5. But now another combination is on the scene.

19.♗f7!+- ♔h8

Or 19...♖f7 20.♘f7 ♔f7 21.♘g5+-.

20.♘c8

Also not bad is the improvement of the next piece — 20.♖d1.

20...♖f7 21.♘g5! ♖f8 22.♘d6 ♘b6 23.♗e3!

The final important piece enters the game with decisive effect.

23...b4 24.♗b6 ♕b6

A nice counterstrike was prepared by Geller in the case of another capture: 24...♖b6 25.♕a7.

25.♘df7 ♔g8 26.♕b3! 1:0.

Not just squares on the d- or e-files are important — for central influence we can use, for example, the c6 square.

2

▷ **Botvinnik**
▶ **Donner**
Amsterdam 1963 [A14]

1.c4 ♘f6 2.♘f3 e6 3.g3 d5 4.♗g2 ♗e7 5.0-0 0-0 6.b3 b6 7.♗b2 ♗b7 8.cd5 ♘d5 9.d4 c5 10.dc5 ♗c5 11.♘bd2 ♘d7 12.a3

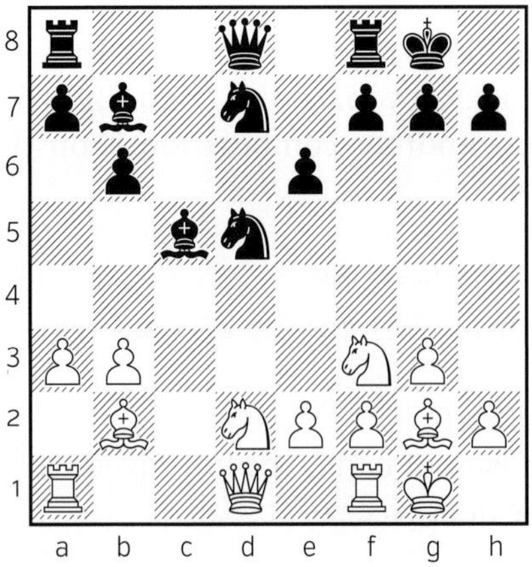

12...♘5f6

Black plays in too relaxed a fashion. It is clear that White is planning some space-seizing activity on the queen's flank, so it is necessary to stop it immediately, so 12...a5!?

13.b4 ♗e7 14.♘d4!

A very useful exchange of bishops, after which it becomes clear that the weakness on c6 will be very serious.

14...♗g2 15.♔g2 ♕c7 16.♕b3!

White is ready to swap queens, the better to control the c6 square.

16...♖fc8 17.♖fc1 ♕b7 18.♕f3

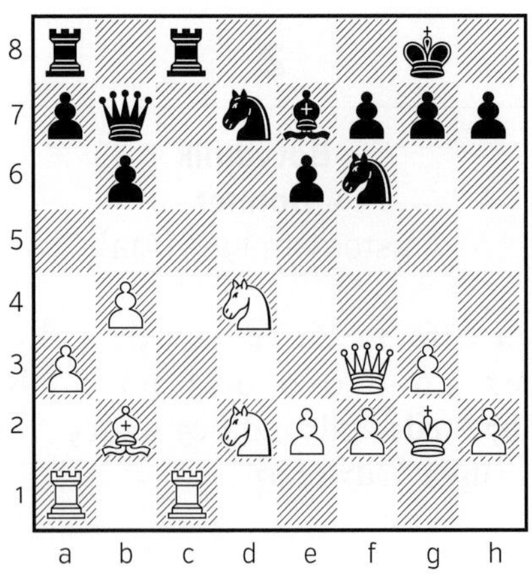

As was said before — White exchanges every defender of c6.

18...♘d5

Another method of development is 18...♕f3 19.♘2f3 ♗f8 20.♘c6 ♘e4 21.♖c2 ♘ec5 22.♖d1! ♖c6 23.♖d7 ♘d7 24.♖c6 and now the rook controls the c6 square and the whole c-file.

19.e4 ♘5f6 20.b5 a6

A very difficult position for Black is reached after 20...♘c5 21.♘c6 h6 22.a4 a6 23.♗d4.

21.♘c6 ♗f8 22.a4

Finally White fixes his grip over the c6 square, and gains a lot of space. The next step will be to create and attack a weakness.

22...ab5 23.ab5 ♖a1 24.♖a1 ♖a8

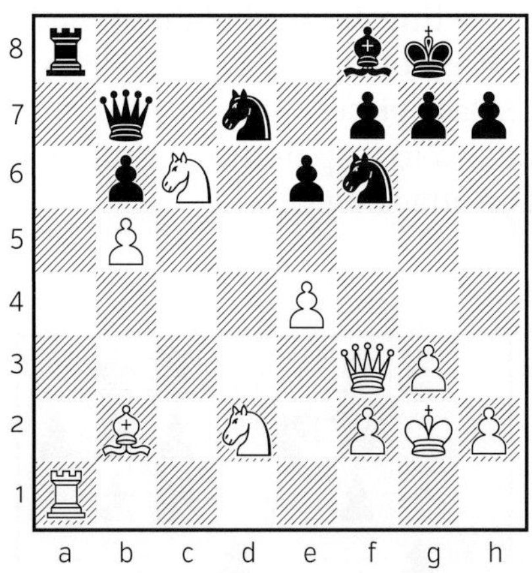

Black tries to reduce White's pressure with the help of full exchanges, but Botvinnik avoids an exchange of the rooks as it will play an important role in the attack of any weakness.

25.♖d1! ♘e8?

A very passive move which allows White to increase his advantage. Much better was 25...♗c5.

26.♘c4

Or immediately 26.e5.

26...♘c5 27.e5

Now there appears a new threat, ♘c4-d6, and after exchanges there White will obtain a dangerous passed pawn,

27...♖c8 28.♖a1!

Now the rook changes direction and penetrates the seventh rank, as Black can no longer fight for the file.

28...♖c7

28...♖a8 29.♖a8 ♕a8 30.♘e7.

29.♖a7 ♕a7

Black decides to sacrifice his queen, but it is too late.

30.♘a7 ♖a7 31.♘b6 1:0.

3

▷ **Dautov**

▶ **J. Polgar**

Istanbul 2000 [E15]

1.d4 ♘f6 2.c4 e6 3.♘f3 b6 4.g3 ♗a6 5.♕a4 ♗b7 6.♗g2 c5 7.dc5 ♗c5 8.0–0 0–0 9.♘c3 ♘e4 10.♕c2 ♘c3 11.♕c3 d5!? 12.♖d1 ♘d7

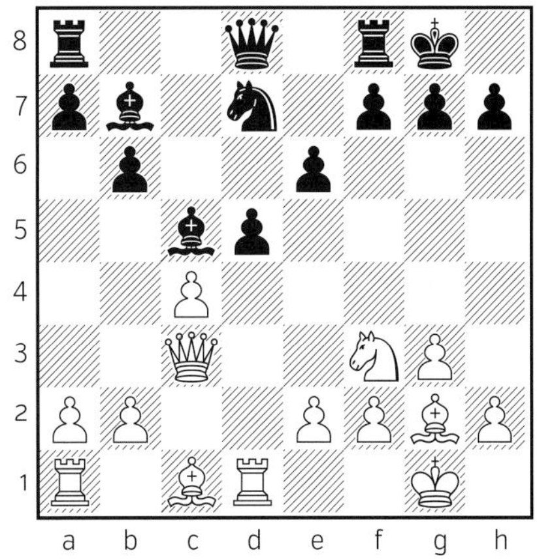

It is risky here to try 12...d4!? 13.♘d4? (13.♕d3 ♘c6 14.a3 a5 15.♘g5 g6 16.♘e4±) 13...♗g2 14.♔g2 e5 15.♘f5! (15.♕f3 ♘a6) 15...♕d1 16.♕e5 f6 17.♕e6 ♖f7 18.♕e8 ♗f8 19.♕e4 ♘c6 20.♕c6 ♖d8.

13.♗g5!

Much stronger than the dull 13.cd5 ♗d5 14.e4 (14.♘e5? ♖c8.) 14...♗e4 15.♘e5 ♗d5 16.♗d5 ed5 17.♖d5 ♕f6 18.♗f4 ♘e5=.

13...♕e8?

Almost any other defence promises Black more than the game continuation.

13...f6 14.♗e3 ♖c8 15.cd5 ♗d5 16.♗c5 ♖c5 (16...♘c5 17.♕e3.) 17.♕e3; 13...♗e7! 14.♗e7 ♕e7 15.cd5 ♗d5 16.♖ac1 ♘c5! 17.b4 ♘a4! (17...♘e4 18.♕b2 ♖fc8 19.♘e5.) 18.♕c2 (18.♕a3 b5 19.♘d4 ♗g2 20.♔g2 ♖ac8=.) 18...b5 19.a3 (19.e4 ♗b7=.) 19...a5=.

14.cd5 ♗d5

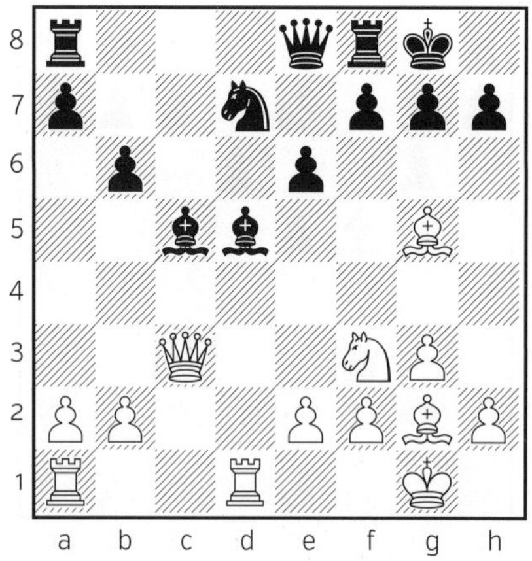

White's next is not just gaining space on the queenside, but the start of a strategy to occupy the c6 square.

15.b4! ♗e7 16.♗e7 ♕e7 17.♖ac1

The start of a plan to gain total control over the open c-file.

17...♖fd8

The attempt to start immediate counterplay on the queens flank does not work: 17...a5? 18.♕c7±, threatening to exploit the unpleasant pin with 19.e4. 17...♘f6 18.♘e5.

18.♘d4

The second step is to exchange the defender of c6, the bishop on d5, and then with b4-b5 White will complete the first part of the operation.

18...♘f6 19.b5 ♗g2 20.♔g2 ♖d5 21.♘c6 ♕d7 22.♕c2!

Tempting, but wrong, was 22.♖d5? ♕d5 23.♕f3 ♕f3 24.♔f3 a6=.

22...♕b7 23.a4 h6 24.e4 ♖c5 25.♕d3 ♖c1 26.♖c1 a6

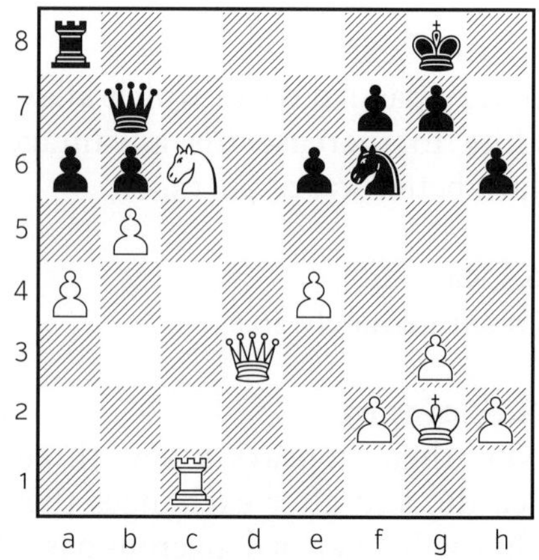

27.♖c4!

White has to find an object of attack with the help of knight c6, which limits the possibilities of his opponent's pieces. The rook is placed in front of the queen for more powerful co-ordination, but the other way was possible also: 27.♖d1!?

27...ab5 28.ab5 ♕c7

28...♘d7?! The transfer of the knight to the strong square c5 is illogical, as it will leave the kingside without serious protection. 29.♖d4 ♘c5 30.♕d1 ♕c7 31.e5±.

29.♖d4± e5?

This creates more weaknesses in the position, so better was the simple 29... g6.

30.♖c4

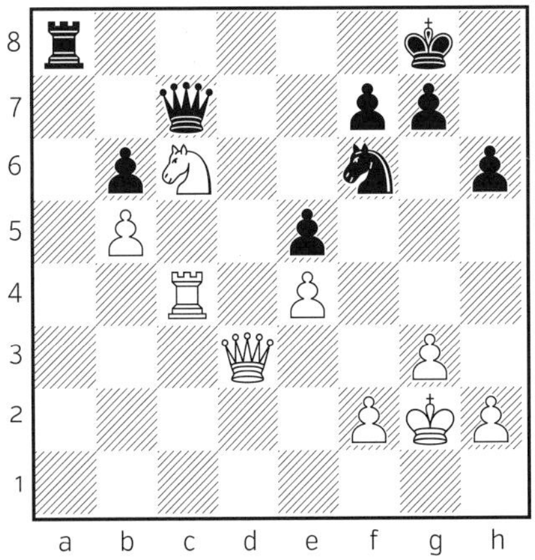

30...♕d7?!

Black decides to sacrifice a pawn for what is only the illusion of activity. No big difference was made by 30...♔h8 31.♕c3 ♖e8 32.♖a4 ♕d6 33.♕c2!± and the white rook plans to start attacking the 7th rank from a7.

31.♘e5

Other moves are simply incorrect: 31.♕d7? ♘d7 32.♘e7 ♔h7 33.♖c6 ♖a2; 31.♕c2? ♕d6=. **31...♕e6?!**

Transitions into the endgame are perfectly controlled by White: 31...♕d3 32.♘d3 ♖a5 33.♖b4 ♘e8 34.♘e5 ♘c7 (34...♘d6? 35.♘c6 ♖b5 36.e5!! ♖b4 37.ed6+-) 35.♖c4 (35.♘c4 ♖b5 36.♖b5 ♘b5 37.♘b6.) 35...♖b5 36.♘f7+-.

32.♘c6 ♖a2 33.e5 ♕d5

Things go very quickly after 33... ♘g4? 34.♘e7 ♕e7 35.♖c8+-.

34.♕d5 ♘d5 35.♖d4 ♘c3 36.♖d8 ♔h7

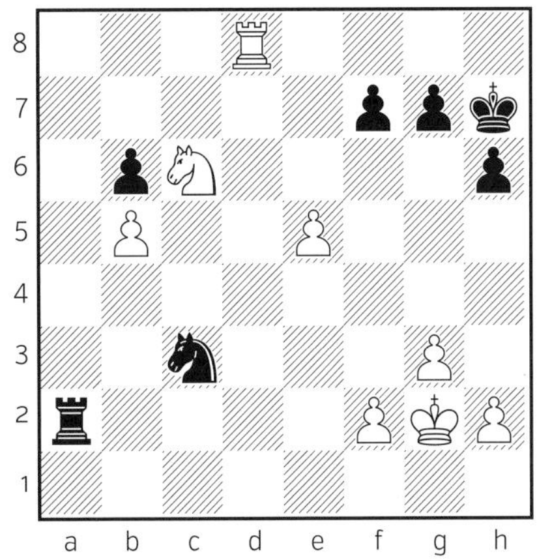

37.♖d7

Also possible was 37.♖f8+-.

37...♘b5 38.♖f7 ♖c2 39.♘b4 ♖e2 40.♘d3 ♘a3 41.♔f3 ♖c2 42.e6 ♖c8 43.♔e4 ♖e8 44.♔d5 b5 45.♖b7 ♘c2 46.e7 ♔g6 47.♔e6 1:0.

CREATION OF THE PASSED PAWN

Pawns can be formed into structures, but at some moment a passed pawn can be created in the center. It can be used as a powerful weapon, but it can also be attacked by the opponent. Let's take a look at how we can use the power of the passed d-pawn, which frequently appears from openings such as the Grunfeld Defence.

1

▷ **Petrosian**
▶ **Korchnoi**
Il Ciocco 1977 [D41]

1.d4 d5 2.♘f3 ♘f6 3.c4 e6 4.♘c3 c5 5.cd5 ♘d5 6.e4 ♘c3 7.bc3 cd4 8.cd4 ♗b4 9.♗d2 ♗d2 10.♕d2 0–0 11.♗c4 ♘c6 12.0–0 b6

There exist other ways of fighting the kind of center which can be transformed into a passed pawn — e.g. 12...♕d6.

13.♖fe1 ♗b7 14.♖ad1

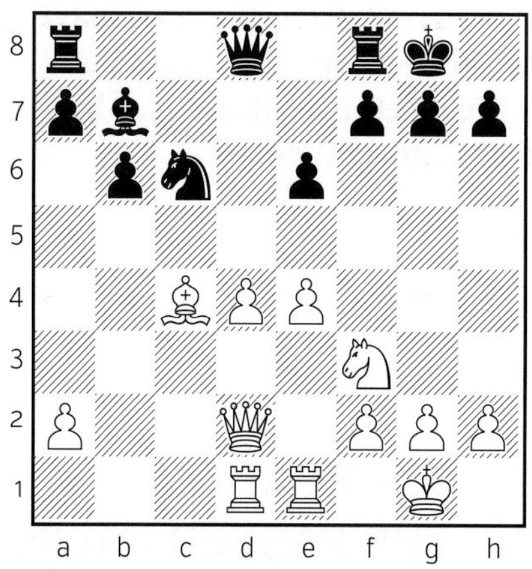

14...♘e7?!

Two other options were playable: 14...♖c8; 14...♕d6.

15.d5!

This is principled and it is also best, although a waiting/improving attitude is also possible and applied by many players:

15.♕e3 ♖c8 16.♗b3 ♕c7 17.h4.

15...ed5 16.ed5 ♘f5 17.♘e5!

With this activity White starts to fight the blockade of the d5-pawn by the knight, but not in a direct way. It is a very useful idea and technique to study.

Worse was the slow 17.♗d3 ♘d6=.

17...♘d6 18.♘c6!±

Of course, classics state that the best plans are conducted in the best way with the help of small tactics.

18...♗c6?

Bad was 18...♘c4 19.♘d8 ♘d2 20.♘b7±, but perhaps better was to place the queen in a more active position with 18...♕f6!?, but clearly the knight on c6 causes much more problems for Black than the knight d6 does for White.

Now there occurs a typical and instructive change of passed pawns — instead of a d-pawn, White obtains a c-pawn, which helps to control the central files much more powerfully.

19.dc6 ♘c4 20.♕f4!

It was too early to try to use the power of the advanced passed pawn:

20.♕d8?? ♖ad8 21.♖d8 ♖d8 22.c7 ♖f8 23.♖d1 b5! 24.♖d8 ♘b6–+.

20...♘d6

Worse was 20...♕f6 21.♕c4 ♖ac8 22.c7! as the pawn c7 completely paralyzes Black's pieces.

21.♖d6 ♕c7

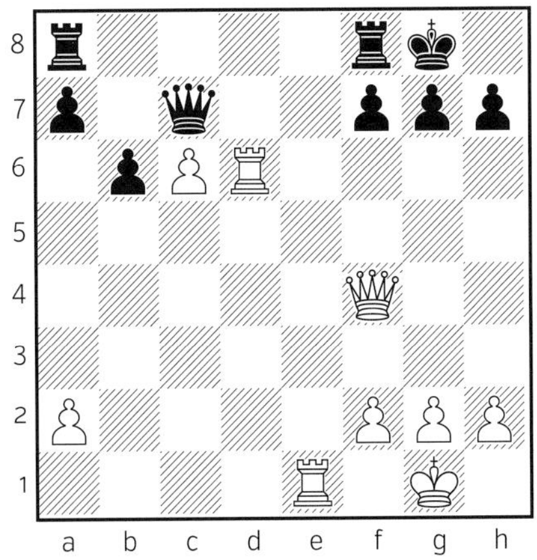

22.g3

White has complete control over the central files, but it is not so easy to use the power of the golden child — the pawn c7.

So, White's plan is to improve the positions of all his pieces, to make his own king safe, and then to set about creating a second weakness in his opponent's position.

22...h6 23.♕e5 ♖ac8

The other rook move does not help: 23...♖ae8 24.♕e8 ♖e8 (24...♕d6 25.♕d7+-.) 25.♖e8 ♔h7 26.♖d7 ♕c6 27.♖ee7+-.

24.♕d5 ♔h7

After 24...♖fd8 25.♖d7! ♖d7 26.cd7 ♖f8 27.♖e8 it is not possible to stop the d-pawn.

25.♖e4 ♔g8 26.♔g2 a6 27.h4 b5

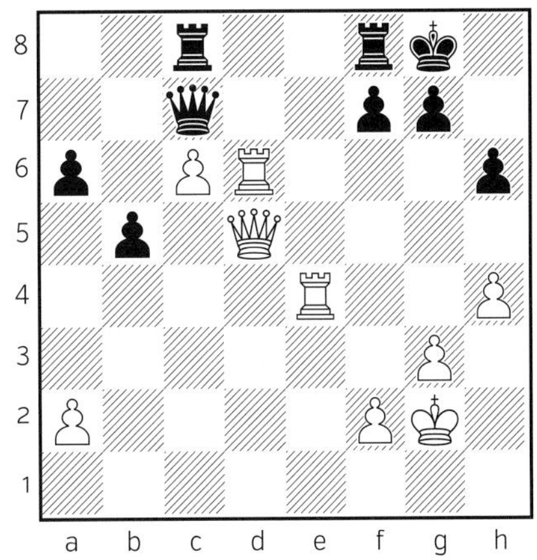

28.g4!

White has improved the positions of every piece to the maximum and now begins the creation of the second weakness — it is, incidentally, on the kingside, so the target is the king!

28...♔h7 29.♖e2 ♔h8 30.g5 h5

30...hg5 31.hg5 ♖ce8 32.♖e8 ♖e8 33.g6 fg6 34.♖d7 ♕f4 35.♕f3! ♕g5 36.♕g3 and the c-pawn has the decisive word in a few moves time.

31.♖d2 ♖fe8 32.♕f3 g6 33.♖f6

Simpler was to close the diagonal with 33.♖2d5 and next ♖d7 then ♕f7.

33...♕e7?

A longer, but ultimately unsuccessful, defence would occur after 33...♖e7 34.♖dd6 ♔g7 35.♕d5 ♖f8 36.♖d7.

34.♖d7 ♕e1 35.♖g6! ♕e5 36.♕h5# 1:0.

The top young players have studied the classics deeply and profoundly, as we can see from the next example.

2

▷ **Andreikin**
▶ **Stupak**
Chotowa 2010 [A40]

1.d4 e6 2.c4 ♗b4 3.♗d2 ♗d2 4.♕d2 ♘f6 5.♘c3 d5 6.♘f3 c6 7.e3 ♘bd7 8.♗d3 dc4 9.♗c4 ♕e7 10.e4 e5

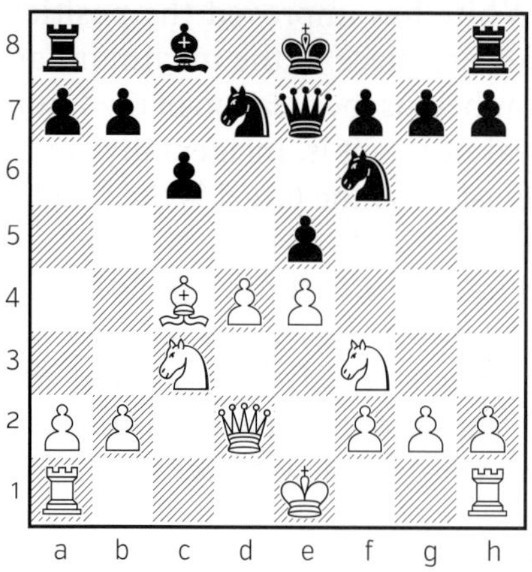

Now White creates a passed pawn, which will eventually prove to be the decisive factor in the game.

11.d5 cd5

After 11...♘b6 12.♗b3 cd5 13.ed5 ♕d6 14.♖c1 ♗d7 15.0–0 0–0 16.♖fe1 ♖fe8 17.♘g5 White will try to unblock the d5-pawn with ♘e4. 17... ♖ac8 18.♘ce4.

12.ed5

12.♘d5 ♘d5 13.♗d5 ♘f6.

12...♕c5 13.♗b3 0–0

It is more desirable to try to drive the opponent's knight from the center: 13...b5 14.0–0 b4 15.♘e2 ♗a6.

14.0–0 ♕d6 15.♖fe1 a6

It's necessary to lose time securing the blockading piece, but it is known to all from Nimzowitsch that the queen is the worst blockading piece.

16.♕e3

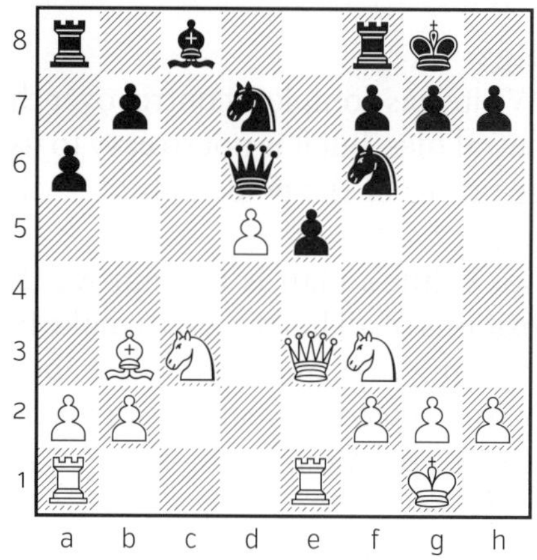

16...♖e8?

It is necessary to continue attacking the d5 pawn with 16...b5 17.♘g5 ♗b7 18.♘ge4 ♘e4 19.♘e4 ♕b6 20.♖ad1 ♖ad8.

17.♘d2!

Now begins the operation to release the passed pawn.

17...b5 18.♘ce4 ♕b8

The other retreat is no better: 18... ♕f8 19.♖ac1 a5 20.a3.

19.d6

Once the passed pawn starts to roll it increases Black's problems.

19...♗b7

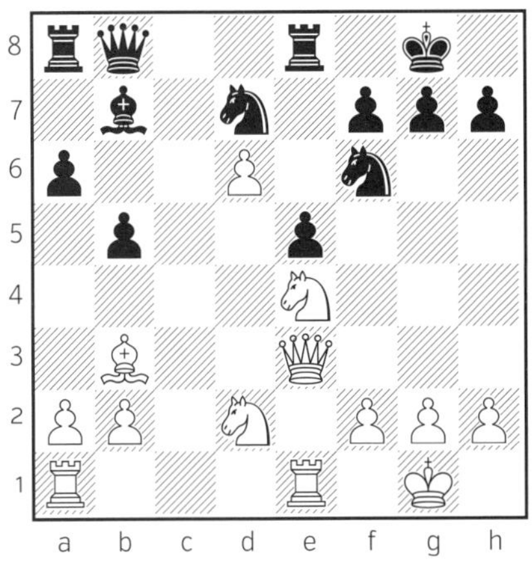

20.♖ac1!

This move has to be supported by exact, although not complicated, calculation.

20...♗e4 21.♘e4 ♘e4 22.♕e4 ♕d6 23.♖ed1 ♘f6 24.♗f7!

A final small combination in Capablanca's style.

24...♔f7 25.♕b7 ♕e7 26.♖c7 1:0.

3

▷ **Mikhalchishin**
► **Filipenko**
Vladikavkaz 1978 [D12]

1.♘f3 d5 2.d4 ♘f6 3.c4 c6 4.e3 ♗f5 5.♗d3 ♗d3 6.♕d3 e6 7.0–0 ♘bd7 8.♘c3 ♗e7 9.e4 de4 10.♘e4 ♘e4 11.♕e4 0–0 12.♗f4 ♕b6 13.♕e2 ♖fe8 14.♖ad1 c5 15.♖d3 ♗f6 16.♗e3 ♕c7 17.b3 e5 18.de5 ♘e5 19.♖d5 ♘g4 20.♕d3 b6 21.♖d7 ♕c6 22.♗f4 ♖ad8 23.♖d5 ♖d5 24.cd5 ♕d7

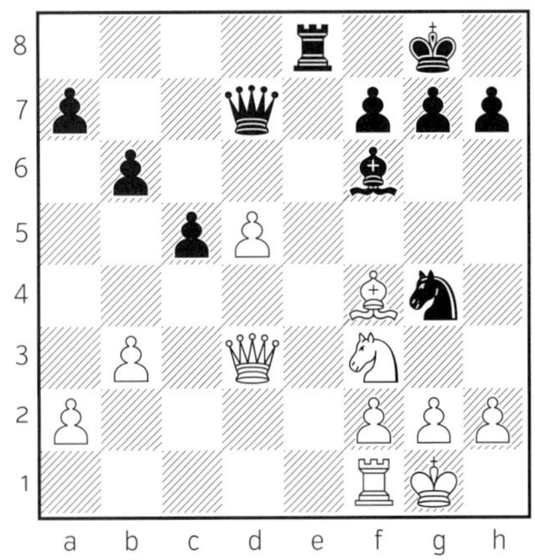

25.d6

If there is even a small chance to move, then the passed pawn has to run!

25...♗e5

There is no real difference after 25...♖e6 26.h3 ♘e5 27.♘e5 ♗e5 28.♗e5 ♖e5 29.♖d1 g6 and the position is similar to the game.

26.♗e5 ♘e5 27.♘e5 ♖e5 28.♖d1 h6

Black is blocking the white pawn and so White's plan has to be to create a second weakness on the queens or kingside. It is not easy, so White tries to combine threats. Black's plan should be to create his own passed pawn on the queenside, deflecting the white pieces from supporting the d-pawn.

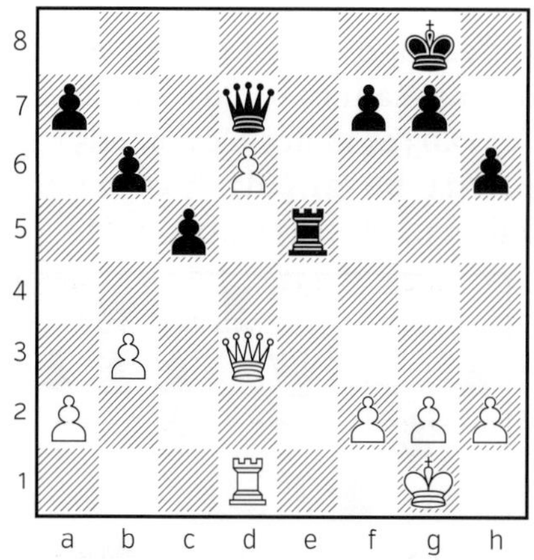

29.f4

It is possible to start more slowly, but this move will be necessary sooner or later. 29.h3.

29...♖e6 30.♕d5 g6 31.h3 ♔g7 32.♔h2

Now White creates the threat f4-f5, so Black has to stop it.

32...♖e2 33.a4

Possibly better is to begin a minority attack, but White did not want to reduce the material just yet. 33.b4! cb4 34.♕c4 ♖e8 35.♕b4.

33...♖e3

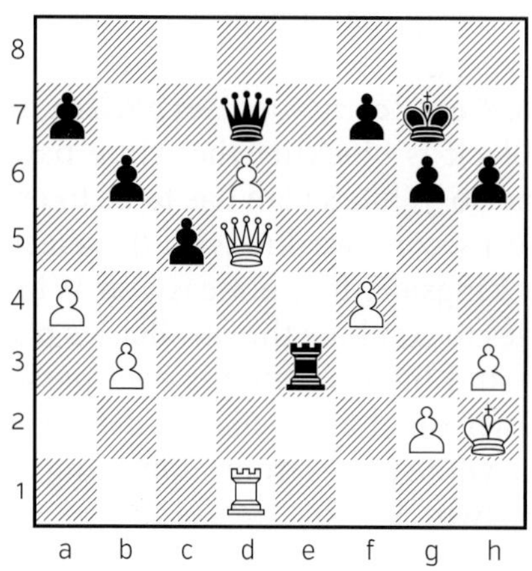

After 33...a5 34.♕d3 ♖e8 35.g4 White is ready to combine threats on both flanks f4-f5 with ♕b5.

34.a5

Very strong now would be 34.b4!? White's threats include a5-a6 and then ♕b7 unblocking his pawn on d6.

34...ba5 35.♕c5 ♖b3

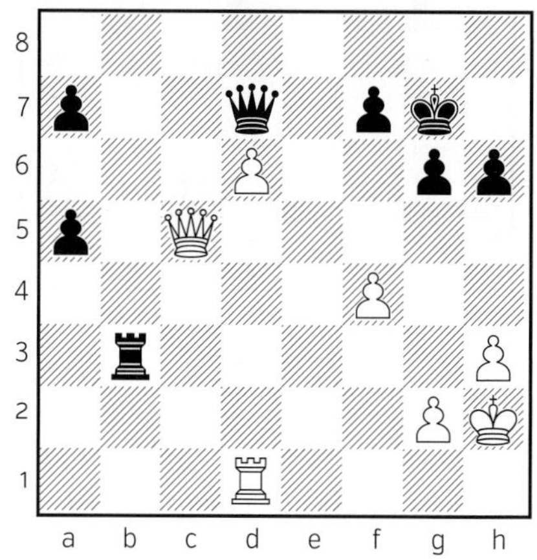

36.♕d4?

White wants to use the absence of his opponent's rook on the e-file, but better was simply to take the pawn with 36.♕a5.

36...♔h7 37.♖e1 ♖b8?

Better was to transfer into a rook endgame, even with the pawn minus on one flank: 37...♖b4 38.♕f6 ♕f5! 39.♕f5 gf5 40.♖d1 ♖b8 41.♖d5 ♖d8 42.♖f5 ♔g6 43.♖d5 a4.

38.♖e7 ♕f5 39.d7 g5

39...♖d8 40.♖e8.

40.♖e8 1:0.

1

▷ **Davidovic**
▶ **Fernandez Garcia**
Manila 1992 (D76)

1.♘f3 ♘f6 2.c4 g6 3.g3 ♗g7 4.♗g2 d5 5.cd5 ♘d5 6.0–0 ♘b6 7.♘c3 0–0 8.d4 ♘c6 9.d5 ♘a5 10.e4 c6 11.♗f4! cd5 12.ed5 ♗c3!?

Such pawns are 'untasty' and Black will have problems with the squares around own his king.

13.bc3 ♘d5 14.♗h6 ♖e8 15.♕d4! ♘f6 16.♕h4 ♘c6 17.♖fe1 ♗g4 18.♘d4! ♖c8 19.♗g5 ♘d4 20.cd4 ♕d7 21.♗f6 ef6 22.♕f6

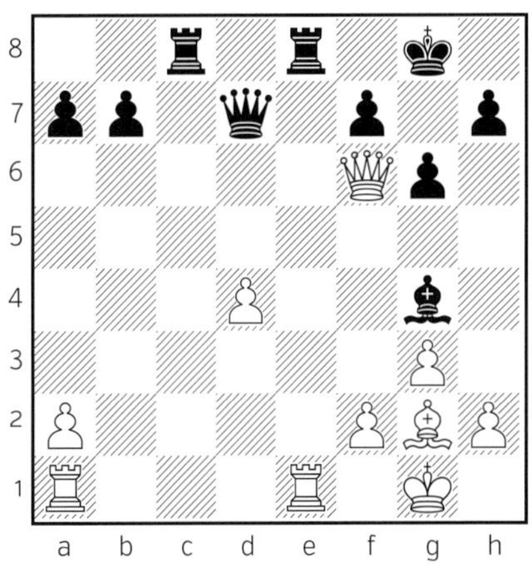

Finally a position with a central passed pawn has appeared. In addition, the power of White's bishop on g2 adds a lot to the pawns power.

22...♖e6?!

It is necessary to start blocking the annoying passed pawn 22...♗e6 and no good is 23.d5 ♗d5 24.♖e8 ♖e8 25.♖d1 ♕a4 26.♖d5 ♖e1 27.♗f1 ♖f1 28.♔f1 ♕c4.

23.♕f4 ♗h3?

It is now necessary to start defending with 23...♗f5 24.d5 ♖a6 25.♖e5 or to start flank counterplay with 23...b5.

24.♗h3! ♖e1 25.♖e1 ♕h3 26.♖e7

Now, forced into complete passivity, Black can do nothing to prevent the advance of White's passed d pawn.

26...♖f8 27.d5 ♕c8 28.h4 b5 29.d6 ♕c5 30.♕f6 a5 31.d7 ♕d5

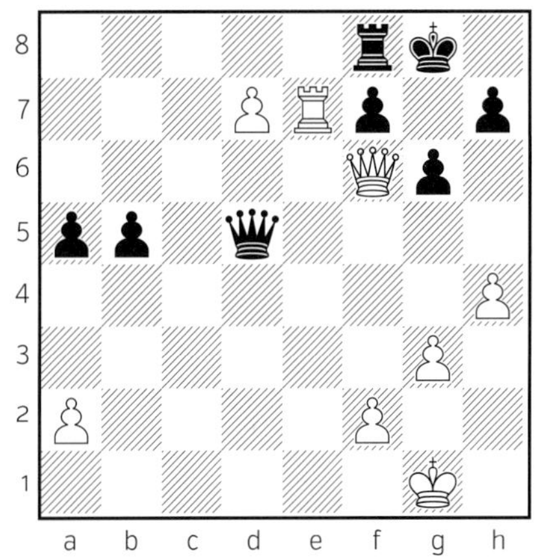

32.♕e5!

The offer to exchange queens forcing his opponent's pieces to leave crucial squares.

32...♕d1 33.♔g2 ♕d3

Material concessions do not help: 33...h5 34.♕b5.

34.♕c5! 1:0.

The threat of 35.♖e8 is unstoppable.

But of course, passed pawns are not always a successful weapon; there exist positions in which methods of blocking and attack are more successful.

2

▷ **Mikhalchishin**
▶ **Sax**
Bled 1998 [E01]

1.d4 ♘f6 2.c4 e6 3.♘f3 c5 4.g3 cd4 5.♘d4 d5 6.♗g2 e5 7.♘f3 d4 8.0–0 ♘c6 9.e3 ♗e7 10.ed4 ed4 11.♗f4 0–0 12.♘e5 ♘e5 13.♗e5 ♗c5

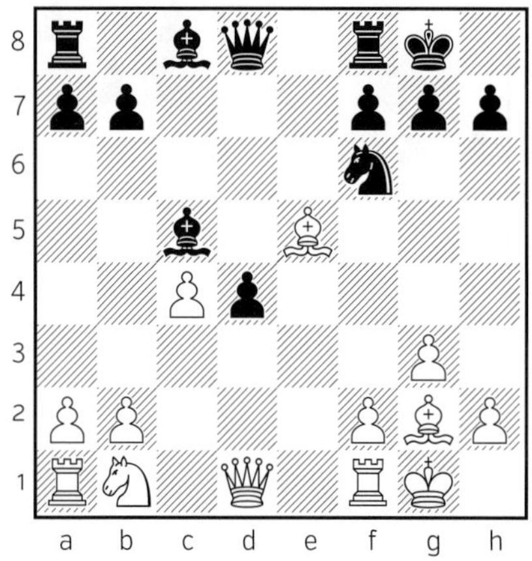

This position from the opening has seen one important element emerge- the passed pawn on d4, but it is sometimes not an important asset for one side, but rather an important target for the opponent.

14.♘d2
Here there are two completely different approaches:14.b4!? ♗b4 15.♕d4 or 14.♗f6!? ♕f6 15.♘d2.

14...♖e8
It is possible to try to get rid of the unpleasant centralized bishop immediately: 14...♘g4 15.♗f4 g5 (15...♘e3? 16.fe3 de3 17.♕h5±) 16.♘b3 gf4 17.♘c5 fg3 18.hg3±.

15.♗f6 ♕f6 16.♘b3
It is possible to reach a central square, but White's task is to attack the central pawn:
16.♘e4!? ♕e5 17.♕d2 ♗f5 18.♖fe1.

16...♕b6

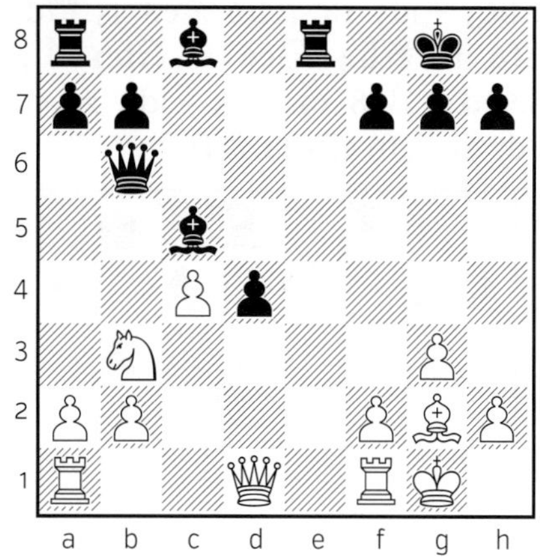

17.♕d3!
Blockading with the queen is often possible when there are no knights on the board! 17.♕h5?! was tried here before but without special success.

17...♖b8
White keeps a big advantage after 17...♗g4 18.♖fe1 ♖e1 19.♖e1 ♖b8 20.♖e5±.

18.♖fe1
Much weaker is the immediate exchange of the better knight 18.♘c5

♕c5 19.♖ad1 ♗e6 20.♕d4 ♕c4 21.♕a7 ♕a2=.

18...♗e6 19.♖e5!?

There were two other tempting options, but the rook on e5 conducts a double function: 19.♖ac1!? or 19.♖ad1!?

19...♗e7

The rook belongs here, on its way to d7, as it protects the pawn and support its advance.

20.♖c1!

Worse would be 20.♖ae1 ♗f6 21.♖5e2 (21.♖b5 ♕c7 22.♘c5 a6! 23.♘e6 ♖e6! 24.♖e6 ab5).

20...♗f6?

Correct was to defend stubbornly with 20...♖ed8.

21.♖b5 ♕c7

Or 21...♕a6 22.♖a5 ♕b6 23.c5±.

22.♗e4!±

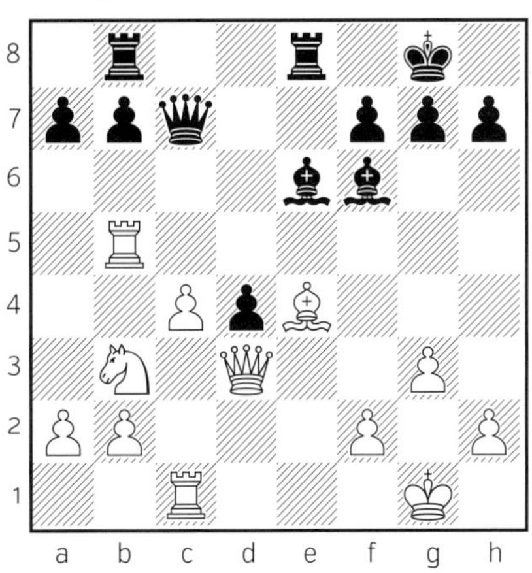

22...g6 23.♘d4

White has achieved his aim — the passed pawn is liquidated!

23...♗d7

No better is 23...♗g4 24.b3 ♖ed8 25.♖d5±.

24.♖d5 ♖bd8

White keeps a big advantage after 24...♗c6 25.♘c6 bc6 26.♖d7 ♕e5 27.♗c6 ♕b2 28.♖f1 ♕a2 29.♕f3 ♔g7 30.♗d5 ♖f8 31.c5±.

25.b3 ♗h3

White would achieve a better endgame with an extra pawn after 25... ♗c6!? 26.♘c6 bc6 27.♖d8 ♖d8 28.♕f3±.

26.♘b5! ♕e7

26...♖d5 27.♘c7 ♖d3 28.♘e8+-.

27.♘d6!

This move guarantees White a decisive advantage.

27...♖d6

27...♖f8 28.♘b7! ♖d5 29.♕d5 ♖e8 30.♘d8+-.

28.♖d6 ♗e5 29.♖d5 ♗b2 30.♖e1+- ♕b4

30...f5 31.♖d7+-.

31.♖e2

1:0.

PAWN SACRIFICES IN THE CENTER

Sometimes central pawns can be sacrificed with the idea of mobilizing all the pieces on the opened central files.

1

▹ **Korchnoi**
▸ **Beliavsky**
Leon 1994 [D45]

1.c4 c6 2.d4 d5 3.e3 ♘f6 4.♘c3 e6 5.♘f3 ♘bd7 6.♕c2 ♗d6 7.b3 0–0 8.♗b2?! e5 9.cd5 cd5 10.de5 ♘e5 11.♗e2 ♘f3 12.♗f3

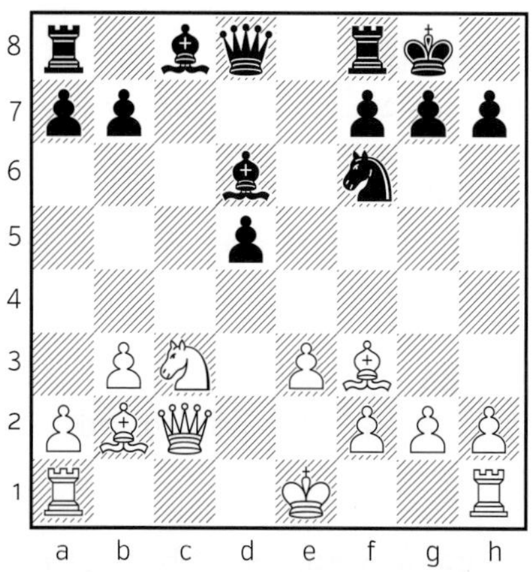

12...d4!!

The idea of this pawn sacrifice in the center is to speed up the development of his own pieces, exploiting some problems facing the white king.

13.ed4?

After the game it became clear that it would be better not to accept the pawn sacrifice, but to try to sacrifice a pawn himself:

13.♘e4 ♘e4 14.♗e4 de3 15.0–0 ef2 16.♕f2 .

13...♖e8 14.♔f1

Other defences do not solve the problems either:

14.♘e2 ♗b4 15.♗c3 ♗f5! 16.♕d2 ♗c3 17.♕c3 ♖c8 18.♕b4 ♗d3;

14.♗e2 ♗g4 15.f3 ♗h5 16.0–0 ♕c7 17.h3 ♗g6 18.♗d3 ♘h5 (Korchnoi).

14...♕a5 15.♕d1 ♗b4 16.♖c1 ♗d7

This simple developing move looks to be better than other bishop moves.

16...♗f5 17.g4;

16...♗e6!?

17.a3

Capture of the pawn would be met by a double -attack with check:

17.♗b7? ♗c3 18.♗c3 ♕b5–+

17...♗c3 18.♖c3

The other capture was no better:

18.♗c3 ♕a3 19.♗b7 ♖ab8 20.♖a1 ♕e7 21.♗f3 ♘e4 22.♗e4 ♕e4.

18...♘d5 19.♗d5

Or 19.♖c5? ♗b5 20.♔g1 ♖e1–+.

19...♕d5 20.a4 ♖ac8 21.f3 ♖c3 22.♗c3 ♖e3

Now it becomes clear how powerful is the activity of Black's pieces.

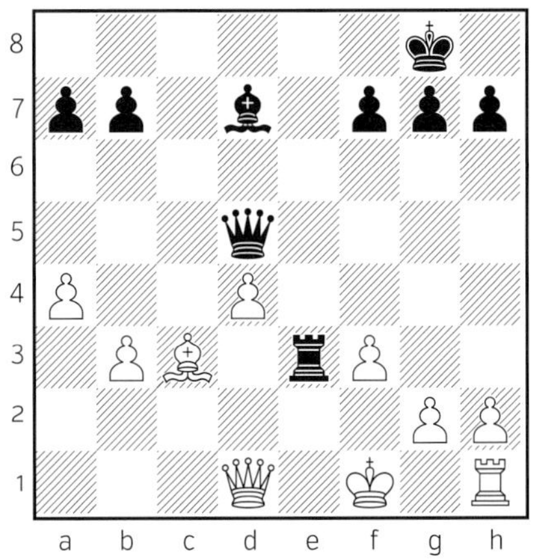

23.♗a1

Black had prepared powerful tactics after 23.♕d2? ♖f3 24.gf3 ♕f3 25.♔g1 ♗c6–+.

23...♖b3 24.♔f2 ♗a4 25.♖e1

Useful prophylaxis, as White has his own tactics as well.

25...f6

25...♖b2?? 26.♗b2 ♗d1 27.♖e8#.

26.♕c1 ♗c6 27.♕f4 h5 28.h4 ♖a3 29.♔g3 ♖a2 30.♗c3 ♕f7 31.♕f5

White would last a bit longer after the king's retreat: 31.♔h2 ♕g6 32.♗d2 ♕d3 33.♗b4 ♗f3 34.♖e8 ♔h7–+.

31...♕c7 0:1.

Such pawn sacrifices are even typical: they are conducted in several special central structures.

2

▷ **Anikaev**
► **Mikhalchishin**
Cheliabinsk 1974 [D88]

1.d4 ♘f6 2.c4 g6 3.♘c3 d5 4.cd5 ♘d5 5.e4 ♘c3 6.bc3 ♗g7 7.♗c4 c5 8.♘e2 ♘c6 9.♗e3 0–0 10.0–0 ♘a5 11.♗d3 b6 12.♕d2 ♗b7 13.♖ac1 cd4 14.cd4 e6

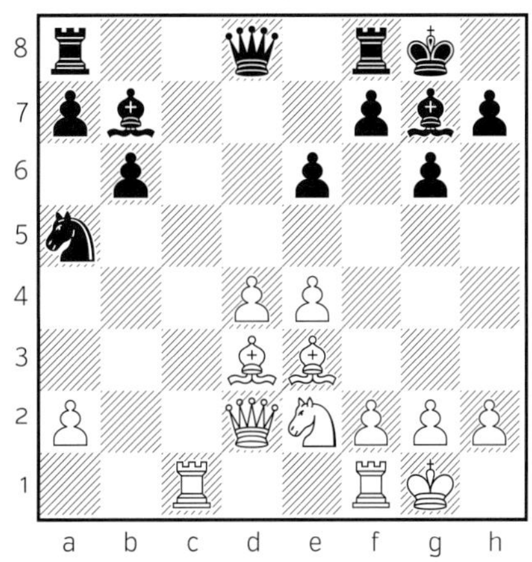

An evaluation of typical Grunfeld structures is not easy at all — it is obvious that White has a very strong center, but Black's bishops b7 and g7 create powerful cross-pressure on the pawns e4 and d4. Of course, the key issue is which plans should be chosen based on these evaluations for both sides? White will try to create some weakness on the kingside, and Black on the opposite side, exploiting the c-file.

15.♗h6

The first step. It is necessary to get rid of the important bishop, which conducts two important functions — attacking White's center and protecting his own king.

15...♕e7 16.♖fe1

Another option is to try immediate action: 16.♗g7 ♔g7 17.♕f4 ♖ac8 18.h4 h6 19.h5 g5 20.♕g3, preparing f2-f4.

16...♖ac8 17.♗g7 ♔g7 18.♘f4

Now it becomes clear that White want to combine a kingside attack with the exploitation of the powerful central push d4-d5.

18...♖fd8

Simplification would not be very successful: 18...♖c1 19.♖c1 ♖c8 20.♖c8 ♗c8 21.♕c3 ♗b7 22.d5 ♕f6 23.♕c7 ed5 24.ed5 and the knight a5 is the source of Black's problems.

19.♕e3

A serious alternative was 19.♖c8 ♖c8 20.d5 ♘c4 21.♗c4 ♖c4 22.de6 fe6 23.e5.

19...♖c1 20.♖c1

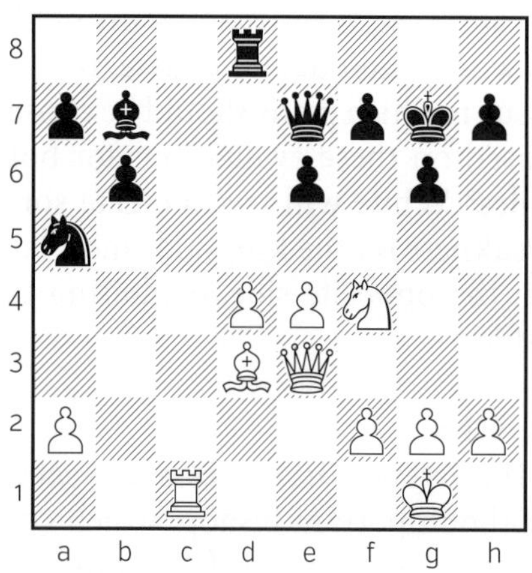

20...♕d6

It was possible to destroy White's center more directly: 20...e5 21.de5 ♕e5 22.f3 ♖c8.

21.d5!?

A typical central pawn sacrifice in such structures, but also a very risky one. Another central push was sufficient only for a draw: 21.e5 ♕d4? (21...♕d7 22.♘h5 gh5 23.♕g5 ♔f8 24.♗h7 ♕d4 25.♕g8 ♔e7 26.♖c7 ♖d7 27.♕g5) 22.♘e6 fe6 23.♖c7 ♔g8 24.♕h3.

21...ed5 22.e5 ♕e7 23.e6 ♘c4

It is high time to bring the knight back into the action.

24.♕g3 ♗c8

A more precise defence is 24...♖f8.

25.ef7 ♕f7 26.h4!?

Better is to bring the rook into play with 26.♖e1.

26...♗f5 27.♖e1 ♘d6

Safer is 27...♔g8.

28.♘h5 ♔f8 29.♕e5 ♘e4 30.♗e4 ♗e4?

Perpetual is the normal result after the correct capture: 30...de4 31.♕h8 ♔e7 32.♕e5 ♕e6 33.♕g7 ♕f7 34.♕e5.

31.♘f6 ♕e7 32.♕g5?

Much better is 32.♕f4! ♔g7 33.♖c1.

32...♖d6?

Nothing much is changed by 32...♔g7 33.♘h5 ♔f8 34.♕f4 ♕f7 35.♘f6.

33.♕h6 ♕g7 34.♕g7 1:0.

3

▷ **Zontakh**
▶ **Ivanovic**
Niksic 2000 [A69]

1.d4 ♘f6 2.c4 c5 3.d5 d6 4.♘c3 g6 5.♘f3 ♗g7 6.e4 0–0 7.♗e2 e6 8.0–0 ♖e8 9.♘d2 ♘a6 10.♔h1 ♘c7 11.a4 b6 12.f4 ed5 13.cd5 ♗a6 14.♗a6 ♘a6

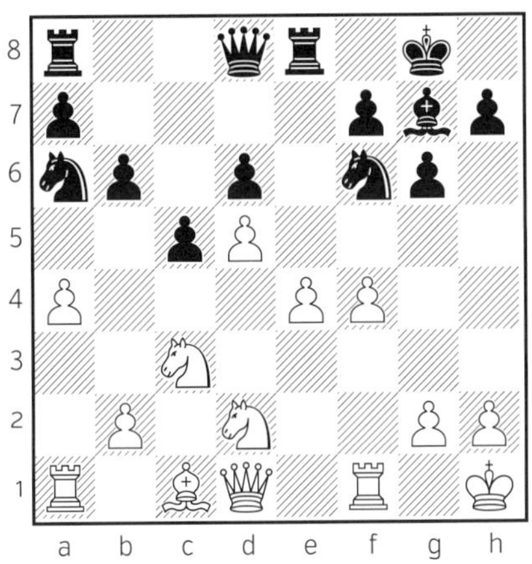

A typical position and structure from the Benoni, where Black's plan is to create strong pressure on the opponents center and try to disturb White's development. A strong center always creates some problems for the opponent, but it is not so easy to maintain the center. Here White applies a typical plan involving a pawn sacrifice, closing the center and transferring the game and events to the king's flank.

15.e5 de5 16.♘c4 ♘b4 17.d6 e4?

Much better is to open the center: 17...ef4 18.♗f4 ♘h5 19.♕f3 ♘f4 20.♕f4 ♕d7.

18.f5 ♕d7

It is very difficult to decide to weaken the king's position, but it would be the best defence. 18...gf5 19.♖f5 ♕d7 20.♖g5 ♔h8 21.♗e3 ♘d3 22.♕e2 ♕e6.

19.♗g5!

White has practically completed his development and finally has some serious attacking threats.

19...gf5 20.♘e3!

Gradually all the pieces start to come closer to the Black King.

20...♖e5 21.♗f6 ♗f6 22.♘f5! ♔h8

Exploiting a simple tactical trick, involving a pin and double attack 22... ♖f5 23.♕g4.

23.♘h6 ♔g7

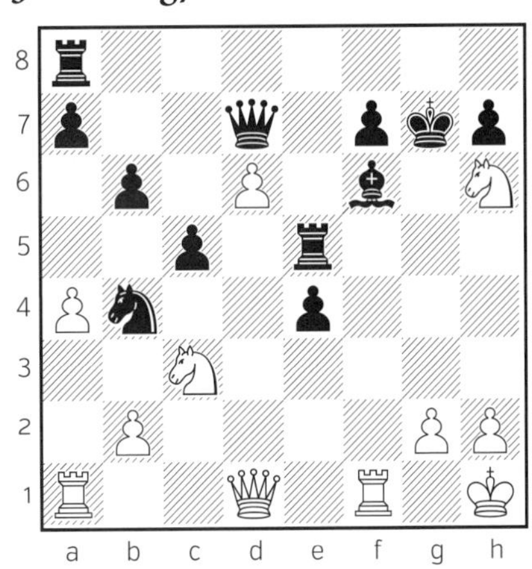

Other defences do not improve the position: 23...♕e6 24.♕e2.

24.♖f6

24.♘g4 was even stronger. Now White ejects Black's king from its defensive shell. Such kings are very vulnerable!

24...♔f6 25.♘g4 ♔f5

Or 25...♔e6 26.♕b3 ♔d6 27.♘b5 ♔e7 28.♘e5.

26.♘e5

Once more stronger was 26.♕e2 trying to add last piece ♖a1 to attack.

26...♔e5 27.♘e4 ♖g8 28.♕e1 ♘c2 29.♕c3 ♘d4 30.♖e1 ♕c6 31.d7 ♕d5 32.♕h3 ♘e2 33.♘c3 1:0.

FLANK STRATEGIES AGAINST THE CENTER

The clash of different approaches is demonstrated in the most dynamic way when it is necessary to attack center not directly, but from a distance. In some cases flank attacks are directed at the heart of the position — against the opponents king, but in many cases the idea is to remove those of the opponents pieces which are protecting important central squares. A master of such strategy was the great champion Mikhail Botvinnik.

1

▷ **Botvinnik**
▶ **Van Scheltinga**
Wijk aan Zee 1969 [E51]

1.d4 ♘f6 2.c4 e6 3.♘c3 ♗b4 4.e3 0–0 5.♗d3 d5 6.a3 dc4 7.♗c4 ♗d6 8.♘f3 ♘bd7 9.b4 e5 10.♗b2 e4 11.♘d2 ♘b6 12.♗e2 ♕e7

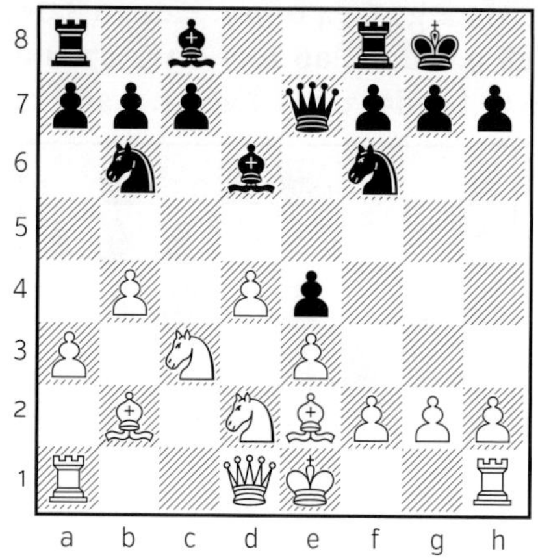

13.g4!!

A typical flank strategy with the aim of attacking his opponent's central pawn. Such attacks are very effective, especially without castling.

13...♘bd5

After 13...h6 14.h4 White would create another threat — to open up the black king.

14.g5 ♘e3?!

The Dutch IM decides to try his last chance — to bluff! But against Botvinnik it has no chance of success.

15.fe3 ♘d5 16.♘d5 ♕g5 17.♘e4!

The easiest way is to return some material for a simplification of the position. The rest is straightforward.

17...♕d5 18.♗f3 ♔h8 19.♘d6 ♕d6 20.0–0 ♗h3 21.♖f2 ♖ae8 22.♕d3 ♕h6 23.e4 ♖e6 24.d5 ♖g6 25.♔h1 ♕h4 26.♕d4 f6 27.♖g1 ♖g1 28.♔g1 ♖e8 29.♔h1 h5 30.♖e2 ♗g4 31.♗g4 ♕g4 32.♕e3 1:0.

2

▷ **Bogoljubow**
▶ **Botvinnik**
Nottingham 1936 (E14)

1.d4 ♘f6 2.♘f3 b6 3.e3 c5 4.c4 ♗b7 5.♘c3 cd4 6.ed4 e6 7.♗d3 ♗e7 8.0–0 0–0 9.b3 d5 10.♗e3 ♘e4 11.♖c1 ♘d7 12.♕e2 ♖c8 13.♖fd1 f5 14.♗f4

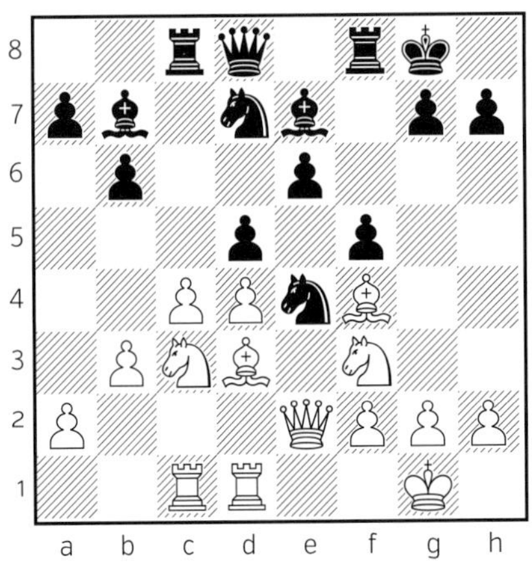

Black has a very strong knight on e4 and the added power of a wing pawn will help to attack the central pawn on d4.

14...g5! 15.♗e5?!

Another retreat looks stronger: 15.♗e3 ♗f6 (Weak is 15...g4 16.♗e4 de4 17.♘e5 ♗a3 18.♖c2 ♘f6 19.♗h6 ♖e8 20.♕e3.) 16.h3 ♕e7 and Black will slowly improve his position in the center before undertaking more decisive action.

15...g4

Now White's pieces lose contact with each other and after an exchange on e5 a weak pawn will appear.

16.♘e1 ♘e5 17.♗e4

Black's pieces start to increase in activity after 17.de5 ♕c7 18.♘b5 ♕e5 19.♘a7 ♗d6 20.g3 ♖a8 21.♘b5 ♗c5.

17...de4 18.de5 ♕c7 19.♘b5 ♕e5 20.♖d7

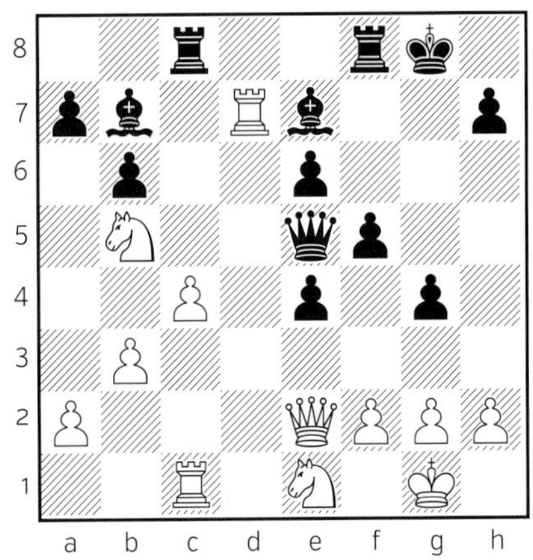

The capture on a7 allows Black to increase the activity of own pieces, e.g. 20.♘a7 ♖a8 21.♘b5 ♗g5 22.♖c3 ♗a6 White instead tries a double attack, but it is refuted by a tactical counterstroke.

20...♗g5! 21.♖cd1 ♗c6 22.♖a7 ♖cd8

Stronger was to fight for the d-file with the other rook: 22...♖fd8. But anyhow, Black now obtains full control of the central file and will penetrate it with decisive effect.

23.a4 ♖d1 24.♕d1 ♖d8 25.♕c2 ♗d2 0:1.

3

▹ **Botvinnik**
▸ **Smyslov**
Moscow 1954 [E45]

1.d4 ♘f6 2.c4 e6 3.♘c3 ♗b4 4.e3 b6 5.♘ge2 ♗a6 6.a3 ♗e7 7.♘f4 d5 8.cd5 ♗f1 9.♔f1 ed5

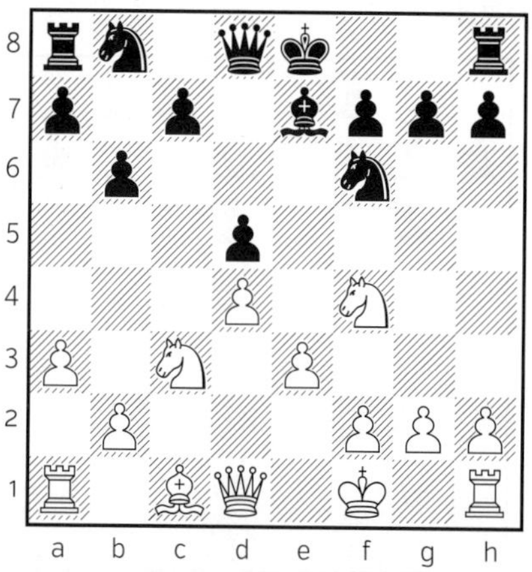

Now the center looks stable, but White found a plan which became classical in such situations. It seems that Black is okay, so what is White‘s compensation for losing the right to castle?

10.g4!

The right moment cannot be missed. By pushing the knight from f6 White creates disharmony among Black‘s pieces, which becomes a crucial factor when the position is opened.

10...c6

10...h6 does not stop White: 11.♕f3 c6 12.h4 and the g4-g5 break becomes even more effective. Probably Black has to match his opponent‘s determination with the response 10...g5, although after 11.♘h5 ♘h5 12.gh5 c6 13.♕f3 and e3-e4 to follow White keeps a solid initiative. (Kasparov)

11.g5 ♘fd7

After 11...♘e4 12.♘e4 de4 13.h4 the pawn on e4 will be attacked soon.

12.h4 ♗d6?

This is a clear mistake. After 12...o-o 13.♕g4 the massive concentration of the enemy‘s forces make the black king feel pretty nervous. The following — not obligatory, but colourful — line shows the potential of White‘s attack:

13...♘a6 14.e4 de4 15.♘e4 f5 16.gf6 ♘f6 17.♕e6 ♔h8 18.h5! ♘e4 19.♘g6 hg6 20.hg6 ♗h4 21.♕e4 ♖f2 22.♔g1 ♔g8 23.♖h4 ♕f6 24.♖f4! (The tempting 24.♗g5? even loses: 24...♕g5 25.♔f2 ♖f8 26.♔e2 (26.♔e1 ♕g1) 26...♕b5 27.♔e3 ♕b3.) 24...♖f4 25.♗f4 ♖f8 26.♗g3 ♘b8 27.d5! with a big advantage. Undoubtedly Black had a number of other opportunities with reasonable chances to defend. (Kasparov)

13.e4! de4 14.♘e4 ♗f4 15.♗f4 0–0 16.h5!

Combining domination in the center with creating threats to the Black king. As you can see the kingside castle doesn't give one full insurance for the safety of the king.

16...♖e8

There are no useful alternatives: 16...♘a6 17.h6 g6 18.♕a4 and the knight has to go back. 18...♘ab8 19.♖e1 leaves Black practically paralysed. (Kasparov)

17.♘d6 ♖e6

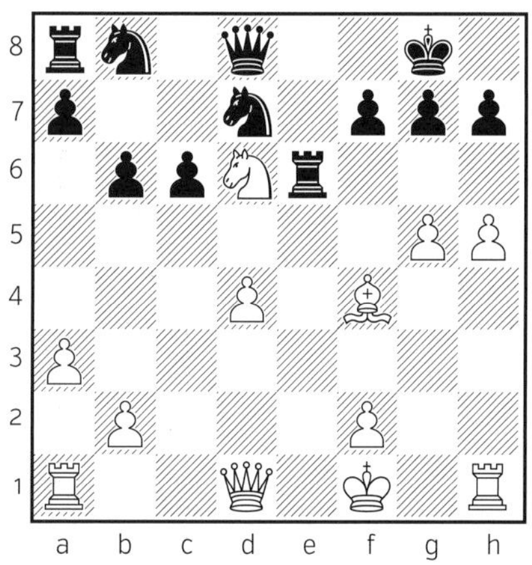

18.d5!

In such situations, as we pointed out before, the best approach is to open the game.

18...♖d6

This exchange sacrifice does not really help, but opening o the game is disastrous:

18...cd5 19.♕d5 ♘a6 20.g6 ♘c7 (20...♘f8 21.gf7 ♔h8 22.h6 ♘c7 23.♘f5!) 21.gh7! ♔h7 22.♕f5 etc. (Kasparov)

19.♗d6 ♕g5 20.♕f3!

Now the primitive 20.dc6 ♘c6 gives Black some hope, so Botvinnik maintains his domination, adding a quality advantage to his material one.

20...♕d5

Keeping queens on the board does not offer any relief:

20...cd5 21.♖g1 ♕d2 22.♗b4 ♕b2 23.♖e1 ♘a6 24.♕d5 etc.

21.♕d5 cd5 22.♖c1 ♘a6 23.b4!

Finishing the hapless knight off.

23...h6 24.♖h3 ♔h7 25.♖d3 ♘f6 26.b5 ♘c5 27.♗c5 bc5 28.♖c5 ♖b8 29.a4 ♖b7 30.♖dc3 1:0.

and the rook exchange is inevitable: 30.♖dc3 ♘e4 31.♖c7, so, Black resigned.

4

▷ **Vidmar**
▶ **Nimzowitsch**
New York 1927 [E11]

1.d4 ♘f6 2.♘f3 e6 3.c4 ♗b4 4.♗d2 ♕e7 5.♘c3 0–0 6.e3?! d6 7.♗e2 b6 8.0–0 ♗b7 9.♕c2 ♘bd7 10.♖ad1 ♗c3 11.♗c3 ♘e4 12.♗e1 f5 13.♕b3! c5 14.♘d2 ♘d2 15.♖d2 e5 16.de5 de5 17.f3

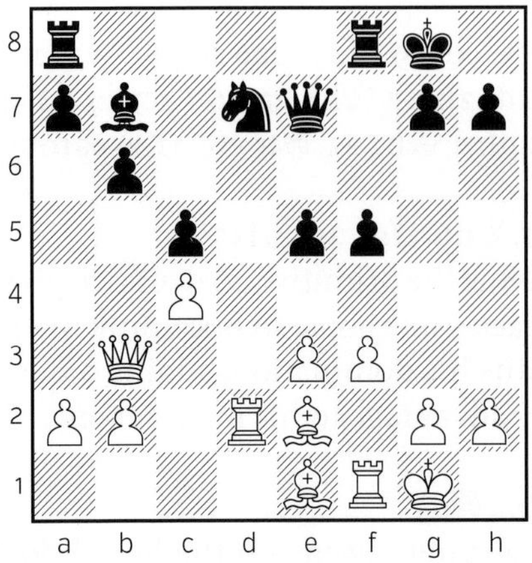

17...g5!!

This is one of the most amazing strategic decisions of the first part of the 20th century. It is illogical to close off his own powerful bishop with 17... e4 18.f4, and after the logical central development White has a nice idea to create an object of attack: 17...♖ad8 18.♕a4 a6 19.♕b3.

Now 17...♘f6 just helps White as it allows the unpleasant pin 18.♗h4.

18.♗f2

The correct way to exploit the d-file is completely different; it is necessary to penetrate Black's position with the queen, not with the rooks!

18.♕d3! It is extremely strange that nobody among the greats — Alekhine, Tartakower, Nimzowitsch, Flohr — saw this resource during their annotations of this game for different magazines!

Everybody praised Nimzovitsch's flank attack, but during the analyses of the classical or top players games it is necessary to establish the key moments and to find the mechanics of how the ideas work.

18...♖ad8 (The tactical solution did not work: 18...♘f6 19.♕f5 ♘e4 20.♕d7.) 19.♕d6 ♕d6 20.♖d6 ♘b8 (The best transfer of the knight — it is necessary to control the d4 square and to protect the e5 pawn at the same time.) 21.♖d8 ♖d8 22.♗c3 ♘c6 23.♖d1 ♖d1 24.♗d1 ♔f7 25.g4 ♔f6 26.♗c2 ♗c8 27.h3 ♘b4 and Black can keep the balance, but it is necessary to play very carefully.

18...♘f6 19.♖fd1 ♖ae8

It makes no sense to try to limit White's activity on the d file, as after 19...♖ad8 20.♕a3 a5 21.♕c3 ♖d2 22.♕d2 ♖c8 23.♕d6 White's control is still strong.

20.♕a4

White tries to exploit his control over the d-file in a tactical way — this threatens ♖d7.

20...♗a8 21.♖d6

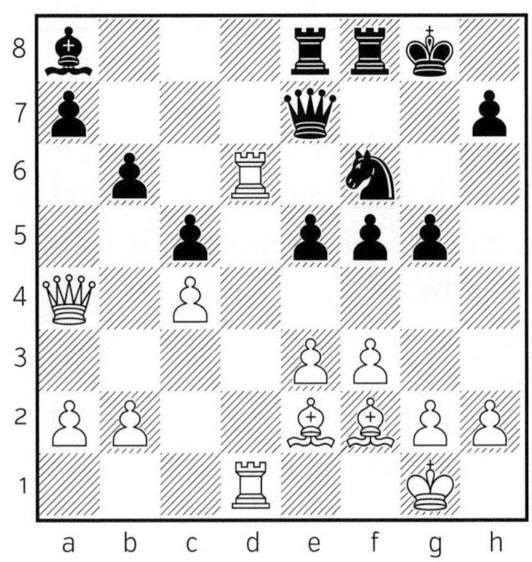

Now White calculated that the following plan does not work tactically: 21.♖d7 ♘d7 22.♖d7 ♕f6 23.♕a7 e4 24.♖h7 f4 25.♗e1 ♕b2.

21...♕g7!
And now it is clear that Black is preparing a powerful attack on the white King after ...g5-g4.
Premature would be 21...e4 22.f4 gf4 23.♗h4 f3 24.♖f6 fe2 25.♖e1.

22.♗f1?
A tactical mistake, which allows the central break. Tartakower recommended as the best defence bringing the queen back 22.♕c2, which is quite logical.
Alekhine's recommendation was completely different: 22.♗e1, activating the bishop on c3. It is remarkable how the greats saw different approaches to the same position.

22...e4! 23.♗e1
White plans to close the position, but now it loses a pawn. 23.f4 gf4 24.ef4 e3. Returning does not help: 23.♗e2 ef3 24.♗f3 ♗f3 25.gf3 g4 26.f4 ♘e4. And a very poor position arises after 23.fe4 ♘e4 24.♖d7 ♕b2.

23...ef3 24.♗c3 ♕e7!
Avoiding the unpleasant pin and switching the object of the attack to e3.

25.♖6d3 fg2 26.♗g2
Of no help is 26.♗e2 f4.

26...♗g2 27.♗f6 ♕e4!
Exploiting the weakness of the white squares for a mating attack.

28.♖1d2 ♗h3 29.♗c3 ♕g4 0:1.

Now for a very dynamic example of a sudden flank attack.

5

▹ Sher
▸ Magerramov
Helsinki 1992 [D32]

1.c4 c5 2.♘f3 ♘f6 3.♘c3 e6 4.e3 d5 5.d4 a6 6.cd5 ed5 7.♗e2 ♘c6 8.♘e5 ♗d6 9.♘c6 bc6 10.dc5 ♗c5 11.0–0 ♕d6 12.♗f3

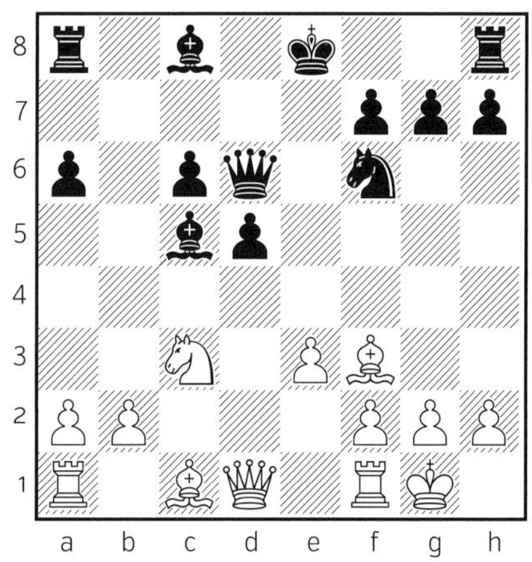

12...h5!
A very risky strategy, but Black correctly evaluates the problems his opponent will face. Normal development promises him nothing spectacular: 12...♗f5 13.♘e2 0–0 14.♗d2

♘e4 15.♖c1 ♖ab8 16.♗e4 ♗e4 17.♗c3 ♗b6 18.♘g3 ♗g6 19.b4.

13.e4

As is written in all middlegame books — a flank attack has to be countered in the center as quickly as possible.

13...♘g4!

Black has chosen such a strategy, so it has to be continued as far as possible.

14.g3 d4

The position is not yet ready for decisive sacrifices:

14...♘h2 15.♗f4 ♘f3 16.♕f3 ♕g6 17.ed5 ♗g4 18.♕e4 ♕e4 19.♘e4.

15.♘e2?

It was necessary to develop the pieces aggressively, which leads to a very unclear position: 15.♗f4 ♘e5 16.♘a4 ♗a7 17.♖c1 h4 18.♗g2 f6.

15...♘e5

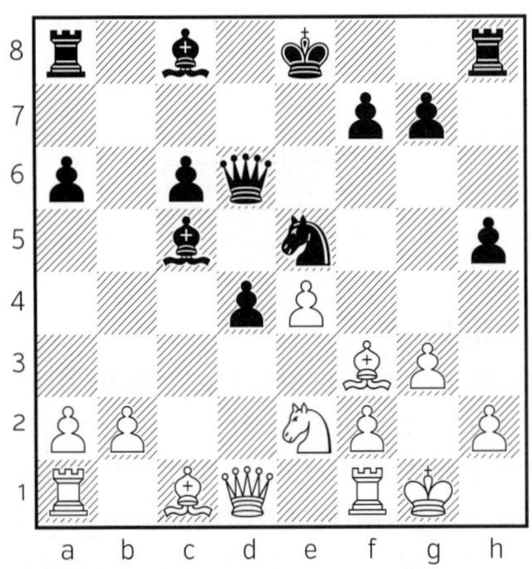

Now White suddenly faces terrible problems with his king and, additionally, his development is incomplete.

16.♘f4

White has no time to retreat with his bishop:

16.♗g2 d3 17.♘c3 ♗g4 18.♕e1 h4 19.♗e3 d2 20.♕d2 ♕d2 21.♗d2 hg3.

16...♗g4 17.♗g4 hg4 18.h4

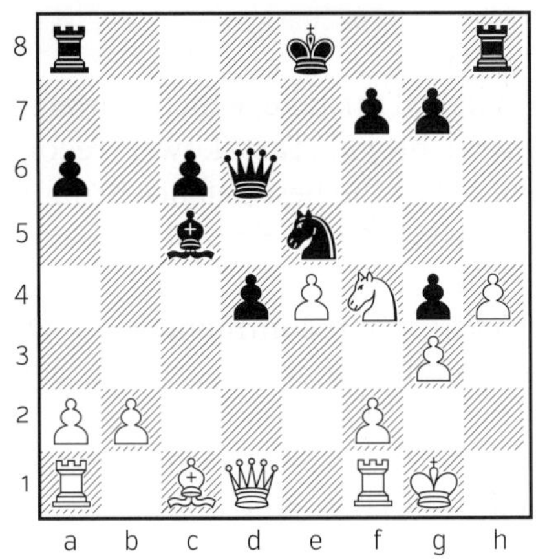

How else to defend against ♘f3?

18...d3

Very strong would be 18...g5.

19.♔g2

Or another try 19.♗e3 ♗e3 20.fe3 g5 21.hg5 ♕b4!

19...♕d4 20.♕e1

20.♘d3 ♕e4 21.♔h2 ♘d3.

20...g5 0:1.

6

▹ **Bojkovic**
▸ **A. Maric**
Novi Sad 1996 [C87]

1.e4 e5 2.♘f3 ♘c6 3.♗b5 a6 4.♗a4 ♘f6 5.0–0 ♗e7 6.♖e1 d6 7.c3 ♗g4 8.h3

White can try to get another form of the center: 8.♗c6 bc6 9.d4 ♘d7 10.h3 ♗h5 11.g4 ♗g6 12.♕a4 ed4 13.♘d4

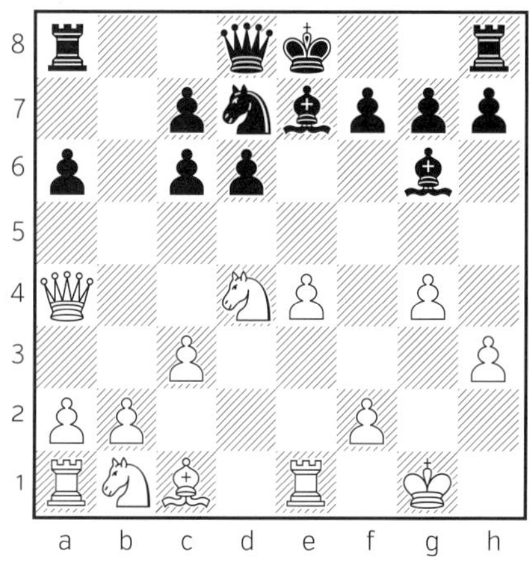

13...c5 14.♘c6 ♘b6 15.♕c2 ♕d7 16.♘e7 ♕e7. Both White's center and king's flank look vulnerable because of the threats ...f7-f5 or ...h7-h5, so the only chance is to try to attack at any price: 17.f4 f5! 18.♕e2 fe4 19.f5 ♗f7 20.♕e4 ♕e4 21.♖e4 ♔d7 22.♗g5 ♖he8 23.♘d2 ♖e4 24.♘e4 ♖e8 25.♘g3 ♘a4 (Finally White's pawn weaknesses come under attack.) 26.♗c1 c4 27.♔f1 ♘c5 28.♘e2 ♘d3 29.♖b1 ♗d5 30.♗d2 ♗g2, 0:1, Wiedenkeller : Mikhalchishin, Stockholm 1980.

8...♗h5 9.d3 ♕d7 10.♘bd2

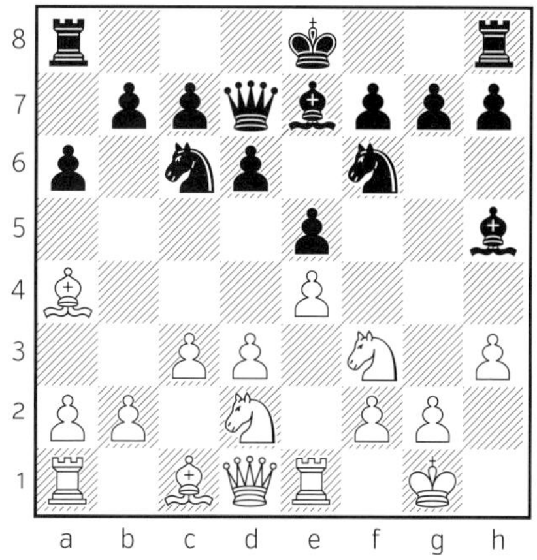

10...g5!

A very risky strategy, but the timing looks to be OK as White has no direct counterstrike in the center. But the small weakness of square f5 could become troublesome soon.

11.♘f1

11.♗c6 ♕c6 12.d4 0–0–0 13.♕b3 g4 14.hg4 ♘g4 15.♘c4 ♖hg8 16.♘a5 ♕b5 17.♕b5 ab5 and once more the endgame is very favourable for Black, this time because of the bishop pair: 0:1 (82), Ceshkovskij : Mikhalchishin, Daugavpils 1997.

11...g4 12.hg4 ♗g4 13.♘e3

White tries to play for exploitation of the weaknesses on d5 and f5, but the counterstrike in the center is playable also. 13.d4 b5 14.♗b3 ed4 — Black does not need to conduct activities in the center; it is possible to continue play on the kingside, for example: 14...♖g8 and White has some serious options here: 15.♗d5, 15.♘g3 or15.♘1h2!?

13...♖g8 14.♔f1

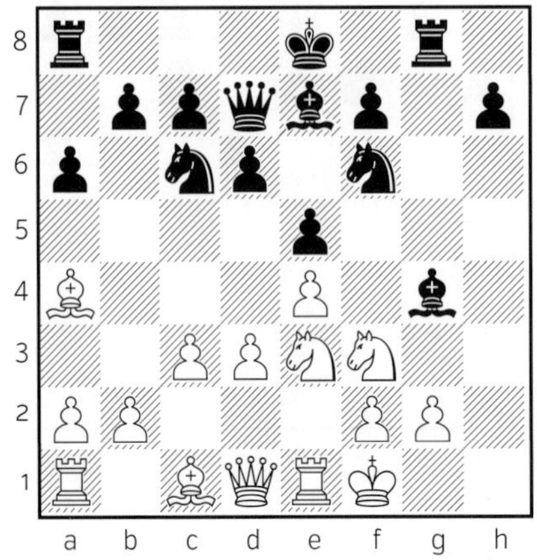

It was possible to try to block the kingside immediately: 14.♘g4 ♕g4 15.g3 h5 16.♔h2 0–0–0 17.♘h4 ♕d1 18.♗d1.

14...♘h5?

This looks logical, but meets with a powerful refutation. The correct way of continuing the attack was demonstrated by a top player: 14...h5 15.d4 b5 16.♗c2 h4 17.de5 ♗f3 18.♕f3 ♘e5 19.♕f5 ♘fg4 20.♘g4 ♘g4 21.♗b3 ♘e5 22.♗f4 ♘c4 23.a4 ♕f5 24.ef5 ♔d7 25.♖e4 ♖gb8 26.ab5, draw, Smirnov : Aronian, Tripoli 2004. As always, a central operation is the best reaction to an opponent's flank activity.

15.d4! b5 16.♗b3 ed4

A normal continuation of the attack has no prospects: 16...♘f4 17.♘d5 ♘d5 (17...♗f3 18.♕f3 ♘g2 19.♘b6! cb6 20.♕f7) 18.ed5 ♘a5 19.de5 0–0–0 20.e6, with a serious advantage.

17.cd4 ♘a5 18.♗c2 ♘f4 19.♘g4 ♕g4 20.♗f4!

White eliminates his opponent's most unpleasant piece and his big advantage in the center allows for a serious attack.

20...♕f4 21.a4!

Typical for Spanish structures, creating weaknesses in Black's flank pawn grouping.

21...b4

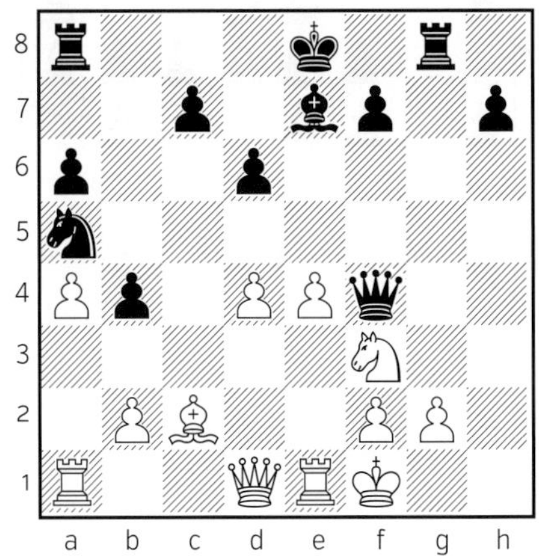

22.e5!

It is clear that White's king is safer than Black's. This move threatens an opening of a central file and launches unpleasant threats.

22...♕g4

After 22...0–0–0 23.g3 ♕h6 24.♔g2 White simply improves the position of his own king and is ready to start attacking Black's king position.

23.ed6 cd6

Nothing is changed by 23...♕g2 24.♔e2 ♕h3 25.de7 ♕e6 26.♔d3 ♕f5 27.♔d2 ♕f4 28.♔e2.

24.g3 ♕h3 25.♔g1 h5

Or 25...♔f8 26.♖c1 ♗f6 27.♕e2 and White's pieces are much-better placed.

26.♘h2

Very strong was 26.♗e4 ♖a7 27.♕d2.

26...♖g5 27.♕d2 f6 28.♗e4 ♖b8 29.♗g2 ♕d7 30.♕d3!

Looking at two flanks — to a6 and to h7.

30...♔f8 31.♕h7 ♘c4 32.♗d5 1:0.

DESTROYING THE OPPONENTS CENTER

Destroying the center with the help of pawn attacks and piece sacrifices -especially piece sacrifices for a central pawn — is the strategy of champions. Sacrificing a piece for a powerful center limits the effectiveness of the opponent's pieces, and further movement of such a center tends to paralyze the opponents pieces.

1

▷ **Euwe**
▶ **Alekhine**
Netherlands 1935 [E18]

1.d4 e6 2.c4 f5 3.g3 ♗b4 4.♗d2 ♗e7 5.♗g2 ♘f6 6.♘c3 0–0 7.♘f3 ♘e4 8.0–0 b6 9.♕c2 ♗b7 10.♘e5 ♘c3 11.♗c3 ♗g2 12.♔g2 ♕c8 13.d5! d6 14.♘d3 e5 15.♔h1 c6 16.♕b3! ♔h8 17.f4 e4 18.♘b4! c5 19.♘c2 ♘d7 20.♘e3 ♗f6

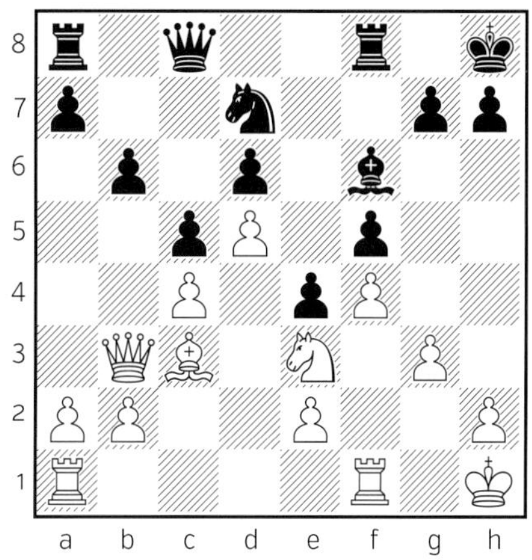

21.♘f5!± ♗c3 22.♘d6 ♕b8 23.♘e4 ♗f6 24.♘d2!

White has destroyed all Black's pawns in the center and is ready to start pushing the e- and d- pawns.

24...g5! 25.e4 gf4 26.gf4 ♗d4 27.e5 ♕e8 28.e6 ♖g8

28...♘f6? 29.♘f3 ...30.♘d4.

29.♘f3?!

29.ed7? ♕e2!; 29.♕h3!:

1. Protecting the king.

2. Threatening the black king (♘f3-g5).
3. Supporting the advance of the passed pawns: 29...♘f6 30.♘f3 ♗b2 31.♖ab1 — Euwe.

29...♕g6 30.♖g1

Now it is a rook sacrifice! 30.♘g5 ♘e5!

30...♗g1 31.♖g1

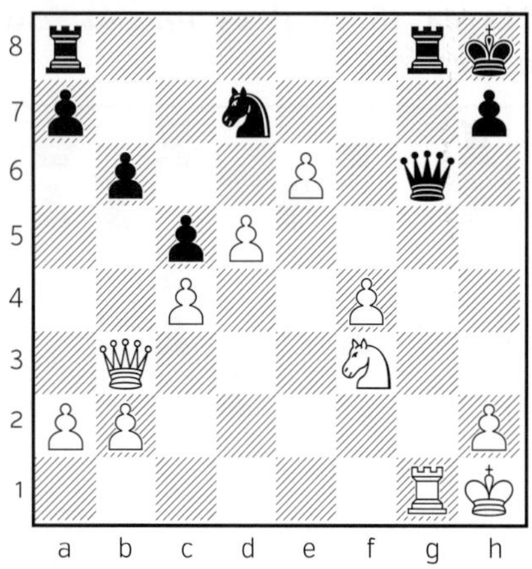

31...♕f6?+-

The only chance for survival was 31...♕f5! 32.ed7 (32.♘g5 h6! — Euwe (32...♖g5 33.fg5 ♕e4 34.♖g2 ♕e1 35.♖g1=, Euwe)) 32...♖g1 33.♔g1 ♕d7 34.♔f2=, Euwe.

32.♘g5! ♖g7

32...♖g5 33.fg5 ♕d4 34.♕c3+-, Euwe.

33.ed7 ♖d7 34.♕e3 ♖e7

34...♕b2 35.♕e6+-.

35.♘e6 ♖f8

35...♕b2 36.d6! ♖ee8 (36...♖d7 37.♘c7 ♖f8 38.♕e5+-) 37.d7 ♖e7 38.d8♕ ♖d8 39.♘d8+-, Euwe: 39...♖e3?? 40.♘f7#.

36.♕e5 ♕e5 37.fe5 ♖f5

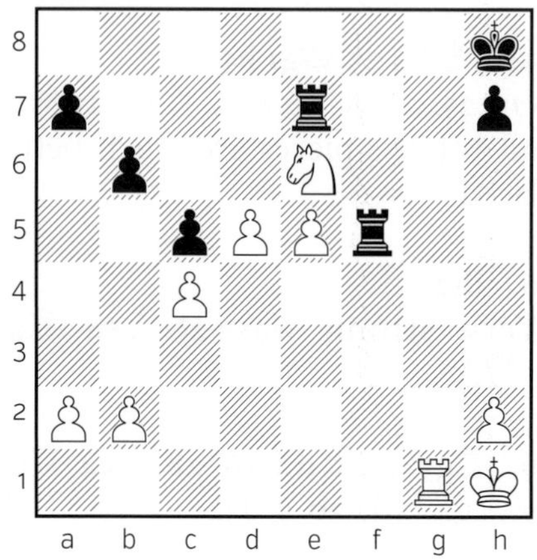

37...♖e6 38.de6 ♖f5! (38...♖e8 39.♔g2 ♖e6 40.♖e1 ♔g7 41.♔f3+-) 39.♖e1 ♔g8 40.♖e3! (40.♔g2 ♔f8 41.♖f1? ♖f1 42.♔f1 ♔e7) 40...♔f8 41.♖a3 ♖e5 (41...a5 42.♖b3) 42.♖a7 ♖e6 43.b3! ♖e2 44.♖h7 ♖a2 45.♖b7+-, Euwe.

38.♖e1?!

Correct here was to swap rooks: 38.♖g5! ♖g5 39.♘g5 ♔g7 (39...h6 40.d6!+-) 40.d6! ♖e5 (40...♖d7 41.♘e6 ♔f7 42.♘f4 ♔e8 43.♔g2 ♖g7 44.♔f3 ♔d7 45.♔e4 ♔c6 46.♘d5+-) 41.d7 ♖e1 42.♔g2 ♖d1 43.d8♕ ♖d8 44.♘e6+-, Euwe.

38...h6?!

It was better to try to play the rook ending:

38...♖e6! 39.de6 ♔g8 40.♖e3!;

38...♔g8 39.♖g1 ♔f7 (39...♔h8 40.♖g5) 40.♘d8 ♔f8 41.♘c6+-, Euwe.

39.♘d8 ♖f2 40.e6 ♖d2 41.♘c6 ♖e8 42.e7 b5 43.♘d8 ♔g7 44.♘b7 ♔f6 45.♖e6 ♔g5 46.♘d6 ♖e7 47.♘e4 1:0.

2

▹ **Tal**
▸ **Ghitescu**
Miskolc 1963 [C93]

1.e4 e5 2.♘f3 ♘c6 3.♗b5 a6 4.♗a4 ♘f6 5.0–0 ♗e7 6.♖e1 b5 7.♗b3 d6 8.c3 0–0 9.h3 h6 10.d4 ♖e8 11.♘bd2 ♗f8 12.♘f1 ♗d7 13.♘g3 ♘a5 14.♗c2 c5 15.b3 g6 16.♗e3 ♘c6 17.d5 ♘e7 18.♕d2 ♔h7

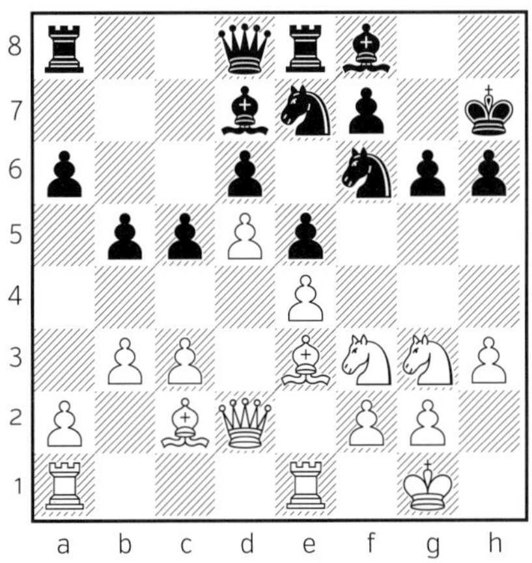

19.♗c5!?
Typical of Tal's style — to destroy an opponent's center and to change the course of the game; here simply to open a closed position. It is also possible to conduct a classical plan of attack with this kind of center: 19.♘h2 ♗g7 20.f4.

19...dc5 20.♘e5 ♘c8 21.f4
Wrong was 21.♘f7 ♕e7 winning the knight.

21...♕e7 22.c4!
White has just two pawns for the piece, but the powerful center makes Black's pieces passive.

22...♗g7 23.♘f3
Better was simply to centralize all the pieces here: 23.♖ad1 ♘d6 24.♗d3.

23...bc4
After 23...♘h5 24.♘h5 ♗a1 25.e5! White would obtain a terrific position for the rook.

24.bc4 ♘d6 25.e5 ♘c4 26.♕c3 ♗b5 27.♖ad1 ♖ad8

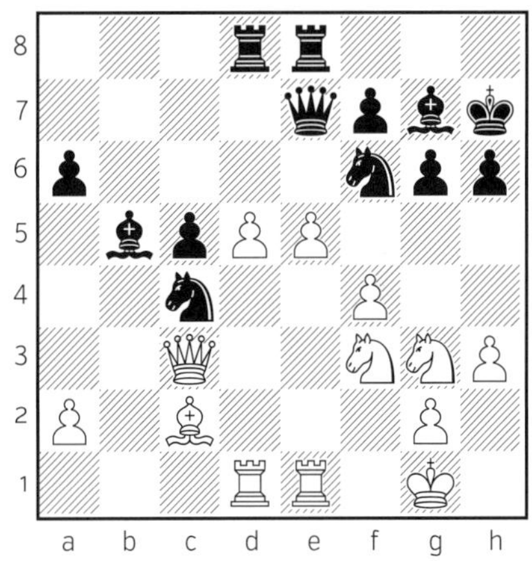

28.d6!
Tal simply pushes his pawns forward, instead of regaining his piece.

28...♘d6 29.ed6 ♕b7?!
Stronger, but not sufficient for equality would be 29...♕f8 30.♕c5.

30.♘e5

30.f5 was strong too. Or even simpler 30.♕c5.

30...♘d7?!

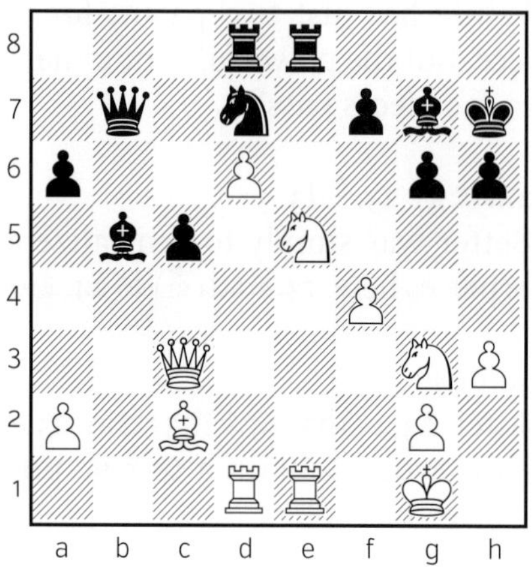

Looking dangerous, but promising some chances for escape, is 30...♘d5 31.♕f3 ♖d6 32.♔h2 ♖dd8 33.♗e4.

31.♘h5!

The start of a very dangerous attack.

31...♗h8 32.♕g3 ♘e5 33.fe5 ♕d7 34.♘f4!

Threatening to sacrifice on g6.

34...♗e5

Or 34...♖g8 35.e6.

35.♗g6! ♔h8

35...fg6 36.♕g6 ♔h8 37.♖e5 ♖e5 38.♕f6.

36.♗f7! ♗d4

36...♕f7 37.♖e5 ♖e5 38.♘g6.

37.♖d4 ♖e1 38.♕e1 ♕f7 39.♕e5 ♕g7 40.♕c5 ♗c6 41.♖d2 1:0.

3

▷ **Romanishin**
▶ **Shijanovsky**
Kiev 1967 (C92)

1.e4 e5 2.♘f3 ♘c6 3.♗b5 a6 4.♗a4 ♘f6 5.0–0 ♗e7 6.♖e1 b5 7.♗b3 d6 8.c3 0–0 9.h3 ♕d7 10.d4 ♖e8 11.♘bd2 ♗f8 12.♗c2 ♗b7 13.a4 g6 14.d5 ♘e7 15.b3 ♗g7 16.♘f1

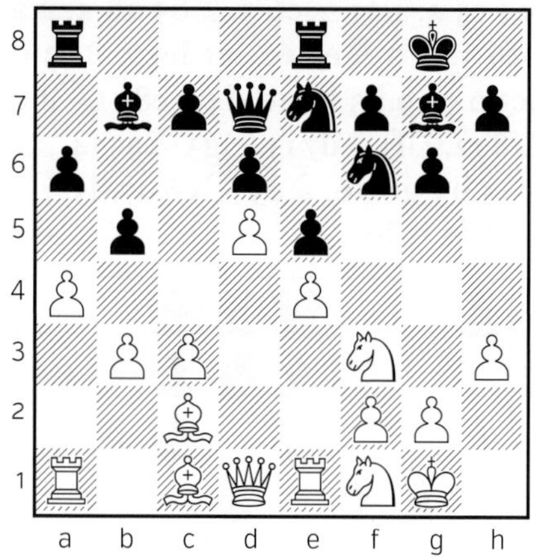

16...♘ed5!

Why suffer without space after c3-c4, when it is possible to destroy the wall constructed by White?

17.ed5 ♘d5 18.♗b2

Better is to try to stop the creation of a big pawn center:

18.♗d2 f5 19.♖c1 c5 20.c4.

18...♘f4 19.♖b1

Interesting would be 19.♘e3.

19...e4 20.♘d4 c5 21.♘e2

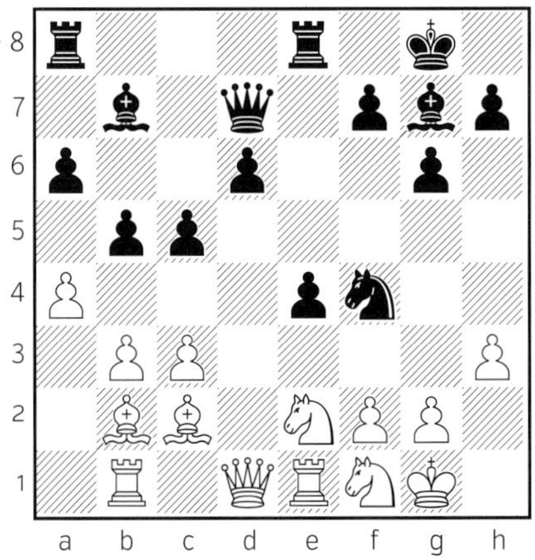

Suddenly Black starts a fierce attack against his opponent's king.

21...♘g2! 22.♔g2 e3 23.f3 ♗f3! 24.♔f3 ♕b7 25.♔g3 ♗e5 26.♘f4 ♗f4

The attack is insufficient after 26...g5 27.♘e3 gf4 28.♔f2 fe3 29.♖e3.

27.♔f4 ♕g2

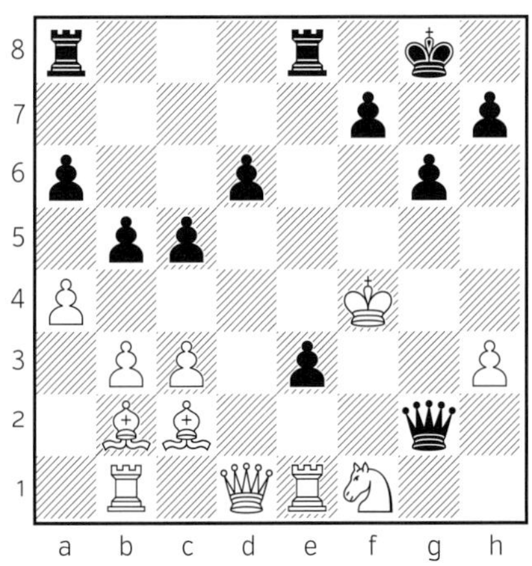

28.♖e3

Very nice mates occur after 28.♕g4 ♕f2 29.♔g5 ♖e5 30.♔h6 ♕f4 31.♕f4 ♖h5# or 28.♕f3 g5!

28...♖e3 29.♘e3 ♕f2 30.♔e4

The queen is lost after 30.♕f3 g5 31.♔g4 h5.

30...♖e8 31.♔d5 ♕e3 32.♕g4 ♕d2 33.♔c6 ♕c2 34.♕d1 ♕e4 35.♔b6 ♖b8 36.♔a5 ♕c6 0:1.

4

▷ **J. Polgar**
▶ **Spassky**
Budapest 1993 [C95]

1.e4 e5 2.♘f3 ♘c6 3.♗b5 a6 4.♗a4 ♘f6 5.0–0 ♗e7 6.♖e1 b5 7.♗b3 d6 8.c3 0–0 9.h3 ♘b8 10.d4 ♘bd7 11.♘bd2 ♗b7 12.♗c2 ♖e8 13.♘f1 ♗f8 14.♘g3 g6 15.b3 ♗g7 16.d5 ♘b6! 17.♗e3 ♖c8 18.♕e2 c6 19.c4 cd5 20.cd5

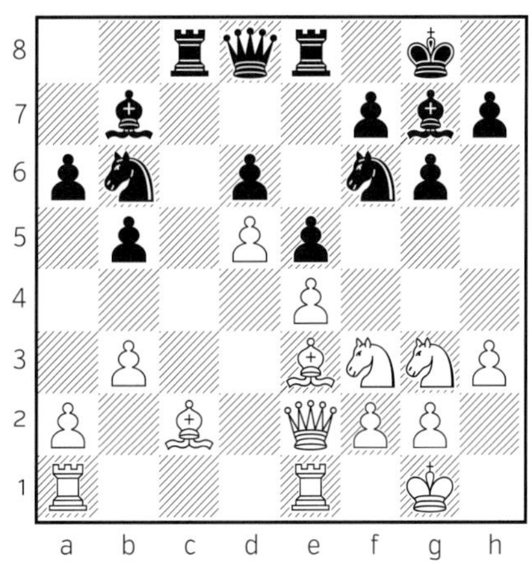

Black has real problems with space, so the piece sacrifice has two ideas — destroying the opponent's center and to free both black bishops.

20...♘bd5! 21.ed5 ♘d5 22.b4?!

Polgar tries to free her bishop, as normal defence would allow Black to start rolling his center.

22.♖ac1 ♘c3 23.♕d2 ♗f3 24.gf3 d5.

22...♘b4

Another serious option would be less materialistic, but sometimes chess players can regret this:

22...♘e3 23.fe3 ♗f3 24.gf3 e4.

23.♗b3

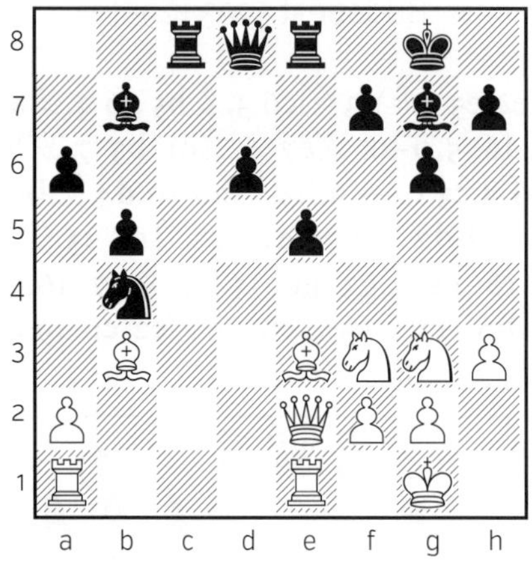

23...♗d5?!

Black has two other serious options: 23...d5 24.a3 ♘c6 25.♕a2 ♘a5 or 23...e4 24.♘d4 ♘d3 25.♖ed1 d5 26.♖d3 ed3 27.♕d3 but in the last variation White would block the position.

24.♖ed1

Black has good compensation after 24.a3 ♗b3 25.ab4 d5 26.♖a6 d4 27.♗g5 f6 28.♕b2 ♗c4.

24...♗c4 25.♕d2

It's not very useful to help Black obtain more central passed pawns: 25.♗c4 bc4 26.♖ab1 ♘d3 27.♘e1 e4.

25...♘d3 26.♗h6 d5 27.♗c2 ♘c5! 28.♖e1?

In such situations it is recommended to create counterplay at any price, or to exchange bishops first.

28.a4.

28...♗h8! 29.♖ad1 ♕b6 30.♕g5 e4 31.♕e3

Only tactical tricks keep White's position playable.

31...♗a2 32.♗b1 ♗b1

It was possible to avoid the exchange of bishops:

32...♗c4! ...a6-a5-a4 etc.

33.♖b1 ♘a4 34.♕b6 ♘b6 35.♗e3 ♘a4

Easier was to simplify the position and start pushing the queenside pawns: 35...ef3 36.♗b6 ♖e1 37.♖e1 b4.

36.♘d4 ♘c3 37.♖bc1 ♖c4 38.♘ge2 ♘e2 39.♘e2 ♖d8

Why not simply try to promote the pawn 39...a5?

40.g4 d4 41.♖cd1 d3

Simpler was 41...a5 42.♘g3 d3.

42.♘g3 ♗c3

In such situations exchanges are recommended — 42...♗e5.

43.♗d2 ♗d2 44.♖d2 ♖dd4 45.f3!

The only chance is to destroy the powerful pawn group.

45...ef3 46.♔f2 b4 47.♔f3 ♖d8

Better was 47...a5.

48.♖e7 ♖b8

A direct winning variation looks to be available here: 48...a5 49.♖a7 b3 50.♖a5 ♖c2 51.♘f1 b2 52.♖b5 ♖c1.

49.♖d7 b3 50.♖7d3! a5 51.♖b2 a4 52.♘e2 ♔g7 53.♔e3 ♖a8 54.♘c3 ♖b4 55.♘a4 ♖aa4 56.♖bb3 ♖f4! 57.♔e2 ♔h6 58.♖f3 ♔g5!

One-flank endings are generally drawish with such material, but here the activity of Black's king is decisive.

59.♔f2 ♖f3 60.♔f3 ♔h4 61.♔g2 ♖a2 62.♔g1 h5! 63.gh5 ♔h5 64.♖f3

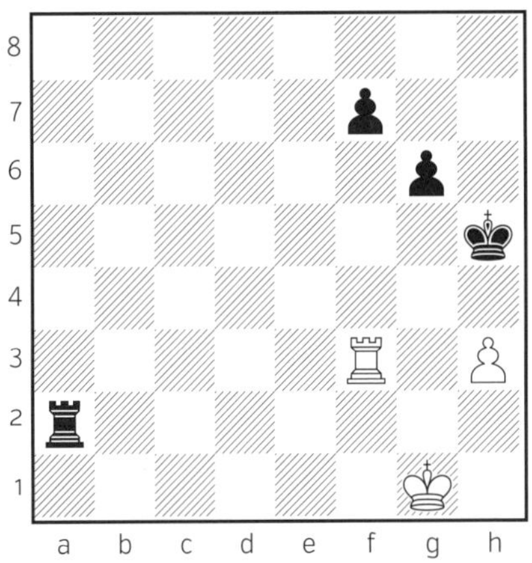

Correct play here was to place the rook behind the pawns:

64.♖b7! f5 65.♖g7.

64...f5 65.♖f4 ♖e2 66.♔h1 ♖e4 67.♖f2 ♔h4 68.♔g2 ♖b4 69.♔h2 ♖e4 70.♔g2 f4! 71.♔f3 ♖e5 72.♖g2

72.♔f4 ♖f5 73.♔e3 ♖f2 74.♔f2 ♔h3–+.

72...g5 73.♖g4 ♔h3 74.♖g3 ♔h4 0:1.

5

▷ **Garcia**
▸ **Medina Garcia**
Tel Aviv 1964 [E68]

1.d4 ♘f6 2.c4 g6 3.g3 ♗g7 4.♗g2 d6 5.♘f3 0–0 6.0–0 ♘bd7 7.♘c3 e5 8.e4 c6 9.♖b1 a6 10.de5 de5 11.b4 b5 12.c5 a5 13.a3 ♖e8 14.♗b2 ♕c7 15.♖e1 ♘f8

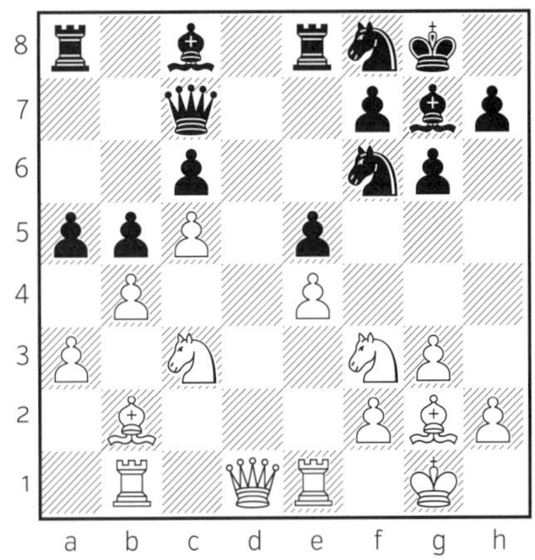

16.♘d5!?

Here is the creation of a powerful center, but without any sacrifice! It means that White believes his powerful pawns in the center are equal at least to the knight — with just one pawn as compensation!

16...cd5 17.ed5 ab4 18.ab4 ♗f5

After 18...e4 19.♘g5 ♗g4 20.♕b3 ♕d7 21.♘e4 ♘e4 22.♗e4 White increases his material compensation, keeping the powerful pawn duo in the center.

19.d6

Interesting is the direct 19.♘e5 ♗b1 20.d6 ♕c8 21.♗a8 ♕a8 22.♕b1 ♘d5 23.♘d3.

19...♕d8

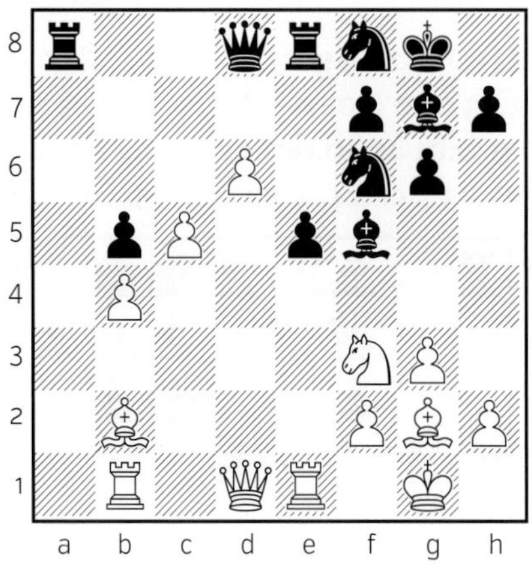

20.♖c1

Once more it was possible to play 20.♘e5?! ♖a2 21.♘c6 ♖e1 22.♕e1 ♕d7 23.♘e7 ♔h8 24.♘f5 ♕f5 25.c6.

20...e4 21.♘e5

Leading to 'disarmament' is the forced line 21.♘d4 ♗d7 22.♕c2 ♘e6 23.c6 ♘d4 24.♗d4 ♗f5 25.d7 ♘d7 26.♗g7 ♔g7 27.cd7 ♕d7 28.♗e4.

21...♖a2 22.♗c3 ♕a8 23.c6 ♖d8

Another good chance is offered by 23...♖c8.

24.c7

It would have been useful to kick away the bishop with 24.g4.

24...♖e8 25.♗f1

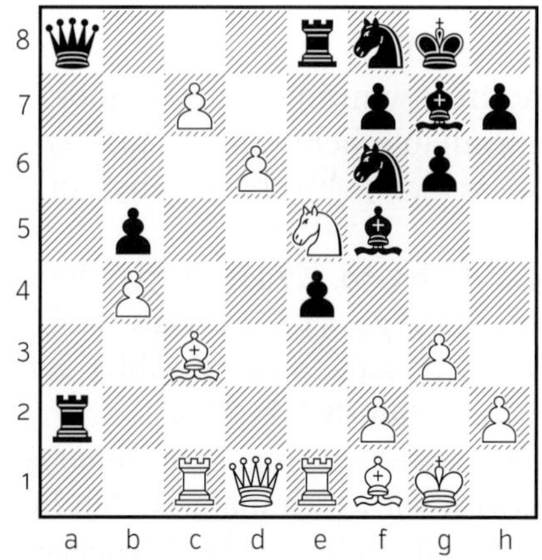

25...♕b7?

Much better is 25...♘d5 26.♗b5 ♘c3 27.♖c3 ♗e5 28.♗e8 ♗c3 29.♕b3 ♕e8 30.♕c3 ♕d7, with a winning position.

26.♗d4?

White could turn the tables with the fantastic opportunity 26.♕b3 ♗e6 27.♗c4!!

26...♗h6?

Still keeping better chances is the simple retreat 26...♖a6.

27.♘c6! ♗c1 28.♘e7 ♖e7 29.de7 ♘8d7 30.♗f6

Even better is 30.♕c1 ♖a8 31.♗b5.

30...♘f6 31.♕d8 1:0.

Pawn attacks against the center have to be conducted very carefully, otherwise the energy of the pieces can be really explosive.

6

▷ **Pavasovic**
▶ **Durarbeyli**
Rijeka 2010 [B22]

1.e4 c5 2.c3 g6 3.d4 cd4 4.cd4 d5 5.e5 ♘c6 6.♘c3 ♗g7 7.h3 f6 8.f4

Of course, the principled decision is to keep fighting in the center, as there are no serious reasons to give it up. 8.ef6 ef6 9.♘f3 ♘ge7 10.♗e2 0–0 11.0–0 g5 12.♖e1 ♗f5 13.♗e3 ♗g6 14.♖c1 ♕d7 15.h4 h6 16.hg5 fg5 17.♘h2 ♔h8 18.♗f3 ♖ad8 19.♘f1 ♘f5 20.♗g4 ♕f7 21.♗f5 ♗f5 22.♘g3 ♗g6 and Black is attacking the center even more directly.

8...♘h6 9.g4 0–0 10.♗g2 e6

The correct decision is to try to create direct counterplay with 10...fe5 11.fe5 e6 12.♘f3 ♘f7 (Weaker is 12... ♗d7 13.♗e3 ♖c8 14.♕d2 ♘f7 15.0–0 ♘a5 16.b3 ♕b6

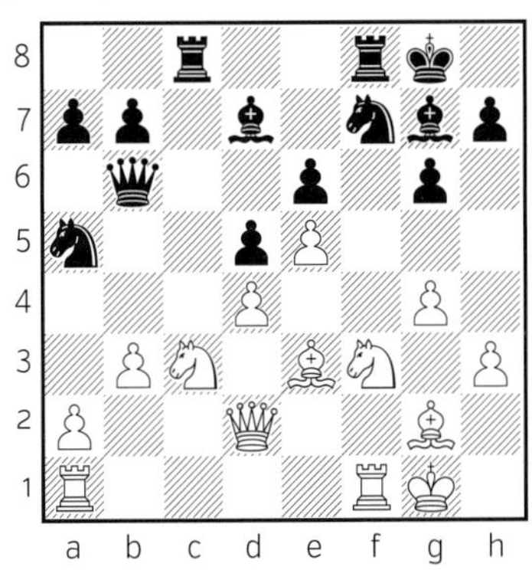

17.h4! (Starting a typical attack while the opponent has no good counterattack in response.) 17...♖c7 18.♖ac1 ♖fc8 19.h5 gh5 20.gh5 ♗e8 21.♗h3 ♕c6 22.h6 ♗f8 23.♔h1 ♘d8 24.♘h4 ♗g6 25.♘g6 hg6 26.♘e2 ♕b5 27.h7, Pavasovic–Lie,C Dresden 2008) 13.0–0 b5! (this is it — a direct counterattack on the queenside.) 14.♗e3 ♗d7?! (14...♗a6 is correct with sufficient counterplay.) 15.♕d2 b4 16.♘e2 ♕b6 17.♔h1

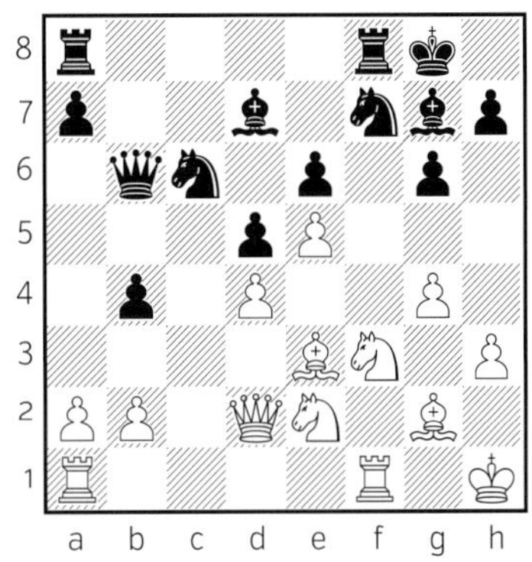

17...b3 (17...♖ac8 18.b3 ♘b8 19.♖fc1 ♗b5 is much better.) 18.ab3 ♕b3 19.♘c1 ♕b6 20.♘d3 ♖fb8 21.♘c5 ♗c8 22.b3 ♗f8 23.♕f2 ♗c5 24.dc5 ♕c7 25.♘g5, Goodger : Indrebo, Caleta 2010.

11.♘f3 ♘f7 12.0–0

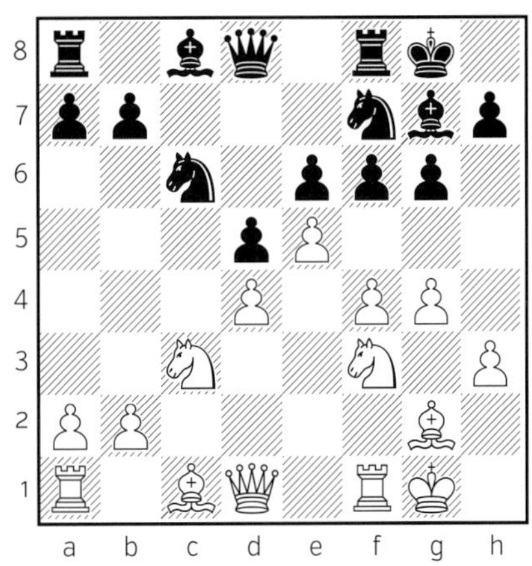

12...g5?!

It looks logical to destroy the opponents center, but Black's pieces are not active enough to do it successfully. Much better is the typical French plan of counterplay on the queenside: 12...♕b6 13.♘a4 ♕c7 14.♗e3 b6 15.♖c1 ♗a6 16.♖f2 ♖ac8.

13.ef6

Another good option is 13.♘e2 gf4 14.ef6 ♗f6 15.♗f4 ♕b6 16.♕d2 e5 17.♗e3 e4 18.♘e5 with better play.

13...♗f6 14.fg5

Here it was possible to transfer to the previous variation 14.♘e2.

14...♘g5 15.♘g5

Direct exchanges allow White to easily develop all his pieces. Slightly unnatural is another possibility: 15.♗e3 ♘f3 16.♖f3 ♗d7.

15...♗g5 16.♖f8 ♔f8 17.♕f3 ♔g7 18.♗g5 ♕g5 19.♖f1

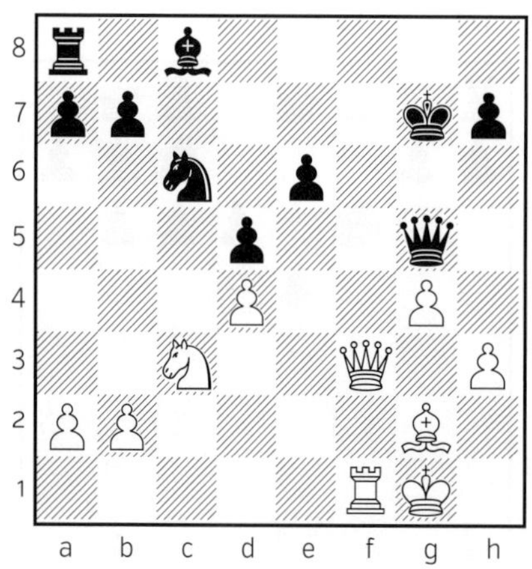

Now Black has to be very careful, as his opponent has mobilized all his pieces.

19...♕e7 20.♕e3

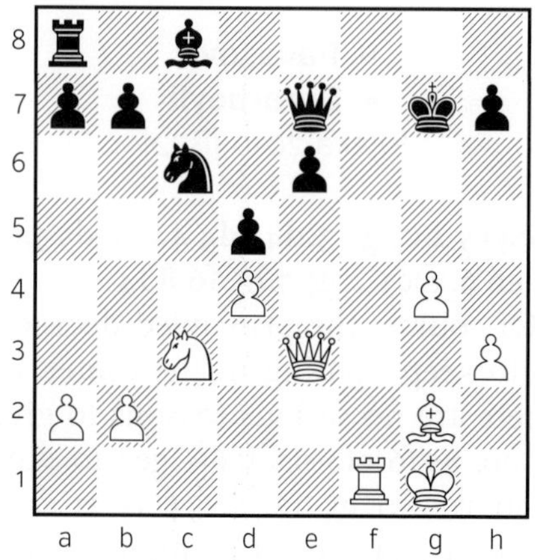

A very interesting possibility is the tactical transition into a sharp endgame:

20.♕f4 ♗d7 21.♗d5! ed5 22.♘d5 ♖f8 (22...♕e2 23.♕f7 ♔h8 24.♕d7 ♕b2 25.♘c7 ♖g8 26.♘e6±) 23.♘e7 ♖f4 24.♖f4 ♘e7 25.♖e4 ♔f6 26.a3 b6 27.♔f2 h6 28.♖f4 ♔g7 29.♔g3

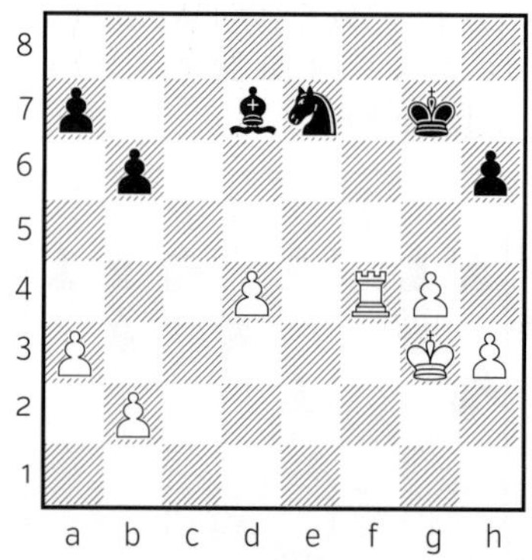

and Black has typical problems defending the ending with rook plus 2 pawns against two pieces.

20...♗d7 21.b4!

A very interesting positional idea — with this flank break White tries to deflect his opponent's knight from controlling the important central e5 square.

21...a6 22.a4
A more timid approach: 22.a3 ♖f8 23.♖f8 ♕f8 24.♘e2 h6 25.♘f4 guarantees White a stable advantage.

22...♕b4?
A very nervous decision, losing on the spot. Much more stubborn is 22... ♖f8 23.♖f8 ♕f8 24.b5 ♘b4 25.♗f1, with a slight White advantage.

23.♕g5 ♔h8 24.♕f6 ♔g8

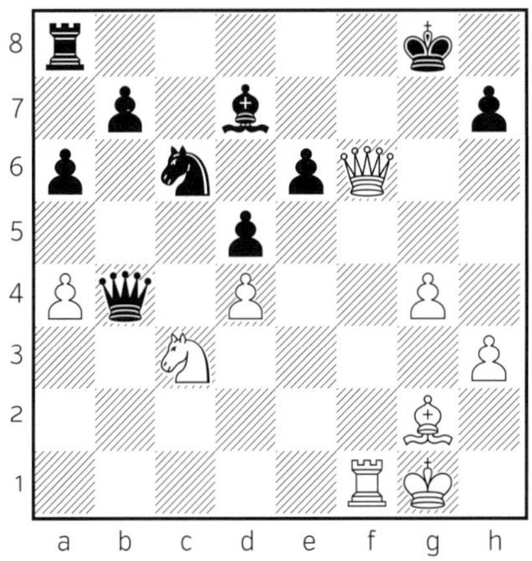

25.♘d5!
It is this blow which was not evaluated properly by young Azerbaijani.

25...♕d4
25...♕f8 26.♕g5 ♕g7 27.♘f6 loses the bishop, as in the game.

26.♕d4 ♘d4 27.♘f6 ♔g7 28.♘d7 ♖d8 1:0.

7

▷ **Mikhalchishin**
▶ **Dzhanoev**
Tbilisi 1976 [A09]

1.♘f3 d5 2.c4 dc4 3.♘a3

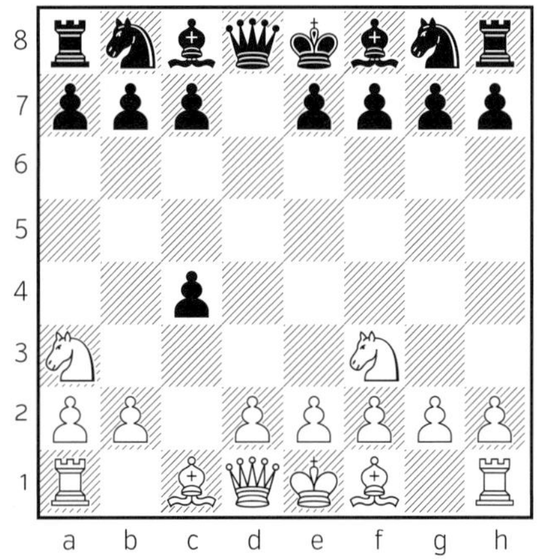

It is possible to try to get another structure in the center: 3.e3 b5 4.a4 c6 5.b3 cb3 6.ab5 cb5 7.♕b3.

3...c5
Now it is possible to launch a special flank strategy with the idea of limiting the power of White's knights in the center: 3...a6 4.♘c4 b5 5.♘e3 ♗b7 6.d4 e6.

4.♘c4 ♘c6 5.g3
It is possible to prevent the creation of the opponent's center with 5.e3, as 5...f6 is powerfully met with 6.d4.

5...f6 6.♗g2 e5 7.0–0 ♗e6
It was not clear whether to start direct development of the kingside, which seemed very logical: 7...♘ge7 8.b3 ♘d5 9.♗b2 ♗e7 10.♘h4! 0–0

11.♕b1 ♖f7 12.♘f5 ♗e6

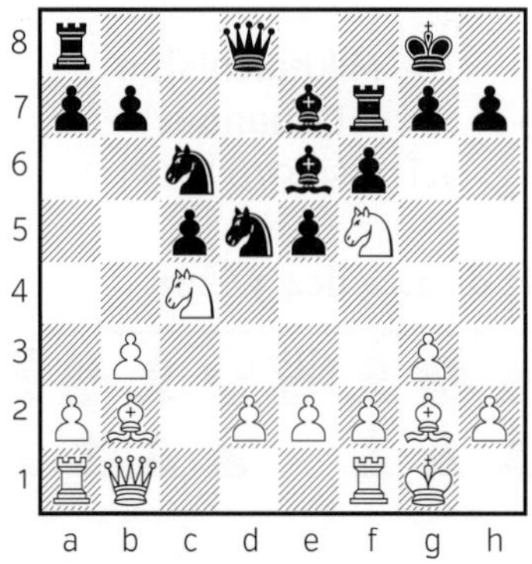

13.f4! ef4 14.gf4 ♘b6!

8.b3 ♘ge7 9.♗b2 ♘d5?

The wrong position for the knight in the center, as it was necessary to stop d2-d4 at all costs. 9...♘f5 10.♘e1 ♕d7=.

10.e3

Now White's intention is clear — to destroy the center and to open the position, exploiting his development advantage.

10...b5

Better is to try to complete development: 10...♗e7 11.d4 cd4 12.ed4 e4 13.♘e1 f5

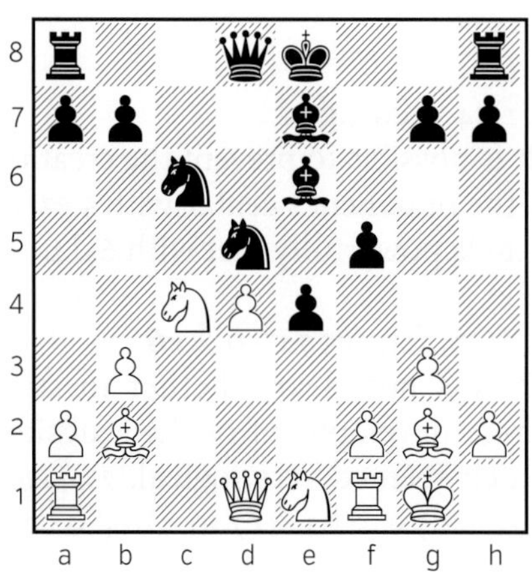

14.f3! (the center must be destroyed at any price!) 14...♘f6 15.fe4 fe4 16.♘c2 0–0 17.♕e2 and White will start to attack the remains of Black's center, but the situation would not be so dangerous as in the game.

11.♘a3 a6 12.d4 ed4

The other option is a bit more complicated: 12...e4 13.♘d2 f5 (Dangerous would be 13...cd4 14.♘e4 de3 15.♘c2 ef2 16.♖f2.) 14.dc5 ♕g5 (An unpleasant pin occurs after 14...♗c5 15.♖c1.) 15.♘c2 ♗c5

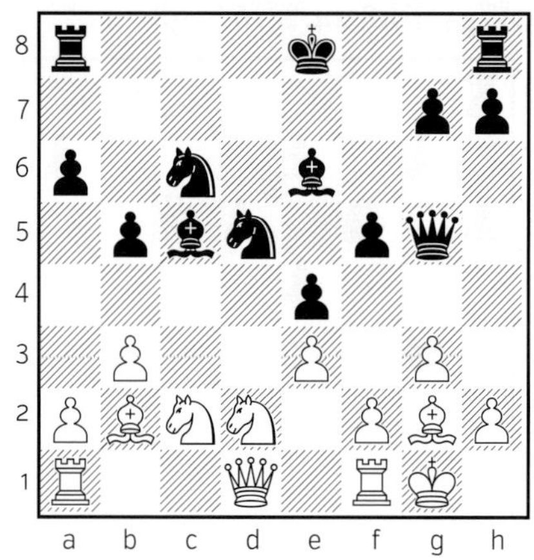

And now White's pieces start to demonstrate their dynamism: 16.♗e4! fe4 17.♘e4 ♕e7 18.♘c5 ♕c5 19.♗g7 ♖g8 20.♕h5 ♗f7 21.♕h7.

13.ed4 ♔f7

Possibly it is necessary to take a huge risk with 13...♕d7 14.♖e1 0–0–0 15.♘c2.

14.♖e1 ♘db4?!

Slightly better is 14...♘cb4.

15.♕e2

Bringing the knight back into the game is very strong: 15.♘c2 ♘c2 16.♕c2 ♖c8 17.d5!

15...♗d5 16.♖ad1 ♕d7 17.dc5 ♖e8

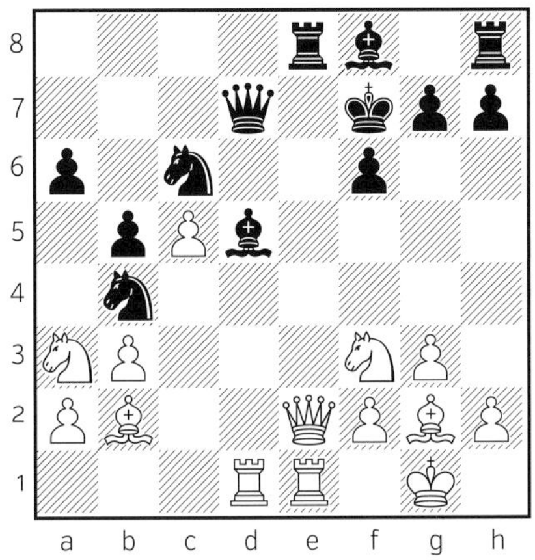

The safer option doesn't help much: 17...♖d8 18.♘c2 ♗c5 19.♘b4 ♘b4 20.♘e5! fe5 21.♕e5 ♗f8 22.a3.

18.♖d5! ♘d5 19.♘g5 fg5 20.♗d5 1:0.

The center can be destroyed with ***pawn counter-strikes in the center***, but in many cases it is necessary to be ready to sacrifice some material for activity.

8

▹ Tseshkovsky
▸ Beliavsky
Tashkent 1980 [C92]

1.e4 e5 2.♘f3 ♘c6 3.♗b5 a6 4.♗a4 ♘f6 5.0–0 ♗e7 6.♖e1 b5 7.♗b3 d6 8.c3 0–0 9.h3 ♗b7 10.d4 ♖e8 11.♘bd2 ♗f8 12.♗c2 g6 13.b3

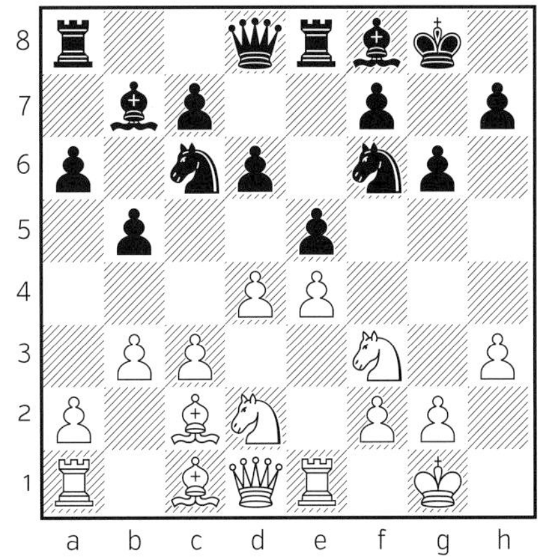

Generally better is to close the center, not allowing the different counter-strikes: 13.d5 ♘b8 14.b3.

13...d5!
Black is slightly better developed in Spanish positions, but with some space problems. So, to play ...d6-d5 in most cases is a success — and secondly it avoids d4-d5 White's space expansion.

14.de5?!
A serious option was the other capture: 14.ed5 ♘d5 15.♘e4 ed4 16.♗g5 f6 17.♘f6 ♘f6 18.♖e8 ♕e8 19.♗f6 ♕f7 20.♗d4 ♘d4 21.♕d4 c5, with very good compensation for the sacrificed pawn in the form of two powerful bishops.

14...♘e5 15.♘e5 ♖e5 16.♘f3
A few years later another top player tried to play this position with an extra exchange, but in vain: 16.f4 ♗c5 17.♔h2?! (17.♔h1) 17...♖e4 18.♘e4 de4 19.♗e3 ♗e3 20.♖e3 ♘d5 21.♗e4 (21.♖e4 ♘c3 22.♕d8 ♖d8) 21...♘e3 22.♕d8 ♖d8 23.♗b7 a5 24.♗c6 ♖d1 25.♖d1 ♘d1 26.b4=, Huebner : Beliavsky, Tilburg 1986.

16...♖e4!

It is interesting that Black is not forced to sacrifice this exchange and can obtain serious counterplay more simply: 16...♖e8 17.♗g5 h6 18.♗f6 ♕f6 19.e5 ♕b6.

17.♗e4 ♘e4 18.♗b2 ♗g7 19.♕c2

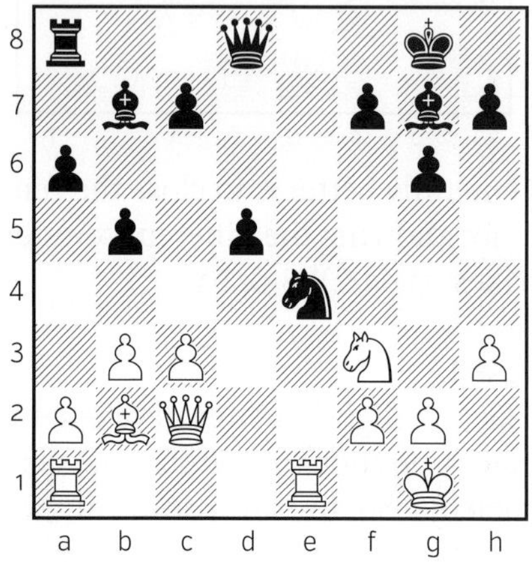

19...♕f6

Also not bad is the prevention of White's blockading strategy with 19...c5 20.a4 ♖c8.

20.b4

20.♖ac1 b4; 20.♖ab1 ♘c3 21.♖e3 b4.

20...c5

It is possible to include the pawn moves: 20...a5 21.a3 ♕c6.

21.bc5

It is not desirable to weaken your own pawn structure even more, so better is 21.♖ab1.

21...♘c5

It's possible to try to increase pressure on the c3 pawn with the rook capture after 21...♖c8.

22.♖e2?

Much better is simply to block the d5 pawn and the big diagonal with 22.♘d4.

22...♖c8 23.♖ae1 ♘e4 24.♕d3

It is very difficult to prevent Black's development of the initiative: 24.♘d4 ♕f4 25.♕b3 h5 26.a4 ♘c5.

24...♕b6 25.♘d4

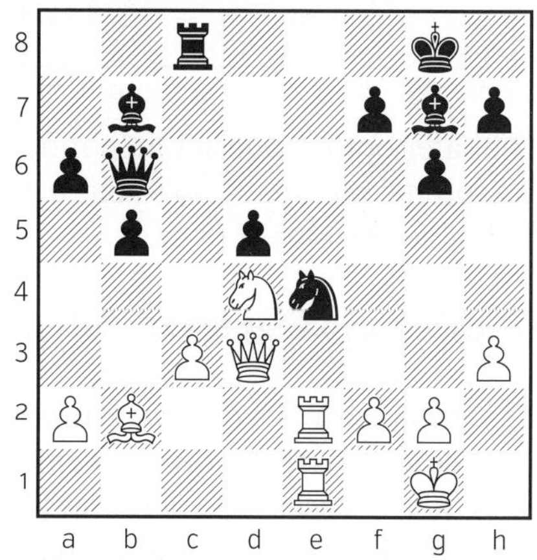

25...h5! 26.♗a1

Simply bad was to try to get rid of knight e4: 26.f3? ♘c3! 27.♖e8 ♔h7! 28.♖c8 ♕d4–+.

26...♖c4

For pressure on the c3 pawn it is better to have the rook in front of the queen, plus the threat will someday be ...b5-b4.

27.♘c2 ♕c7 28.♘e3 ♖c5 29.♘d1 ♗f6 30.♗b2 ♕c6

Black is clearly better, but it is not easy to improve his position immediately.

31.♗a3 ♖c4 32.♗b4 ♔h7 33.a3

Trying to win another exchange doesn't work:

33.♘e3 ♘c3–+.

33...♕c7

Now it is clear that White's bishop on b4 is in trouble.

34.♘e3 a5 35.♘d5

White can't exploit the absence of the Black queen from the defence: 35.♗a5 ♕a5 36.♘d5 ♗d5 37.♕d5 ♘g5 38.♖e3 ♔g7.

35...♗d5 36.♕d5 ab4!

Once more a sacrifice with the idea of exploiting the huge power of the passed pawn.

37.♖e4 ♖e4 38.♖e4 bc3

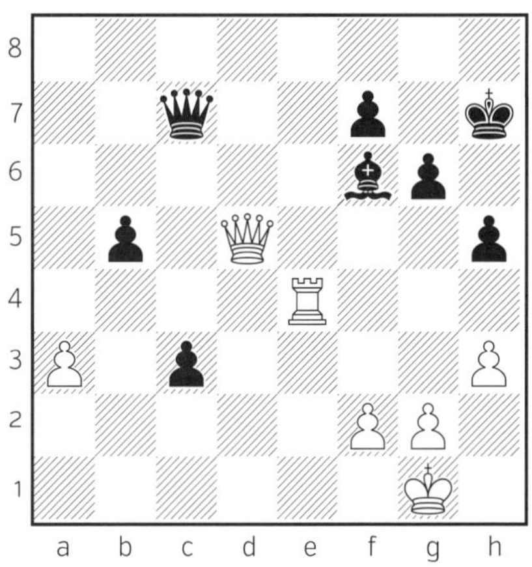

39.♕d1 ♕c5

Faster was 39...c2 40.♕c1 ♗b2.

40.♕c1

40.♕c2 ♕a3.

40...♗g5 0:1.

9

▹ **Suba**

▸ **Mikhalchishin**

Lugano 1987 [D90]

1.♘f3 ♘f6 2.c4 g6 3.♘c3 d5 4.cd5 ♘d5 5.♕b3 ♘b6 6.d4 ♗g7

I liked this kind of play, as White center is not so solid and there are different ways to fight against it.

7.♗g5

7.e4 ♗g4 8.♗e3 ♗f3 9.gf3 ♗d4 10.♖d1 e5 11.h4 ♘c6 12.♘d5 ♕d6 13.♗b5 0–0–0 14.♗g5 ♘d5 15.♗c6 ♕c6 16.♗d8 ♖d8 17.ed5 ♖d5 18.0–0 ♖d7 19.♔g2 a6 20.♖d2 ♕f6

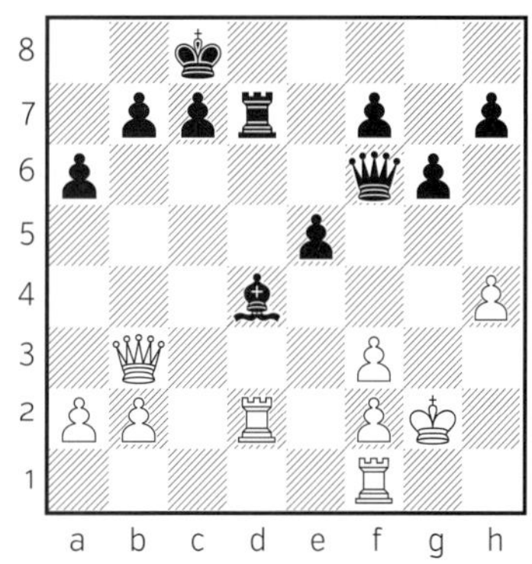

and Black has a fantastic bishop on d4, which is much stronger than the rook (Stajcic : Mikhalchishin, Vienna 1982).

7...♗e6 8.♕c2 h6 9.♗h4 ♘c6 10.♖d1

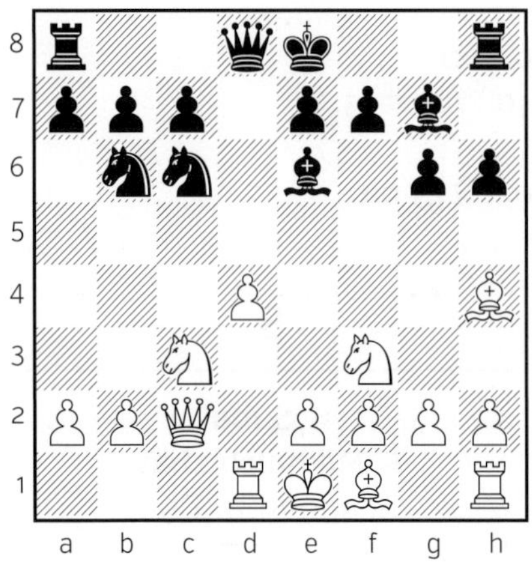

10...0–0

Another way of handling this position was demonstrated much later: 10...♘b4 11.♕b1 0–0 12.a3 ♘4d5 13.♘d5 ♕d5! (A very effective pawn sacrifice.) 14.♗e7 ♖fe8 15.♗b4 ♗g4 16.♘e5 c5 17.♗c5 ♗e5 18.♗b6 ♗f4 19.♗c5 b6 20.♗b4

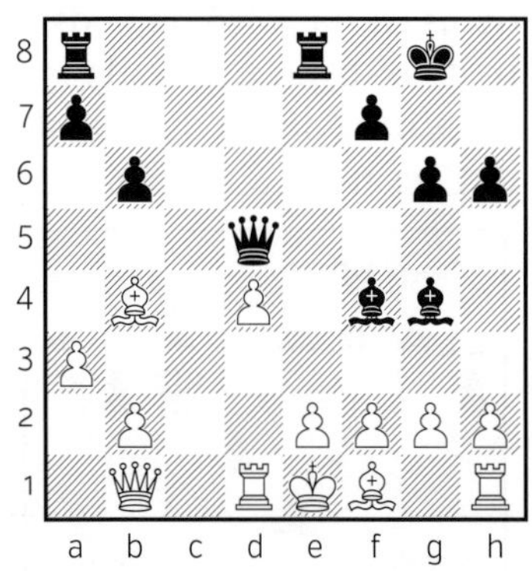

20...♗e2? (Here the correct move order of the sacrifice is different: 20...♖e2! 21.♗e2 ♕g2 22.♖f1 ♖e8) 21.♗e2 ♕g2 22.♖f1 ♖e2 23.♔e2 ♖e8 24.♔d3 ♕f3 25.♔c2 ♖c8 26.♗c3 ♕e2 27.♔b3, draw, Skembris : Mikhalchishin, Portoroz 1993.

11.h3

Here there is a chance to reduce Black's pressure on the center: 11.d5 ♘b4 12.♕c1 ♗g4 13.a3 ♘a6.

11...♘b4 12.♕b1 f5!

Black stops the central expansion with e4, and fights for his own space.

13.e3 g5 14.a3

Better was the simple retreat 14.♗g3 f4 15.♗h2, but Suba was worried about his lack of development and king in the center.

14...♘4d5 15.♗g3 f4 16.♗h2

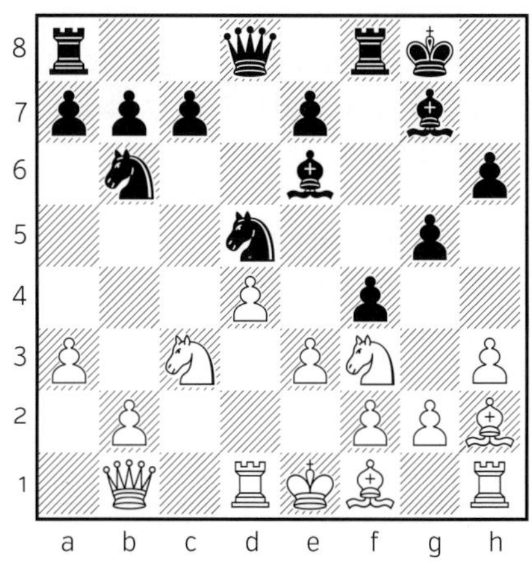

Better is to complicate the position with 16.ef4 gf4 17.♗h4 ♘c3 18.bc3 ♕d6.

16...c5!?

A powerful try to destroy the center, but much simpler was to destroy White's position from the other side: 16...fe3 17.fe3 ♗h3.

17.♘e4?

White misses his last chance to develop:

17.dc5 ♘c3 18.bc3 ♗c3 19.♘d2 ♕e8 20.♗b5 ♕f7 21.0–0 ♘d5.

17...fe3 18.♘c5

The same problems awaits White after 18.dc5 ♘a4 19.fe3 ♗f5.

18...♗f5

Still stronger is the capture 18...♗h3.

19.♗d3 ♕c8 20.fe3

White has to try to defend a slightly worse endgame after 20.♗f5 ♕f5 21.♕f5 ♖f5 22.♗e5 ef2 23.♔f2 ♘c4.

20...♘e3 21.♕a2 ♘bd5

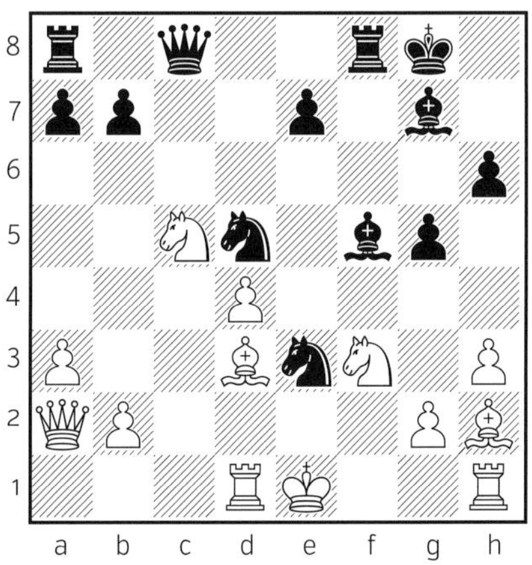

Once more, there was a simpler and better solution: 21...♔h8.

22.♔d2?

Now White's king comes under extremely unfriendly fire. Continuation of the fight was better with 22.♘e5.

22...♗d3 23.♔d3 ♕f5 24.♘e4 ♕e6! 25.♖a1 ♖ac8 26.♘fd2 ♕a6 0:1.

10

▷ **Mikhalchishin**
▶ **Velimirovic**
Yugoslavia 1992 [E62]

1.♘f3 ♘f6 2.c4 g6 3.g3 ♗g7 4.♗g2 0–0 5.0–0 d6 6.d4 ♘c6 7.♘c3 ♗g4 8.h3 ♗f3 9.♗f3 ♘d7 10.♗e3 e5

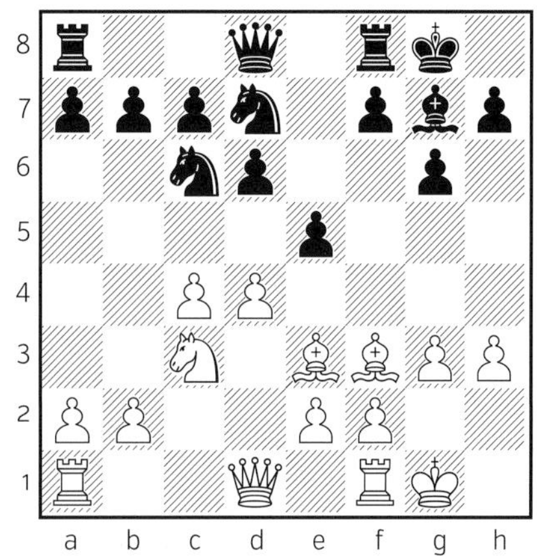

11.♗c6

What to do in such positions? The bishop is so strong that it is a pity to exchange it even for some weakness on c6. On the other hand, closing the center would allow Black unlimited activity on the Kingside. 11.d5 ♘e7 12.♗g2 h6!

11...bc6 12.♕d2

Possible is the neutral 12.b3!? as it's not clear yet how to attack Black's structure.

12...♖e8

In such situations it's wrong to give up the center: 12...ed4 13.♗d4 ♗d4 14.♕d4 ♕f6 15.♕f6 ♘f6 16.b4.

13.b3 ♘f6 14.♔g2 ♕d7

Another position for the queen is possible — 14...♕e7!?

15.♖ad1

Solid centralization, as two other typical changes of the center would be premature: 15.de5 ♖e5 16.♗d4 ♖h5 17.♖h1 ♖e8 or 15.d5 cd5 16.♘d5 ♘d5 17.cd5 c5.

15...ed4

The premature closing of the center 15...e4? 16.b4± allows White to develop a strong initiative on the queenside.

16.♗d4 ♘e4

Another mode of counterplay is more precise: 16...c5 17.♗f6 ♗f6 18.♘d5 ♗e5 19.♕g5 ♗g7 20.e3 a5.

17.♘e4 ♖e4 18.♗g7 ♔g7 19.f3 ♖e7 20.e4

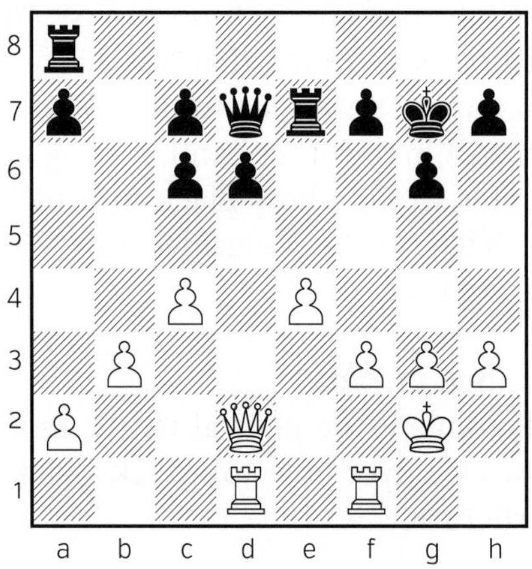

Trying to avoid Black's defence of the center isn't really possible: 20.c5 d5 21.e4 ♖d8 22.ed5 cd5.

20...♕e6?

It was necessary to avoid the typical destructive sacrifice: 20...c5 21.b4 cb4 22.♕b4, with a small advantage.

21.c5!±

With this pseudo sacrifice (as White will get this pawn back soon enough) White completely destroys his opponent's structure on the queenside.

21...dc5 22.♕c3

Even stronger is a different way of exploiting Black's weaknesses: 22.♖c1!? ♕e5 23.♕f2.

22...♕e5 23.♖c1

It is necessary to take care to avoid typical counterplay in the endgame: 23.♕e5 ♖e5 24.♖d7 a5!

23...f5

Now White is ready for his opponent's typical counterplay: 23...a5 24.♕c5 a4 25.b4±.

24.ef5 gf5 25.♕c5 ♖d8

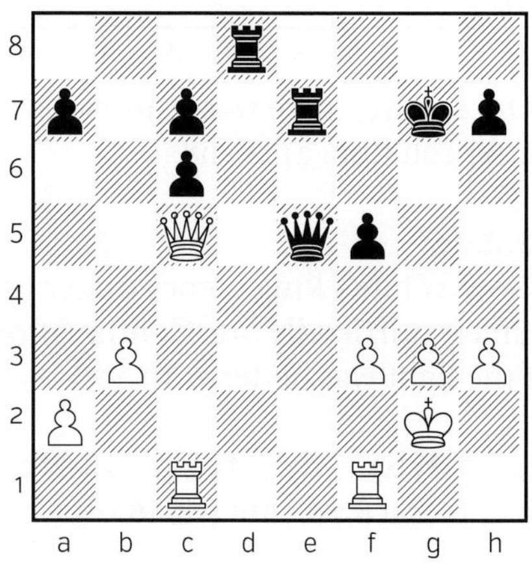

26.♖f2!

Correct prophylaxis for the second rank, as the materialistic approach 26.♕e5 ♖e5 27.♖c6 ♖e2 28.♖f2 ♖dd2 29.♖c7 ♔g6 30.♖e2 ♖e2 31.♔f1 ♖a2 would lead to a position with the white king cut off.

26...♖d6 27.♖c4!

Of course, again not the materialistic 27.♕a7? ♖g6.

27...♕c5 28.♖c5 ♔f6 29.♖fc2 ♖ee6 30.h4

Another way is possible, but it is just a matter of taste. 30.g4 fg4 31.hg4+-.

30...h6 31.♖a5 ♖d5 32.♖a7+- ♖ed6 33.♖c7 ♖d2 34.♖d2 ♖d2 35.♔h3 ♖c2 36.b4 ♖c4 37.a4! f4 38.a5 fg3 39.a6 ♖b4 40.♖c6 1:0.

Destroying the center is a process which has to be started and proceeded with correctly — and also prepared properly.

11

▹ **Bondarevsky**
▸ **Bronstein**
Leningrad 1963 [A48]

1.d4 ♘f6 2.♘f3 g6 3.♗f4 ♗g7 4.e3 0–0 5.♘bd2 b6 6.c3 c5 7.h3 d6 8.♗e2 ♗a6 9.♗a6 ♘a6 10.0–0 ♕d7 11.♕e2 ♘c7

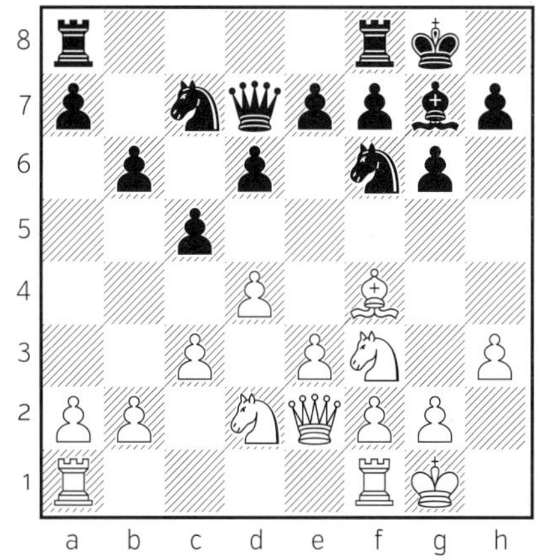

White has a strong central structure — c3-d4-e3 — but somewhat defensive. In such cases the main question is how White will increase the power of his central position? Black has to start to attack his opponent's center with the central strike ...e7-e5 or with the flank expansion ...b6-b5-b4.

12.dc5

The immediate central advance is met by a central counterstrike: 12.e4 ♘e6 13.♗e3 cd4 14.cd4 d5 15.e5 ♘e4 16.♕d3 ♘d2 17.♗d2 ♖ac8 18.♖fc1 ♖c1 19.♖c1 ♖c8, with equal chances, but it was a more logical development than the game line.

12...bc5

The other capture is wrong, as it allows strong White centralization: 12...dc5 13.♘e5 ♕c8 14.♖fd1 ♘cd5 15.♘df3.

13.e4 e5!?

An interesting try to take the whole center.

14.♗e3

Stronger is to leave the opponent with a bad bishop: 14.♗g5 ♘e6 15.♘c4 ♕c6 16.♗f6 ♗f6 17.♖ad1 ♗e7 18.h4.

14...♖ab8 15.b3 ♕c6 16.♕c4 ♘d7

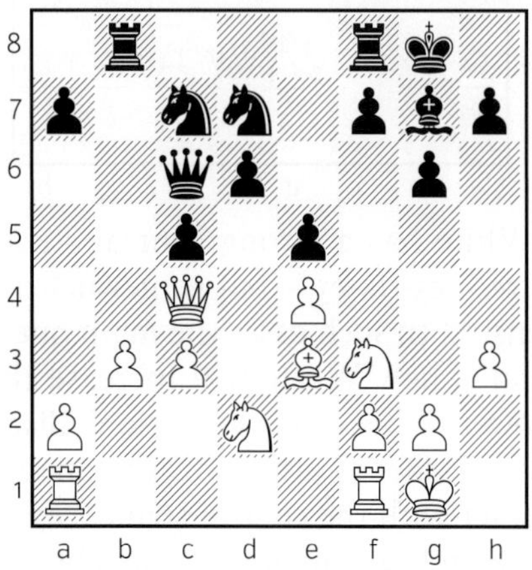

The position of White's queen is too strong and it has to be removed.

17.♘h2?

It was urgently necessary to start an attack on Black's pawn structure: 17.b4 ♘b6 18.♕b3 a6 19.a4.

17...♘b6 18.♕d3 d5

Black starts to move his own center, which will look to expand further.

19.f3

Nothing pleasant awaits White after an exchange in the center: 19.ed5 ♘cd5 20.♘c4 ♖bd8 21.♖fd1 f5.

19...♖bd8

An immediate expansion is possible: 19...d4 20.♗f2 ♘e6.

20.♕c2

The last hope was to launch some sort of attack on the queenside with 20.a4.

20...f5

Continuing to build the powerful center, but possibly simpler was 20...d4 21.♗g5 f6 22.♗h4 d3 23.♕b2 ♘e6.

21.♖ad1 ♘e6

Bronstein did not like the space gaining 21...d4, which was actually even stronger.

22.ed5 ♘d5 23.♘c4 ♘ef4 24.♖f2

After 24.♔h1 ♘e3 25.♘e3 ♖d1 26.♖d1 e4 finally the monster bishop on g7 would be released.

24...♘e3 25.♘e3 ♖d1 26.♕d1 e4

A similar idea as in the above variation.

27.♕c2 ♗h6!

From here the bishop creates even more threats than on the long diagonal.

28.♘hf1 ♘d3 29.♖d2 c4!

This starts a short and powerful attack on the Black squares.

30.♘c4 ♕c5 31.♔h2 ♗f4 32.g3 ♘e1 0:1.

In modern chess such cases are much more complicated — and are conducted in the sharpest of openings.

12

▷ **T. Kosintseva**
▶ **Dembo**
Antakya 2010 [B67]

1.e4 c5 2.♘f3 d6 3.d4 cd4 4.♘d4 ♘f6 5.♘c3 ♘c6 6.♗g5 e6 7.♕d2 a6 8.0–0–0 ♗d7 9.f3 h6 10.♗e3 b5 11.♔b1 ♘e5 12.♗d3 ♗e7

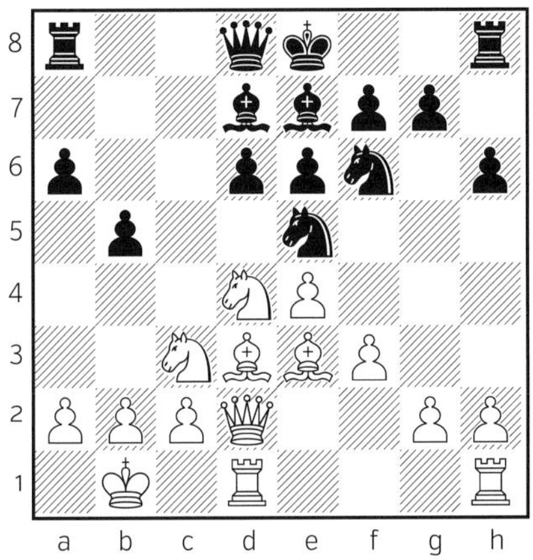

The pawn on h6 is extremely weak for two reasons — it makes White g2-g4-g5 attack very easy plus it makes castling kingside very dangerous, because of a bishop sac on h6. So, it was necessary to try to stop this simple g4 strategy and to play 12... h5!? Other moves were tried in the past (12...♕c7; 12...♖c8!?), but none of them promised sufficient counterplay for Black.

13.g4 b4
Black starts not so much the attack against the king, but prepares counterplay in the center and therefore tries to push White's knight to a worse position.

14.♘ce2 d5 15.ed5 ♘d5 16.♘f4 ♘e3?
16...♘d3 17.♕d3 ♘f4 18.♗f4 0–0 19.♘f5 ef5 20.♕d7 ♕d7 21.♖d7 ♖fe8 22.gf5 ♖ac8 promises Black good chances to hold in the endgame a pawn down.

17.♕e3 ♕a5 18.h4 ♘d3
A more 'Sicilian-like' move would be 18...♖c8.

19.♘d3 ♕c7 20.♘e5
Now the center is destroyed and opened, so the position of White's centralized knights is more powerful than Black's bishop pair. Possible was 20.g5, trying to open the position after g5-g6.

20...♖d8 21.g5

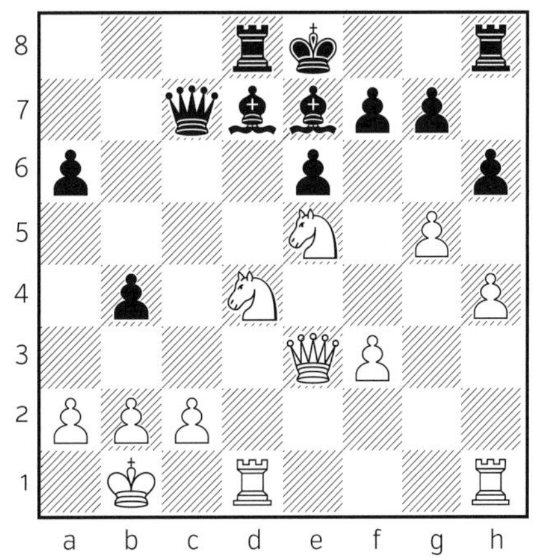

21...g6?
Black is in trouble, which is confirmed by the next variation: 21... ♗d6 22.♘d7 ♖d7 23.g6 ♗e5 24.gf7 ♔f7 25.♘e6 ♔e6 26.f4 ♖d1 27.♖d1 ♖c8 28.♕e2.

22.♕e4

22.h5! ♗g5 23.f4 ♗f6 24.hg6 ♗e5 25.gf7 ♔f7 26.fe5 and Black's king is terribly exposed.

22...h5 23.♘dc6

It is very logical to bring the final undeveloped piece into the game: 23.♖he1.

Another tempting, but slightly weaker possibility is the piece sacrifice: 23.♘g6 fg6 24.♕g6 ♔f8 25.♘e6 ♗e6 26.♕e6 ♔g7 27.♖d8 ♖d8 28.♕h6 ♔g8 29.♕g6 ♔f8 30.♕h5 ♕e5 31.f4, but even here Black faces serious problems.

23...♗c6 24.♖d8 ♕d8

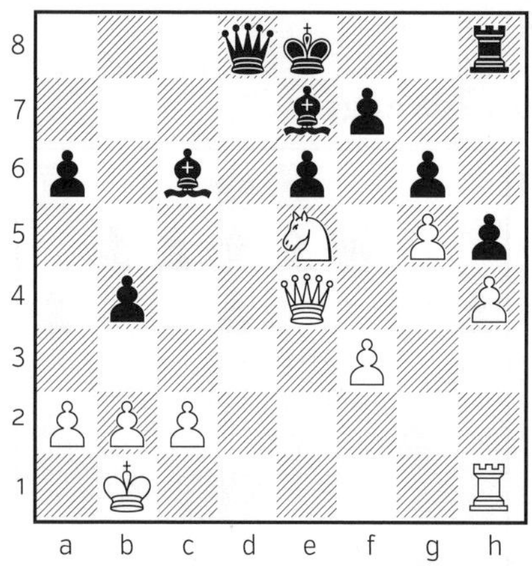

25.♘c6

Another option is 25.♕c6 ♔f8 26.♕a6 ♔g7 27.♕b7 ♕d6 28.f4 winning a pawn and keeping some winning chances.

25...♕d6 26.♘e5 ♕d5 27.♕d5 ed5 28.♖d1 ♗c5 29.♖d5 ♗f2

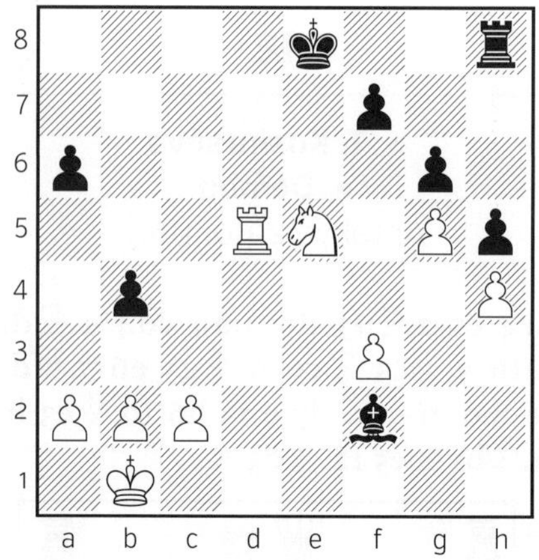

30.♖d8?

30.♘c6 0–0 31.♘b4 ♗h4 32.♘a6 f6 33.gf6 ♖f6 34.♘c5 ♖f3 35.a4

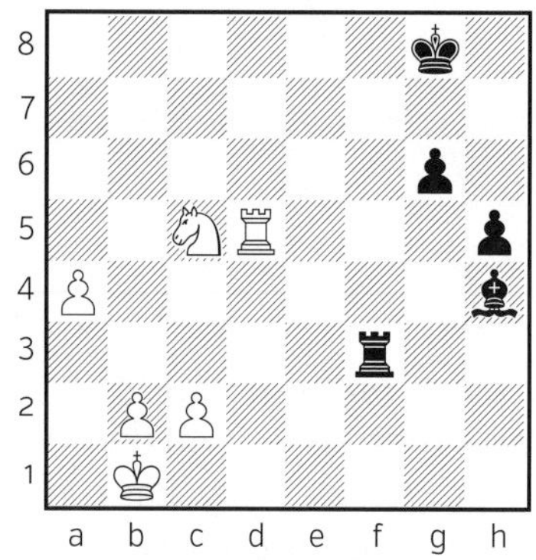

leads to a position with an extra White pawn, but the pawns are on different flanks and in such cases the role of the bishop mustn't be undervalued. Kosintseva overlooked a typical 'cutting-off' move at the end of a variation.

30...♔d8 31.♘f7 ♔e8 32.♘h8 ♗h4 33.♔c1

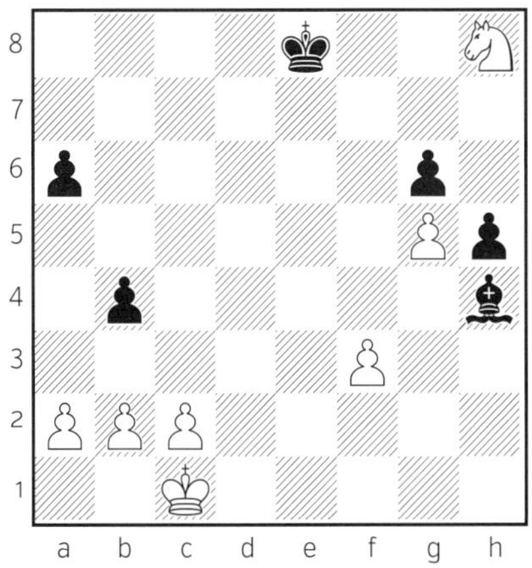

Few chances to save the game were offered by 33.♘g6 ♗g5 34.♘e5 h4 35.♘g4 h3 36.c4 bc3 37.bc3 ♗h4 38.♔c2 ♗g3.

33...♗g3!

This simple move decides the fate of one of the top-seeded players! The knight is arrested.

34.♔d1 ♔f8 35.♘g6 ♔f7 36.♘h8 ♔g7 37.♔e2 ♗e5

Other moves were winning also: 37... h4; 37...♔h8.

38.c4 bc3 39.bc3 ♔h8 40.c4 ♗f4 0:1.

Changing the structure of the center – closing the center

Closing the center is a method that is used for different purposes: sometimes the opponent's pressure is so unpleasant that it is necessary to reduce the tension. Or it is possible to start an attack with the flank majority, which is unable to be met by a successful central counterstrike. This method is very sensitive, as there have been many cases of an incorrect closing of the center.

1

▹ **Steinitz**
▸ **Lasker**
St. Petersburg 1896 (D35)

1.d4 d5 2.c4 e6 3.♘c3 ♘f6 4.♗f4

A similar plan of prematurely closing the center was refuted in the modern QGD: 4.♘f3 ♗e7 5.♗f4 and e.g. 5...0–0 6.c5 b6 7.b4 a5 8.a3 etc.

4...♗e7 5.e3 0–0

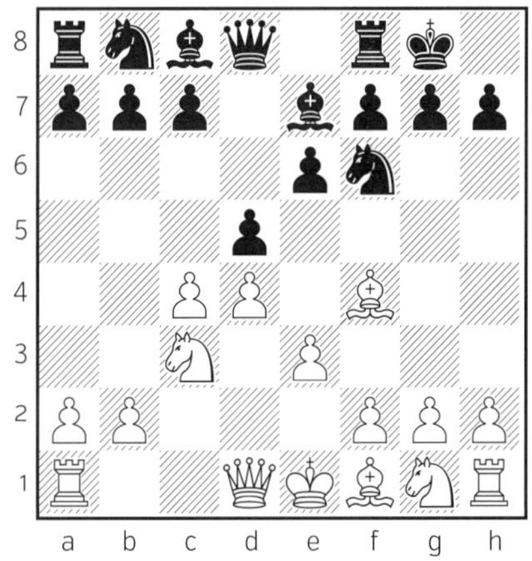

6.c5!?

A very interesting and direct plan.

6...♘e4

Lasker tries to attack in the center. An extremely interesting option is to attack White's pawn chain 6...b6 7.b4 a5 8.a3 ab4 9.ab4 ♖a1 10.♕a1 ♘c6 11.♕a4 bc5!! 12.♕c6 cd4, with a dangerous initiative for the sacrificed piece.

7.♘e4 de4 8.♕c2 f5 9.♗c4 ♘c6 10.a3

Faster development is possible: 10.♘e2.

10...♗f6 11.0-0-0!

A very risky decision — it is possible to simply complete development (11.♘e2).

11...♔h8

11...b6? 12.d5! leads to a disaster.

12.f3 ♕e7 13.♗g3!

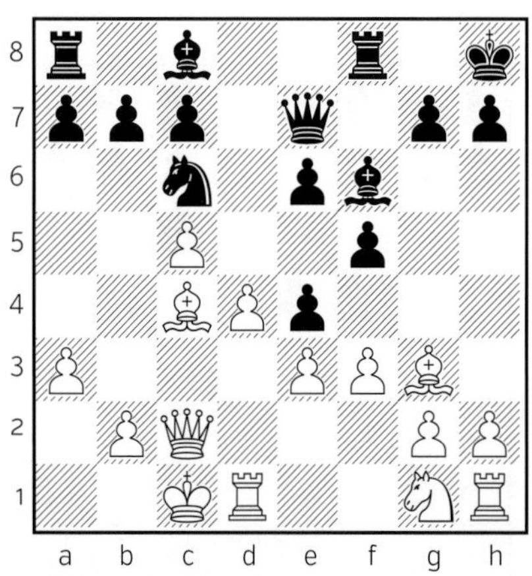

Refusing the pawn sacrifice gives Black an initiative:

13.fe4? e5 14.de5 ♘e5.

13...f4?!

Too risky, as Black's development is incomplete, Better is to play 13...b6.

14.♕e4!?

14.♗f4 e5 15.♗e5 ♘e5 16.de5 ♕e5 17.♗d5 ef3 18.♘f3 ♕e3 19.♔b1.

14...fg3 15.hg3

White has gained only two pawns for the piece, but his initiative will encounter no more obstacles.

15...g6

Lasker gives up a pawn, but better is 15...g5 16.f4 ♗d7.

16.♕g6 ♗d7

16...♖g8 17.♕e4 ♘a5 18.♗d3 ♖g7 19.♘e2, with much better play.

17.f4 ♖f7?!

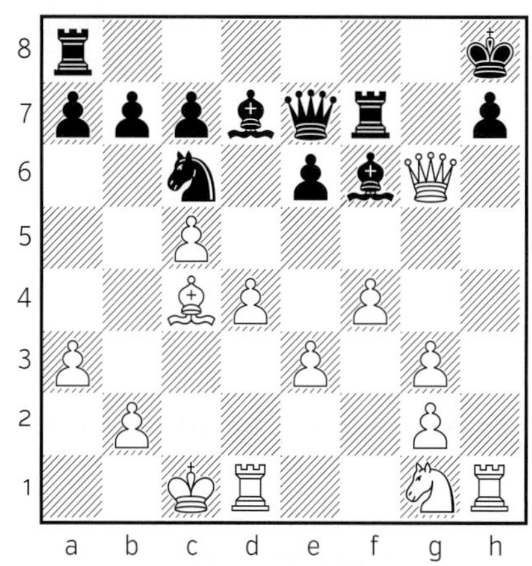

After this mistake Black's game is finally doomed. More interesting is to start counterplay after 17...♘a5.

18.g4 ♖g7

If 18...♖g8, then 19.♕h5 and g4-g5. Now 19.♕h5 allows Black to defend with ♗d7-e8-g6, but...

19.♕h6

19.♕h5 ♘a5 20.♗d3 ♗a4 21.g5!

19...♖g4 20.♗d3 ♖g7

Wrong is 20...♖h4 21.♖h4 ♗h4 22.♘f3 ♗f2 23.♖h1 ♗e3 24.♔b1, winning.

21.♘f3 ♕f7 22.g4!

The white attack rolls by itself and the space for Black pieces is constantly shrinking.

22...♖ag8 23.g5 ♗d8

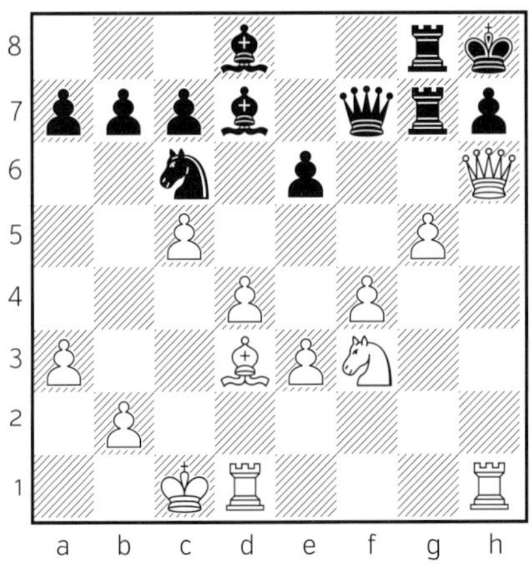

24.♖h2!

A disaster on h7 is unavoidable. The rest is simple.

24...♖g6 25.♕h5! ♖6g7 26.♖dh1! ♕h5 27.♖h5 ♖f8 28.♖h7 ♖h7

28...♔g8 29.♖g7 ♔g7 30.♖h7.

29.♖h7 ♔g8 30.♖d7 ♖f7 31.♗c4 1:0.

31.♗c4 ♖d7 32.♗e6 ♖f7 33.g6.

2

▷ Rubinstein
▶ Mieses
Germany 1909 [D34]

1.d4 d5 2.c4 e6 3.♘c3 c5 4.cd5 ed5 5.♘f3 ♘c6 6.g3 ♗e6 7.♗g2 ♘f6 8.0–0 ♗e7 9.♗g5 ♘e4 10.♗e7 ♕e7 11.♖c1 ♘c3 12.♖c3

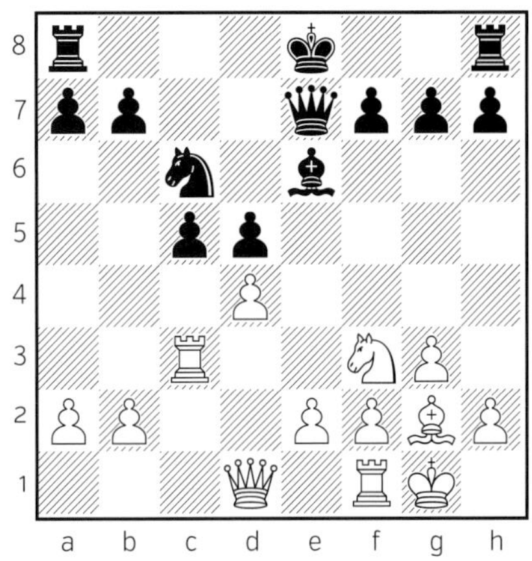

12...c4

A more-or-less forced closing of the center, as with an isolated pawn Black has huge problems because of White's control of c file: 12...cd4 13.♘d4 ♘d4 14.♕d4 0–0 15.♖fc1.

13.♘e5 0–0

The best chance is 13...♘e5 14.de5 ♕c5!, protecting the d5-square and controlling another important point — d4.

14.b3?

Correct in such situations is firstly to fix the structure and only then try to attack it, so 14.♘c6 bc6 15.b3 ♖fc8 16.bc4 dc4 17.♕a4.

14...♕b4

Correct here is to keep the powerful central structure with 14...♘e5 15.de5 ♖fd8 16.♕d4 b5.

15.♕d2 ♖ac8

Again possible is the exchange on e5: 15...♘e5 16.de5 ♖ad8 17.♕d4 b5.

16.♖d1

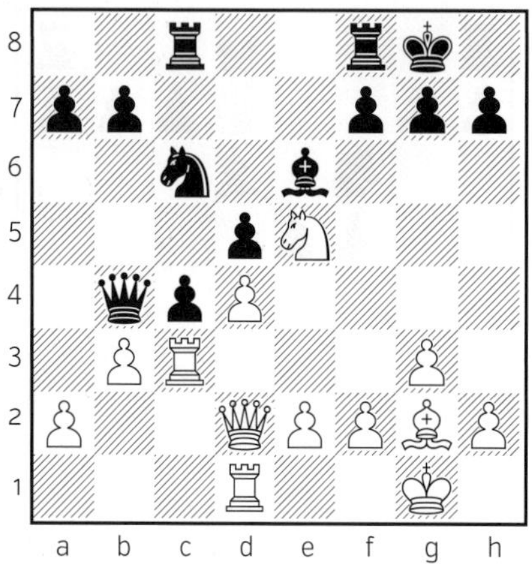

Here White could create a powerful passed pawn in the center:
16.a3 ♕b6 17.♘c6 ♖c6 18.bc4 ♖c4 19.♖c4 dc4 20.d5.

16...b5

Even now it is necessary to exchange knights: 16...♘e5 17.de5 b5 18.a3 ♕e7 19.b4 ♖fd8 20.♕d4 ♖a8!, with the idea, after a7-a5, of attacking the opponent's pawn chain on the queenside.

17.f4 ♘e5 18.fe5 a5 19.bc4

Possible is 19.e4.

19...♖c4 20.♖b3 ♕a4

Very good chances are offered by a transition into the endgame, with a pawn majority on the queen's flank: 20...♕d2 21.♖d2 b4.

21.e3 ♖fc8 22.♗f1 ♖c2 23.♕e1 b4 24.♗d3 ♕a2! 25.♗c2 ♖c2 0:1.

3

▹ **Munguntuul**
▸ **Zhang Xiaowen**
Subic Bay 2009 [C11]

1.e4 e6 2.d4 d5 3.♘c3 ♘f6 4.e5 ♘fd7 5.f4 c5 6.♘f3 ♘c6 7.♗e3 ♗e7 8.♕d2 0–0 9.0–0–0 c4!?

Both sides have castled, but on different sides — and this is usually the signal for flank attacks. However this one looks to be somewhat premature, so possibly better is to attack the center differently, with ...a6 and ...b5 or ♕a5.

10.f5 b5

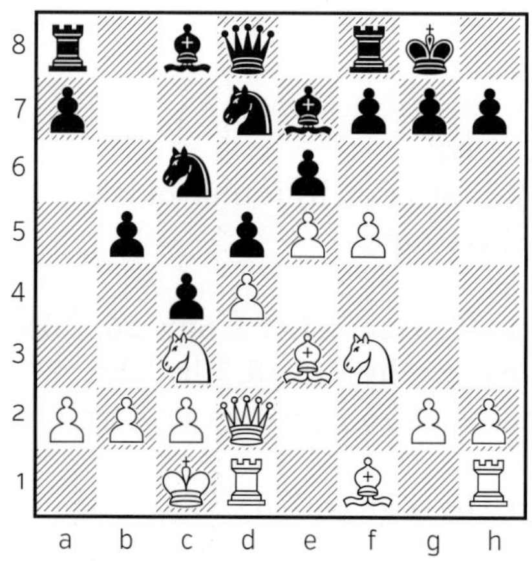

11.g4

Here White has a thousand different possibilities for the attack (11.fe6;

11.f6, 11.♗g5), but it appears everywhere that Black's closing of the center was a very good decision!

11...b4 12.♘e2 ♕a5

Every Black move creates some threat and improves a piece.

13.♔b1

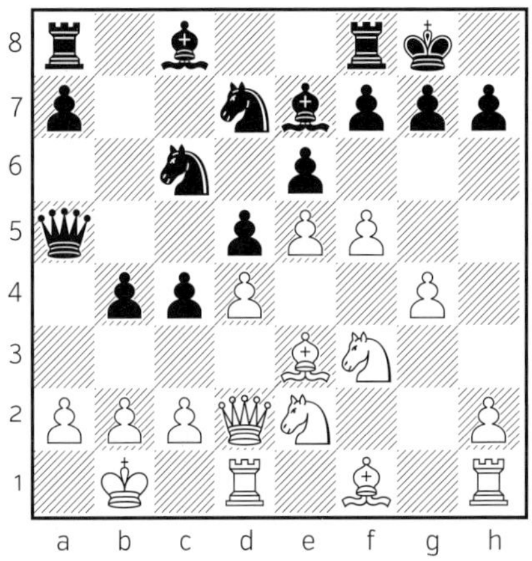

13...c3!

Immediately showing up the weakness of White's king position.

14.♕e1

No better is another retreat closer to her king: 14.♕c1 cb2 15.♕b2 ♘b6.

14...cb2 15.f6 gf6 16.♕h4

Desperate trying to drum up some even minimal attacking chances for herself.

16...♗a6

Another development move, and preparation of the attack with ...♗c4.

17.♘g3 b3!

Every move is like a nail being hammered in- now she threatens ...♘b4.

18.cb3 ♘b4 19.a4 ♕c7

Black is able to attack even in retreat!

20.♘e1 ♕c3 21.♗d3 ♗d3 22.♖d3 ♘d3 0:1.

4

▷ **Kortschnoj**
▶ **Lputian**
Wijk aan Zee 2000 (D37)

1.d4 e6 2.c4 d5 3.♘c3 ♘f6 4.♘f3 ♗e7 5.♗f4 0–0 6.e3 ♘bd7 7.cd5 ♘d5 8.♘d5 ed5 9.♗d3 c5 10.0–0

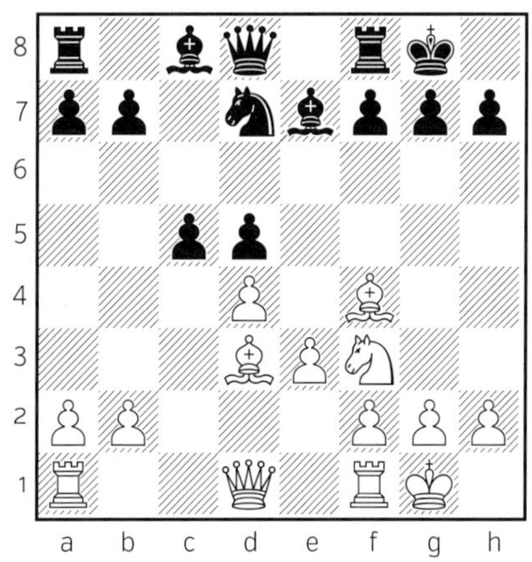

10...c4

It was possible to play with an isolated pawn: 10...cd4 11.♘d4 ♘c5.

11.♗c2 b5 12.e4 ♘b6 13.♖e1 ♗e6 14.♕b1 ♔h8 15.♗e5 ♗f6!

Remarkable: it is impossible to force Black to move any pawn on the king side!

16.♗f6 ♕f6 17.e5 ♕h6 18.♖e3

Due to the awkward location of White's pieces he has problems — how to create threats on the king side?

18...b4 19.♕e1 a5 20.g3

20.h4!?, with the idea of ♘g5.

20...♘c8?!

Black could now play 20...c3 21.bc3 ♘c4 22.♖d3 ♗f5 23.cb4 ab4 24.♕b4 ♗d3 (24...♖fb8!? 25.♕b8! ♖b8 26.♖b3 ♖b3 27.ab3, also with roughly equal chances.) 25.♗d3, with about equal play.

21.♘h4 ♘e7 22.f4 g6 23.♕d2 ♖fb8 24.♗a4!

Black will also have difficulties in carrying out his plan!

24...♖b7 25.♘f3 ♖c8 26.♘g5 ♕f8 27.♖f1 ♘f5 28.♖ef3 c3 29.♕f2 ♘e7

29...♖c4 30.bc3 bc3 31.♗b3 ♖d4 32.♖c3.

30.♘e6

30.f5? gf5 31.g4 ♕g7.

30...fe6 31.g4 ♖bc7 32.bc3 ♖c3 33.♗d7 ♖f3 34.♕f3 ♖c3 35.♕e2

35.♕f2?! ♕f7 36.♕h4 ♔g7.

35...♘c6!= 36.♗c6 ♖c6 37.♕b5 ♖c4 38.♕d7?

38.♕a5 ♖d4 39.♕b6=.

38...♖d4 39.♕e6 ♖f4 40.♖c1??

Big mistake, as White could keep his drawing chances after 40.♖f4 ♕f4 41.♕e8 ♔g7 42.♕e7 ♕f7 43.♕d6=.

40...♔g7 41.g5 ♕f7! 42.♕c8

After the exchange of queens Black could recapture either way with a decent advantage. Still, it was the lesser evil.

42...♕a7 43.♔h1 ♕f2–+ 44.♕d7 ♖f7 45.♕d5 ♕e2 46.h4 ♕g4 47.e6 ♕h3 0:1.

5

▷ **Koneru**
▷ **Chiburdanidze**
Doha 2011 [E42]

1.d4 ♘f6 2.c4 e6 3.♘c3 ♗b4 4.e3 c5 5.♘ge2 cd4 6.ed4 d5 7.c5!

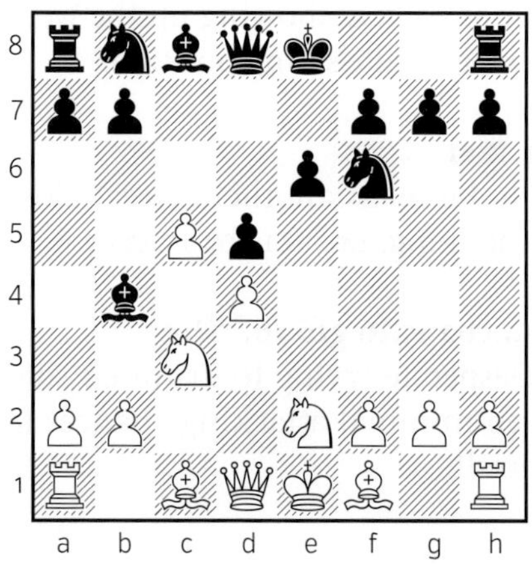

The most serious positional plan — White want to create a pawn majority on the queen's flank and to avoid Black's counterplay in the center.

7...♘e4

A very serious alternative here is the direct attack on the center 7...e5 8.de5 ♘g4 9.e6!

8.♗d2 ♘c6

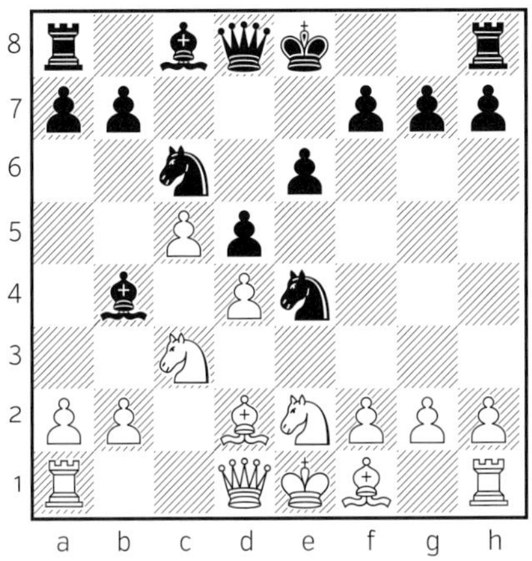

This looks to be the best try.

9.♘e4

Maja had successfully applied this variation in the same tournament before, so Koneru's preparation was aimed very precisely.

9.a3 ♗c3 10.♘c3 ♕h4 11.♘e4 ♕e4 12.♗e3 e5 13.♕a4 0–0 14.0–0–0 ed4

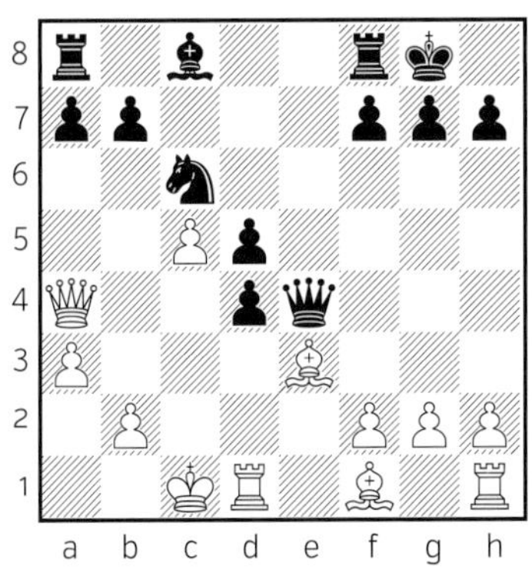

15.♗d3 ♕e5 16.♗d2 ♗f5 17.♕c2 ♗d3 18.♕d3 ♕e4 19.♕g3 a5 20.♖he1 ♕f5, with better play (0:1), Mkrtchian : Chiburdanidze, Doha 2011.

9...de4 10.♗b4 ♘b4 11.♕a4

11.♘c3 f5 12.♗b5 ♗d7 13.0–0 ♗b5= 14.♘b5 0–0 15.f3 e3=, Bareev : Aseev, URS 1990.

11...♘c6 12.♖d1 ♕g5

An interesting new idea. More consistent seems to be:

12...0–0 13.♘c3 e3!? (13...f5 14.♗b5±) 14.fe3 ♕g5 15.♔f2 (15.♔d2 ♖d8! 16.♘b5 e5) 15...♗d7 (With idea ♘e5.) 16.♕c2 (16.♗b5? a6; 16.d5!?; 16.h4 ♕f5 17.♔g1 ♘e5 18.♗b5 ♘g4 19.♖f1 ♗b5 20.♕b5 ♕c2 21.♖h3±, Rossiter–Piper, London 1994) 16...b6! 17.♕e4! bc5 18.dc5 ♗e8 (18...♘e5? 19.♕f4±) 19.♗d3 g6 20.♕f4 ♕c5 21.♘e4 ♕e5 22.♖hf1, with approximately equal play, Knaak : Skembris, Thessaloniki 1988.

13.g3

The transfer into endgame looks a bit artificial: 13.♕b3 0–0 14.♕e3 ♕e3 15.fe3 f5 16.♘c3 ♗d7. A direct attack on the pawn is possible, but unclear whether it offers some chances for the advantage: 13.♘c3 e3 14.f3 0–0 15.♘e4 ♕g6 (15...♕h6!? 16.♗b5 ♗d7 17.0–0 a6 18.♗e2 ♖ad8, idea e5, ♘e7, ♘c6) 16.♕b3! f5 17.♘d6 f4 18.♕d3 ♕g5 (18...e5!? 19.♕g6 hg6 20.♗c4 ♔h7 21.d5 ♘d4) 19.♕e4 g6 20.a3 ♗d7 (20...a5!?) 21.b4 (21.♘b7? ♖ab8 22.d5 ♘e7 23.d6? ♘c6 24.♗b5 ♕g2–+) 21...♘e7, with very active counterplay after transferring the knight to f5, Lugovoi : Aseev, St. Petersburg 1995.

13...e3

Development leads to White's slight advantage: 13...0–0 14.♗g2 f5 15.0–0 ♖d8 16.f3 ♕e3 17.♖f2 ef3 18.♗f3, but an interesting idea would be to head for the endgame 13...♗d7 14.♕b3 ♕d5 15.♘c3 ♕b3 16.ab3 f5 17.♗c4 e5 18.♘b5 ed4 19.♘d4 ♘e5 20.♗e2 ♖c8 21.♘f5 ♗f5 22.♖d5, Iljushin : Andreikin, Russia 2005 and here the best chance for Black is 22...♔e7.

14.fe3 ♕e3 15.♗g2 ♗d7 16.♕c4!

With this move White starts an operation to allow him to castle, after driving her opponent's queen from e3.

16...0–0 17.♖d3 ♕h6 18.0–0 ♖ab8

Centralization of the rook would be met by strong flank development: 18...♖ad8 19.b4 a6 20.a4 ♗c8 21.b5 ab5 22.ab5 ♘e7 23.c6.

19.b4 e5

Maja desperately tries to avoid White's pawn-mass advance, but a different attempt to create some counterplay on the queenside contains its own flaws:

19...a6 20.a4 a5 21.b5 ♘b4 22.♖dd1 ♘d5 23.♗d5 ♕e3 24.♔g2 ed5 25.♕d3 ♖fe8 26.♕e3 ♖e3 27.♘f4.

20.d5 e4?

Maja tries desperately to escape from the positional grip. Black is in troubles after 20...♘e7 21.♘c3 ♔h8 22.♖e1 ♖fc8 23.d6.

21.♕e4 ♖be8

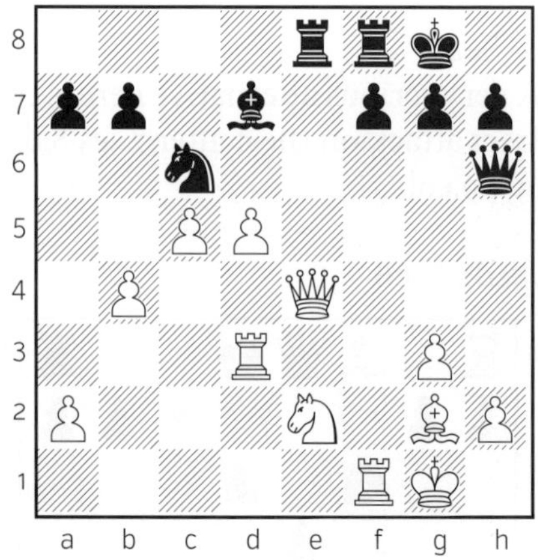

22.dc6! ♗c6

How did Maja manage to overlook 22...♖e4 23.cd7?

23.♕g4 ♗b5 24.♘f4 ♗d3 25.♘d3 ♕e3 26.♘f2

White has two pieces for the rook and the terrific pawn formation c5 plus b4, which guarantees an easy win.

26...♖e7 27.♕f4

An improvement is 27.♕c4 ♖d8 28.♗d5.

27...♕a3 28.♕c4

One more active attacking option is 28.♘e4 ♕a2 29.♘d6 b6 30.♕g5 ♖e2 31.♗d5 ♕d2 32.♘f7.

28...♖d8 29.b5 ♖d2 30.c6 bc6 31.bc6 ♕a5

It was better to try the risky capture-a chance existed that White would not play in the most precise way: 31...♕a2 32.♕b4 ♖e8 33.c7 ♖c2 34.♖e1 ♖f8 35.♗e4 ♖c7

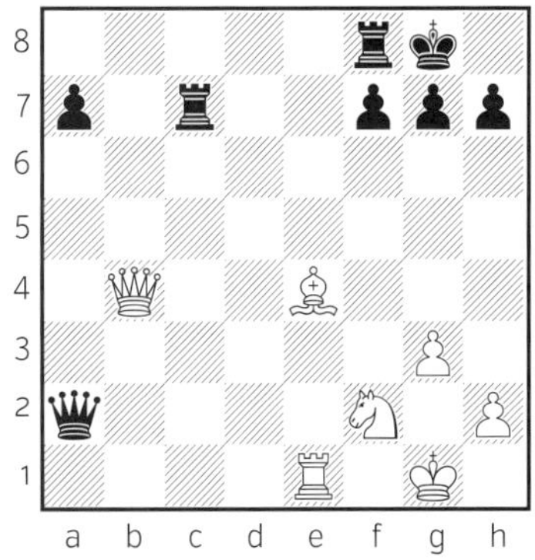

36.♗b1! ♛d5 37.♗h7 ♔h7 38.♕f8.

32.a4 h6 33.♘e4 ♛b6 34.♔h1 ♖d4 35.♕c2 ♛a5 36.♖b1

Slightly better would be 36.♘c5.

36...g6 37.h4 ♔g7 38.♕c5 ♛c5 39.♘c5 ♖c4 40.♘b7 ♖e3

The pawn promotes after 40...♖a4 41.♖c1 ♖c7 42.♘d6 ♔f8 43.♘b5 ♖c8 44.c7.

41.♘d6 ♖c5 42.♖b7 1:0.

There are cases in which the closing of the center looks very dangerous.

6

▷ **Tukmakov**
▶ **Lputian**
Luzern 1993 [D58]

1.d4 e6 2.c4 d5 3.♘f3 ♘f6 4.♘c3 ♗e7 5.♗g5 h6 6.♗h4 o–o 7.e3 b6 8.♖b1 ♘bd7 9.cd5 ♘d5 10.♗e7 ♛e7 11.♘d5 ed5 12.♗e2 ♘f6 13.♕a4 ♗d7 14.♕b3 c5 15.♕a3 ♖fe8 16.♖c1

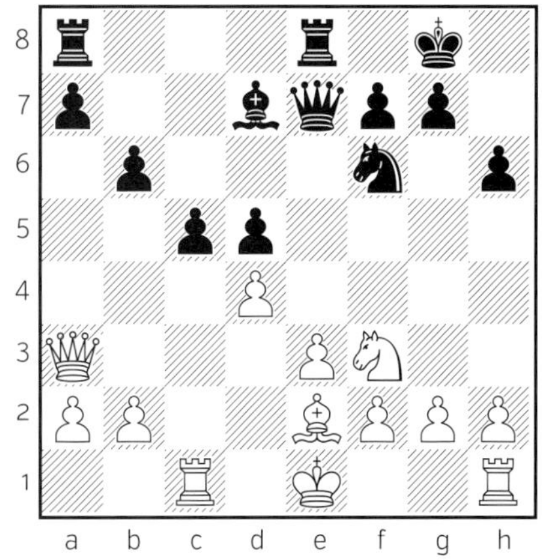

16...c4!

Keeping the central structure with 16...♖ec8 leads to a very passive set up.

17.♕e7 ♖e7 18.♘e5 b5!

Keeping the Black bishop (18...♗e8) was not logical, as Black wants to place his pawns on white squares.

19.♗f3?!

More logical is pawn counterplay on the other side: 19.f3 a5 20.g4 b4 21.h4, but White tries to stop ...b5-b4 with cheap tactics.

19...a5 20.g4 a4

20...b4 21.♖c4 — this is the point.

21.a3 ♖b8 22.h4 g5!

Radically stopping all White's threats on the kingside.

23.hg5 hg5 24.♖h6

White cannot stop his opponent's attack: 24.♗d1 b4 25.♘d7 ♖d7 26.♗a4 ♖a7 so he decides instead to destroy his structure with an exchange sacrifice.

24...♔g7 25.♖f6 ♔f6 26.♗d5

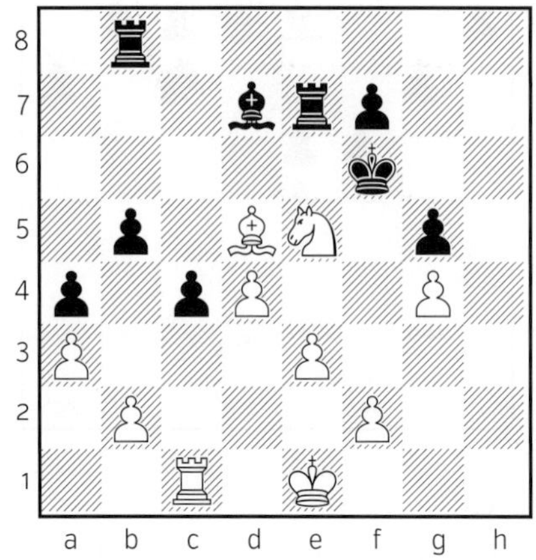

26...♖e5!

The best decision, returning the material and eliminating the strong knight on e5. Much weaker is the positional continuation 26...♖h8 27.♔e2 ♗e8.

27.de5 ♔e5 28.♗f7

The simple retreat does not work: 28.♗f3 ♗e6 29.♔d2 ♖d8 30.♔e1 ♖d3 31.♖c3 ♖d6 32.♖c1 ♗d5 33.♗d5 ♖d5 and in the rook ending Black's king and rook are tremendously active.

28...♗g4 29.♗g6

No help is offered by the small pawn sacrifice 29.f4 gf4 30.ef4 ♔f4 31.♔d2 ♖d8.

29...♖d8

Now White will have additional problems with his king.

30.♗c2 ♗f3 31.♖a1 g4 32.♖c1 ♖d6 33.♖a1 ♖h6

After the improvement of every piece follows the decisive penetration.

34.♖c1 ♖h1 35.♔d2 ♖h2 36.♔e1 ♔f6 37.♗b1 g3! 38.fg3 ♖e2 39.♔f1 ♖b2 40.♗c2 ♖a2 41.♔e1 ♖a3 42.♖b1 ♖a2 0:1.

Even World Champions make wrong decisions.

7

▷ **Hort**
▶ **Karpov**
Amsterdam 1981 (D58)

1.d4 ♘f6 2.♘f3 e6 3.c4 d5 4.♘c3 ♗e7 5.♗g5 h6 6.♗h4 0–0 7.e3 b6 8.♖c1 ♗b7 9.cd5 ed5 10.♗e2 ♘bd7 11.0–0 c5 12.♕c2 a6 13.♖fd1

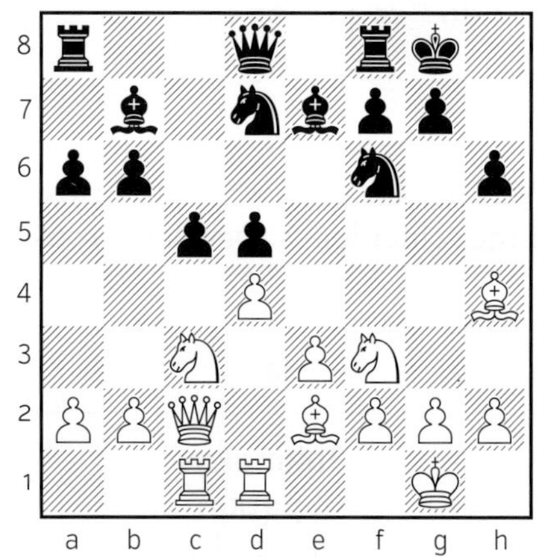

13...c4?!

Closing the center here is very risky: Black has to be very careful and to play immediately 13...♘e4.

14.a4!

A very important move, preventing Black from supporting his pawn formation with ...b6-b5 and preparing to destroy it with b2-b3, thereby creating some weakness on b6 or d5.

14...♗c6?!

Karpov tries to force through this important pawn move, but better would be to do it with the help of knight — 14...♘e8.

15.♘e5 ♕c7 16.♘c6

A very strong could be unleashed with the central break 16.e4! de4 17.♘c4 ♗d6 18.♘d6 ♕d6 19.d5.

16...♕c6

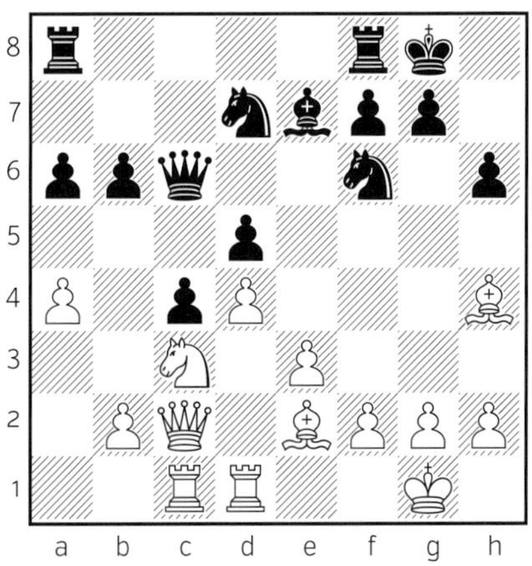

17.♗f3

The original plan is not bad either: 17.b3 b5 18.bc4 bc4 19.e4 de4 20.d5 ♕c5 (20...♘d5 21.♘d5 ♗h4 22.♕e4.) 21.♘e4 ♘e4 22.♕e4 ♗h4 23.♕h4 and the c4-pawn is very weak.

17...♗b4?

This move allows tactical tricks, but other moves don't help either: 17...♖ae8 18.b3! b5 19.ab5 ab5 20.♗f6 ♘f6 21.bc4 bc4 22.e4; 17...♖fe8 18.e4±; 17...g5 18.♗g3±.

18.♘d5!+- ♘d5 19.♕f5

It is also possible, but bad, to enter the tricky position after 19.♕c4? ♕c4 20.♖c4 b5!

19...♕a4 20.♗d5 ♖ac8 21.b3!

A small tactical operation with the idea being to open files and the opponent's king.

21...cb3 22.♖c8 ♖c8 23.♕f7 ♔h8 24.♗b3 ♕b5 25.♗e6 ♖f8 26.♗d7! ♖f7 27.♗b5 ab5 28.♖b1 ♖c7 29.g4 1:0.

Closing the center can take different forms. In each case there appears different plans for both sides to attack their respective targets.

8

▷ **Tsetselian**
▶ **Mikhalchishin**
Tbilisi 1979 (D91)

1.♘f3 ♘f6 2.d4 g6 3.c4 ♗g7 4.♘c3 d5 5.♗g5 ♘e4 6.cd5 ♘g5 7.♘g5 e6 8.♕d2 h6 9.♘f3 ed5 10.e3 0–0 11.♗e2 c6 12.0–0

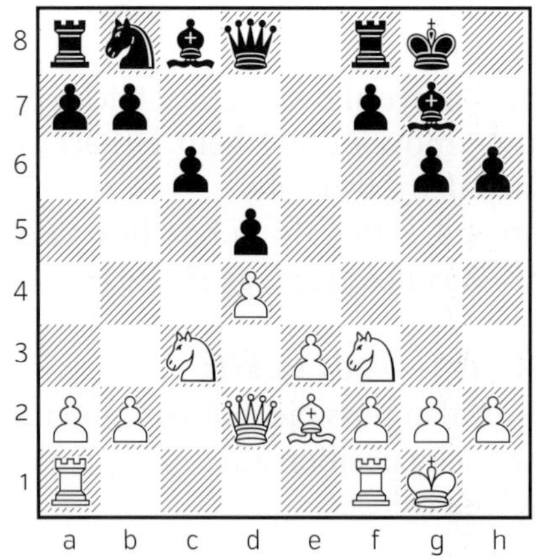

At the moment the structure is typical for Queen's Gambit Exchange variations, with the most natural White plan being b2-b4-b5, the so-called minority attack. The idea of this plan is to create a weakness on c6 or d5. For this reason Black has to counterattack on the other side, but first it is useful to improve the position of his own pieces, preventing for some time his opponent's plans.

12...♕d6

Another possible option is 12...♕e7. At the moment it is not clear where the queen is better placed.

13.♘a4

13.a3 is too slow so White decides to apply another typical plan — activation of the pieces, with the idea being to force some weakening of Black's position on the queenside.

13...♗g4 14.b4

Of course White did want to obtain a stupid bishop: 14.h3 ♗f3 15.♗f3 ♘d7 16.♖ac1 f5 and then ...♘d7-f6-e4.

14...♘d7 15.♘c5 ♘c5

Black can keep the position balanced after 15...b6 16.♘d7 ♗d7 17.♖ab1 ♖fe8.

16.bc5 ♕e7

Nothing special, but this retreat shows that earlier it was better to place queen on e7. Now Black obtains a weakness on b7 and White is ready to extend his pressure by doubling rooks on the b-file. But Black prepares to attack on the other side and plans to retreat bishop to c8 to protect his b7-pawn. Sometimes the position of the piece on c8 is very strong!

17.♖ab1 ♖ae8 18.♖b3 ♗c8!

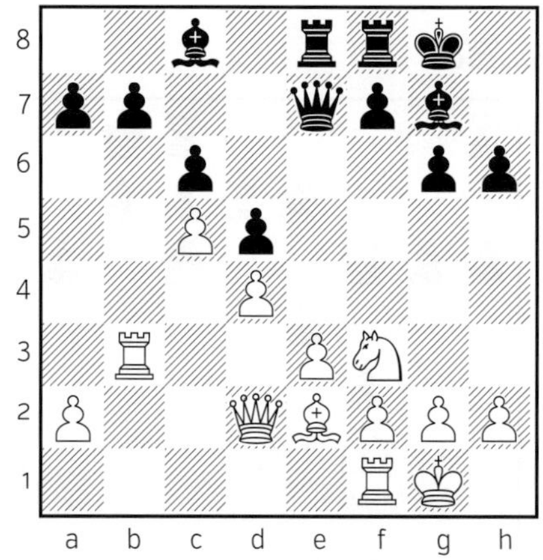

With this move Black shows his intentions and White understands that his attack on b7 is a failure.

19.♘e1 h5

Black has to proceed with his plan very carefully. If, for example, 19...f5 20.f4 ♔h7 21.♘f3 and White knight will obtain a strong square on e5.

20.♕b2

Wrong is 20.♘d3 ♗d4.

20...h4

Creating the unpleasant threat ...h4-h3.

21.h3 g5 22.♘d3 ♕e4!

Premature is 22...f5 23.♗h5 ♖d8 and Black's pieces are uncoordinated.

23.♗f3 ♕e6

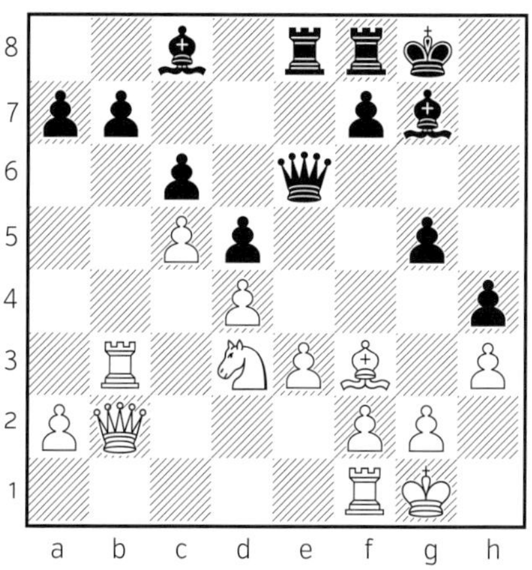

Not bad is the other position of the queen, 23...♕g6. White is sick and tired of prospective ...f7-f5 and ...g5-g4 advances, so he tries to change the course of the game with an exchange sacrifice.

24.♖b7?! ♗b7 25.♕b7 ♖e7 26.♕a6 f5

It's better to attack immediately and not to defend, e.g. 26...♖b8 27.a3!, with ♘b4 next.

27.♘b4 g4 28.♗d1?

It was necessary to continue changing the position 28.♘d5 gf3 29.♘e7 ♕e7 30.♕c6 fg2 31.♕d5 ♕f7 32.♕f7 ♔f7 33.♔g2 ♔e6 34.♖b1 and White has real counterplay.

28...♖f6 29.♘d3

Very sharp play arises after 29.♗a4 ♖c7 30.♗c6 ♖c6 31.♘c6 ♕c6 32.♕a7 gh3 33.♖b1 ♖f8 34.♖b6 ♕e8, but here White will be struggling sooner-or-later.

29...g3!

A very unpleasant opening of the white king's position.

30.♘e5 gf2 31.♖f2 ♖h6

Now the bishop g7 is finally ready to enter the game with decisive effect.

32.♗c2 ♗e5 33.♗f5 ♗h2 34.♔h2 ♕e3 35.♖f3 ♕d4

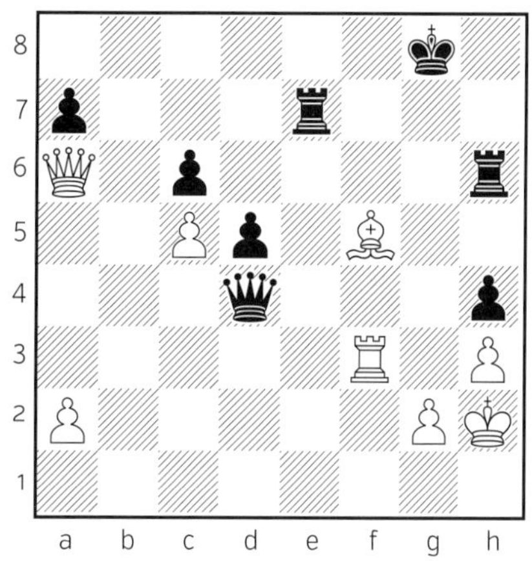

Materially White does not stand badly, but the weakness of the black squares proves fatal.

36.♕c8 ♔g7 37.♗d3 ♖f6 38.♖f6 ♕f6 39.♕g4 ♔f8 40.♕c8 ♔f7 41.♕g4 ♕e5 0:1.

BLOCKADE OF THE CENTER

A special method which is used to limit the mobility of the opponent's center, with the idea of conducting a powerful attack on it, after correct preparation.

1

▷ **Rubinstein**
► **Salwe**
Lodz 1908 [D33]

1.d4 d5 2.♘f3 c5 3.c4 e6 4.cd5 ed5 5.♘c3 ♘f6 6.g3 ♘c6 7.♗g2 cd4
Modern theory prefers development with 7...♗e7.

8.♘d4 ♕b6 9.♘c6 bc6 10.0–0 ♗e7

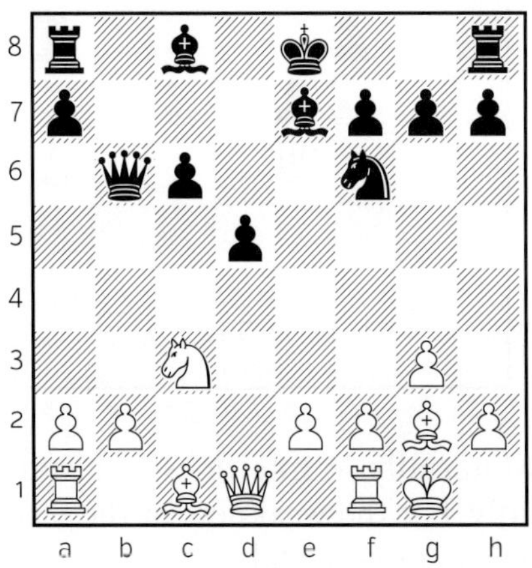

11.♘a4!
This was the first game in which a plan of ‚pawn-structure blockade' was demonstrated. White has to obtain maximum control of the weak c5 square.

11...♕b5 12.♗e3 0–0 13.♖c1 ♗g4 14.f3!
Rubinstein did not like to calculate complicated lines such as 14.♖e1 ♗b4 15.♘c3 ♗c3 16.♖c3 ♕b2 17.♗d4 ♕a2 18.♗f6 gf6 19.♕d4.

14...♗e6 15.♗c5!
The correct procedure is to exchange the opponent's pieces which control this weak square.

15...♖fe8

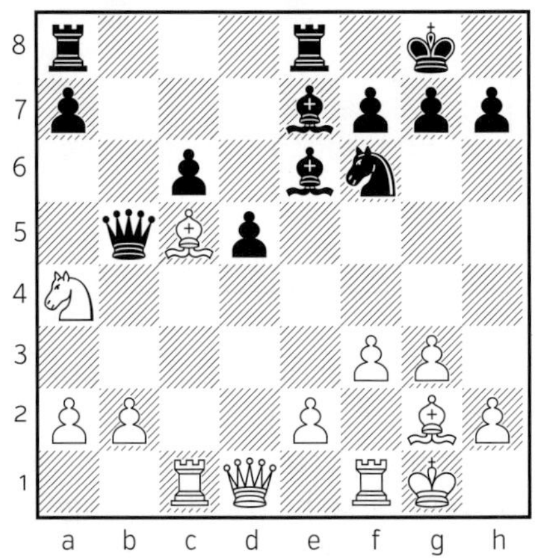

16.♖f2!?
A great transfer of the rook, which could also be started with 16.e3.

16...♘d7
Nothing is changed by 16...♗c5 17.♖c5 ♕b7 18.♕d4 ♘d7 19.♖c1.

17.♗e7 ♖e7 18.♕d4 ♖ee8 19.♗f1!

Rubinstein camouflages his plans, which are soon-or-later to be conducted with 19.e3.

19...♖ec8 20.e3 ♕b7

A bit more preparation is needed: 20...♕a5 21.b3 ♖ab8 22.♘c5.

21.♘c5 ♘c5 22.♖c5 ♖c7 23.♖fc2 ♕b6

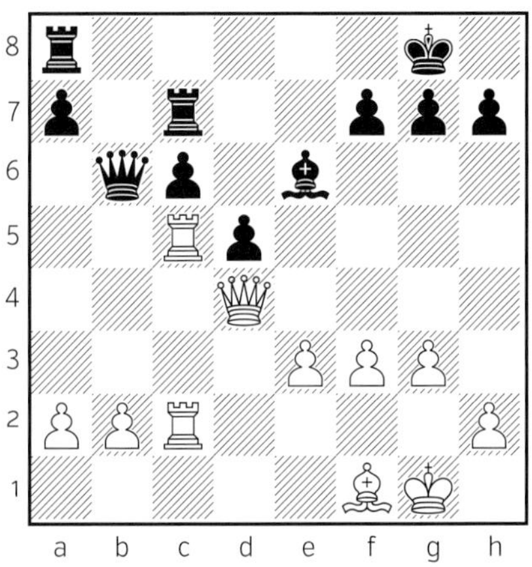

24.b4!

White increases his control of the c5 square to the maximum.

24...a6 25.♖a5 ♖b8

No help was offered by 25...♕b7 26.a3 ♖cc8 27.♕d3.

26.a3 ♖a7 27.♖c6

The pawn is lost and the game is practically over; realization of the extra pawn is very easy.

27...♕c6 28.♕a7 ♖a8 29.♕c5 ♕b7 30.♔f2 h5 31.♗e2 g6 32.♕d6 ♕c8 33.♖c5 ♕b7 34.h4 a5 35.♖c7 ♕b8 36.b5 a4 37.b6 ♖a5 38.b7 1:0.

2

▷ **Kasparov**
▶ **Illescas Cordoba**
Linares 1994 (D34)

1.c4 ♘f6 2.♘c3 c5 3.g3 e6 4.♘f3 ♘c6 5.♗g2 d5 6.cd5 ed5 7.d4 ♗e7 8.0–0 0–0 9.♗g5 cd4 10.♘d4 h6 11.♗e3 ♖e8 12.♖c1 ♗f8 13.♘c6 bc6

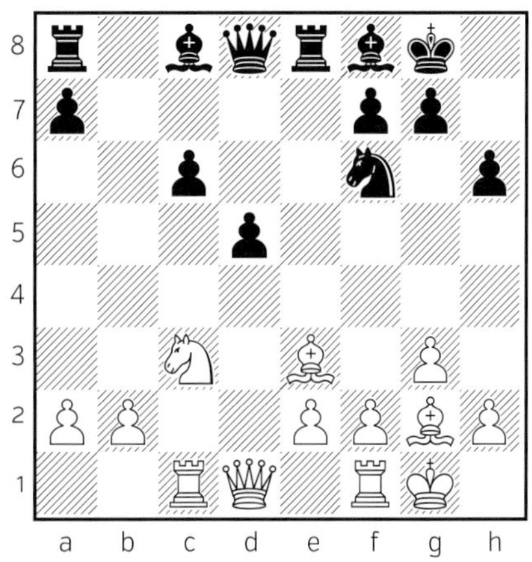

14.♘a4!

Kasparov starts Rubinstein's plan.

14...♗d7 15.♗c5 ♗c5 16.♘c5 ♗g4 17.♖e1

It is not so easy to follow Rubinstein's plan, as Black can block White's structure himself! 17.f3 ♗f5 18.♖f2 ♖e3 19.♕d4 ♕e7.

17...♕a5 18.h3

The typical tactical defence was not possible: 18.♕c2? ♕a2! 19.♖a1 ♖e2!!

18...♗f5

It was worth a try to keep the bishop on the same diagonal: 18...♗h5!?

19.♘d3 (19.a3!? ♖ab8 20.♘d3 ♕b6 21.b4.) 19...♕a2 20.♖c6 ♗g6! 21.♘f4 ♗e4 22.f3!? (22.♕d4 ♗g2 23.♔g2 ♖e4.) 22...♗f5 23.♕d4 ♗e6! 24.♖ec1.

19.♕d4!

Kasparov prefers this way to the direct queen swap 19.♕a4.

19...♖ab8 20.a3 ♕b5

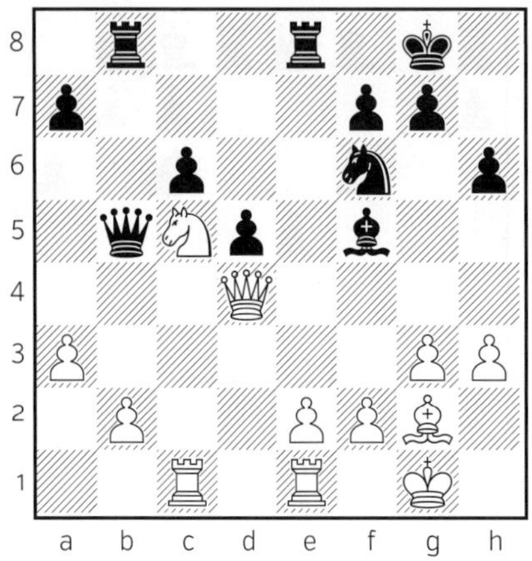

21.b3!

White has just a small edge after 21.b4 a5 22.♕f4!? ♗g6 23.♘b3 ab4 24.♘d4 ♕b7 25.ab4 ♕b4 26.♘c6.

21...♘e4?!

Bad is 21...♖e2?? 22.♖e2 ♕e2 23.♕f4+–, but worth a shot is 21...a5!?

22.b4! a5

Illescas wants to destroy the blockading grip and so sacrifices a pawn. Slightly better was 22...♕b6.

23.♘e4 ♗e4 24.♖c5 ♕b6 25.ba5 ♕b2 26.♕b2 ♖b2

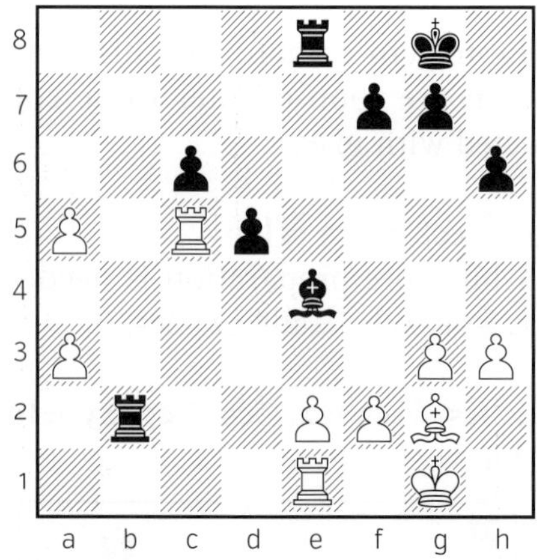

27.♖c6

27.♗f1!? ♖a8±.

27...♖a2?

Black has drawing chances in the rook endgame, trying to get the classical 3 against 4 pawns on one flank.

27...♗g2! 28.♔g2 ♖a2

(28...♖ee2? 29.♖e2 ♖e2 30.a6 ♖e8

(30...♖e4 31.♖c8 ♔h7 32.a7+–)

31.a7 ♖a8 32.♖c7!+–)

29.♖c3!

a) 29.♖d6 ♖a3 30.♖d5 ♖a8;

b) 29.♖c5 ♖a3 (29...d4 30.♖d1 ♖ee2 31.♖f5 ♖a3 32.♖d4 g6 33.♖b5 ♖aa2 34.♖f4 ♖e7 35.♖b8 ♔g7 36.♖a8±) 30.♖d1! (30.♖d5 ♖a8±) 30...♖e2 31.♖dd5±;

29...d4 30.♖d3 ♖a8 31.♖d4 ♖a3 32.♖b1 ♖3a5 33.♖b7 ♖5a7.

28.♖ec1!

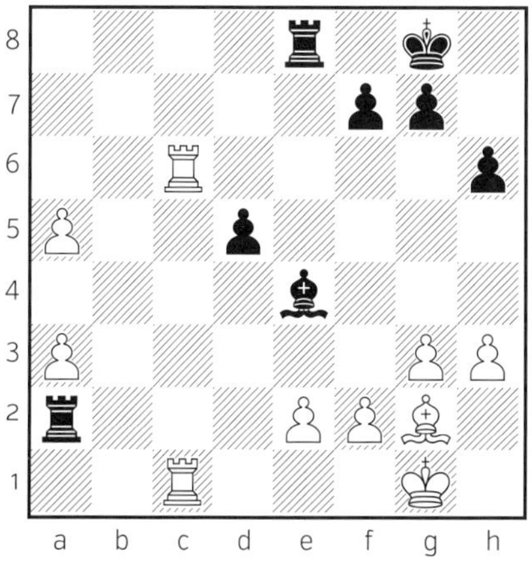

28...♖a3?

Now the rook ending with one rook is much worse: 28...♗g2 29.♖c8! ♖c8 30.♖c8 ♔h7 31.♔g2 ♖a3 (31...♖e2? 32.a6 ♖e7 33.♔f3! ♔g6 34.♖d8 ♖a7 35.♖d6 f6 36.♔e3 ♔f7 37.♔d4 ♔e7 38.♖b6+–) 32.♖c5 d4 33.h4! d3 34.ed3 ♖d3 35.h5, with winning chances.

29.♖c8 ♖c8

White keeps serious winning chances after 29...♔f8 30.♖e8 ♔e8 31.♗e4 de4 32.♖c5 ♔d7 33.e3 ♔d6 34.♖f5 f6 35.g4!

30.♖c8 ♔h7 31.f3!

No rook endings any more!

31...♗f5?!

31...♗g6 32.♖c5 d4 33.g4±.

32.♖c5+– ♗e6 33.♔f2

From this moment on the realization of the extra pawn is easy.

33...g5 34.f4 gf4 35.gf4 d4 36.♗e4 ♔g7 37.f5 ♗a2 38.♗d3! ♔f6 39.a6 ♔e7 40.♖c6 f6 41.♖c7 ♔d6 42.♖h7 ♖a4 43.♖h6 1:0.

3

▹ **Taimanov**
▸ **Karpov**
USSR 1973 [E55]

1.d4 ♘f6 2.c4 e6 3.♘c3 ♗b4 4.e3 c5 5.♗d3 0–0 6.♘f3 d5 7.0–0 dc4 8.♗c4 cd4 9.ed4 b6 10.♕e2 ♗b7 11.♖d1 ♘bd7 12.♗d2 ♖c8 13.♗a6?

White believes that this exchange is good, but much better was 13.♗d3.

13...♗a6 14.♕a6 ♗c3 15.bc3

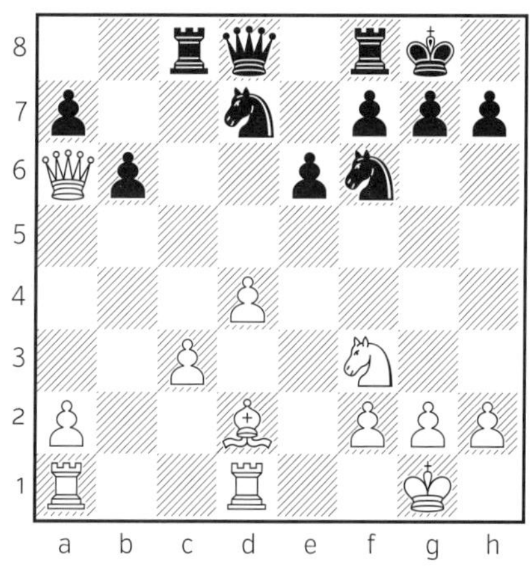

15...♖c7!

A great preventative and preparatory move, as Karpov starts here his plan to establish control over c4 and to block White's central pawn structure.

16.♖ac1

Nothing is promised by 16.c4 ♕c8 17.♕a3 ♖c4 18.♕a7 ♕a8! 19.♕a8 ♖a8 and the pawn on a2 will be a terrible weakness.

16...♕c8 17.♕a4 ♖c4!

The blockade must be completed! But in this case it is also necessary to sacrifice a pawn!

18.♕a7 ♕c6 19.♕a3 ♖c8 20.h3 h6 21.♖b1 ♖a4

Black could easily regain the pawn, but in the endgame his opponent would have drawing chances: 21...♘e4 22.♖b3 ♘d2 23.♘d2 ♖c3 24.♖c3 ♕c3 25.♕c3 ♖c3 26.♘f1.

22.♕b3 ♘d5 23.♖dc1 ♖c4 24.♖b2

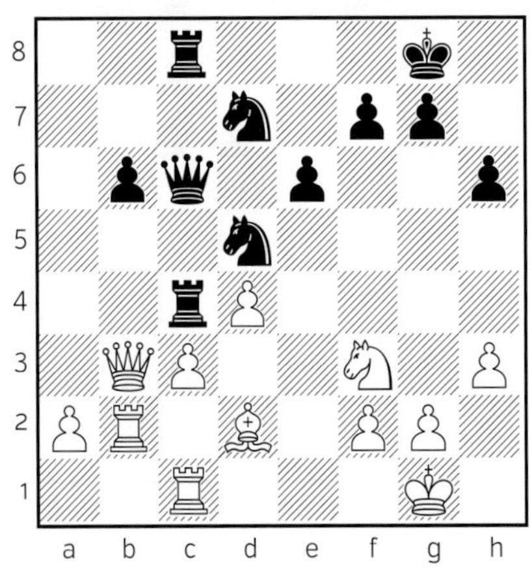

Better chances for a draw are offered by the queen swap: 24.♕b5 ♕b5 25.♖b5 ♖a8=.

24...f6!?

A very risky attempt to play for a win. A draw would be a normal result after mutual exchanges: 24...♘c3 25.♗c3 ♖c3 26.♖c3 ♕c3 27.♕c3 ♖c3 28.♘e5.

25.♖e1 ♔f7 26.♕d1 ♘f8 27.♖b3 ♘g6

Karpov still does not want a draw after the return of the pawn: 27...♘c3 28.♖c3 ♖c3 29.♗c3 ♕c3 30.d5 ♖d8 31.de6 ♘e6 32.♕e2 ♖d6.

28.♕b1 ♖a8 29.♖e4

It was better to start a counterattack: 29.♕d3!? ♖a2 30.♖e6!? ♔e6 31.♕g6.

29...♖ca4 30.♖b2 ♘f8 31.♕d3 ♖c4

Safer is 31...♕c4.

32.♖e1 ♖a3 33.♕b1 ♘g6

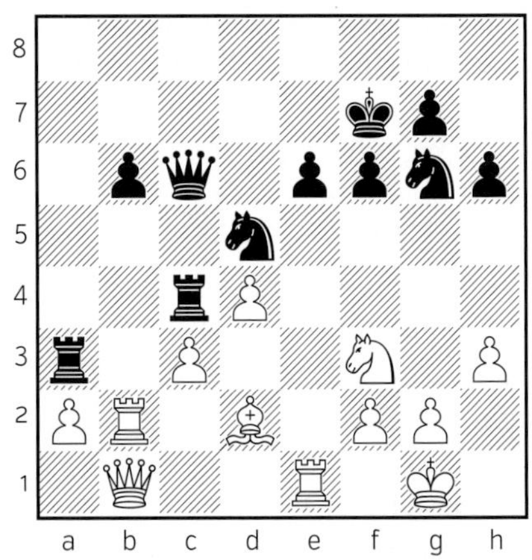

34.♖c1?

Necessary to hold is 34.♕d3! ♘df4 35.♕f1 ♖ca4 36.♖eb1 ♘d5 37.♖c2.

34...♘c3 35.♕d3

Taimanov overlooked a check at the end of the variation 35.♗c3 ♖ac3 36.♖c3 ♖c3 37.♖b6 ♖c1 38.♔h2 ♕c7.

35...♘e2! 36.♕e2 ♖c1 37.♗c1 ♕c1 38.♔h2

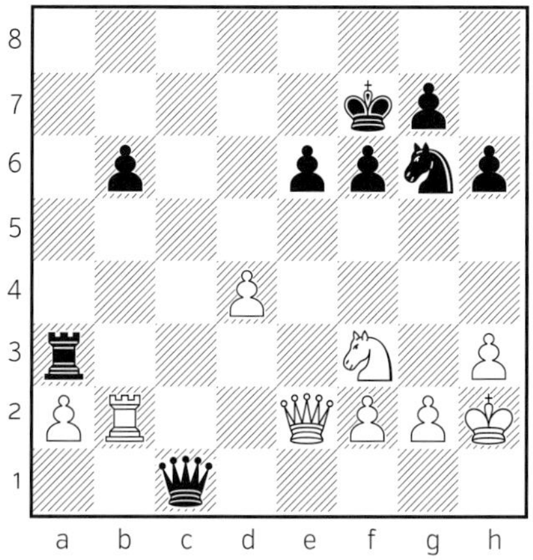

38...♖f3?!

More normal is a slower realization: 38...♕c7 39.g3 ♘e7 40.♖c2 ♕d8 41.♘d2.

39.gf3 ♘h4

White lost on time, but the position here is equal:

39...♘h4 40.d5! (40.♖b6? ♕c7; 40.♔g3 ♕g5–+; 40.♖b3 ♕g5 41.♕f1 ♕f4 42.♔g1 ♘f3.) **0:1.**

4

▷ **Rivas Pastor**
▶ **Huebner**
Linares 1985 [E12]

1.d4 e6 2.c4 ♘f6 3.♘f3 b6 4.♗f4 ♗b7 5.e3 ♗e7 6.h3 c5 7.♘c3 cd4 8.ed4 0–0 9.♗d3 d5 10.0–0 dc4 11.♗c4 ♘c6 12.♖c1 ♖c8 13.♗d3 ♘d5 14.♗g3 g6 15.♖e1 ♘a5

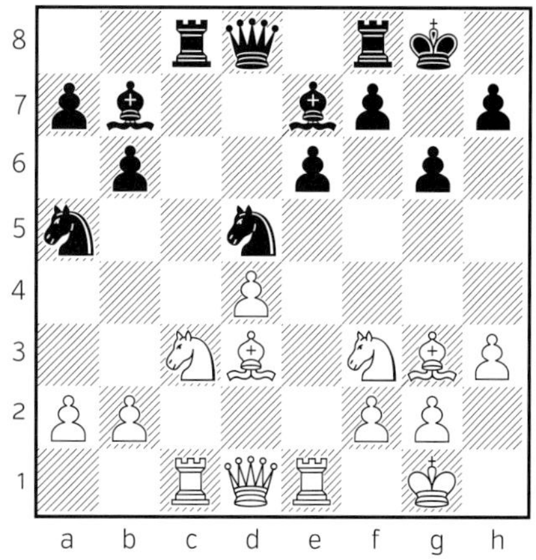

16.♕e2?!

Better is to avoid exchanges with 16.♘e4 ♘b4 17.♗b1.

16...♘c3 17.bc3 ♗f6 18.♘d2

Activity was very good here: 18.♘e5 ♕d5 19.♕f1 ♗e5 20.♗e5 f6 21.♗f4 ♕a2 22.♖a1 ♕b3 23.♗d6 ♖fe8 24.♗b4 ♕d5 25.♗b5 ♗c6 26.♗a6 ♖c7 27.♖e3.

18...♗g7 19.♘f1

Hmm, why not in the central direction — 19.♘e4?

19...♕g5 20.♘e3 h5 21.♗a6 ♕e7

Similar would be 21...♗a6 22.♕a6 ♕e7.

22.♗b7 ♕b7 23.♗h4 ♕e4 24.♗g5 ♘c4!

Starting the blockading process.

25.f3

Even worse would be 25.♘c4 ♕e2 26.♖e2 ♖c4 27.♗d2 ♖a4.

25...♕c6!

Increasing control over the blockade.

26.g4 ♘e3 27.♕e3

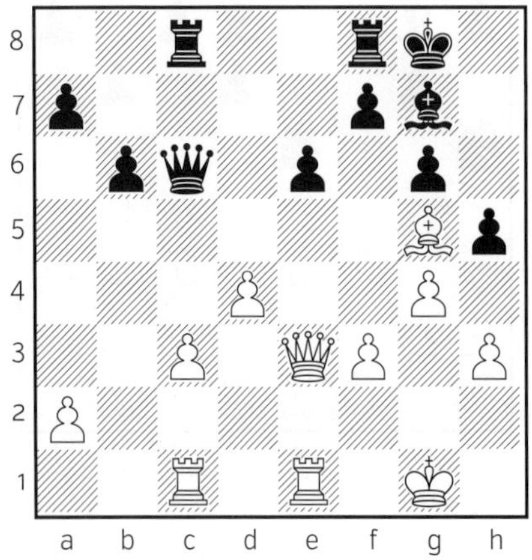

27...♕d5! 28.♔g2

Avoiding bad tactics 28.gh5 ♖c3 29.♖c3 ♗d4.

28...hg4 29.hg4 ♖c6

Black is not interested in losing tempii for the winning of some material: 29...♕a2 30.♔g3 ♕d5.

30.♗h6 ♖fc8?!

Again possible is 30...♕a2.

31.♗g7 ♔g7 32.♖h1 ♕a2

And here also 32...g5 33.♕d2 b5 34.a3 a5.

33.♔g3 ♕d5 34.♕h6 ♔f6 35.♖h5 ♕d6 36.♖e5?

The balance could be kept by 36.♔g2 ♔e7 37.♕g5 ♔d7 38.♖h7.

36...♔e7 37.g5 ♖c3 38.♖a1 ♕d4 39.♕g7 ♖f3! 40.♔f3 ♖c3 41.♔e2 ♖c2 42.♔f3 ♖f2 43.♔g3 ♕f4 0:1.

5

▹ **Kharitonov**
▸ **Mikhalchishin**
Volgodonsk 1981 [D76]

1.d4 ♘f6 2.c4 g6 3.g3 ♗g7 4.♗g2 d5 5.cd5 ♘d5 6.♘f3 0–0 7.0–0 ♘b6 8.e3 e5 9.♘c3 ♘c6 10.d5 ♘e7 11.e4 ♗g4 12.♕b3 c6 13.♘h4?! cd5 14.ed5 ♘ec8!

The best plan is always to block the central structure and only then try to destroy it. Another option is much weaker: 14...♖c8 15.♗g5 h6 16.d6!+-.

15.h3 ♗d7 16.♘e4 ♗a4 17.♕b4 ♗c2! 18.♗g5?

Better was to continue the plan: 18.♘c5 ♘d6, with an unclear position.

18...f6 19.♗e3

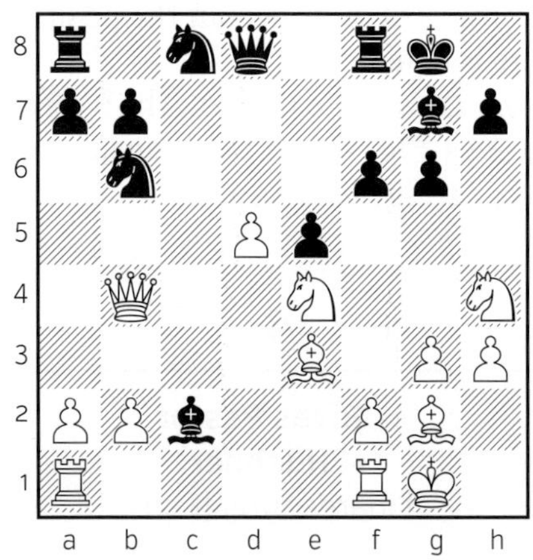

19...♗e4!

It is necessary to eliminate the knight which fights for the most important square d6.

20.♗e4 ♘d6 21.♗g2

Now it is too late to fight for control over the d6 square: 21.♗c5 ♘bc4 22.♖fc1 a5!

21...♘bc4 22.♗c1 a5 23.♕e1

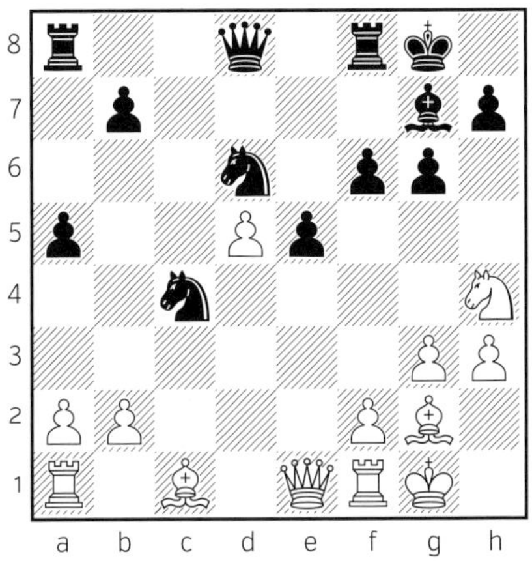

No better was another retreat 23.♕b3 a4 24.♕c2 f5.

23...e4!

It's part of the Black central expansion, plus the knight on h4 is left out of the game.

24.b3 f5 25.♖b1

An exchange sacrifice does not improve White's position: 25.bc4 ♗a1 26.c5 ♘f7.

25...♘e5

Now two powerful black knights control everything in the center.

26.♕e3 ♘d3 27.♗a3 ♖e8 28.♗d6 ♕d6

An exchange of the blockading knight causes no lasting harm to Black, as the pawn d5 will come under fire.

29.♖bd1 ♘b4?!

It was possible to take the pawn immediately, but Black did not want to offer an escape to the knight: 29... ♕d5 30.♘f3 ♖ad8 31.♘e1 ♕b5.

30.♖d2 ♕f6

Simpler was to take the pawn with 30...♘d5.

31.d6 ♖ad8 32.d7

There was a threat to capture the knight: 32.♖fd1 g5.

32...♖e7 33.♖fd1 ♘d3 34.♗f1

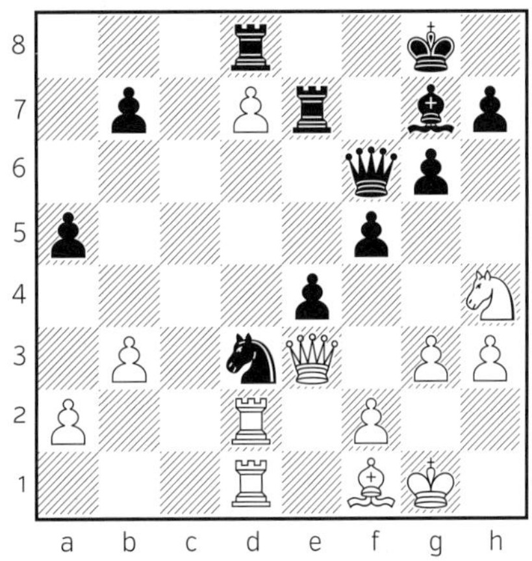

Or 34.♖d3 ed3 35.♕d3 g5–+.

34...f4!–+

A very important blow, and now White is lost.

35.♕e2 ♖dd7 36.♕g4 fg3 37.♕g3

A quicker defeat awaits 37.♗d3 ♖d3 38.fg3 ♕d4.

37...♗h6 38.♖c2

The same happens after 38.♗d3 ♗d2 39.♗c4 ♔g7 40.♘g2 ♕f3.

38...♗f4 39.♕g4 ♘e5 40.♖c8 ♔g7 0:1.

6

▷ **Loncar**
▸ **Nepomniachtchi**
Rijeka 2010 [D85]

1.d4 ♘f6 2.c4 g6 3.♘c3 d5 4.cd5 ♘d5 5.e4 ♘c3 6.bc3 ♗g7 7.♘f3 c5 8.♗e3 ♕a5 9.♗d2 0–0 10.♗e2 ♘d7 11.♕c2 e5
Starting the plan to change the central structure.

12.♖b1?!
A possible change of the structure goes like this: 12.0–0 ♕c7 13.de5 ♘e5 14.♘e5 ♕e5 15.f4 ♕e7 16.♗f3 ♗e6 17.e5 ♖ad8, with Black having counter chances.

12...♕c7 13.d5 ♘f6
Of course, Black's plan in such positions is to transfer his knight to the blockading square d6 and then he prepares ...f7-f5.

14.0–0 ♘e8 15.c4 ♘d6 16.♗c3

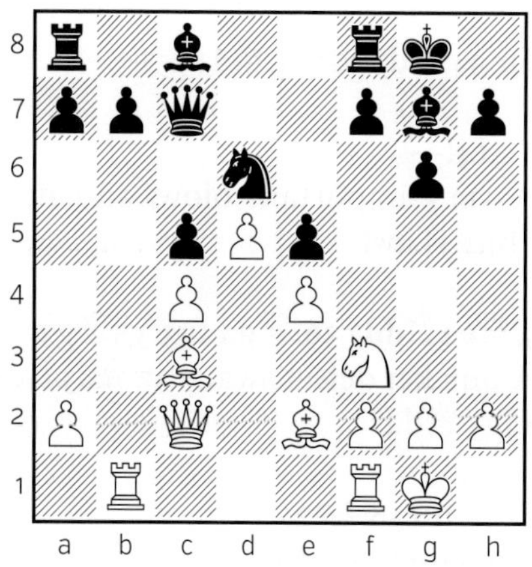

16...♖e8
Possible is an immediate continuation of the plan: 16...f5 17.♘d2 fe4 18.♖bd1 ♖f4 (Even better looking is 18...♗f5 19.g4 ♗d7 20.♘e4 ♗a4.) 19.g3 ♖f7 20.♘e4 ♗f5 21.f3 ♖af8.

17.♗d3 f5 18.♘d2 f4
In such situations Black cannot keep the tension around e4 for too long and it is better to close the center as soon as possible.

19.♗e2
In this typical structure White has to start play on the queen's wing — 19. a4.

19...♕f7 20.♕d1 h5

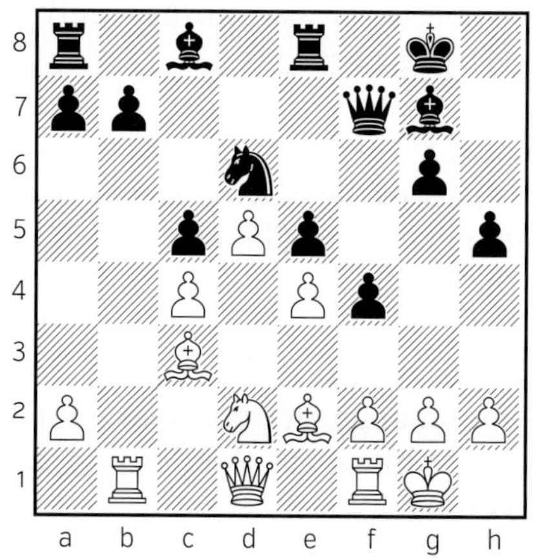

Black slowly prepares his pawn advances on the kingside.

21.g4?!
Sometimes such plans for stopping the opponents pawn advances work. But here White had to continue his own plan: 21.a4 ♗d7 22.a5.

21...hg4 22.♗g4 ♗f6

Preparing ...♔g7 and a transfer of the rook to the h-file, when White will feel the weakness of own king.

23.♗c8 ♖ac8 24.f3 ♔g7 25.♖f2

White has no intention of playing on the other side and prefers instead to improve the position around his king. 25.a4.

25...♖h8 26.♖g2 ♖h3 27.♕e2 ♖ch8 28.♔h1 ♕e7 29.♖bg1 g5 30.♘f1

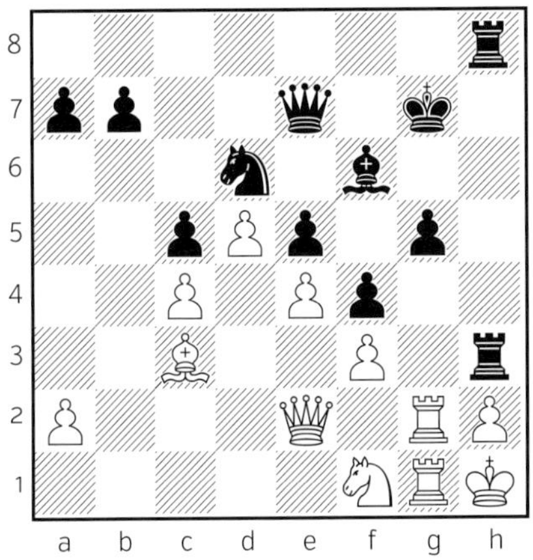

30...♘f7!

A nice manoeuvre, as the pawn d6 has no possibility to advance. Black protects the important pawns g5 and e5 and then prepares a transfer of his queen closer to White's weaknesses.

31.♕d1 ♕d6 32.♖b2 ♕a6 33.♕d3 ♖8h5 34.♖bg2 ♔f8 35.d6?

Finally White understands, that Black will improve the positions of all his pieces and will then start an attack on the c4 and a2 pawns. So Loncar tries to activate own pieces with the sacrifice of his central pawn.

35...♕d6 36.♕b1

An instructive variation was 36.♕e2 g4! 37.♖g4 ♘g5.

36...♖f3 37.♖d2 ♕c6 38.♗b2 ♖fh3 39.♖d5 b6 40.♕d1 ♕e6 41.♘d2 0:1.

DOUBLED PAWNS IN THE CENTER

Doubled pawns limit the mobility of one's own pawn structure and can be attacked by the opponent. But there are cases when the doubled pawns leave important files in the center open.

1

▷ **Johner**
▶ **Nimzowitsch**
Dresden 1926 [E41]

1.d4 ♘f6 2.c4 e6 3.♘c3 ♗b4 4.e3 0–0 5.♗d3 c5 6.♘f3 ♘c6 7.0–0 ♗c3 8.bc3 d6 9.♘d2

This move presents the idea of an immediate attack in the center, before Black can start his attack on the weak c4 pawn. 9.e4 e5 10.d5 ♘a5 11.♘e1, with the idea of fighting for the black squares after f2-f4 was also possible, but not so good.

9...b6

With the idea 10...e5 11.d5 ♘a5 12.♘b3 ♘b7, according to Nimzowitsch Black's typical plan. 9...e5 10.d5 ♘a5 (10...♘e7 11.e4!, Nimzowitsch) 11.♘b3.

10.♘b3?

The knight on b3 only prevents an attack of c4 after ...♘a5. Instead it is necessary to immediately start an attack in the center: 10.f4! e5 11.fe5 de5 12.d5 ♘a5 13.♘b3 ♘b7 14.e4 ♘e8, with the idea ...♘e8-d6.

10...e5 11.f4

It's necessary to keep the central tension, so clearly worse is 11.d5 e4! 12.♗e2 (12.dc6 ed3) 12...♘e5!

11...e4

Another plan is 11...♕e7 12.fe5 de5 13.d5 ♘d8 14.e4 ♘e8, with the idea being to block the d5-pawn with the knight.

12.♗e2

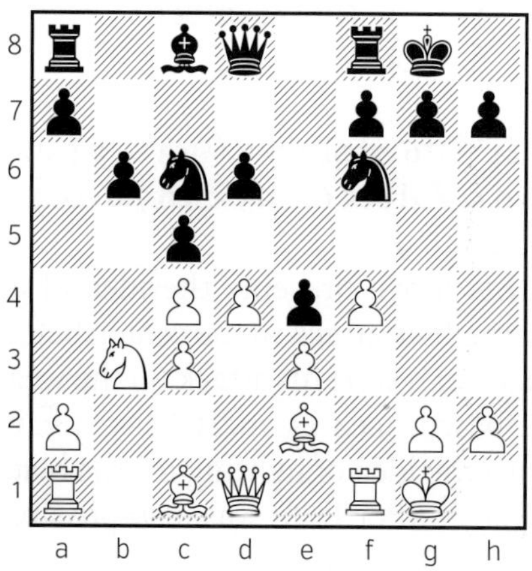

12...♕d7!

A very difficult and complicated restrictive manoeuvre is initiated with this move. Another way of fighting White's center was 12...♘e8! 13.g4 (13.f5 ♕g5) 13...f5 14.d5 (14.dc5!? dc5 15.♕d5 ♕d5 16.cd5 ♘e7 17.♖d1 ♘d6) 14...♘e7 15.g5, leads to petrification — Nimzowitsch.

13.h3?

No annotations by Nimzowitsch, but the move weakens g3.

13.f5!? (Szabo)

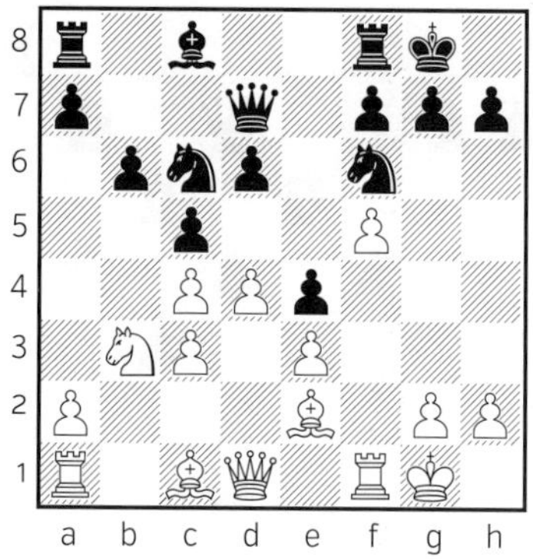

13...♘e7 14.g4 h5!;

13.♗d2!? (Larsen) 13...♘e7 14.♗e1 ♘f5? (14...♘g4 15.♕d2 f5 and it's not easy to storm the white position.; 14...♗a6!? 15.♗h4? ♘f5 16.♗f2 cd4!) 15.♗f2;

13.a4! (Larsen) 13...a5 14.♗d2.

13...♘e7 14.♕e1

After 14.♗d2 Black has two options:

a) 14...♘f5 (With the idea ...♘g3, to exchange the ♗e2, which covers c4.) 15.♕e1 g6 16.g4 ♘g7 17.♕h4 ♘fe8 (With idea f7-f5.) 18.a4 (To prevent ♗d7-a4.) 18...f5 19.g5 ♘c7

20.d5 ♗a6 (A preventive measure directed against 21.a4-a5, for now the reply could be 21...b6-b5.) 21.♔f2 ♕f7 22.♖fd1 (22.♕h6? ♘d5! 23.cd5 ♗e2 24.♔e2 ♕d5 25.♘c1 ♘h5!, with permanent imprisonment of White's queen. Black wins by promoting the pawns.) 22...♔h8± with the idea ...♘h5, ...♔g7 and finally ...h7-h6 — Nimzowitsch;

b) 14...h5! (Larsen) 15.♗h5 (15.♗e1 ♘f5 16.♗f2 g6) 15...♘h5 16.♕h5 ♕a4! (16...♗a6 17.f5!) 17.f5 f6 18.♖f4? ♗f5.

But, better was 14.♔h2! or even 14.g4!? (Szabo).

14...h5!

The start of the process of tying White up.

15.♗d2

A tactically refutation awaits 15.♕h4 ♘f5 16.♕g5 ♘h7 17.♕h5 ♘g3.

15...♕f5!

Making her way to h7. This was the original point of the restraining manoeuvre.

16.♔h2 ♕h7!

The restraining manoeuvre ...♕d8-d7-f5-h7 represents one of the most remarkable conceptions invented by Nimzowitsch.

17.a4 ♘f5

With the idea 18...♘g4 19.hg4 hg4 20.♔g1 g3 etc.

18.g3

The only chance was 18.a5! (Larsen) 18...♘g4 19.♗g4 hg4 20.ab6 gh3 21.gh3 ♘h4 22.♕g3. It's not easy to prove a clear win for Black — Larsen.

18...a5

It's easier to defend the weakness on b6 than the weakness on a4.

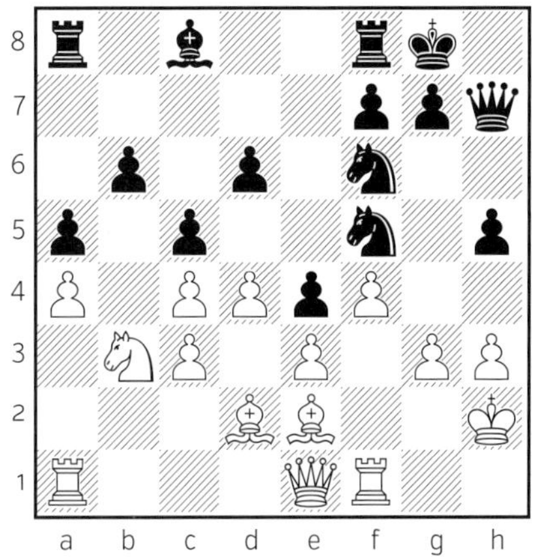

19.♖g1 ♘h6 20.♗f1 ♗d7 21.♗c1 ♖ac8

Black has enough play on the kingside, so he is not worried about the center being closed by d4-d5.

22.d5 ♔h8 23.♘d2

23.♔g2 ♖g8 24.♔f2 g5–+.

23...♖g8

Black prepares the opening of the g-file with the doubling of his rooks, attacking the g3 pawn

24.♗g2 g5 25.♘f1 ♖g7 26.♖a2 ♘f5 27.♗h1 ♖cg8 28.♕d1 gf4! 29.ef4 ♗c8 30.♕b3 ♗a6 31.♖e2

Correct defence. Very bad was 31.♗d2 ♖g6! 32.♗e1 ♘g4 33.hg4 hg4 34.♔g2 ♗c4! 35.♕c4 e3–+

31...♘h4!

Very strong, as was another mode of attack: 31...h4 32.g4 ♘g3.

32.♖e3

After 32.♘d2 Black would include his bishop in the attack: 32...♗c8! (32...♕f5? 33.♕d1! ♗c8 34.♕f1) 33.♘e4 (33.♕d1 ♗h3! 34.♔h3 ♕f5) 33...♕f5! 34.♘f2

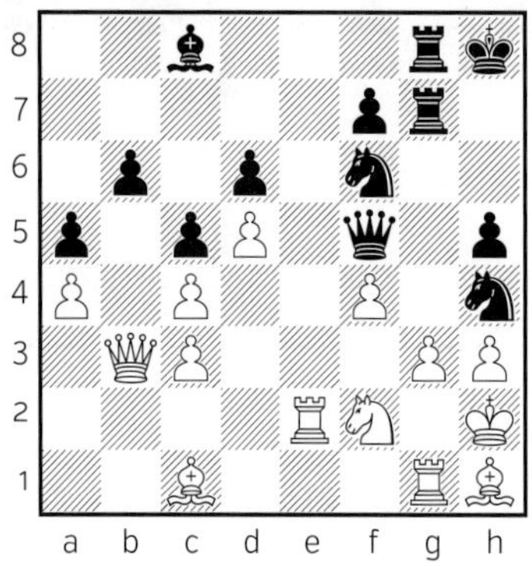

34...♕h3! 35.♘h3 ♘g4#.

32...♗c8 33.♕c2 33...♗h3! 34.♗e4

A quicker end is reached after 34.♔h3 ♕f5 35.♔h2 ♘g4 36.♔h3 ♘f2 37.♔h2 ♕h3#.

34...♗f5

The best, since ...h5-h4 can no longer be stopped; after the fall of the ♗h3 the defence has become hopeless.

35.♗f5 ♘f5 36.♖e2 h4 37.♖gg2 hg3 38.♔g1 ♕h3 39.♘e3 ♘h4 40.♔f1 ♖e8! 0:1.

2

▷ **Spassky**
▶ **Fischer**
Reykjavik 1972 [E41]

1.d4 ♘f6 2.c4 e6 3.♘c3 ♗b4 4.♘f3 c5 5.e3 ♘c6 6.♗d3 ♗c3 7.bc3 d6 8.e4 e5 9.d5 ♘e7

White wastes no time and immediately starts preparation of an attack on Black's center with f2-f4, trying to increase power of his black squared bishop.

10.♘h4

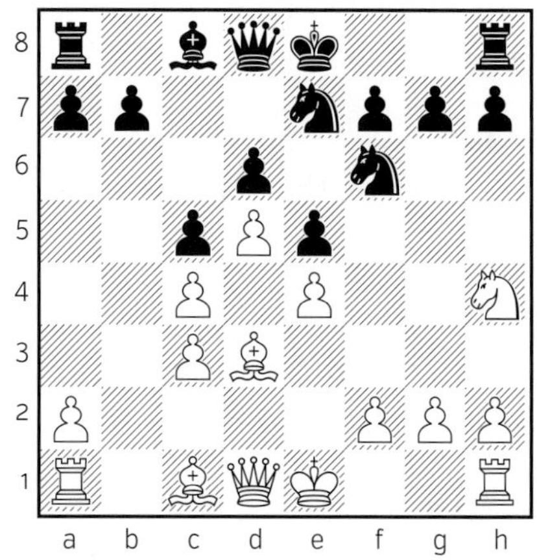

10...h6!

After 10...♘g6 unpleasant for Black is 11.♘f5! Black would like to play ...g7-g5, completely blocking his opponent's bishop on c1.

11.f4!?

White utilises a tactical idea, but the other option (11.f3) was playable.

11...♘g6!

Black cannot win the piece, as this try is countered powerfully: 11...ef4!? 12.♗f4 g5 13.e5! ♘g4 14.e6!

12.♘g6 fg6 13.fe5

It is not necessary to define the central structure so fast, better was the simple 13.0–0.

13...de5 14.♗e3

The immediate 14.♖b1 is possible.

14...b6 15.0–0 0–0

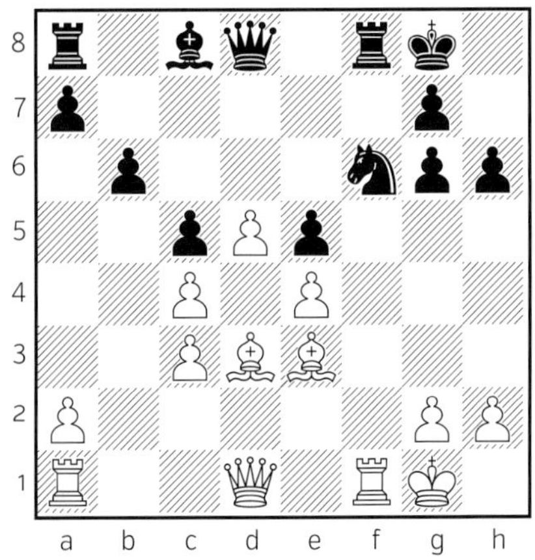

16.a4?

This move is a bit risky and somewhat strange — we already know that the a4-pawn will be weaker than the pawn on b6, therefore it was necessary to prepare play on the kingside with 16.♕e2.

16...a5!

Of course, it is not recommended to allow a4-a5, which would create a weakness on the queen's wing.

17.♖b1 ♗d7 18.♖b2 ♖b8 19.♖bf2?

Better was to begin with a different move — 19.h3.

19...♕e7 20.♗c2 g5!

An important part of Black strategy: it is necessary to block White's bishop.

21.♗d2 ♕e8!

Another way is to transfer the bishop to g6 for attack on the weakness at e4: 21...♗e8.

22.♗e1 ♕g6 23.♕d3 ♘h5

It is necessary to exchange all rooks to eliminate all possibilities of white counterplay.

24.♖f8 ♖f8 25.♖f8 ♔f8 26.♗d1 ♘f4!

Nothing special is promised after another knight retreat 26...♘f6 27.♗c2.

27.♕c2??

A simple oversight. Correct was a different retreat 27.♕b1 ♔e7

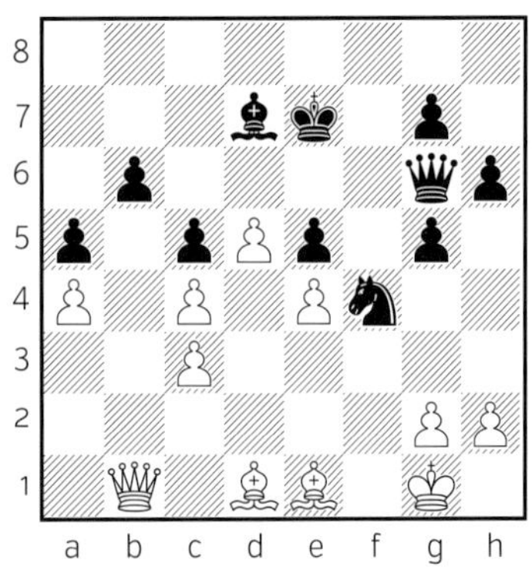

and Black would transfer his king to c7, protecting the pawn b6, thus freeing his queen for attacking purposes.

27...♗a4! 28.♕a4 ♕e4 0:1.

Chess is the game of double attack, as taught by the great David Bronstein.

Doubled pawns sometimes create strongholds for powerfully-placed, centralised pieces. Next we will look at two fantastic classical games in which the great Champion Mikhail Botvinnik instructively conducts such a strategy.

3

▷ **Botvinnik**
▶ **Kan**
Leningrad 1939 [E24]

1.d4 ♘f6 2.c4 e6 3.♘c3 ♗b4 4.♘f3 c5 5.a3 ♗c3 6.bc3 ♕a5 7.♗d2 ♘e4 8.♕c2 ♘d2 9.♘d2 d6 10.e3 e5

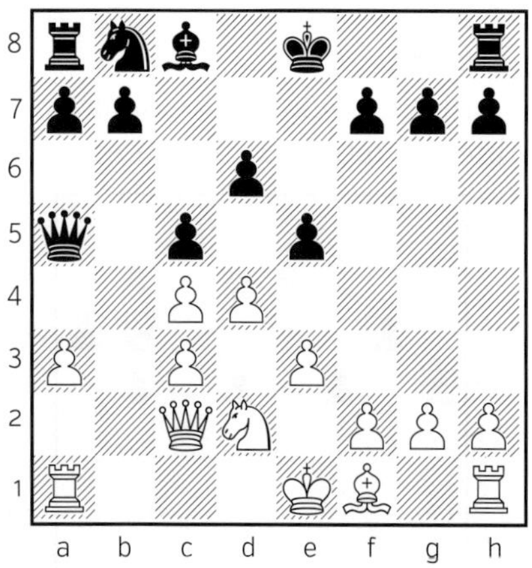

11.de5!

This looks very illogical, as White create a more exposed weakness on c4, but an important idea is to exploit the weakness of the d5-square for his own purposes. In other words, to make his own stronghold there as his opponent is unable to protect it properly.

11...de5 12.♗d3 h6 13.0–0 0–0 14.f4!

Premature is 14.♗e4 f5 15.♗d5 ♔h8 16.e4 f4, as only the bishop d5 would be outside and the other White pieces would not be very useful. The role of the bishop on d5 is only possible to evaluate in conjunction with the coordination of other pieces.

14...♘d7?

Clearly better would be 14...ef4 15.ef4 ♘d7 16.♘e4 ♕c7 17.♖ad1 f5 18.♘g3 g6 and Black sticks to his strategy of preventing occupation of the central squares.

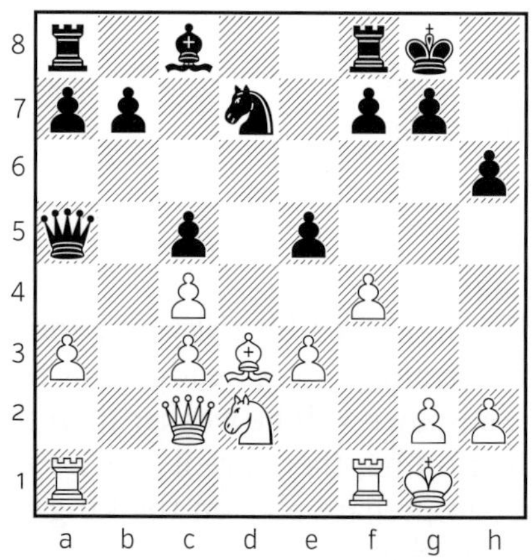

15.f5! ♘f6

Now White exchanges the only real defensive piece which his opponent has.

16.♘e4 ♕d8 17.♘f6 ♕f6 18.♗e4 ♖b8 19.♖ad1 b6 20.h3 ♗a6

Another kind of position arises after 20...♗b7 21.♖d7 ♗e4 22.♕e4 ♖fd8 23.♖fd1 a6 24.♖7d5 ♖d5 25.cd5, changing the position from 'doubled pawns' to 'dangerous central passed pawn' — a very typical and instructive case.

21.♗d5 b5

Exchanging off the opponent's doubled pawns is an extremely unusual operation — generally players try to avoid it — but Black wants to create some counterplay on the b-file. If Black waits:

21...♖fe8 22.e4 ♖ed8 23.♖f3, White would prepare a plan of attack on the kingside: g2-g4, ♕f2, h3-h4 and then prepare g4-g5 with a decisive attack.

22.cb5 ♖b5 23.c4 ♖b6 24.♖b1!

The correct technical decision — after exchanging one pair of rooks Black will have no real threat along the b-file.

24...♖d8 25.♖b6 ab6 26.e4 ♗c8

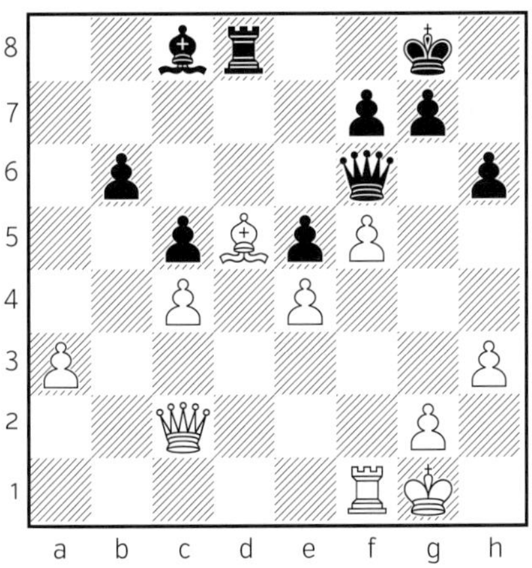

27.♕a4!

Now Black's weaknesses are on the queen's flank — the pawn b6 and the squares around it.

27...♗d7 28.♕a7 ♗e8 29.♖b1 ♖d6 30.a4!

With the manoeuvre a4-a5, White will change the weakness to c5, but additionally will obtain the important b-file.

30...♔h7 31.a5 ba5 32.♕a5 ♖a6 33.♕c5 ♖a2 34.♕e3!

Now we have the 'realization' phase of the game and the most important task is to eliminate threats such as ...♕g5.

34...♕a6 35.♖b8 ♕a4 36.♔h2 ♖a3 37.♕c5 ♖a2 38.♖a8 ♕a8 39.♗a8 ♖a8 40.♕e5 ♗c6 41.♕c7 1:0.

4

▷ **Botvinnik**
▶ **Chekhover**
Leningrad 1938 [E21]

1.d4 ♘f6 2.c4 e6 3.♘c3 ♗b4 4.♘f3 0–0 5.♗g5 d6 6.e3 ♕e7 7.♗e2 e5 8.♕c2 ♖e8 9.0–0 ♗c3

Black uses tactics to create doubled pawns in his opponent's position, as it is not possible to capture on c3 with the queen because of ...♘e4.

10.bc3 h6 11.♗h4 c5

More efficient is to place the bishop on the other diagonal, trying to force e3-e4. 11...b6 12.♘d2 ♗b7.

12.♖fe1 ♗g4

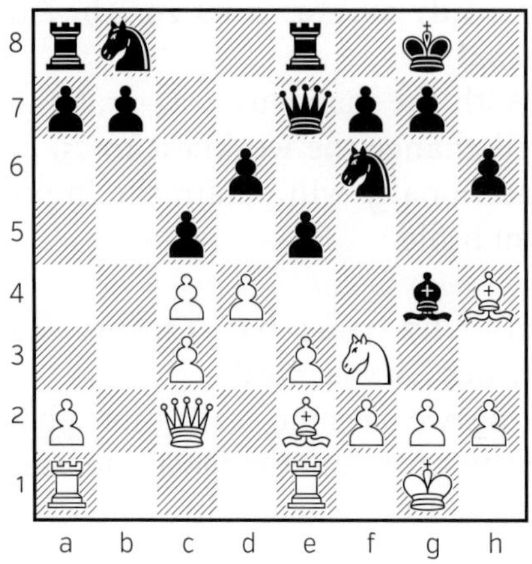

Very interesting developments follow after 12...g5 13.♗g3 ♘h5 14.dc5 ♘g3 15.fg3! The open f-file will be extremely useful. 15...dc5 16.e4 ♘d7 17.♘d2 transferring the knight to e3, from which square where it will be possible to jump to d5 or f5 later.

13.♗f6! ♕f6 14.♕e4!

With this two-move strategic operation Botvinnik fights for the center and white squares. Of course, the bishop retreat to c8 means an admission of the wrong plan, but possibly it was better.

14...♗f3 15.♗f3 ♘c6 16.dc5 dc5 17.♖ad1 ♖ad8 18.♖d5

Now White is able to control the central d5 square with the rook, which is a tremendously powerful piece, and an exchange on d5 means an undoubling of the pawns plus the creation of a terrifying central passed pawn.

18...b6 19.♖ed1 ♘a5 20.h3

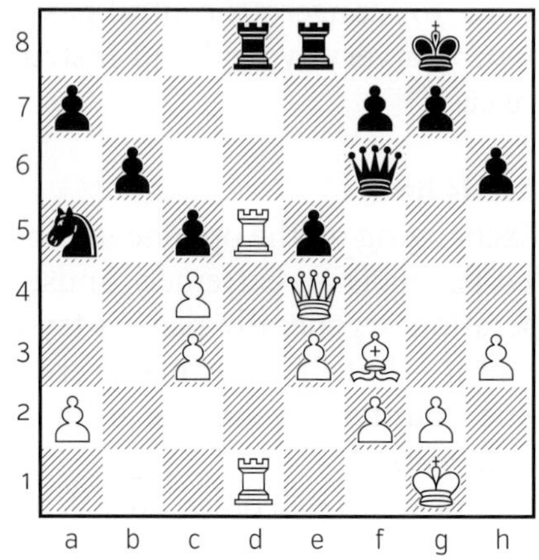

20...♖d5?

This exchange is wrong. Correct is the attempt to limit the activity of his opponent's bishop and to put the pawns on white squares (20...g6).

21.♖d5 ♕e7 22.♗g4

Now it is clear that d7 is a terribly vulnerable square.

22...♕b7

Still better was to try to tame this bishop: 22...g6 23.♖d7 ♕f6.

23.♗f5!

White is ready to play ♕g4 and to transfer his bishop to e4.

23...♕b8 24.♖d7 ♖d8 25.♕e5

Small tactics leads to a final activation of White's pieces.

25...♘c4 26.♕b8 ♖b8

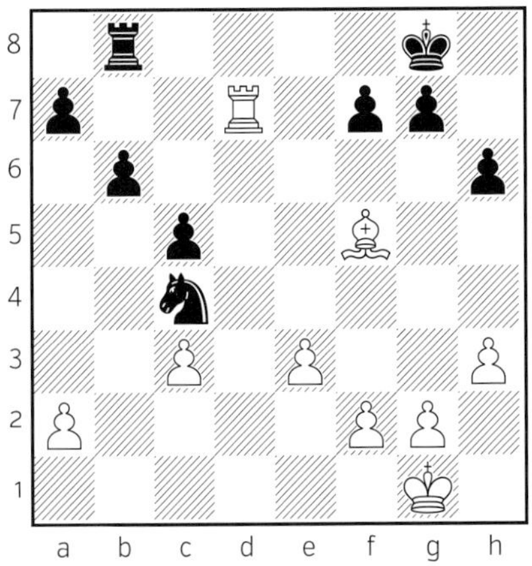

27.♗e4

Centralization is always powerful. Possible also was prosaic materialism 27.♖a7.

27...♘a3 28.♗d5 ♖f8 29.e4 a5 30.c4

White plays as if he is not interested in material — a magnificent improvement of the position!

30...b5 31.cb5 ♘b5 32.e5 a4 33.f4 ♘d4

Of no help is 33...♘c3 34.♗c4 ♘e4 35.f5 a3 36.e6.

34.♔f2 g5 35.g3 gf4 36.gf4 ♘e6 37.♔e3 c4

Or 37...♘d4 38.♗c4 ♘f5 39.♔e4 ♘g7 40.f5, squeezing his opponent.

38.f5 ♘c5 39.♖c7 ♘d3 40.e6 fe6 41.fe6 1:0.

5

▹ **Larsen**

▸ **Portisch**

Porec 1968 [C28]

1.e4 e5 2.♘c3 ♘c6 3.♗c4 ♘f6 4.d3 ♘a5!? 5.♘ge2!?

This is in Rubinstein's style — White gives up his bishop and accepts doubled pawns, but this allows him to control the central file very effectively.

5...♘c4 6.dc4

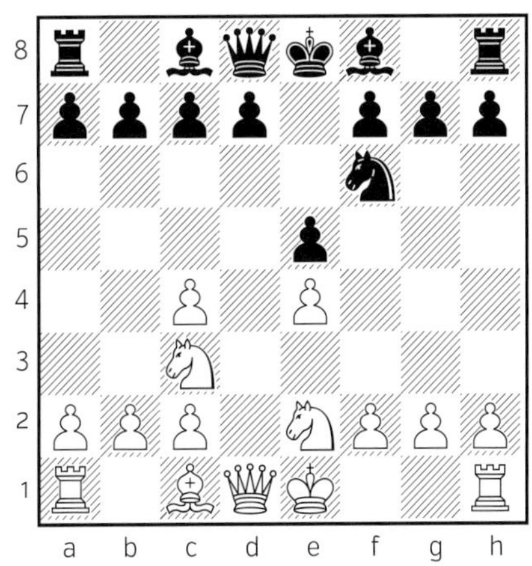

6...♗e7 7.0–0 d6 8.b3 0–0 9.♘g3 c6

It's not the best idea to create a potential weakness on d6, so a better plan is 9...♘e8, with the idea of ...f7-f5, trying to activate his white-squared bishop. Or an additional idea here, ...♗g5! and if 10.♕h5 g6 11.♕h6 c6.

10.♗b2 ♕a5?!

It's not clear what the queen's function is there. Again better is to aim for ...f7-f5.

11.♕e1

A good alternative is 11.a4!?

11...♕c7 12.a4 ♗e6 13.♖d1 a6

Still better was to create counterplay on the other side: 13...g6, with ...♘g4 and ...f7-f5.

14.♕e2 ♗g4 15.f3 ♗d7 16.♔h1 ♖ab8

Now Black realizes the problems with his queenside counterplay: 16... b5? 17.ab5 ab5 18.cb5 cb5 19.♘f5 ♗f5 20.ef5 ♕c6 21.♘b5.

17.♘f5 ♗f5 18.ef5 ♖fe8

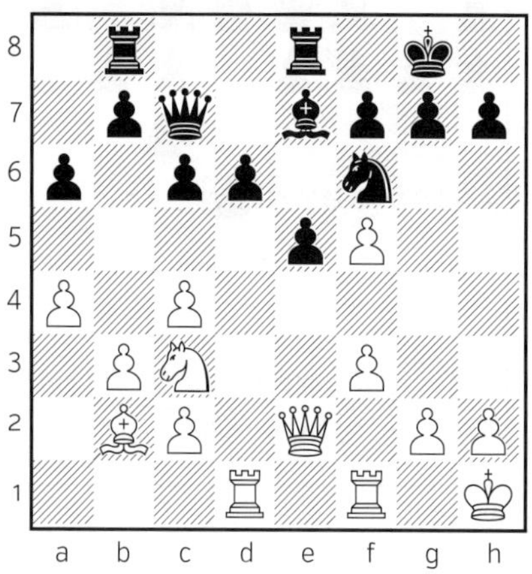

19.♖d2

In such situations White generally thinks about advancing his pawns on the king's wing, not just with idea of attacking but more importantly to push the knight away from f6, thereby obtaining an extremely strong position for his own knight on e4, e.g. 19.g4 h6 20.h4.

19...♖bd8 20.♖fd1 ♘h5?

Better would be 20...g6! or 20...♕a5.

21.♗a3

Slowly it becomes clear that d6 is a weakness — sooner or later!

21...♘f4 22.♕f2 ♕a5?

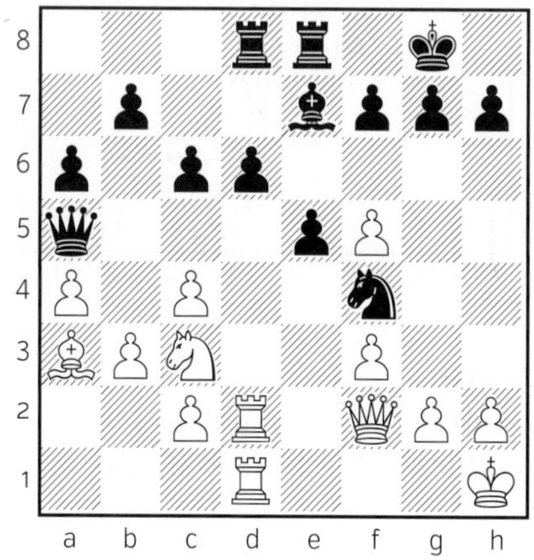

Better is to retreat to f6, so 22...♘h5.

23.♘e4

Now Black is forced into combinational play for which his opponent's pieces are better coordinated.

23...d5 24.♗e7 ♖e7 25.♕h4! ♖ed7

The knight will be surrounded after 25...f6 26.g3 ♖f8 27.♘f2.

26.g3 ♘e2

The tactics are well seen in the case of 26...de4 27.♕d8!

27.f6! ♕b4 28.♕g4 1:0.

Files can be opened on the flanks, but the main events will happen in the center anyhow.

6

▷ **Beliavsky**
▶ **Jussupow**
Linares 1989 (A90)

1.d4 e6 2.c4 f5 3.g3 ♘f6 4.♗g2 d5 5.♘f3 c6 6.0–0 ♗d6 7.♗f4 ♗f4 8.gf4 0–0 9.e3 ♘bd7 10.♕e2 ♔h8 11.♘c3 ♕e7

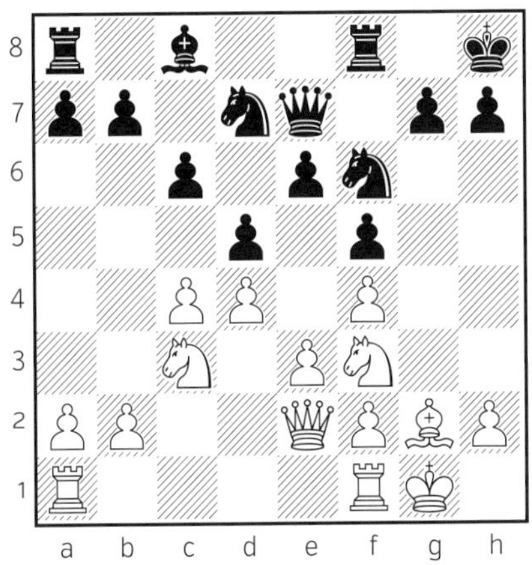

In such center configurations White can combine his play on the g-file with an attack on the other side. A second plan is demonstrated in the variation 11...♘e4 12.♖fc1!? ♕e7 13.♖ab1 and then b2-b4.

12.♔h1 ♖g8 13.cd5! ed5
Another capture 13...cd5 14.♖ac1± allows White to conduct the attack on the c file.

14.♗h3 ♘g4
Or 14...g6 15.♖g1 ♘e4 16.♖g2±.

15.♖g1 ♘df6 16.♖g2 ♗e6 17.♖ag1 ♖af8

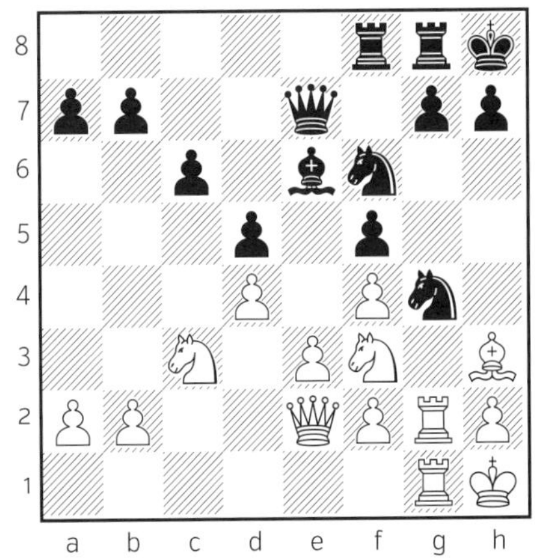

White has maximum concentration on the g-file, but Black has built a sufficient defence, so it is necessary to start the second part of the plan — activity on the other side.

18.a3!!± ♗d7
18...a5 19.♘a4, trying to transfer the knight via c5-d3-e5.

19.b4 ♗e8
The counterattack would be refuted: 19...a5 20.♕b2 ab4 21.ab4 ♗e8 22.b5±.

20.♗g4! ♘g4 21.♖g3! ♗h5 22.♕b2 ♘f6 23.♘e5 ♘g4

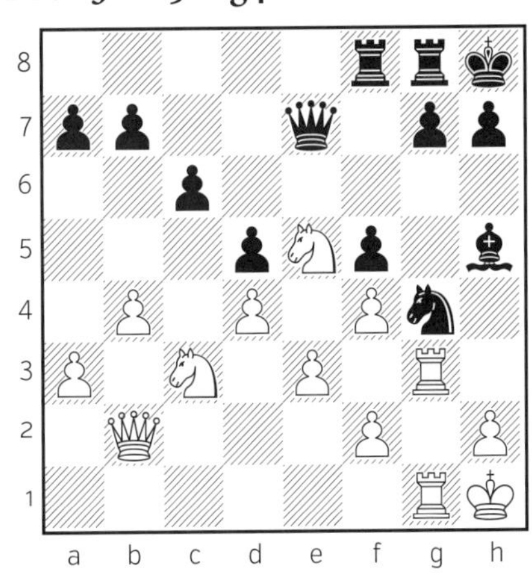

The knight in the center will be kicked away:

23...♘e4 24.♖h3 g6 25.f3±.

24.f3! ♘e5

There is a tactical refutation of 24...♘e3? viz. 25.♕e2 ♘c4 26.♘g6+-.

25.de5

White's idea is to put his knight on d4. From this square it will exert a strong influence over the opponent's position.

25...h6

After 25...g5 26.♘e2 gf4 27.♘f4± White's knight becomes extremely powerful.

26.♘e2 b6 27.♘d4 c5

Black drives the knight from its powerful square, but it finds an even better spot on d6.

28.♘b5 ♔h7 29.♘d6 g5 30.♕c2 ♕e6 31.♖h3 ♕g6

Or 31...♗e8 32.bc5 bc5 33.♕c5+-.

32.fg5 hg5 33.e6 ♔h6 34.♘f7 ♖f7 35.ef7 ♕f7 36.bc5 bc5 37.♕c5- ♖g6 38.♕d4 ♖g8 39.♖c1 ♕e6 40.♖g3 g4 41.♕f4 1:0.

A similar strategy was invented by Alexander Alekhine and used as sharp weapon by many other great champions.

7

▹ **Botvinnik**

▸ **Ragozin**

Leningrad 1930 (D37)

1.d4 d5 2.c4 e6 3.♘f3 ♘f6 4.♘c3 ♘bd7 5.♗f4 dc4 6.e3 ♘d5 7.♗c4 ♘f4 8.ef4

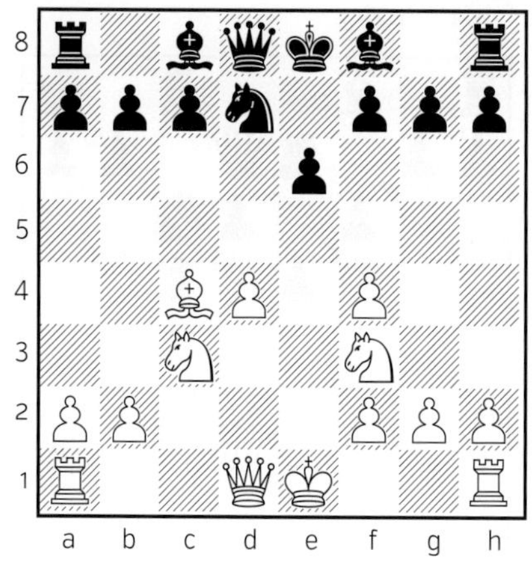

On the one hand White has given up his bishop and suffered doubled pawns, but on the other hand the center is opened. Coupled with his strong control over the e5 square, he has sufficient compensation for such damage. This strategy was a favourite of such greats as Alekhine and Rubinstein, so Botvinnik borrows from the classics for his own use.

8...♗d6 9.g3 ♘f6 10.0–0 0–0 11.♕e2 a6

Another plan was chosen by the first women's World Champion: 11...b6 12.♖fd1 ♗b7 13.♖ac1 ♕e7 14.a3 ♖fd8 15.♘e5 c5 16.♘b5 cd4 17.♘d4 ♗e5 18.♕e5 (A very useful idea was to aim for an occupation of the c6 square.

18.fe5 ♘e4 19.♗b5.) 18...♕d6 19.♗b3 ♕e5 20.fe5 ♘e8 21.f4 a6 22.♔f2 ♔f8 23.f5 ♗d5 24.fe6 ♗b3 25.e7, 1:0, Botvinnik : Menchik,Hastings 1934.

12.♖fd1

The rooks have to be placed on d1 and e1 — this structure demands such a set up!

12...b6

It's better not to weaken the c5 square with the aggressive flank strategy 12... b5 13.♗d3 ♗b7 14.♘e4. **13.♖ac1 ♗b7 14.♗d3 ♕e7 15.♘e4 ♖fd8**

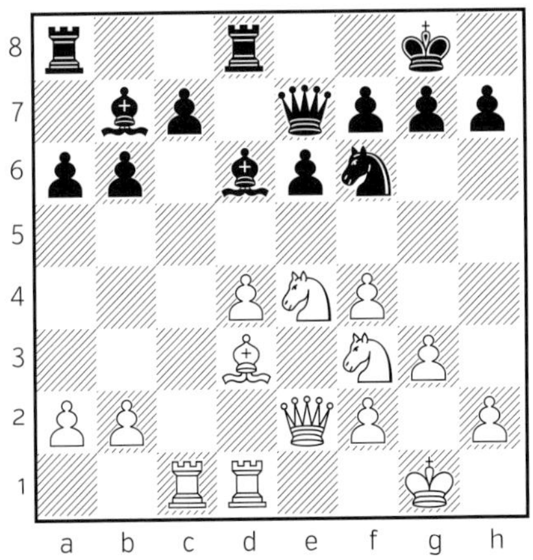

White keeps a clear advantage after 15...♘d5 16.a3 ♖fd8 17.♘e5.

16.♘f6 ♕f6 17.♗e4!

The correct plan to eliminate Black's best piece and increase control over the e5 square. **17...♗e4 18.♕e4 c5**

At least c6 will not be so weak as it is now.

19.♘e5 cd4 20.♖d4 ♗c5

A much more comfortable heavy pieces endgame would arise after exchanging on e5: 20...♗e5 21.fe5 ♕e7 22.♕c6 ♖d4 23.♕a8 ♖d8 24.♖c8 ♖c8 25.♕c8 ♕f8 26.♕a6.

21.♖d7! ♕f5

A better solution is to sacrifice a pawn: 21...♖d7 22.♘d7 ♕d8 23.♘c5 bc5 24.♖c5.

22.♕b7 ♖ab8 23.♕f3

Even simpler is 23.♖d8 ♖d8 24.b4 ♗f8 25.♕b6.

23...f6? 24.g4 1:0.

8

▷ **Kramnik**
▶ **Lputian**
Debrecen 1992 [D37]

1.d4 ♘f6 2.c4 e6 3.♘f3 d5 4.♘c3 ♗e7 5.♗f4 0–0 6.e3 c6 7.♕c2 ♘bd7 8.h3 a6 9.♖d1 h6 N 10.a3 dc4 11.♗c4 ♘d5

Transferring into a classical structure.

12.0–0!

12.♗g3 ♘c3 13.♕c3.

12...♘f4 13.ef4 ♕c7

13...♖e8 14.♘e5 ♘f8 15.f5 ♗f6 16.♘e4 ♕e7 17.♘g4 ♘h7 18.♖fe1±.

14.♘e5 ♘f6

Also possible is the immediate attack on the center:

14...c5 15.♗a2!? (15.d5 ♘e5 16.fe5 ♕e5 17.♖fe1±) 15...♘e5 (15...cd4 16.♗b1

♘f6 17.♘d5!-; 15...f5 16.♘d5! ♕d8 17.♘e7 ♕e7 18.♘g6-) 16.de5 b5 17.♗b1 g6 18.♖d3!±, with complete control over the d-file.

15.♗a2 ♗d7 16.♗b1

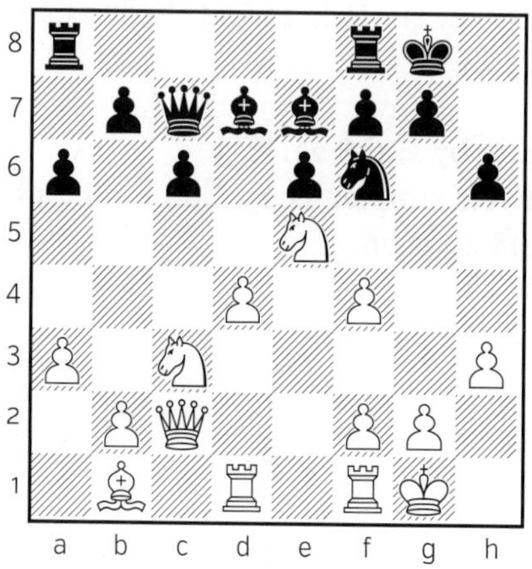

16...♗e8?

It is better not to block the rook:

16...♖fd8 17.♘e4 ♔f8 18.♘f6 ♗f6 19.♕h7! ♔e7 20.♖fe1 ♖h8 21.♕c2±.

17.d5!!

This strike is possible because of the faulty previous move, but it has to come quickly. 17.♘e4? g6.

17...♖d8

All captures are bad:

17...cd5 18.♘d5!+-;

17...ed5 18.♘d5!+-.

White now demonstrates his power, but the capture on e6 guarantees an advantage also.

18.♖fe1!?

18.de6 fe6 19.♘e4 g6 20.♘g3 ♗d6 21.♘g6 ♗g6 22.♕g6 ♕g7 23.♕g7 ♔g7 24.♘e2 ♘d5 25.g3±.

18...♔h8 19.de6 ♖d1 20.♖d1 fe6 21.♘e4 g6

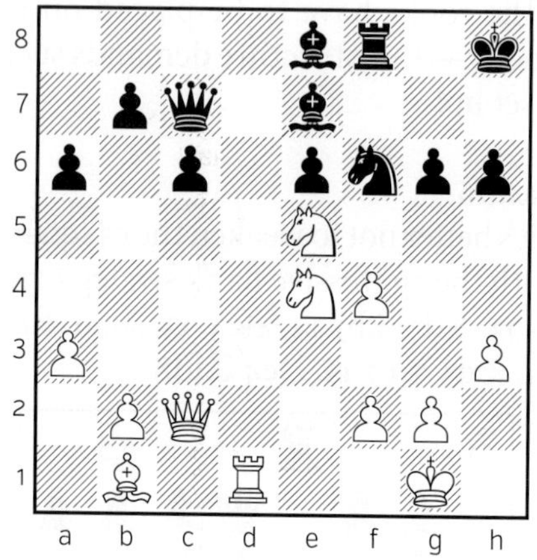

22.♘c5!

The powerful white knights keep Black's pieces in very poor positions.

22...♗c5

22...♕c8 23.♘g6! ♗g6 24.♕g6 ♗c5 25.♕h6 ♔g8 26.♕g5 ♔h8 27.♕c5+-.

23.♕c5 ♖g8

Or 23...♕g7 24.♖d8 (24.♗g6?? ♖g8) 24...♖g8 25.♕d6+-.

24.♗a2+- ♔g7

24...♗f7 25.♕d6!;

24...♘d5 25.♗d5 ed5 26.♖d5.

25.♗e6 ♖f8 26.♘d7! ♗d7 27.♕e7

1:0.

CHANGING THE CENTRAL STRUCTURE

A very important topic: when to exchange pawns, when to close the center and when to keep tension there? Problems involving these decisions can be seen in the Spanish game (Ruy Lopez). And here we can see that not only the position is important, but also the tastes and experience of the players. The great Robert Fischer preferred to exchange in the center and to try to control the central squares with the pieces.

1

▷ **Fischer**
▶ **Shocron**
Mar del Plata 1959 [C97]

1.e4 e5 2.♘f3 ♘c6 3.♗b5 a6 4.♗a4 ♘f6 5.0–0 ♗e7 6.♖e1 b5 7.♗b3 0–0 8.c3 d6 9.h3 ♘a5 10.♗c2 c5 11.d4 ♕c7 12.♘bd2 ♗d7 13.♘f1 ♖fe8 14.♘e3 g6 15.de5 de5

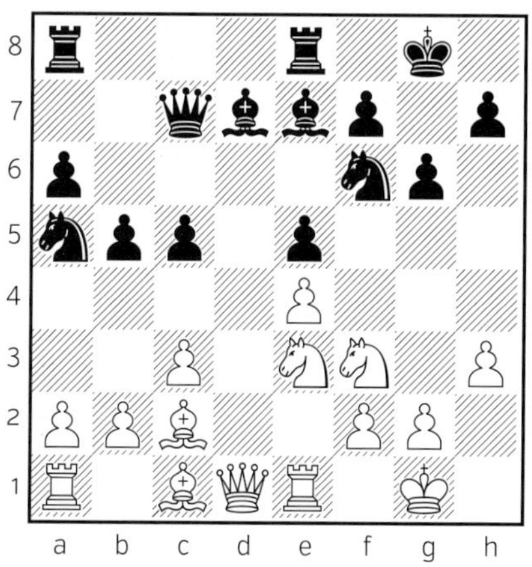

This is Fischer's favourite center in the Spanish structure, and here he won many games. His plan was to combine control over d5 and f5, with preparation for the attack against the king.

16.♘h2! ♖ad8 17.♕f3 ♗e6 18.♘hg4 ♘g4 19.hg4

Yes, just so! The capture with the knight is much weaker: 19.♘g4 ♗g4! 20.hg4 c4=.

19...♕c6?!

An improvement on Black's play is to bring the knight back to the center: 19...♘c4! 20.♘d5 ♗d5 21.ed5 ♘b6 22.♖d1 ♖d6 23.a4 ♖ed8 24.ab5 ab5 25.♗e3 c4=, Keres : Matanovic, Bled 1961.

20.g5

Here there was an even stronger method of attack: 20.♕g3! f6 (20...♕c7 21.♘f5!; 20...♗f6 21.g5 ♗g7 22.♕h4→) 21.g5 ♔h8 22.b3 ♖f8

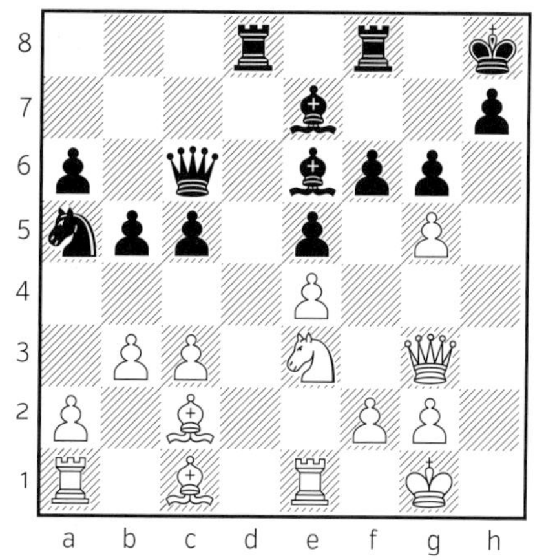

23.♘d5! ♗d5 24.ed5 ♕d5 25.gf6 ♗f6 26.♗h6±, Boleslavsky : Tal, Tbilisi 1957.

20...♘c4

It is interesting that the dangerous-looking grabbing of the pawn was possibly the best solution: 20...♗g5 21.♘d5! ♗c1 (21...♗d5? 22.♗g5±) 22.♘f6 ♔h8! 23.♖ac1 (23.♘e8 ♗g5 24.♘f6 ♘c4∞) 23...♖f8 (23...♖e7 24.♕g3 ♕c7 25.♕h4) 24.♕g3 ♕c7 25.♕g5 ♔g7=.

21.♘g4 ♗g4 22.♕g4 ♘b6!

Much weaker is 22...f6? 23.gf6 ♗f6 24.a4 ♘b6 25.ab5 ab5 26.♗e3± with weaknesses on both flanks.

23.g3 c4

Possible is the same plan but conducted differently. 23...♘d7

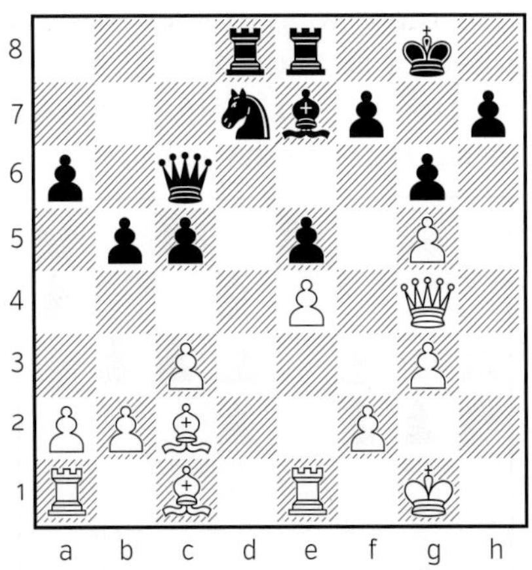

24.a4 c4! (24...b4? 25.cb4 cb4 26.♗b3±) 25.ab5 ab5=.

24.♔g2 ♘d7= 25.♖h1 ♘f8

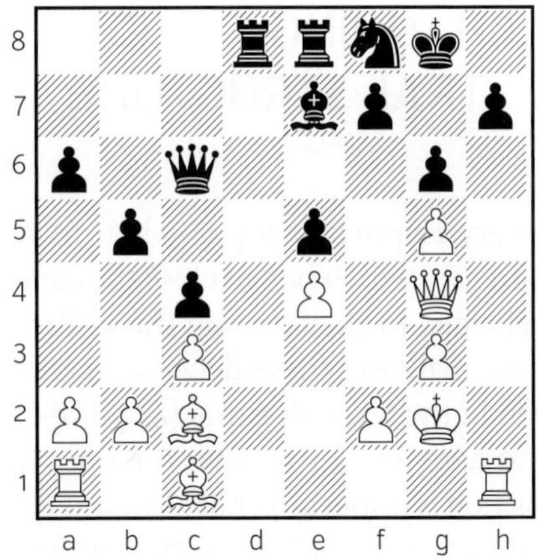

26.b4!

A very fine plan as White prepares to open a file in the correct way: 26.b3 b4! 27.cb4 c3!∞; 26.a4 b4! 27.cb4 ♗b4 28.a5 ♕c7=.

26...♕e6

Risky is grabbing the pawn with 26...cb3?! 27.♗b3 ♕c3 28.♗e3, but possibly better is to counterstrike here with 26...a5!? 27.a3 ♖a8=.

27.♕e2 a5! 28.ba5 ♕a6 29.♗e3 ♕a5 30.a4 ♖a8

Also possible is 30...♕c3 31.ab5=.

31.ab5 ♕b5

31...♕a1? 32.♖a1 ♖a1 33.♕c4±; 31...♕c3!?

32.♖hb1 ♕c6 33.♖b6! ♕c7 34.♖ba6 ♖a6 35.♖a6

White has the initiative as the pawn c4 is weak and the rook a6 is quite active.

35...♖c8 36.♕g4 ♘e6

Somewhat weaker is 36...♗c5?! 37.♗c5 ♕c5 38.♗a4!±.

37.♗a4 ♖b8 38.♖c6

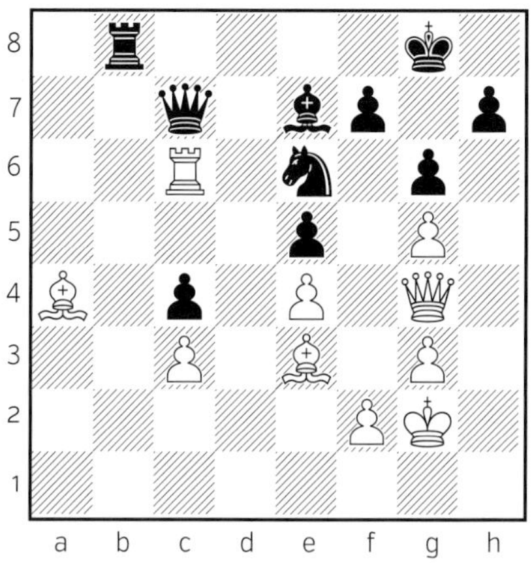

38...♕d8?

Black can save the game with an 'only' move 38...♕d7!! 39.♔h2 (39.♖c4? ♕d3! 40.♖c6 ♖b1∓) 39...♖b1! 40.♖b6 (40.♖c4 ♕d3 41.♖c8 ♔g7 42.♕h4 ♗g5! 43.♗g5 ♖h1! 44.♔h1 ♕f1 45.♔h2 ♕f2=) 40...♕d3 41.♖b1 ♕b1 42.♗d7 ♘c7 43.♗c6 ♕d3.

39.♖e6! ♕c8

39...fe6 40.♕e6 ♔f8 41.♕e5+-.

40.♗d7! ♕d7 41.♖g6 1:0.

On the other hand, the great Mikhail Tal preferred to keep the tension in the center till the end.

2

▷ **Tal**
▸ **Kholmov**
Moscow 1969 [C98]

1.e4 e5 2.♘f3 ♘c6 3.♗b5 a6 4.♗a4 ♘f6 5.0–0 ♗e7 6.♖e1 b5 7.♗b3 d6 8.c3 0–0 9.h3 ♘a5 10.♗c2 c5 11.d4 ♕c7 12.♘bd2 ♘c6 13.a3

Tal's way! A small-but-useful move, preventing ...♘b4 in some lines and preparing b2-b4 in others!

13...cd4

Here other central treatments are possible: 13...♘d7 14.de5 de5 15.a4! or the more modernistic approach: 13...ed4 14.cd4 ♘d7.

14.cd4 ed4

Kholmov decides to open the center immediately, but it was also possible to choose a semi-open version of it: 14...♗b7 15.d5 ♘a5 16.♘f1 ♖fc8 17.♗d3.

15.♘b3

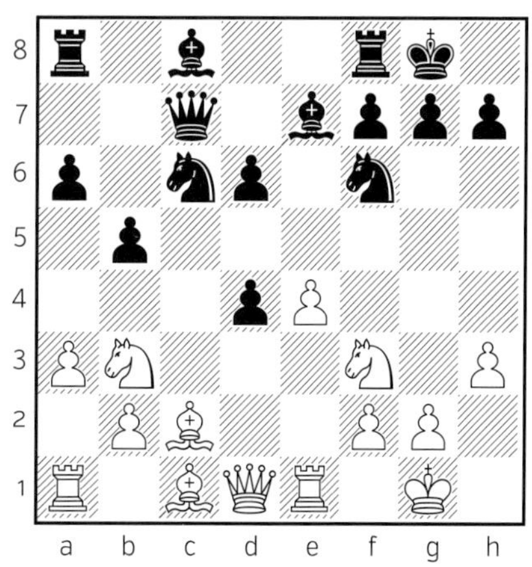

15...♘d7

In such positions, when one side gives up his center, he tries to attack the opponent's part of the remaining center:

15...♖e8 16.♘bd4 ♘d4 17.♘d4 ♗b7.

16.♘bd4 ♘d4 17.♘d4 ♗f6

A useful move and it is not clear where Black's knight belongs — e5 or to c5?

18.♗e3

Development is almost always correct and must be completed, as a more aggressive approach is not effective yet:

18.♘f5 ♘e5! 19.a4 ♗e6.

18...♘e5

Possible is 18...g6, with ...♖e8 next.

19.b3!

A useful reaction — preventing ...♘c4 and preparing to exploit the c-file

19...♗d7

Transition into an endgame is a bit risky: 19...♘c6 20.♖c1 ♘d4 21.♗d4 ♗d4 22.♕d4 ♕c5± 23.♕c5 dc5 24.♗d1 ♗e6 25.♖c5 ♖ac8 26.♖c8 ♖c8 27.♖e3 ♖c1 28.♖d3 f5, with some compensation for the pawn.

20.♖c1± ♖ac8

Or 20...♕b7 21.f4 ♘c6 22.♕d3±.

21.f4 ♘c6

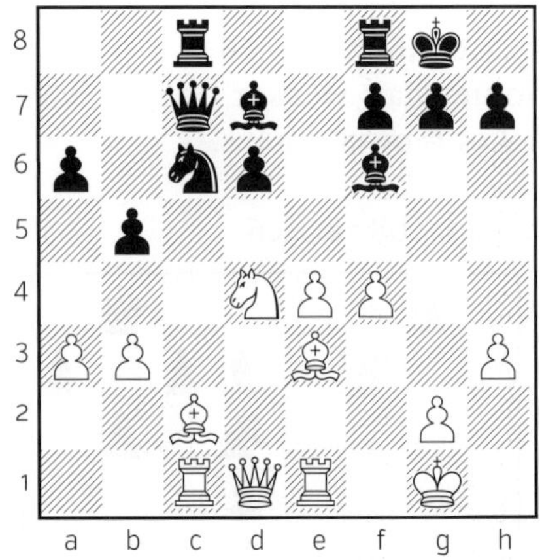

22.e5!

Tal's typical reaction, as the bishop retreat leads to a complicated middlegame:

22.♗b1 ♕a5 23.♘c6 ♗c6 24.♕d6 ♗c3 25.♖e2 ♖fd8 26.♕e7 ♖d7 27.♕g5 h6 28.♕g4 ♖cd8.

22...de5 23.♘c6 ♗c6 24.♗e4 ♖fd8

Here there are two other options, which both players had to calculate:

24...♕b7 25.♖c6 ♖c6 26.fe5 ♗e7 27.♕h5 h6 28.♕f5 g6 29.♕f3 ♖fc8 30.♗d5, with attack or 24...♗e4 25.♖c7 ♖c7 26.♕d5+-.

25.♕g4 ♗d7

Weak is 25...♕b7 26.♖c6 ♖c6 27.fe5+-, but slightly better chances for defence are given by the queen sacrifice 25...♕d6 26.♖ed1 ♕d1 27.♖d1 ♖d1 28.♕d1 ♗e4 29.fe5 ♗e5 30.♕d7 ♖b8 31.♕e7 f6.

26.♗h7 ♔f8 27.♗f5 ♕b7

27...♗f5 28.♕f5 ♕b7 29.♕h7+-.

28.fe5 ♖c1 29.♖c1 ♗f5

A horrible bad pin would result after 29...♗e5 30.♖d1.

30.♕f5 ♕d5 31.♗f4

Now Black has just minimal compensation for the pawn.

31...♔g8 32.b4 ♗h4 33.♔h2 ♖e8 34.♖c7 ♗f2? 35.♖c8+- ♖f8

35...♖c8 36.♕c8 ♔h7 37.♕c2+-.

36.♗g5 1:0.

3

▹ **Kuzmin**
▸ **Averbakh**
USSR 1974 [C98]

In the Spanish, the problem of 'the center' is the most important thing. There are three possible strategies for White in Spanish structures:

Closing of the center and exploitation of the space advantage, plus the creation of an attack on one of the flanks.

Exchanging pawns and planning to exploit important, weakened squares at d5 and f5.

Trying to keep the center open and under pressure, which allows the slightly-better-placed White pieces to start different attacks earlier than Black in the center.

1.e4 e5 2.♘f3 ♘c6 3.♗b5 a6 4.♗a4 ♘f6 5.0–0 ♗e7 6.♖e1 b5 7.♗b3 d6 8.c3 0–0 9.h3 ♘a5 10.♗c2 c5 11.d4 ♕c7 12.♘bd2 ♘c6 13.d5

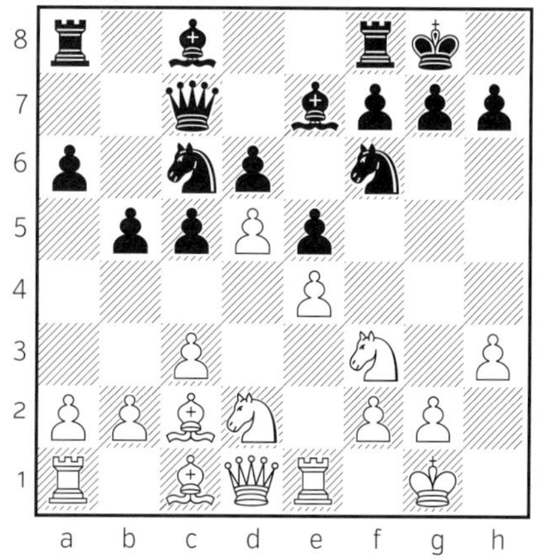

13...♘a5

Black has another retreat, recommended by the great Akiba Rubinstein — 13...♘d8, with the idea being to conduct a fantastic reshuffling of his own pieces: ...♘e8, ...g6, ...f6, ...♘g7 and ...♘f7 and after that to try to attack White's center with ...f6-f5! A fantastic mountain of a plan and White's best answer is to immediately launch an attack on the queen's flank: 14.a4 ♖b8 15.ab5 ab5 16.b4.

14.b3

Typical elastic prophylaxis, as White tries to stop any activity on the queen's flank. Another continuation of White's plan allows Black to activate his bad knight — 14.♘f1 ♘c4!

14...♗d7 15.♘f1 ♖fb8

It is very difficult to understand the role of the rook here. 15...♘b7, with the next direct plan ...a6-a5-a4.

16.♗d2

It is always unclear, where this bishop should be placed. Possible is 16.♗e3 or to immediately support his own attack on the kingside with 16.g4.

16...g6 17.♘g3

White decides on a plan with f2-f4, as other option would start with 17.g4 and only then ♘g3, ♔h1, ♖g1 and ♘f5.

17...♘b7 18.♘h2 ♗e8?!

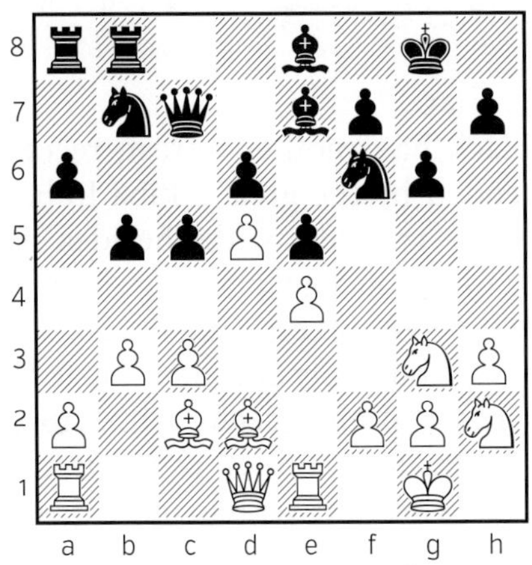

Better is 18...♘e8, to try to meet White's opening of the center with the activation of his black-squared bishop: 19.f4 ♗f6 20.f5.

19.f4! ef4

Another option is to wait for White's next few steps and to start an attack on the other side with 19...c4 20.b4 a5. But Black dreams about controlling the e5 square.

20.♗f4 ♘d7 21.♘g4 ♘e5 22.♖f1!±

It is possible to exchange on e5 first (22.♗e5), but White can improve the position of all his pieces first. 22...de5 23.♖f1.

22...♔h8

It is necessary to try a sharper way, as 22...♘g4 looks dangerous after 23.♕g4 ♗f6 24.♘f5 ♗c3 25.♖ad1.

23.♕d2 ♘g4

Still better was to counterattack immediately with 23...c4.

24.hg4 f6

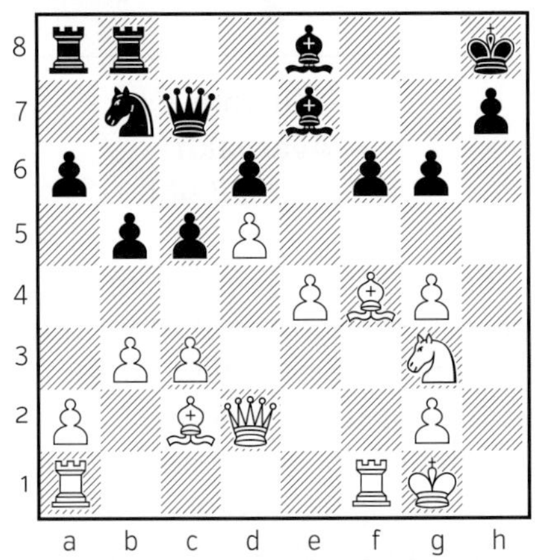

A decisive weakening of the king's position. The last try is 24...a5.

25.♗h6! ♘d8?!

After 25...g5 26.e5 fe5 (26...de5 27.♘e4, with a decisive activation of the knight.). It's time to launch tactics, according to Capablanca: 27.♕g5! ♗g6 28.♗g7 ♔g7 (Simpler for White is 28...♔g8 29.♗f6 ♗f6 30.♖f6.) 29.♘f5 ♔h8 30.♘e7, with a decisive attack.

26.g5 fg5 27.c4 1:0.

The central counterstrike can be very effective, but it must be conducted with the possibility of tactical blows, as happened in the next game.

4

▷ **Yudasin**
▶ **Mikhalchishin**
Lviv 1983 [C55]

1.e4 e5 2.♘f3 ♘c6 3.♗c4 ♘f6 4.d3 h6 5.0–0 d6 6.c3 g6 7.♖e1 ♗g7 8.♗b3 0–0 9.♘bd2 ♖e8 10.h3

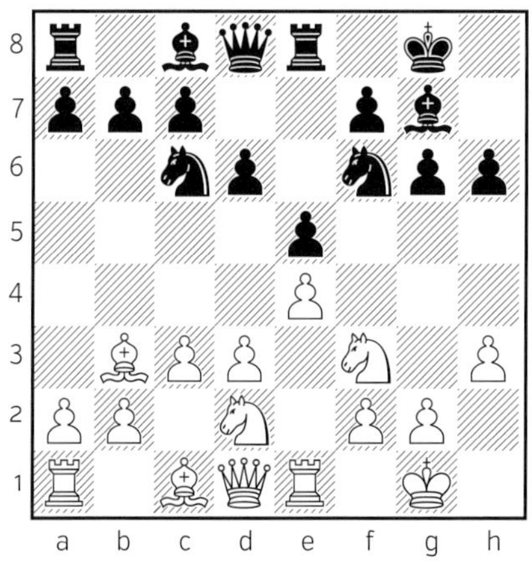

10...d5?!

Black decides to counterattack in the center immediately, but we can see the clear lack of proper development. Much simpler was to try to exchange bishops first: 10...♗e6.

11.ed5

The typical pin is not dangerous for Black: 11.♗a4 de4 12.de4 ♗d7 (12...♘d7=.) 13.♘c4 ♘h5=. **11...♘d5 12.d4!±**

This is the problem — the knight on d5 will not be protected in the event of exchanging rooks on e8. **12...♘b6**

Desperate tries to develop the bishop are powerfully countered in the center: 12...♗e6 13.c4 ♘f4 14.d5 ♗h3 15.gh3 ♘h3 16.♔f1±;

12...♗f5 13.♘f1! e4 14.♘g3! ef3 (14...♘a5 15.♘f5 gf5 16.♗d5 ♕d5 17.♘h4.) 15.♖e8 ♕e8 16.♘f5 gf5 17.♗d5±.

13.♘e5 ♘e5 14.de5 ♖e5

14...♗e5? 15.♘f3 ♕d1 16.♗d1+-.

15.♖e5 ♗e5 16.♕f3!

16.♘f3 ♕d1 17.♗d1 ♗g7 18.♗f4 ♘d5=.

16...♕e7

16...♕f6 17.♕f6 ♗f6 18.♘e4 ♗g7 19.♗f4 c6 20.♖d1 ♘d5, with the idea of 21.♗d5 cd5 22.♖d5 (22.♘d6!±) 22...♗e6 23.♖b5 b6.

17.♕e3! g5

17...h5 18.♘f3 ♗f6 19.♕e7 ♗e7 20.♘e5+-;

17...♗d6 18.♕h6 ♕e1 19.♘f1 ♗f5 20.♗e3! ♕a1 21.♗d4+-;

17...♗f6 18.♕h6 ♕e1 19.♘f1 ♗f5 20.♗g5! ♗g5? 21.♗f7! ♔f7 22.♕h7+-.

18.h4! ♗d6

18...♗g4 19.♕e4! ♗h5 20.g4+-; 18...♗f6 19.♘e4 gh4 20.♕h6 ♕e4 (20...♗g7 21.♕h5! ♕e4 22.♕f7 ♔h7 23.♕h5+-) 21.♕f6; 18...gh4 19.♘f3 ♗f6 20.♕h6.

19.♘e4 ♗f4 20.♕f3 ♗g4
20...♗f5 21.hg5 hg5 22.♗f4 ♗e4 (22...gf4 23.♖e1+-) 23.♕g3+-.

21.♕g4 ♕e4 22.g3!
22.♗f4 ♕f4 23.♕f4 (23.♕h5 ♔g7) 23...gf4 24.♖e1.

22...♕e1 23.♔g2 ♗c1
23...♕e4 24.♔h2 ♕e1 25.♗f4 ♕a1 26.hg5+-.

24.♕f5! gh4
24...♖f8 25.♕g6 ♔h8 26.♕h6 ♔g8 27.♗c2 f5 (27...♖e8 28.♗h7-) 28.♗b3 ♖f7 29.♕g6+-; 24...♕e7 25.♕g6 ♔f8 26.♕h6 ♔g8 27.♖c1+-.

25.♕f7 ♔h8 26.♗c2 h3 27.♔h2 1:0.

TYPICAL CHANGES OF THE STRUCTURE

There are many different changes of the center possible with the help of pawns, but sometimes piece exchanges lead to new plans.

1

▷ **Harikrishna**
▶ **Vovk**
Cappelle la Grande 2011 [E63]

1.d4 ♘f6 2.c4 g6 3.♘f3 ♗g7 4.g3 0–0 5.♗g2 d6 6.0–0 ♘c6 7.♘c3 a6 8.b3 ♖b8 9.♘d5

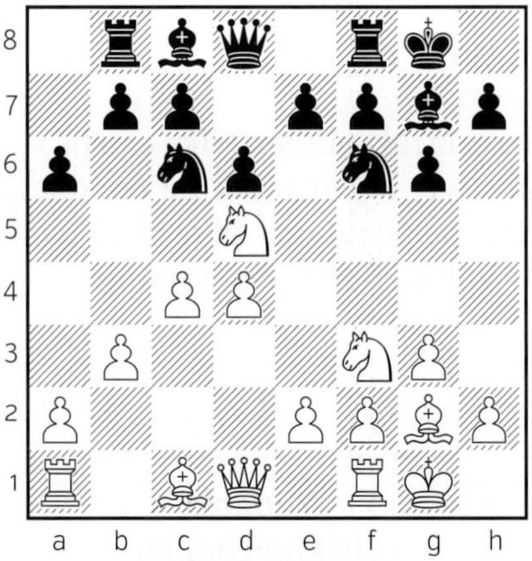

An interesting attempt to change the position in the center. Another possible plan is 9.♗b2 b5 10.cb5 ab5 11.♖c1

9...♘h5
This is the main move. The point of playing 9.♘d5 is seen in the line 9...b5?! 10.♘f6 ♗f6 11.♗h6 ♖e8 12.♖c1 — by blocking the b-file with b2-b3 and protecting the c4-pawn with ♖c1, White has taken the sting out of the ...b5 plan. Not very convincing is 9...♘d5 10.cd5 ♘a7 11.♗b2 c6 12.dc6 ♘c6 13.♕d2, with the plan d4-d5, obtaining a huge space advantage.

10.♗b2 e6 11.♘c3 ♗d7
After 11...b5 White can choose between 12.cb5 (and 12.d5 ♘e7 13.de6 ♗e6 14.cb5 ab5 15.♕d2) 12...ab5 13.♖c1, for example: 13...b4 14.♘a4 ♘a5 15.♕c2 ♗a6 16.♖fe1 c6 17.e4 ♗b5 18.e5, Romanishin : Nijboer, Essen 2001.

12.d5 ♘e7 13.de6 ♗e6

13...fe6 is better, as the pawn controls the most important square d5.

14.♕c2 ♗f5

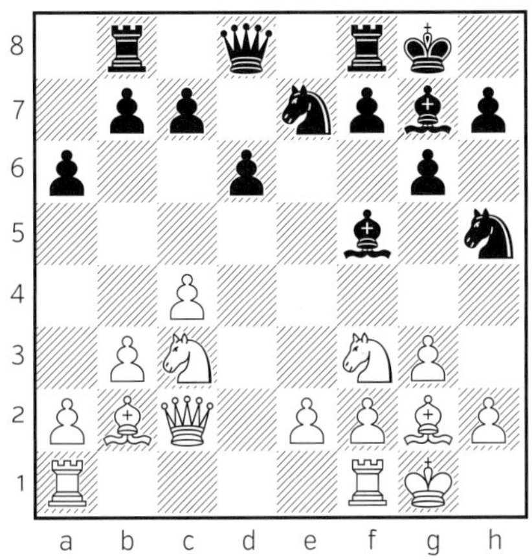

Now 14...b5 can be met with 15.c5! dc5 16.♖ad1 ♕e8 17.♘e4 ♗b2 18.♕b2 c4 19.♘e5.

15.♕d2

A very nice, more direct plan was possible: 15.e4!? ♗g4 16.♖ac1 ♖e8 17.h3 ♗f3 18.♗f3 ♘f6 19.c5, trying to open the center, and the bishop pair will start to co-ordinate dangerously.

15...♘f6

Nothing is changed by the immediate typical counterstrike on the queen's flank: 15...b5!? 16.e4 ♗d7 17.cb5 ab5 18.♖ac1 b4 19.♘d5 ♗b2 20.♕b2 ♘d5 21.ed5 ♘f6 22.♘d4 and the pawn c7 will be weak forever!

16.♖fd1 ♖e8

More natural seems to be 16...♕d7.

17.h3 ♘c6

It seems that this is Black's last chance to play ...b5.

18.♘d5! ♗e4 19.♖ac1 ♗d5 20.♗f6!

This bishop is not important — important will be the structure with a weakness on c7. The long diagonal will be emptied and nothing will take place on it.

20...♗f6 21.cd5 ♘e5 22.♘d4!

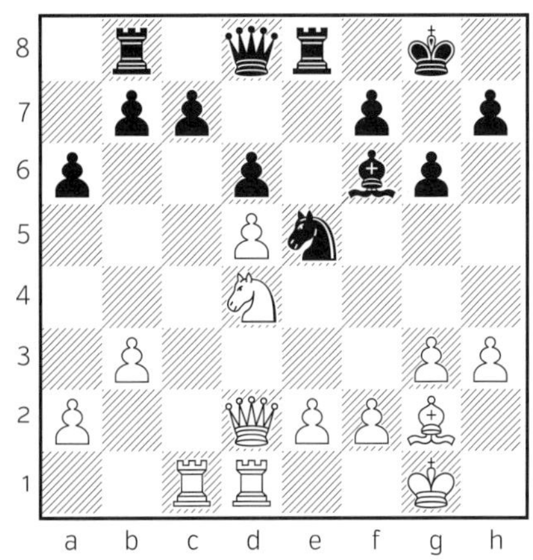

The pawn structure has been fixed and it benefits White. He can put pressure on the c7-pawn. Of course, Black can easily defend that pawn, but that will make his pieces passive, which may enable White to start an attack on the kingside. In such positions Black's counterplay is non-existent.

22...♘d7 23.e3 ♖e7 24.♖c2 ♗g7 25.♖dc1 ♘f6 26.♖c4 ♘e8

Black correctly decides to protect the pawn with his knight. Now White has to prepare the second part of the plan — to create another weakness.

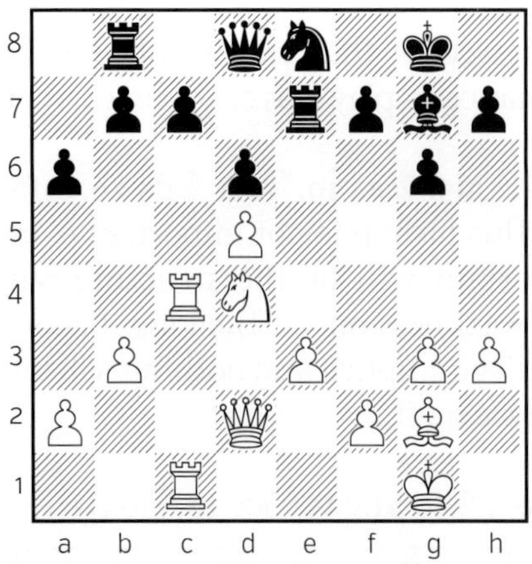

27.a4!

The correct technical operation — blocking the queenside.

27...♖a8 28.a5 ♕b8 29.b4 ♕d8 30.♖1c2 ♕d7 31.♕c1 ♕d8 32.♕b1 ♕d7 33.♕b3 ♕d8 34.♖c1 ♕d7 35.♕c2 ♕d8 36.♗f3 ♔h8 37.♔g2! ♕d7 38.h4!

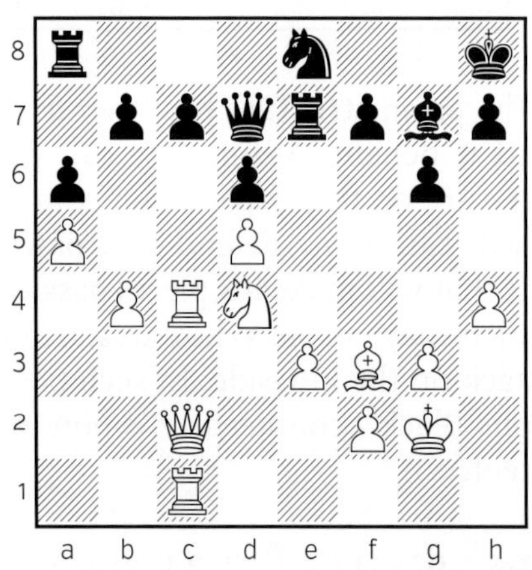

After some manoeuvring White begins the second part of his plan; as we mentioned before, the creation of a second weakness. Now Black has to worry about h4-h5-xg6, as then White might utilise the open h-file.

38...h5

This move is practically forced, but it does weaken Black's structure a bit.

39.♘e2 ♗e5 40.♘f4

40.♘g1 followed by ♘h3-g5 was very strong also.

40...♗f4

Otherwise White might play ♘d3, followed by ♗e2, f2-f4 and e3-e4.

41.♖f4 ♖e5 42.♖c4 ♔g8 43.♔g1 ♕b5 44.♕d2 ♖e7 45.♗g2 ♕d7 46.e4 ♔h7 47.♕d4 ♕b5 48.f4

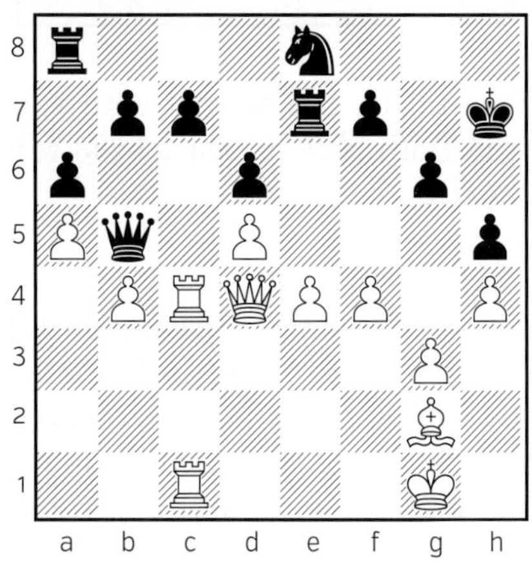

After the next set of manoeuvres White starts to roll his pawns. Sooner or later e4-e5 will appear.

48...♕d7

After 48...b6 49.♖a1 ba5 50.♖a5 ♕b6 51.♔h2 Black obtains another weakness on a6.

49.♖4c3 ♕b5 50.e5 ♖d8 51.♗f3 ♖dd7 52.♗e4?!

A small inaccuracy. Preferable is 52.♖e3 ♘g7 53.♗e4.

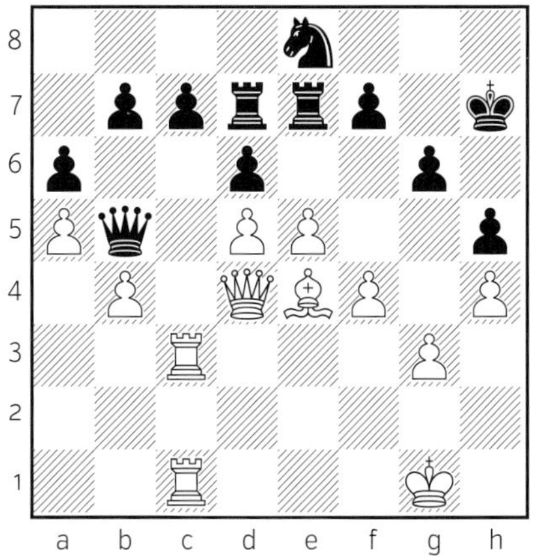

52...♘g7?
Black had to try mudding the waters with 52...de5! 53.fe5 c6.

53.e6! fe6 54.♕f6
After this break, White gets the opportunity to launch an attack on the king.

54...♕b4 55.♗g6 ♔g8 56.♖b1 ♕a4 57.♖e3
A very good idea was to try to outflank Black's king with 57.♖cb3.

57...e5 58.♖b7
Here there is a quicker, more decisive option:
58.fe5! ♕d4 59.♖f1 ♕e3 60.♔h1+-.

58...♕d1 59.♔h2 ♕d2 60.♔h3 ♕d5 61.♖b8 ♖e8 62.♗e4 ♕f7 63.♖e8 ♘e8 64.♕g5 ♘g7 65.f5 d5 66.♗c2 ♖d6
Slightly better would be to close down the bishop with 66...e4.

67.♖e5 c6

The more stubborn 67...♔f8 would demand a few more moves from White.

68.♗d3 c5 69.f6! ♕f6 70.♖e8 ♔f7 71.♗g6! 1:0.

2

▹ **Pelletier**
▸ **Jenal**
Zurich 2008 [B36]

1.♘f3 c5 2.c4 ♘c6 3.d4 cd4 4.♘d4 g6 5.e4 ♘f6 6.♘c3 ♘d4 7.♕d4 d6 8.♗g5 ♗g7 9.♕d2 0–0 10.♗d3 ♗e6 11.0–0 ♖c8 12.b3 a6

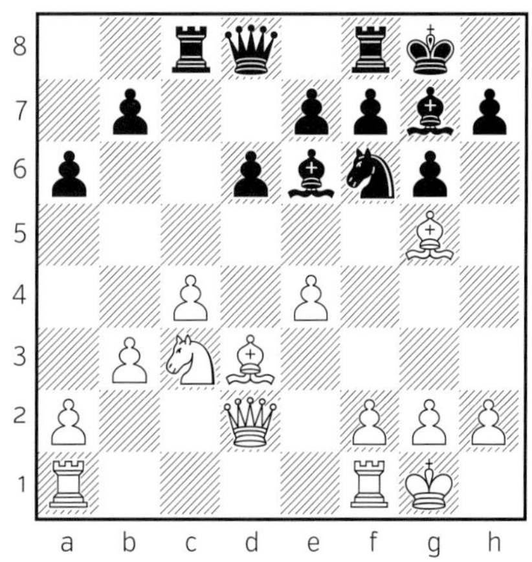

This is the so-called Maroczy structure and White has 3 plans:
1. Attack on the kingside with f2-f4-f5.
2. Attack on the queenside with b2-b4 and c4-c5.
3. A central strategy with ♘c3-d5.

Black's plans are simpler: Counterstrike at the center with ...b7-b5 or

...f7-f5. And fight to control the dark squares.

13.♖ac1 ♘d7 14.♖fe1

Now we can see that Pelletier has chosen the third plan.

14...♖e8 15.♘d5 ♗d5 16.ed5

Sometimes possible is 16.cd5, especially in those cases when it is possible to fight for control over the c-file.

16...♘e5

Better would be a dark-squared strategy here:

16...a5, followed by ...♕b6 and ...♕b4.

17.♗f1 ♕b6 18.h3!

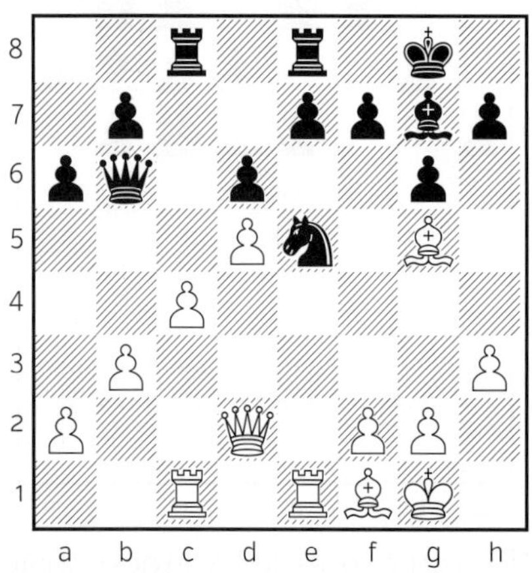

A prophylactic move, and now White is ready to play b2-b4 and c4-c5.

18...e6

Black feels helpless against his opponent's plans and decides to destroy White's center, but at the same time he creates weaknesses in his own position.

19.♖cd1 ed5 20.♕d5 ♕b4

More stubborn defence is available by activating the rooks:

20...♖e6 21.♖e2 ♖c5.

21.♖e2

Doubling rooks on the d-file increases the pressure on the weak pawn at d6.

21...♖e6 22.f4 ♖c5 23.♕d2

We can't call it a tactic, but with this smart retreat White wins a pawn.

23...♕d2 24.♖dd2 ♘c6 25.♖e6 fe6 26.♖d6 ♗d4 27.♔h1 e5 28.g3!

Not allowing his opponent to gain control over the e5 square.

28...ef4 29.gf4 ♖f5 30.♗g2 ♗c5 31.♖d7 1:0.

3

▷ **Mikhalchishin**
▶ **Pfleger**
Roma 1977 [E65]

1.♘f3 ♘f6 2.c4 c5 3.♘c3 g6 4.d4 cd4 5.♘d4 ♗g7 6.g3 0–0 7.♗g2 d6 8.0–0 ♘bd7

Of course, much better is to start fighting in the center with 8...♘c6.

9.b3 a6 10.♗b2 ♖b8 11.♖c1 ♘c5 12.♕d2

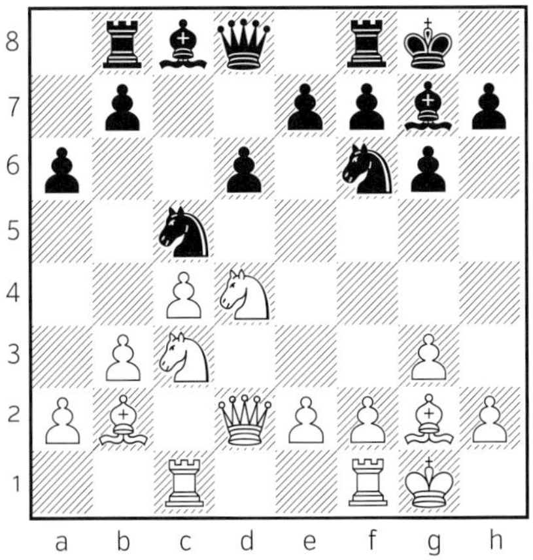

Another option is to try to eliminate the active black knight: 12.b4 ♕b6 13.a3.

12...♗d7 13.♖fd1

Another serious option is to continue the b4 strategy with 13.♗a1 ♕b6 14.♖b1.

13...♖e8

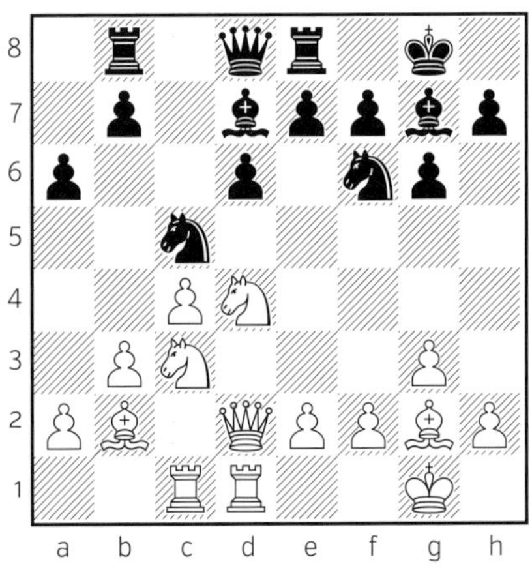

14.♘d5 ♘fe4

Counterplay does not work: 14...b5 15.cb5 ab5 16.♘c6!±; 14...♘d5 15.cd5 ♕b6 16.♖c4. White would start a plan to control the c-file after b4.

15.♕c2 f5 16.b4 ♘a4

Even worse would be 16...♗a4?! 17.♘b3±.

17.♗a1 ♘g5

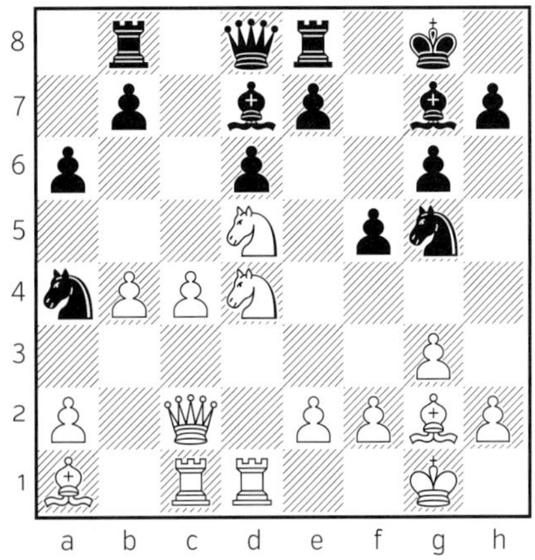

The pawn sacrifice was not a serious option: 17...e6 18.♘e3 ♕e7 19.♗e4 fe4 20.♕e4.

18.c5!

A typical break as we have seen. White's active central pieces have to start working.

18...♖c8 19.c6!±

Very strong was 19.♕b3 ♔h8 20.h4 dc5 21.♘f5 ♗a1 22.hg5 gf5 23.♖a1 cb4 24.♕b4.

19...bc6 20.♕a4 cd5 21.♗d5 e6 22.♗c6! ♗c6 23.♘c6 ♕d7 24.♗g7 ♕g7

Or another recapture 24...♔g7 25.♕a6+-.

25.♖d6 ♘e4 26.♖d3!

Protecting Black's target, the c3 square.

26...♕b7 27.♖c4!- ♔g7 28.♕c2 ♖c7 29.♘a5 ♖c4? 30.♕b2 1:0.

4

▹ **Gligoric**
▸ **Sax**
Vrbas 1977 [D86]

1.d4 ♘f6 2.c4 g6 3.♘c3 d5 4.cd5 ♘d5 5.e4 ♘c3 6.bc3 ♗g7 7.♗c4 0–0 8.♘e2 b6 9.0–0

Brave souls can start an immediate attack here, keeping the king in the center, with 9.h4!?

9...♗b7

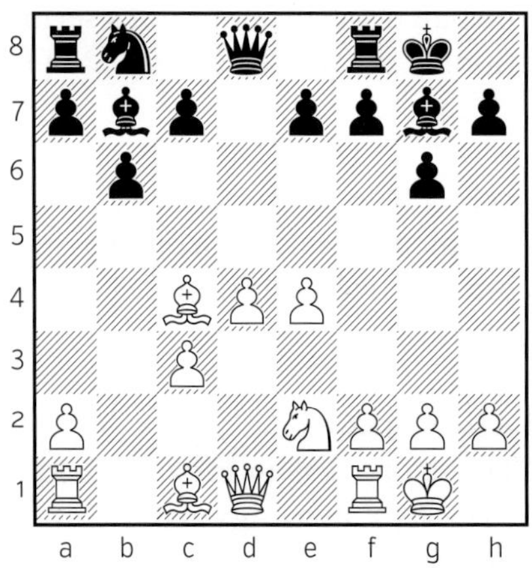

10.e5

It is a difficult decision as to how to change the center? On the one side White opens the bishop from b7, but its ability to attack is very limited after f2-f3. On the other hand it is important to close down the more important black-squared bishop and to prepare an attack on the kingside. Other possibilities (10.f3; 10.d5) were not so effective.

10...♘c6 11.♘f4 ♘a5 12.♗d3 c5 13.♗e3 ♖c8

Black continues classically, trying to control squares on the c-file.

14.♕g4 ♘c6

14...cd4 15.cd4 ♘c4 16.♖ac1 ♘e3 17.fe3 just leads to the strengthening of White's center.

15.♖ad1 cd4 16.cd4 ♘b4!

Black has an obvious idea to exploit the weaknesses of the white squares in the center, but there are no serious objects for attack.

17.♗b1 ♘c2

Black tries to eliminate the bishop forever, but a better position for the knight lies in the center — 17...♘d5!

18.h4 ♗e4!

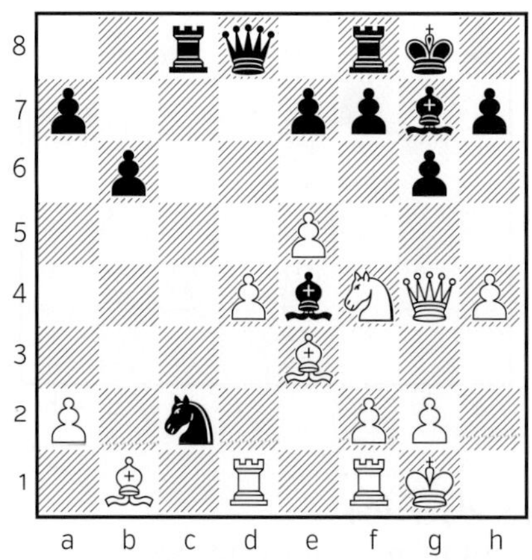

A logical idea to exchange white-squared bishops. A risky strategy — winning a pawn — is also possible, but White's attack could become very strong: 18...♗a6 19.♗c2 ♖c2 20.♖fe1 ♗c8 21.♕g3 ♖a2 22.h5.

19.h5!

It is possible to transfer into an equal endgame: 19.♘e6 ♗f5 20.♕f5 gf5 21.♘d8 ♖fd8 22.g3.

19...♗f5 20.♕g3 ♖c3?

Correct would be to connect the rooks with 20...♕d7 giving Black a comfortable position.

21.♗c2

More serious problems would face Black after the principled 21.♖c1!

21...♖c2 22.♖c1 ♖a2?

Risky materialism. Usually it is better to continue a central strategy, so 22...♖c1 23.♖c1 ♕d7.

23.e6! ♕d6 24.d5!

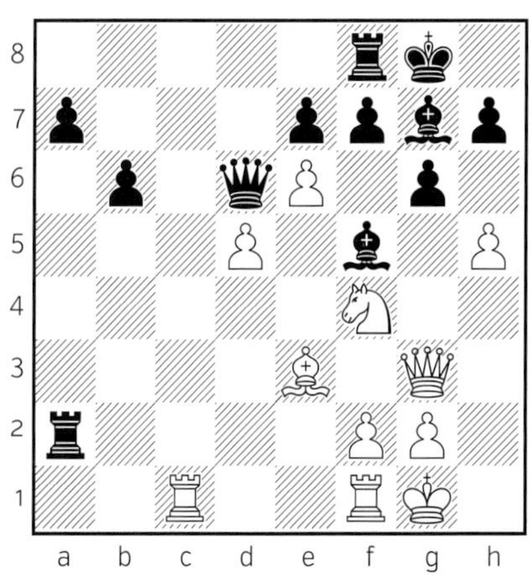

White finally starts to move in the center after sacrificing the queen's flank, plus he has an attack on the opponent's king.

24...♗e5

It was necessary to continue his risky material strategy with the weak king: 24...fe6 25.de6 ♗e5 26.hg6 hg6 27.♖fd1 ♗f4 28.♗f4 ♕e6 29.♗h6 ♖e8.

25.♖c6 ♗f4 26.ef7! ♖f7

Of course, the king capture is much more risky — 26...♔f7 27.♗f4 ♕d5 28.♖c7 ♖c8.

27.♗f4 ♕d5 28.♖fc1 ♖c2?

Black should try to reduce White's attacking power with exchanges: 28...♖a1 29.♖g6 hg6 30.♖a1 a5 31.♗e5 ♖h7 32.hg6 ♖h6!

29.♖6c2 ♗c2 30.♗h6 e5 31.♕c3 ♗f5 32.♕c8 1:0.

5

▷ **Foguelman**
▶ **Stein**
Mar del Plata 1965 [E62]

1.d4 ♘f6 2.c4 g6 3.g3 ♗g7 4.♗g2 0–0 5.♘f3 d6 6.0–0 ♘c6

Another example of such a central strategy is 6...♘bd7 7.♘c3 e5 8.e4 a6 9.h3 ♖b8 10.de5 de5 11.♕c2 c6 12.♖d1 ♕c7 13.♗e3 b5 14.c5!

(Now the idea is clear — occupation of the important d6 square.)

14...a5 15.b3 ♖e8 16.a4 b4 17.♘b1 ♘f8 18.♘bd2 ♗a6 19.♗f1!

(It's necessary to exchange the a6-bishop, which is preventing the transfer of White's knight.)

19...♗f1 20.♔f1 ♘e6 21.♘c4 ♘d7 22.♘d6

(White has reached the main idea for this kind of strategy — he has occupied the important d6 square, and Black has no time to fight for the d4 square.)

22...♖ed8 23.♘g5 ♘g5 24.♗g5 ♗f6 25.♗h6 ♕a7 26.♕c4 ♘f8 27.♗f8 ♔f8 28.♖d3 ♔g7 29.♖ad1 ♖a8 30.f4 ef4 31.gf4 ♕e7 32.e5 ♗h4 33.f5 h5 34.f6 ♗f6 35.ef6 ♕f6 36.♔g2 ♕g5 37.♖g3, A. Maric : Repkova, Yerevan 1996.

7.♘c3

7.h3 e5 8.♗e3 ♘e4 9.de5

(The wrong decision once again — much better is to keep the center closed:

9.d5 ♘e7 10.♕c2 f5 11.♘fd2.) 9...de5 10.♕c1 ♗e6 11.♘a3 f5 12.♘g5 ♘g5 13.♗g5 ♕d7 14.♔h2

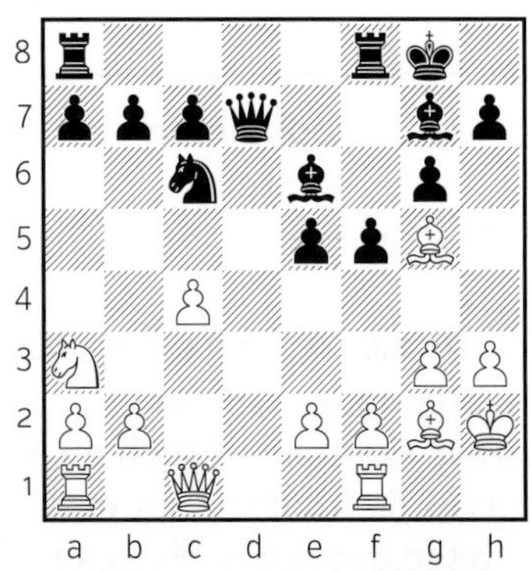

14...f4! 15.gf4 ef4 16.♖d1 ♕f7 17.e3 f3 18.♗f1 ♗e5 19.♗f4 ♕g7 20.♖b1 ♕h6 21.♗e5 ♘e5 22.♖d4 ♖f5 23.e4 ♖g5 24.♘b5 ♗h3 25.♕g5 ♕g5 26.♗h3 ♕h4, 0:1, A. Maric : Rasik, Winterthur 1996).

7...e5

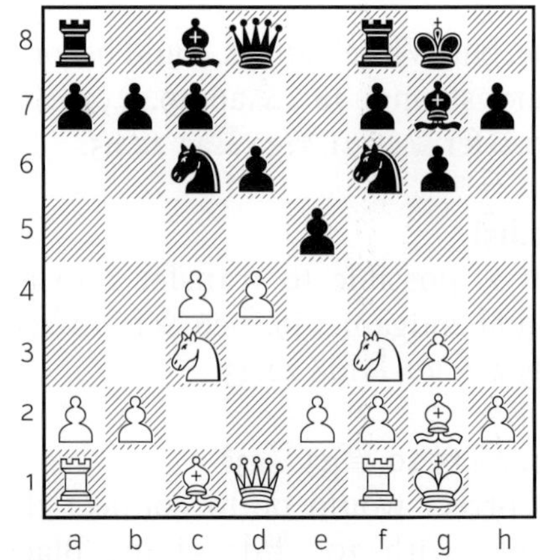

8.de5

Such exchanges have to be conducted very carefully as the typical weakness of the central black squares are sometimes fatal to White. More usual is firstly to close the center, forcing the opponent's pieces to less-active positions — and only then try to open the center:

8.d5 ♘e7 9.e4 ♘e8 10.♘e1 f5 11.♘d3 ♘f6 12.♗g5 h6 13.♗f6 ♗f6 14.f4.

8...de5 9.♘b5?!

Correct would be the centralised developing strategy (9.♗e3.), otherwise White's strategy is based on nothing more than tactical threats.

9...♕e7 10.b3 ♖d8 11.♕e1 a5!

A very strong reaction, as the bishop sortie to a3 will be met with the blockading ...♘b4.

12.e4 ♘b4 13.♗a3 ♗g4

The fight for the central d4 square has started! Another possible strategy is 13...c6 14.♘c3 ♖d3.

14.♕e2 c6 15.♘c3 ♘d7!

Yet another typical, and key, move — increasing control over the dark squares in the center.

16.♖ad1 ♘c5 17.♖d8
Or 17.h3 ♗f3 18.♗f3 ♘e6.

17...♖d8 18.♖d1 ♘e6 19.♖d8 ♕d8 20.♕d2
Exchanges do not make White's life easier, as the knight on d4 will dominate the entire position.

20...♘d4 21.♔f1

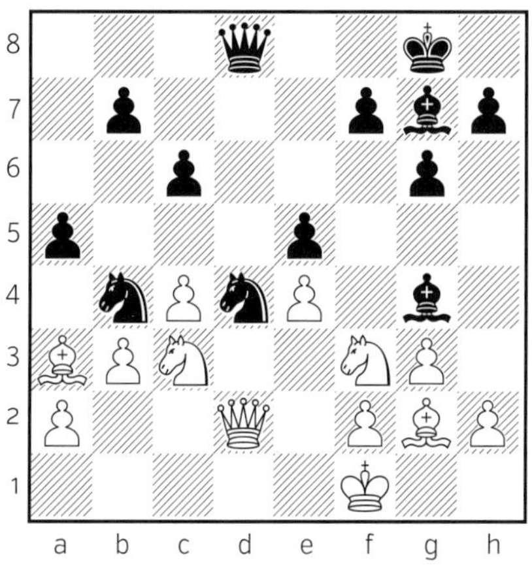

21...♗f6!
Threatening exchanges on f3 and ♗g5. White decided to exchange on d4, which creates a tremendously strong passed pawn on the d-file.

22.♘d4 ed4 23.♘a4 d3 24.f3 ♗g5 25.f4 ♗e7 26.♗b2 b5! 27.cb5 cb5 28.♘c3
No real threats exist on the long diagonal: 28.♕c3 f6.

28...♕d4 29.♕f2

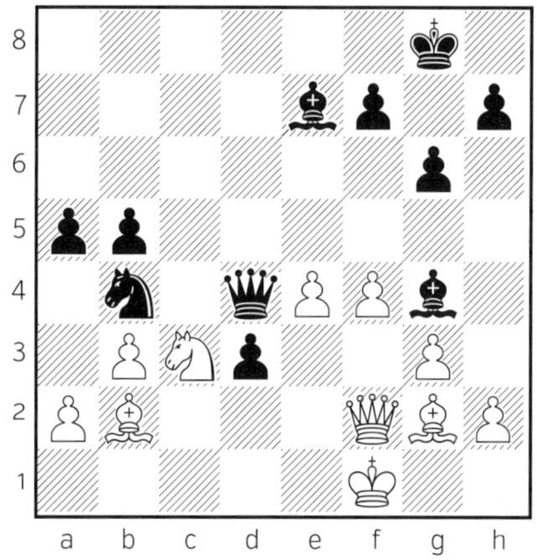

29...♗e2!
A decisive cheap trick!

30.♘e2 ♕b2 31.♗f3 de2 32.♗e2 ♕a2 0:1.

6

▷ **Carlsen**
▶ **Jakovenko**
Nanjing 2009 [D31]

1.d4
This is Carlsen's big ability, which was spotted many years ago by top trainer Arshak Petrosian — he is able to serve with both hands equally. In Dortmund 2009 he won against Jakovenko in the Berlin Wall, but just a few months later he decided to try to find winning chances in a different opening.

1...d5 2.c4 e6 3.♘c3 ♗e7
Before this game Magnus had only a little experience in the Carlsbad structure: 3...♘f6 4.cd5 ed5 5.♗g5

c6 6.e3 ♗f5 7.♕f3 ♗g6 8.♗f6 ♕f6 9.♕f6 gf6 10.♘f3 ♘d7 11.♘h4 ♗b4 12.♖c1 ♘b6 13.a3 ♗c3 14.♖c3 ♘c8 15.f3 ♘d6 16.g3 a5 17.b3 a4 18.b4 ♗b1 19.♔f2 ♗a2 20.♖c1 ♗c4 21.♗h3 ♘b5 22.♖a1, Carlsen : Azmaiparashvili, Khanty-Mansiysk 2005.

4.cd5 ed5 5.♗f4 c6 6.♕c2

6.e3 ♗f5 7.g4 is Botvinnik's complicated line, which was applied by Karpov and Kasparov, so it would be interesting to know why Magnus did not follow in their steps? Play there is extremely sharp and interesting.

6...♗d6

A possible plan for Black, as White's bishop position on f4 is considered to be unpleasant for Black. 6...g6 was always considered to be the mainline here, but such a creative player as Alexey Shirov invented here 7.f3 ♗g5 8.♗g5 ♕g5 9.e4 with initiative to White.

7.♗d6

7.♗g3 would be more appropriate, as exchanging on g3 is useful only to White. But Magnus is so convinced in his technique that exchanges don't disturb him, or his chances to play for a win.

7...♕d6 8.e3 ♘e7 9.♗d3 b6?!

This is a bit strange — to create his own weakness on c6. Of course, Black's plan is to seek an exchange of his white-squared bishop. The most natural and classical way to do so would be 9...g6, with ...♗c8-f5 next. In the 'legends' match there occurred 9...♘d7 10.♘ge2 h6 11.0–0 0–0 12.a3 a5 13.♖ad1 b6 14.e4 de4 15.♘e4 ♕b8 16.♘2c3 ♗a6 17.♗a6 ♖a6 18.d5 ♘d5 19.♘d5 cd5 20.♖d5 ♖a7 21.♕d2 ♘c5 and here Kasparov did not win a pawn, but rather started a mating attack: 22.♘f6 gf6 23.♕h6 f5 24.♕g5 ♔h8 25.♕f6 ♔g8 26.♖f5 ♘e4 27.♕h4 ♖e8 28.♖h5 f5, 1:0, Kasparov : Karpov, Valencia 2009.

10.♘f3 ♗a6 11.0–0

11.♗a6 ♘a6 12.0–0 0–0 13.♖ad1 ♘c7 14.♘e5 is possible also, as it is not clear if the black knight is well-placed on c7 or not.

11...♗d3 12.♕d3 ♘d7

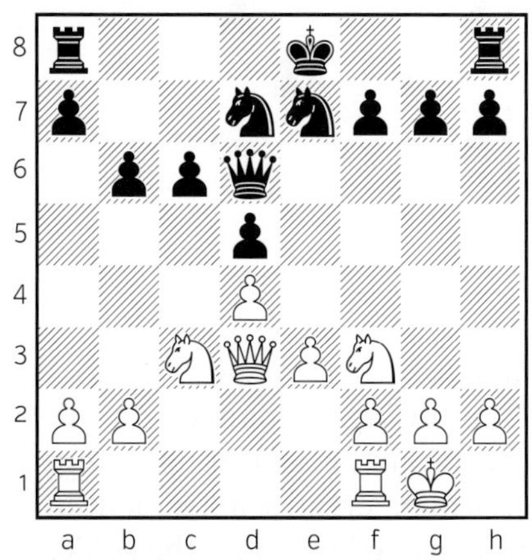

13.e4

There is no other active plan in this situation.

13...0–0

13...♕g6 would retain much more tension. If 13...de4, then after 14.♘e4 ♕g6 15.♕a3! Black's king is kept in the center, which is terribly dangerous for him.

14.e5! ♕e6

14...♕g6 15.♕d2 ♖fe8 is more logical, preparing ...f7-f6.

15.♖ae1 ♖fe8

Counterplay on the other side with 15...c5 would be premature because of 16.♘b5. Now and on the next move.

16.♘h4

Magnus plays directly, threatening f2-f4. He does not care about the prophylactic plan on the other side (16. b4).

16...♘g6 17.♘g6 ♕g6

17...hg6 18.♖e3 ♕f5 19.♕d2 keeps White's advantage at the same level.

18.♕d2 ♘f8

Black tries to block the position on the king's flank. 18...f5 would be met by a transfer of the knight to f4 (19. ♘e2).

19.f4 ♕f5

It is known -and not just to Grandmasters! — that blockading the opponent's pawn with the queen is a useless task, especially when a knight is still on the board. A lowly knight can easily remove a more powerful blockading piece. Here 19...f5 is also possible, but then White can start play on the other side — 20.b4!

20.♘d1! f6 21.♘e3 ♕d7 22.♕d3

22.ef6 gf6 23.f5, with an attack on the pawn f6 is possible. The knight on e8 would also be cut off from all the important squares. But Carlsen has a different idea, to go with his knight to f5 and d6.

22...fe5 23.de5 ♘e6 24.f5 ♘c5

24...♘g5 allows 25.♘c4, occupying the square d6.

25.♕d4 ♘e4

25...♕f7 26.♘g4 ♘e4 27.e6 ♕h5 28.♘e5. But now Carlsen wins a pawn for no compensation.

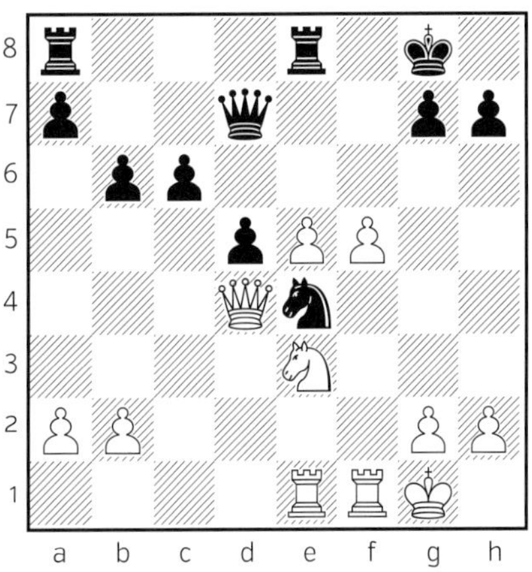

26.♘d5! ♕d5

Giving up, although the last attempt to catch some fish in muddy water fails also: 26...♘c5 27.f6 ♖ed8 28.e6! ♘e6 29.f7! ♔f8 30.♕h4 ♕d5 31.♕h7 ♕d4 32.♖f2 ♔e7 33.♕f5 ♕d5 34.♕g6 leads to a decisive attack.

27.♕e4 ♖ad8 28.e6 ♕e4 29.♖e4 ♖d6

Once more — during the whole game we get the impression that Jakovenko is under terrible pressure and does not think about aiming for even the smallest activity with 29...♖d2. White can try the sharp way 30.g4 (30.b4 ♖a2 31.♖c1) 30...♖b2 31.g5 ♖b5 32.h4 ♔f8 33.f6 gf6 34.gf6 or play more safely. **30.g4**

Now White's plan is easy — to create connected passed pawns, which every player knows is a fearful weapon.

30...♔f8 31.g5 ♔e7 32.♔g2 ♖d5

32...♖d2 33.♔g3 would be similar to the previous variation.

33.♔g3 ♔d6 34.h4 c5 35.f6 gf6 36.gf6 ♖d3 37.♔h2

You can go forward or back, by now everything wins.

37...♖d2 38.♔h1 1:0.

In some cases the building of the center is a very complicated process, and to perform such plans properly it is necessary to have serious experience and knowledge.

7

▷ **Botvinnik**
▶ **Keres**
Moscow 1952 [D36]

1.d4 ♘f6 2.c4 e6 3.♘c3 d5 4.cd5 ed5 5.♗g5 ♗e7 6.e3 0–0 7.♗d3 ♘bd7 8.♕c2 ♖e8 9.♘ge2 ♘f8 10.0–0 c6 11.♖ab1 ♗d6 12.♔h1

A prophylactic move, avoiding ...♗h2 and ...♘g4.

12...♘g6

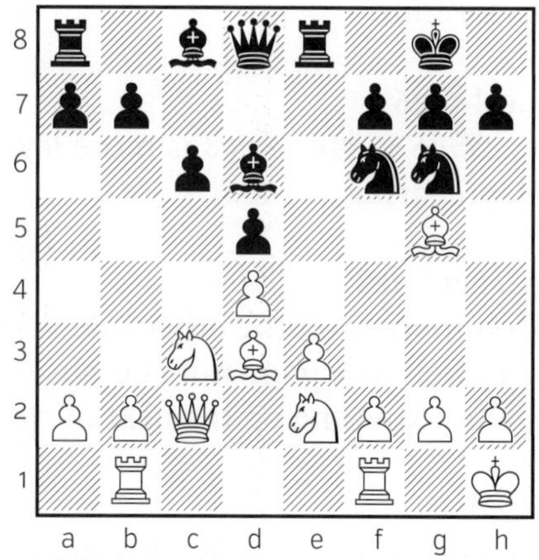

Now the sacrifice does not work: 12...♗h2? 13.♗f6.

13.f3!

Here White has the typical minority attack plan b2-b4-b5, but Botvinnik prefers central expansion — the creation of a powerful center.

13...♗e7 14.♖be1

A question arises — why put the rook firstly on b1, and then to e1? But in chess, the correct plans are not immediately obvious in every position.

14...♘d7 15.♗e7 ♖e7

An immediate central 'roll' was possible after the other recapture: 15...♕e7 16.e4 ♘b6 17.e5 ♕h4 18.f4 ♘e7 19.♘g3.

16.♘g3

If now White starts his central plan 16.e4 de4 17.fe4 ♘df8, there could be certain problems with the weakness of his pawn on d4.

16...♘f6 17.♕f2

White protects the d4-pawn and doubles on the f-file. Now everything is ready for e3-e4.

17...♗e6 18.♘f5

Here White has another option to play for space expansion:

18.f4 ♘g4 19.♕g1 ♘f8 20.f5 ♗c8 21.e4 de4 22.♘ge4 f6 23.h3 ♘h6 24.♘g3.

18...♗f5 19.♗f5 ♕b6 20.e4

Finally White creates a powerful center and is ready to grab more space.

20...de4 21.fe4 ♖d8 22.e5 ♘d5 23.♘e4

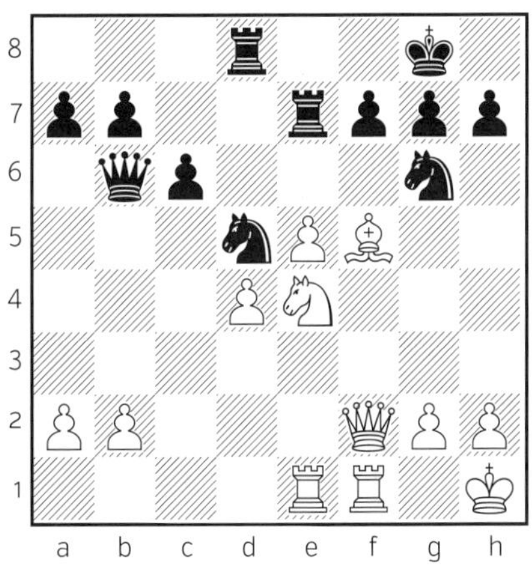

On the one hand Black has a strong knight on d5, but on the other the white knight on e4 is more powerful — it can be placed on d6 or g5, which is much more dangerous.

23...♘f8

Maybe the best defence is to sacrifice the exchange on d6 for one pawn and try to hold:

23...♕c7 24.♗g6 hg6 25.♘d6 ♖d6 26.ed6 ♕d6 27.♖e7 ♕e7 28.♖e1 ♕d8.

24.♘d6 ♕c7 25.♗e4!

Not threatening to take on d5 yet, but opening a file for his queen and rook.

25...♘e6 26.♕h4 g6

Another defence was bad also: 26...h6 27.♗d5 cd5 28.♖c1 ♕d7 29.♘f5 ♖ee8 30.♖c3 and the rook will be transferred to the kingside.

27.♗d5 cd5

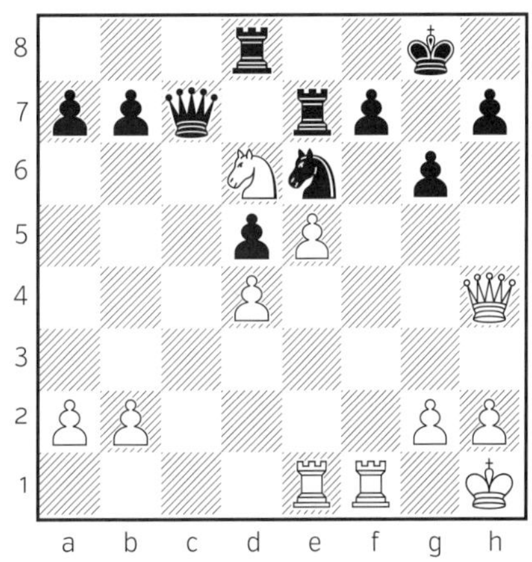

28.♖c1 ♕d7 29.♖c3!

The same typical transfer of the rook via the third rank — a rook 'lift'.

29...♖f8 30.♘f5!

With cheap tactics, White includes his knight in the attack on the king.

30...♖fe8

Simple is 30...gf5 31.♖g3 ♘g7 32.♕f6.

31.♘h6 ♔f8 32.♕f6 ♘g7 33.♖cf3

All White's pieces are attacking! A very instructive picture!

33...♖c8 34.♘f7 ♖e6 35.♕g5 ♘f5 36.♘h6 ♕g7 37.g4 1:0.

Let's examine a very typical case, one in which the young player does not care about his center and development. His aim is to start direct counterplay on the kingside.

8

▷ **Znidaric**
▶ **Suta**
Bled 2016 [E68]

1.♘f3 ♘f6 2.c4 g6 3.d4 ♗g7 4.g3 0–0 5.♗g2 d6 6.0–0 ♘bd7 7.♘c3 e5 8.e4 ♖e8 9.♖e1 a5 10.h3

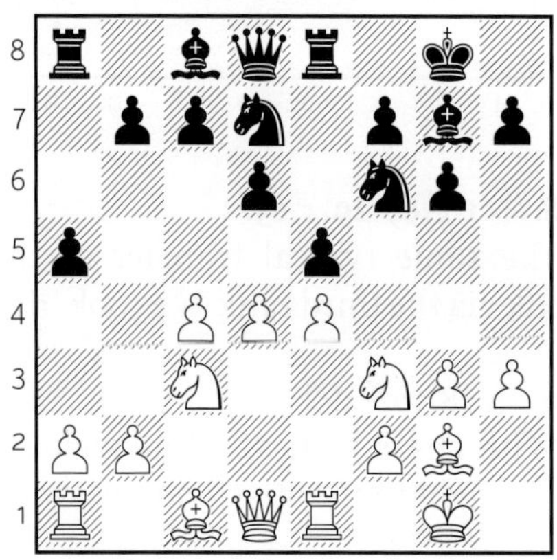

10...♘h5?

Black decides to begin flank activity before completing his development. Classical plans are much more logical here:

10...ed4 11.♘d4 ♘c5 or 10...c6.

11.♗g5 f6 12.♗e3 ♖f8

It is still possible to play logical improving moves, such as 12...c6 or 12...♗f8.

13.♖c1

It is possible to destroy the opponent's center immediately, with the instructive:

13.c5! dc5 (13...ed4 14.♘d4 ♘c5 15.g4) 14.dc5 c6 15.♘d2 ♕e7 16.♘a4 ♖d8 17.♕b3 ♔h8 18.♘c4.

13...f5?

Still better was 13...c6.

14.ef5 gf5 15.de5 de5

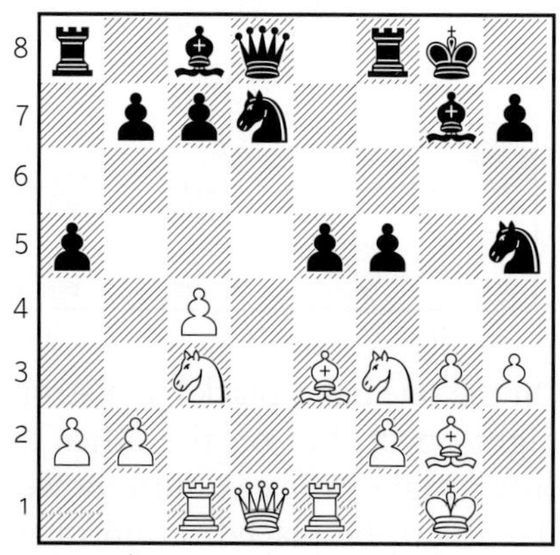

16.♘e5! ♘e5 17.♕h5 ♘c4 18.♗d5 ♔h8 19.♗c4 1:0.

9

▷ **Mikhalchishin**
▶ **A. Ivanov**
USSR 1979 [E43]

1.d4 ♘f6 2.c4 e6 3.♘c3 ♗b4 4.e3 b6 5.f3 ♘h5

A very interersting flank strategy for the attack on White‘s center. A more classical way is 5...c5!?

6.♘h3 f5 7.e4 0–0

7...fe4 8.fe4 ♕h4 9.♘f2 0–0 10.♗e3±.

8.♗g5 ♕e8

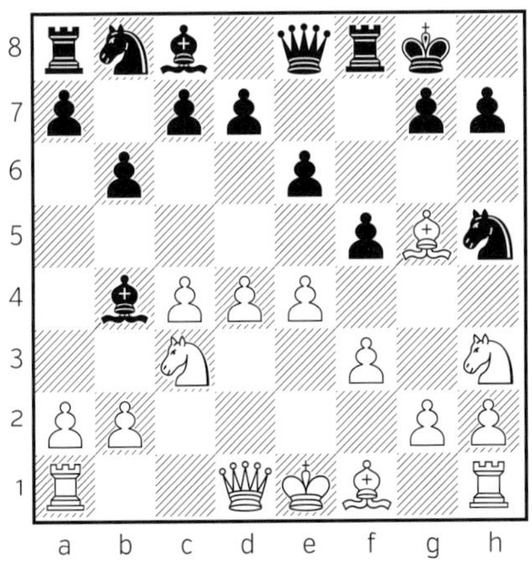

9.ef5

White decided to change form of the center, but clearly not worse was 9.♗e2!?

9...ef5

9...h6 10.♗d2 ♘c6 11.♘b5 ef5 12.♗e2 ♕d8 13.d5±.

10.♗e2 ♘c6 11.d5

Tactically wrong would be 11.0–0? ♘d4, but 11.♕d2!? is possible.

11...♘a5?!

Obvious decentralization. Much better is the central approach: 11...♘e5 12.d6 ♗b7 (12...cd6 13.♕d5+–) 13.dc7 ♖c8!

12.0–0

12.d6 ♗d6 13.♕d5 ♕f7 14.♕a8 ♗b7 15.♕a7 ♖a8.

12...♗a6?

Better would be to double White‘s pawns: 12...♗c3 13.bc3 ♗a6 14.♖e1 ♕f7 15.c5.

13.♘b5! ♗b5 14.cb5 f4?

14...♕e5 15.f4 ♕e3 16.♔h1 ♘f6 17.d6 ♗d6 18.♗f6 gf6 19.a3±.

Here it was correct to return the knight to the game: 14...♘b7 15.♖c1 ♗d6.

15.♗d3 ♕e5 16.♕c2 h6 17.♗h4 ♘f6

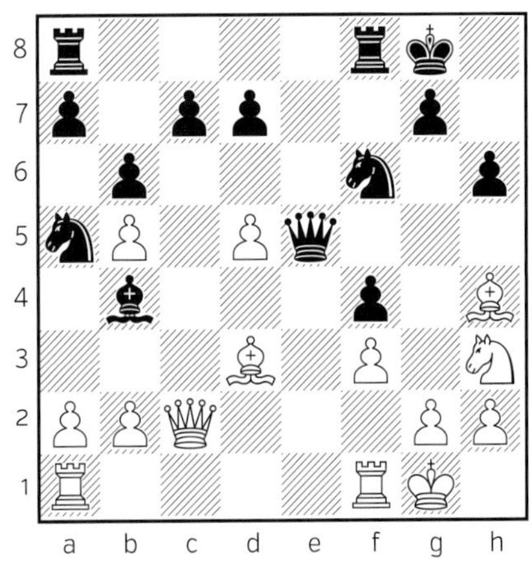

It is very risky to win the pawn 17...♕d5 18.♔h1!

18.♗f6! ♕f6 19.♘f2

Now White understands, that it is necessary to activate his own knight — finally.

19...♖ac8 20.♔h1 ♘b7 21.♘g4
Even now 21.d6! is possible 21...♗d6 22.♘g4 ♕g5 23.♕c4 ♔h8 24.♕e4.

21...♕g5?
21...♕d6 22.a3 ♗c5 23.♖ae1 with better play.

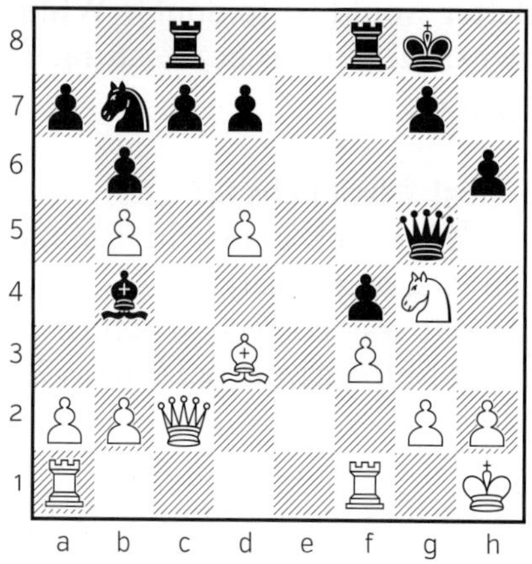

22.d6!+– ♗d6 23.♕c4 ♖f7 24.♕e4 ♘c5 25.♕h7 ♔f8 26.♖ae1 1:0.

10

▹ **Taulbut**
▸ **Mikhalchishin**
Mexico City 1978 (C87)

1.e4 e5 2.f3 ♘c6 3.♗b5 a6 4.♗a4 ♘f6 5.0–0 ♗e7 6.♖e1 d6 7.♗c6!? bc6 8.d4 ed4 9.♘d4 ♗d7 10.♘c3 0–0 11.♕f3 ♖b8
Better is a central strategy with 11...♖e8.

12.♖b1
Simpler is 12.b3 c5 13.♘f5 ♗f5 14.♕f5 with better play.

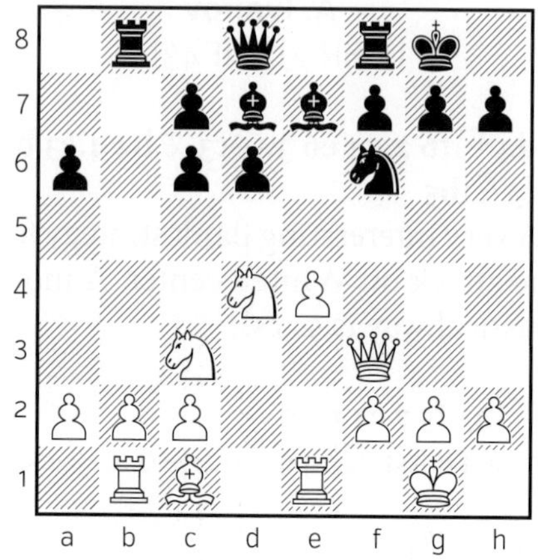

12...♖b6?!
Once more it is better to play in the center: 12...♖e8 13.♗f4 c5 14.♘f5 h6.

13.h3 g6 14.♘b3
Black would gain some clear counterplay after 14.♗g5 ♘h5 15.♗e7 ♕e7 16.♕e3 ♖e8 17.b3 g5.

14...♘h5 15.♗e3 ♖b8

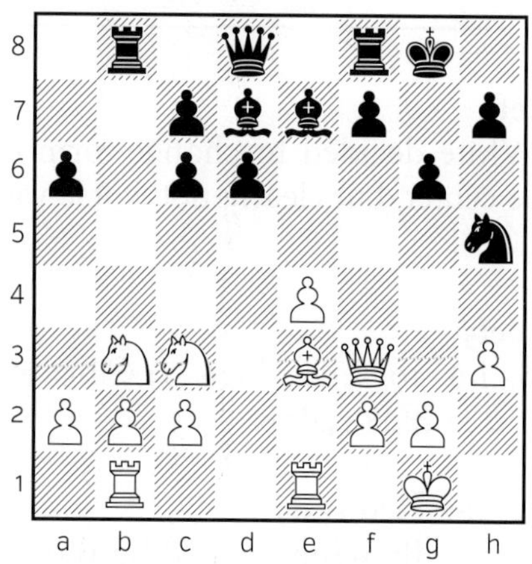

16.e5!

We know that when one side controls the center and his pieces stand better, it is necessary to try to open the position up.

16...de5

It is better not to open the central file: 16...♘g7 17.♖bd1 d5 18.♗c5 ♖e8 (18...♖b3 19.♗e7 ♖c3 20.♕f6) 19.♗e7 ♕e7.

17.♗h6 ♖e8 18.♖e5 ♘g7 19.♖d1

White has a dominant position after 19.♘e4 ♘f5 20.♖e7 ♕e7 21.♘bc5.

19...♘e6?

The correct defence was to close the d-file with 19...♗d6.

20.♘e4! ♖b5

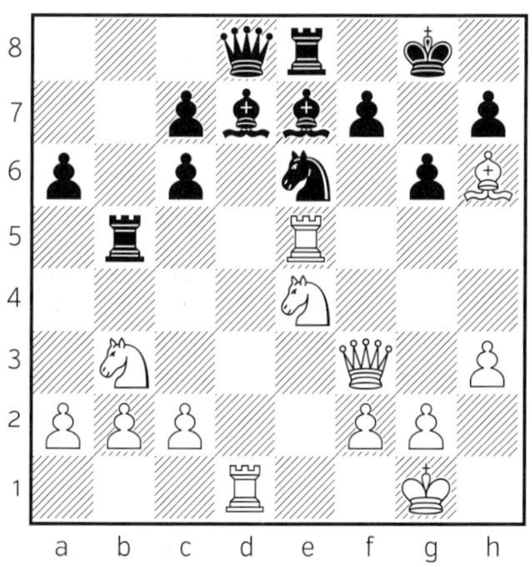

Now begins a forcing variation.

21.♖e6! fe6 22.♕c3 e5 23.♕c4 ♔h8 24.♕f7 ♖g8 25.♘f6 ♗f6 26.♖d7 ♕d7 27.♕d7 1:0.

11

▷ **S. Garcia**
► **Mikhalchishin**
Baku 1980 [C84]

1.e4 e5 2.♘f3 ♘c6 3.♗b5 a6 4.♗a4 ♘f6 5.0–0 b5 6.♗b3 ♗b7 7.♘c3 ♗e7 8.d3 0–0 9.♗d2 Another way is 9.a4 b4 10.♘d5 ♘a5! 11.♘e7 ♕e7 12.♗a2.

9...d6 10.♘d5?! ♘d5 11.ed5?

More logical is to keep the center intact with 11.♗d5 ♕c8 12.c3 ♘d8.

11...♘b8

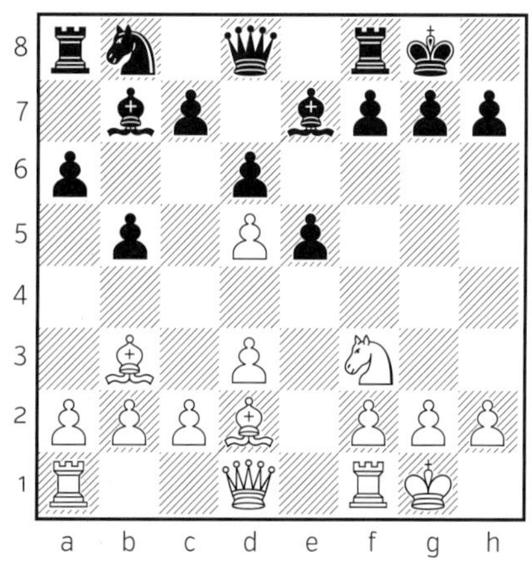

12.♗a5

Even if White returns to a central strategy now, Black would have no real problems. 12.♖e1 ♘d7 (12...f5? 13.♘e5! de5 14.d6 ♔h8 15.de7 ♕e7 16.a4 ♘d7 17.d4 e4 18.♕e2 with pressure on the queenside pawns.) 13.d4 ed4 14.♘d4 ♘c5 15.♕f3 ♗f6.

12...♘d7 13.d4?!

Now activity had to be exercised on the other flank — 13.c4!? f5 14.♖c1.

13...e4

An aggressive attitude, creating a pawn majority. Possible and logical too is 13...♗f6.

14.♘d2 f5!

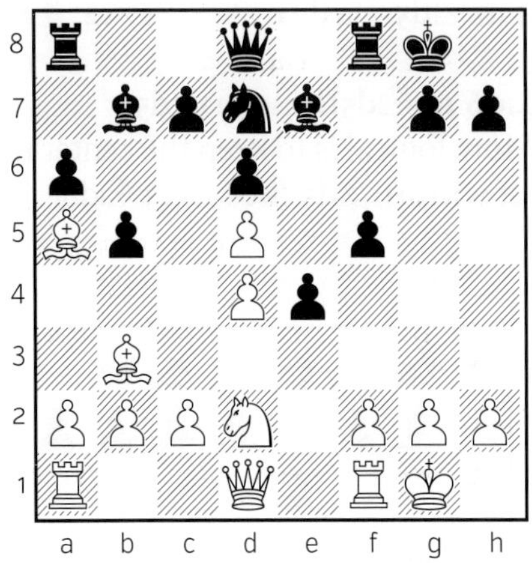

It is absolutely necessary to support the pawn and not to allow the opponent to simplify the situation.

14...♘f6 15.♖e1 ♗d5 16.♗d5 ♘d5 17.♘e4 ♕d7.

15.♘b1

In such situations it is urgently necessary to create some pressure on the opponents position — 15.a4.

15...♘f6

Another logical set up was 15...♘b6 16.♘c3 ♗f6.

16.♘c3 ♕d7 17.♕e2 ♖ae8 18.a4 ♗d8!

Unclear complications would arise after 18...f4 19.ab5 ab5 20.♘e4 ♘e4 21.♕e4 f3.

19.ab5 f4!

The pawn majority must roll forward!

20.f3

The capture of one more pawn would allow Black to launch a mating attack:

20.ba6 f3 21.gf3 ♗a6 22.♕a6 ef3 23.♔h1 ♘g4! 24.♘d1 ♘h2! 25.♖g1 ♕h3 26.♖g3 ♕h5 27.♔g1 ♘g4–+.

20...ef3 21.♕f3 ab5

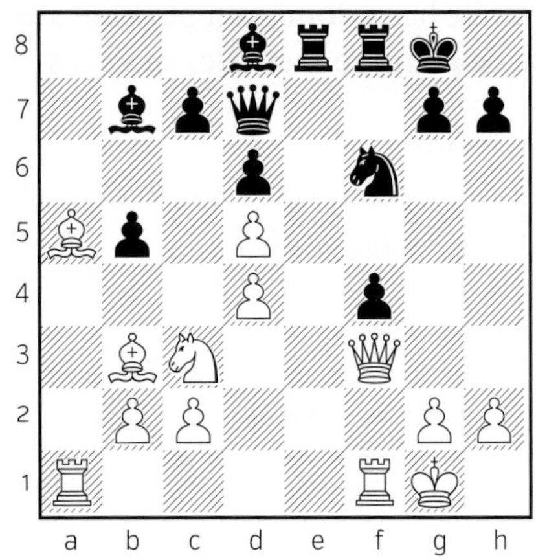

22.h3?

There was a great opportunity for White to survive in the forced line 22.♕f4 ♘g4 23.♕d2 ♖f1 24.♖f1 h6!

22...g5 23.♕d3

Better was to try for exchanges 23.♖fe1.

23...♕g7!

Preparing the opening of the g-file, closer to the opponent's king.

24.♖f3
24.♕b5 g4! 25.♕b7 gh3 26.♖f2 ♘g4–+.

24...♗c8!
Now the bishop enters the game.

25.♖af1 ♘h5 26.♘b5 g4–+ 27.hg4 ♗g4 28.♖e1 ♗f3 29.♕f3 ♖e1 30.♖e1 ♘g3 31.♗c4 ♔h8 32.♗d3 ♕h6 33.♗c3
Of no help is 33.♗g3 fg3 34.♕g3 ♗h4 35.♕h3 ♗f2 36.♔h2 (36.♔f1 ♕c1 37.♔e2 ♕e1#) 36...♗g3! 37.♔g3 ♕f4#.

33...♕h1 34.♔f2 ♕c1 0:1.

12

▷ **Logar**
▶ **Mihalcisin**
Murska Sobota 2010 [C84]

1.e4 e5 2.♘f3 ♘c6 3.♗b5 a6 4.♗a4 ♘f6 5.0–0 b5 6.♗b3 ♗b7 7.d3 ♗e7 8.♘c3 0–0 9.♗g5 d6 10.a3

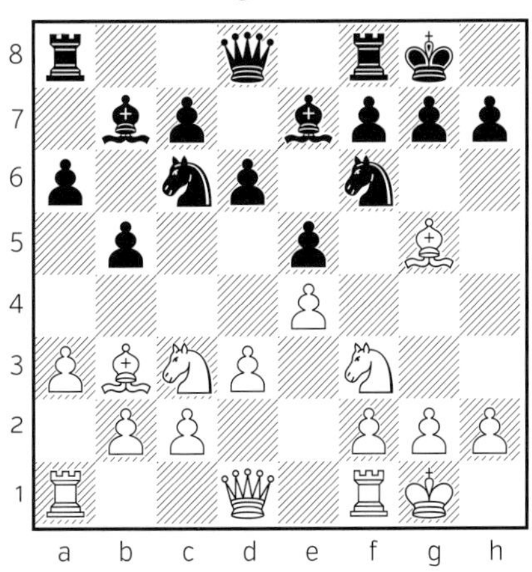

Now it is a question of how Black should start his plan aimed at the center -which flank options are possible here?

10...h6
One option was 10...♕d7, with the typical manouevre ♘c6–d8–e6. Another option allows White to activate in the center: 10...♘d7 11.♗e3 ♘c5 12.♗d5 ♘e6 13.d4 ed4 14.♘d4 ♕d7 15.♘f5.

11.♗f6 ♗f6 12.♘d5 g6
The plan is simple — to prepare ...f7–f5 after ...♗g7 and ...♔h8. At the same time it is clear that Black totally controls the central square d4.

13.♘f6 ♕f6 14.♕d2
In any case it was necessary to activate the bishop (14.♗d5).

14...♔g7 15.♖ad1

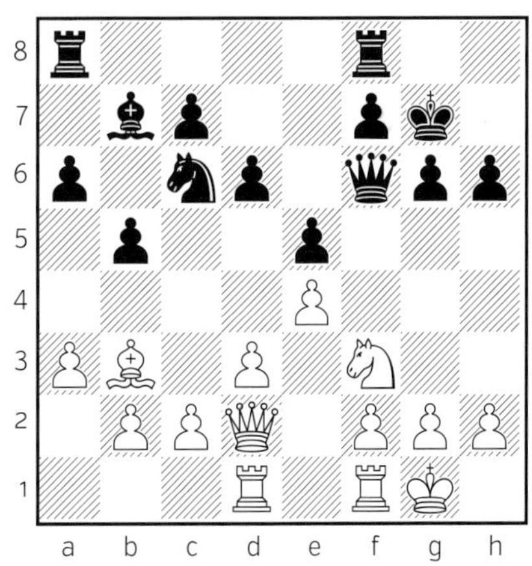

Black faces no problems after White's central build-up: 15.c3 ♘d8 16.♖fe1 ♘e6 17.d4 ♘g5.

15...♘e7

Very logical also is the other route — 15...♘d8 16.♖fe1 ♖e8 17.a4.

16.♖fe1 g5!

White's central play can't be stopped with 16...c5 17.c3 ♗c8 18.d4 cd4 19.cd4 ♗g4 20.♖e3.

17.h3 ♕g6

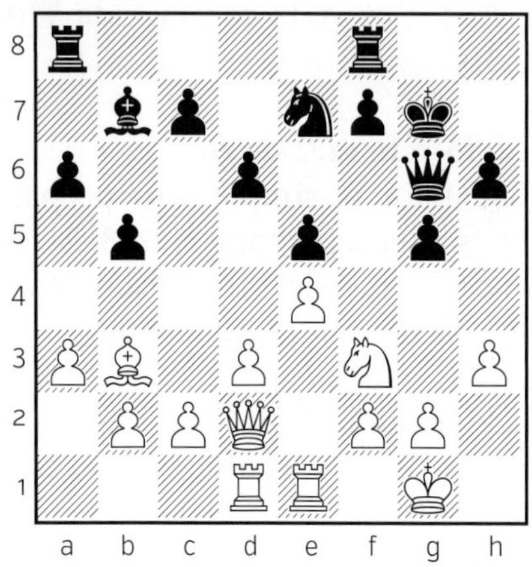

18.c3

The best chance here was to try to win a pawn for some unclear threats on the other flank: 18.♕a5 ♖ac8 19.c4 f5 20.cb5 ab5 21.♕b5 ♗c6 22.♕c4 fe4 23.de4 ♖f4.

18...f5

Finally Black has achieved his goal — ...f7–f5 is executed.

19.♘h2?

Much more stubborn defence was 19.ef5 ♘f5 20.♘h2 ♘h4 21.f3.

19...fe4 20.de4 ♗e4 21.f3 ♗f5 22.♘f1 ♗e6 23.♗c2 ♕f7 24.♗e3

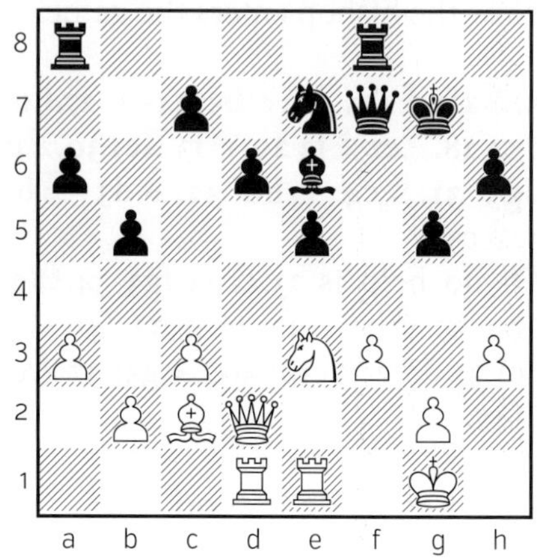

24...♘g6

Also possible here was an exchanging strategy — 24...♘f5.

25.♕d3 ♖h8 26.♕e4 ♘f4 27.♖d2 h5!

The attack is not over yet.

28.♖ed1 ♖af8

A faster attack was 28...g4 29.hg4 hg4 30.fg4 ♖af8.

29.a4 ♕f6! 30.ab5 ab5 31.c4

Or 31.♖f1 g4 32.fg4 hg4 33.♖df2 ♕g5.

31...bc4 32.♕c6 ♖f7 33.♘c4 g4 34.♘e3 ♕g5 35.fg4 ♘h3! 36.gh3 ♕e3 0:1.

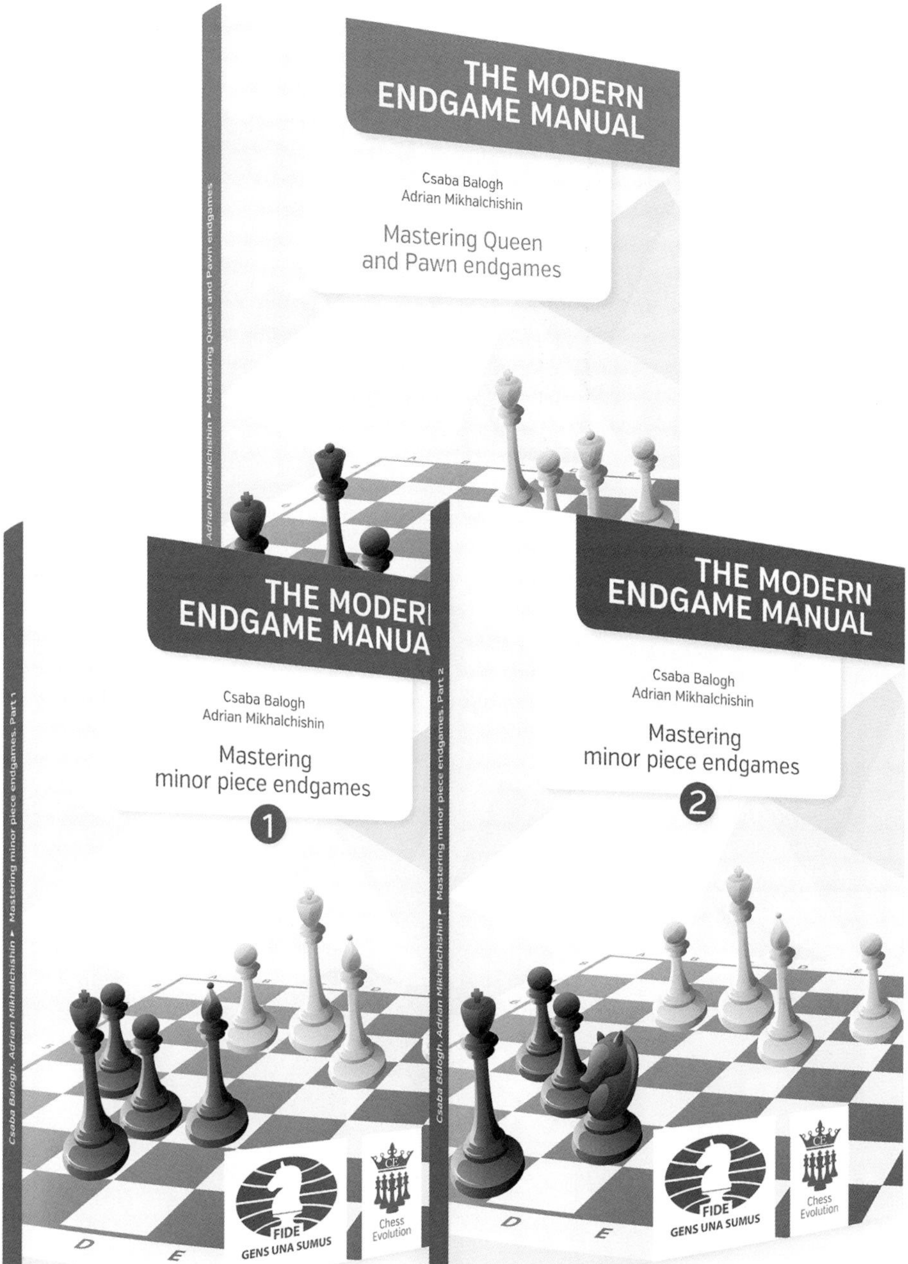

www.chess-evolution.com

Greatest
365 Puzzles
Balogh Csaba
From practical games of 2012
Part I
Greatest
501 Puzzles
Balogh Csaba
From practical games of 2012
Part II
Tactics, Tactics, Tactics!
Csaba Balogh
Volume 3
Fun edition
Tactics, Tactics, Tactics!
Csaba Balogh
Volume 4
Thoughtful edition

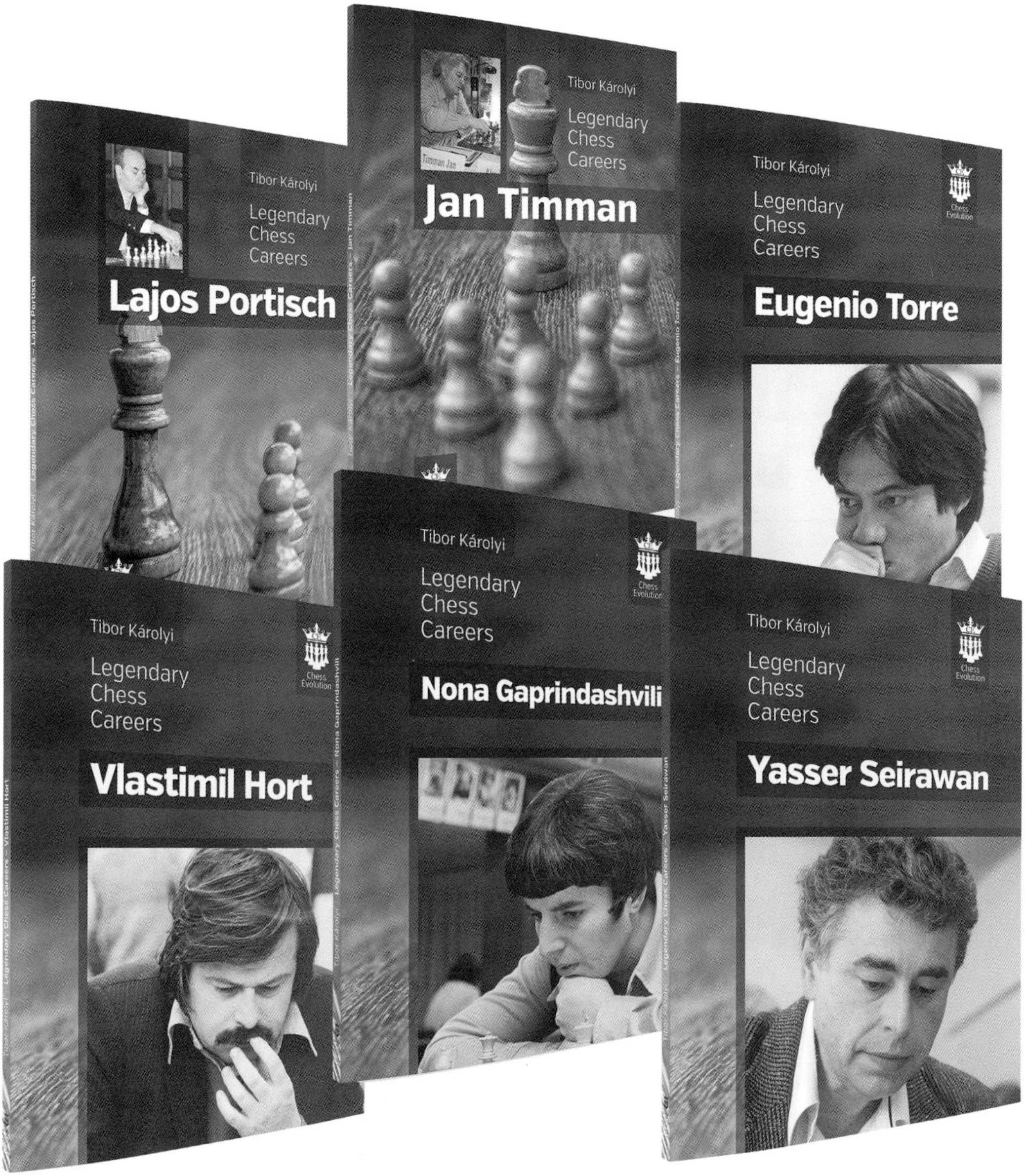
Tibor Károlyi
Legendary Chess Careers
Jan Timman
Tibor Károlyi
Legendary Chess Careers
Lajos Portisch
Tibor Károlyi
Legendary Chess Careers
Eugenio Torre
Chess Evolution
Tibor Károlyi
Legendary Chess Careers
Nona Gaprindashvili
Chess Evolution
Tibor Károlyi
Legendary Chess Careers
Vlastimil Hort
Chess Evolution
Tibor Károlyi
Legendary Chess Careers
Yasser Seirawan
Chess Evolution

Arkadij Naiditsch
Csaba Balogh
Best attacking
games of 2012–2015
Arkadij Naiditsch
Csaba Balogh
Most instructive
endgames of 2012–2015
Arkadij Naiditsch
Csaba Balogh
Caruana vs Gelfand
33... ♖e3!!
Arkadij Naiditsch
Csaba Balogh
Carlsen vs Anand
25.♘h3!!
Arkadij Naiditsch
Csaba Balogh
Best fighting
games of 2012–2015
Carlsen vs Li Chao
24.d5!!
Chess Evolution